MORE THAN TWENTY YEARS AGO, IN THE MIDST OF WIDESPREAD VIOLENCE in Israel and Palestine, a group of Israeli and Palestinian teachers gathered to address what to many people seemed an unbridgeable gulf between the two societies. Struck by how different the standard Israeli and Palestinian textbook histories of the same events were from one another—whether of the Balfour Declaration or the 1967 War—they began to explore how a new understanding of history itself might open up different kinds of dialogue in an increasingly hostile climate. Their express goal was to "disarm" the teaching of Middle East history in Israeli and Palestinian classrooms.

The result is a riveting and unprecedented "dual narrative" of Israeli and Palestinian history. *Side by Side* comprises the history of two peoples, in separate narratives set literally side by side, so that readers can track each against the other, noting both where they differ and where they correspond. This unique and fascinating format, translated into English from Arabic and Hebrew, reveals surprising juxtapositions and allows readers to consider and process the very different viewpoints and logic of each side of the Israeli-Palestinian conflict.

An eye-opening—and inspiring—new approach to thinking about one of the world's most deeply entrenched conflicts, *Side by Side* is a now-classic book that offers readers a way to discuss and perhaps even help find a bridge to peace in the Middle East.

PEACE RESEARCH INSTITUTE IN THE MIDDLE EAST (PRIME) is a nongovernmental organization established by Palestinian and Israeli researchers with the help of the Peace Research Institute in Frankfurt, Germany.

A co-founder with the late **DAN BAR-ON** of PRIME and its current co-director, **SAMI ADWAN** has published widely on the role of education in peacebuilding.

PRIME co-director **EYAL NAVEH** is a professor of U.S. history at Tel Aviv University and teaches history and history education at the Kibbutzim College of Education.

SIDE BY SIDE

Parallel Histories of Israel-Palestine

Sami Adwan, Dan Bar-On, Eyal Naveh
PRIME (Peace Research Institute in the Middle East)

Requests for permission to reproduce selections from this book should be made through our website: https://thenewpress.com/contact.

Published in the United States by The New Press, New York, 2012
Distributed by Two Rivers Distribution

LIBRARY OF CONGRESS CATALOGING-IN-PUBLICATION DATA

Side by side : parallel histories of Israel-Palestine / edited by Sami
Adwan, Dan Bar-On, Eyal Naveh, and the Peace Research Institute in the
Middle East (PRIME).
   p. cm.
Includes bibliographical references.
 ISBN 978-1-59558-683-4 (pb)
1. Palestine--History--1917-1948. 2. Israel--History--1948-1967. 3.
Israel--History--1967-1993. 4. Jews--Israel--Identity. 5. Palestinian
Arabs--Ethnic identity. I. 'Adwan, Sami 'Abd al-Razzaq. II. Bar-On, Dan,
1938-2008. III. Naveh, Eyal J., 1952- IV. Peace Research Institute in the
Middle East.
 DS125.S54 2011
 956.9405--dc22

                                    2011016429

The New Press publishes books that promote and enrich public discussion and understanding of the issues vital to our democracy and to a more equitable world. These books are made possible by the enthusiasm of our readers; the support of a committed group of donors, large and small; the collaboration of our many partners in the independent media and the not-for-profit sector; booksellers, who often hand-sell New Press books; librarians; and above all by our authors.

www.thenewpress.com

Composition by Influx House
This book was set in Garamond

CONTENTS

IN MEMORY OF PROFESSOR DAN BAR-ON

Professor Dan Bar-On devoted many years to the study of the Israeli-Palestinian conflict, with a sincere commitment to know the "other" and to look at the reflection of the "other" within us. This book is one of the significant products of his groundbreaking work with colleague Professor Sami Adwan, expressing an innovative conception of the meaning of history and its place in the development of conflicts and their reconciliation.

To the very end, Dan never wavered in his concern for the progress and completion of the project he had created with Sami, entitled "Learning Each Other's Historical Narratives." While building a unique and warm partnership, Dan and Sami brought together Palestinian and Israeli teachers to write this dual-narrative history book.

To our great regret, Dan did not live to see this publication. A noble man of many dimensions, Dan was an inspiration to everyone working on the project, enabling them to persevere and learn together throughout the delicate process. We greatly admired his ability to embrace differences between the perspectives of the conflict and to see how the acknowledgment of differences makes dialogue possible and creates a basis for reexamining the different narratives as well as the substance of the conflict, in preparation for future reconciliation.

Dan and Sami were able to construct the project to become personally meaningful to everyone involved. We were greatly influenced by Dan's special charisma, his dedication and insight, and his extraordinary capacity to change without losing the self, to learn new "languages" and move between them, while working tirelessly to "translate" the "other."

Dan touched each one of us and became a fundamental part of our professional journeys and our individual life stories. We were greatly honored and privileged to have worked with him and to have shared his vision integrating greater closeness, understanding, differentness sensitivity, and self-examination.

Dan will be greatly missed by all of us.

The PRIME Team
Israelis and Palestinians

Professor Dan Bar-On died of cancer on September 4, 2008.

THE DUAL-NARRATIVE APPROACH:
JEWISH-ISRAELI AND PALESTINIAN PUPILS LEARN
THE HISTORY OF THE OTHER PARTY IN THE CONFLICT[1]

SAMI ADWAN AND DAN BAR-ON[2]

This book is the outcome of a creative educational approach developed by a group of Palestinian and Israeli teachers, all of whom have served as our co-authors: Mysoun Al-Husaini, Khalil Bader, Nir Cohen, Natalia Gotkobiski, Niv Keidar, Eyal Keren, Eshel Klinhouse, Sara Maor, Shai Miselman, Rula Musleh, Lila Noy, Yiftach Ron, Yousef Tumaizi (1957–2002), Naom Vered, Sahar Yousef, Rachel Zamir, and others. Supervised by two historians, Professor Eyal Naveh and Professor Adnan Musallam, the group worked together for seven years, between 2002 and 2009, under the auspices of PRIME (Peace Research Institute in the Middle East). The text's editors also serve as the co-directors of PRIME. The shared aim was the development of an original idea: a history text comprising two narratives for events that happened in the lives of the two nations during the last century. For these two peoples, as for many others, the twentieth century was devoted to the building of their own nationhood. Whereas that process ordinarily has a positive meaning for a society, in this case, unfortunately, the development of these two nations proceeded in opposition to the other and even, to some extent, at one another's expense (Bar-Tal, 2000). The intractable conflict between the two societies over the last hundred years buttressed the construction of their separate collective identities, at the price of poisoning the relationship between the people of the two societies.

Hence the new approach embodied in this book: portraying the separate historical narratives of these two peoples in a joint textbook—so high school and postsecondary students, teachers, teachers' instructors, and parents will be exposed to the other national narrative in a way that lets them acknowledge it as new and valuable information for themselves. Using this book, the habitual stance of simply ignoring one another's historical narrative gives way to a process of developing mutual respect and understanding of each side's "logic," as a necessary (if not sufficient) step toward developing a better relationship with the "other" and between the two peoples.

In choosing this approach, we relinquished the possibility of developing a single "bridging narrative" that the people of both societies could identify with. After the renewal of widespread violence—after the breakout of the Al-Aqsa Intifada—in October 2000, we reached the painful conclusion that no such bridging narrative appears likely to be viable among our people at the grassroots level for some time, perhaps not for generations to come. The mutual suspicion, hatred, and poisoning of the minds among both peoples in relation to the "other" have become so intense that sustaining a common bond has become impossible, except within very small and exclusive elite groups on each side. We asked ourselves at that point what could be done, given the current hostile climate, aside from standing by and watching the negative dynamic accelerate. We decided to initiate a process that would allow both peoples—especially the younger generation—to move beyond the one-dimensional identification with their own narrative and become equipped to acknowledge, understand, and respect (without having to accept) the narrative of the other. The fact that the idea might sound naive or even utopian, given the overwhelmingly hostile political climate at the time, did not deter us.

In an earlier paper, we portrayed the process: how a group of Israeli and Palestinian teachers developed these parallel texts and tested them in their respective classrooms (Adwan and Bar-On, 2004; 2006). Over the first five years (2002–2007), while developing their respective narrative texts, the teachers themselves went through a remarkable process that deserves a separate discussion. We will briefly refer to some of the issues that arose:

1. Perceiving and managing multiple narratives: children versus adults.

2. Introducing multiple narratives in stressful situations: a process of dealing with mourning and working through it, so as to enable a group to cease demonizing the other and its collective existence.

3. Coping with asymmetry of power alongside the symmetry between narratives: a constant tension.

4. Understanding the narratives as a reflection of different stages in the development of nationhood: the monolithic and the neo-monolithic stages in the two societies, Palestinian and Israeli.

PERCEIVING AND MANAGING MULTIPLE NARRATIVES: CHILDREN VS. ADULTS

Coleman and Lowe (2005) suggest that, in conflict situations, people differ in their capacity to tolerate opposing ideas and that those with higher tolerance would be helpful in the constructive conflict resolution processes. What can generate that tolerance? Steele, Spencer, and Lynch (1993) suggest that such a tolerance is related to personality attributes—e.g., high self-esteem—or to situational factors that can enhance such tolerance (Bargh and Chartrand, 1999). Peng and Nisbett (1999) found that cultural differences account for the differential ability to cope with dialectical solutions to social dilemmas: Eastern students showed a higher ability to cope than Western students, who used more formal logical arguments. In addition, when faced with two contradictory explanations for the same event, Western students tended to polarize them, while Eastern students tended to accept them both as valid.

Harris and Giménez (2005) found that young children in Western culture tend to adopt the biological-secular approach to death, while adults have a larger tendency to believe in the possibility of life after death. Comparing children's and adults' attitudes about truth and lies: Fu, Lee, Cameron, and Xu (2001) tested Western and Eastern children to see how they evaluate hiding the truth in the context of prosocial activities. Eastern adults did not view hiding the truth when it was related to a prosocial activity as a lie, while

Western adults did. Both the Eastern and Western children saw such an act as positive, even when they defined it as a lie. Eastern children were more affected by the norms of their adult society regarding these values.

We suggest that children are accustomed to daily situations involving multiple narratives and learn through their own experiences how to navigate among them. For example, they know that their father may subscribe to a different narrative than their mother regarding certain matters, and therefore should be approached differently. Similarly, their siblings are likely to have other narratives than their own and may also differ among themselves (Bonitatibus and Beal, 1996).

One developmental tradition claims that younger children are less capable of managing multiple narratives, in comparison with children at the operational stage (7–11) (Piaget and Inhelder, 1948/1956; Klausmeier, 1979), because they have greater difficulty making sense of another perspective on reality that differs from their own. Younger children have a more concrete and dogmatic way of thinking and hence have trouble understanding the difference between empirical and logical problem solving (Morris and Sloutsky, 2001). The inference might be that a dual-narrative approach will therefore be less accessible to younger children.

Another research tradition suggests otherwise. In one study (Ackerman, 1988; Casteel, 1997; Bonitatibus and Beal, 1996), both younger and older children showed similar abilities in accepting two interpretations of an empirical script in which a contradiction was demonstrated between an actor's intention and his actual actions. Both age groups were able to accept the contradiction between the actor's intentions and the outcomes, though the probability for both possibilities was not seen as high. Bonitatibus and Beal (1996) conducted a series of experiments in which younger children showed higher capacities to accept two outcome options to a script, in comparison to children in the operational phase.

The studies cited above dealt with problems of multiple accounts or narratives that could be defined as relatively emotionally distant from the research participants themselves, as individuals and as collectives. However, when the public faces politically and emotionally loaded dual narratives, how well can children or adults cope with the notion that several narratives addressing the same historical event may be equally legitimate and logical—especially when the narratives encompass their own historical account and that of their perceived enemy? Could one expect children or adults to accept the "logic" behind their enemy's historical account when they are so accustomed to hearing it denounced as untrustworthy?

Assuming the intractable conflict between Palestinians and Israelis has had a considerable negative impact on both adults and children, we expected to see relatively little openness to constructively addressing the narrative of the other. We anticipated that, in such circumstances, even very young children will have internalized, identified with, and adopted their parents' and teachers' stance of believing in the moral superiority of their own account of the history of the conflict, while disregarding or morally excluding that of the other side (Opotow, 1990; Bar-Tal, 2000). We therefore knew that implementing our dual-narrative approach in classrooms would not be easy, but we were encouraged to find our teachers' willingness to struggle with these issues.

A PROCESS OF COPING OR MOURNING: GIVING UP DEMONIZING THE "OTHER"

In intractable conflicts, each side creates a monolithic identity by constructing it in opposition to the "other." Historical facts are recruited to support the narratives associated with these monolithic constructions (Bar-On, 2008). Learning to respect the narrative of the other may be seen as a coping process, similar to a mourning process (Freud, 1930): one must learn to give up those parts of one's narrative which are essential to maintaining a negative and morally inferior collective image of the other (and a positive narrative for one's own group). The children and adults who participate in such a learning process sense that they are letting go of something, losing something, and meanwhile may have no clear understanding of what they gain by this loss (Tajfel, 1982).

While working with our teachers on the development of the two narratives (Adwan and Bar-On, 2004), the mourning process became self-evident. Each time that one side had to relinquish a negative definition of the other, there was a crisis in the group of teachers: "How will we be able to teach your text in our class? The pupils are used to thinking about you very differently in this context." This work with our teachers vividly demonstrated the central role of emotions in the teaching and learning of historical accounts: usually positive emotions emerge vis-à-vis your own historical account and negative emotions vis-à-vis that of the other. Historians who focus more narrowly on the historical facts per se are less attuned to this aspect of the teaching and learning process. A few teachers from each group made an effort to mediate and were able to help other teachers manage these crises and successfully navigate the mourning process. Notably, the emotional components of this process required special attention being essential to any progression of processing or mourning (Freud, 1930).

A teacher named Rachel summarized the process she went through over the course of four years in the project:

> When I saw the narrative of the other side, first I was angry and frustrated at how different it is from ours. I felt it was not based on facts but on stories and emotions. Later, I learned to cognitively accept the difference, but still felt that our narrative was superior to theirs. Only recently did I learn to see the logic behind their narrative and even to emotionally feel empathy to what they went through. If this took me four years, imagine what it will take the pupils or their parents.

In these phrases, Rachel actually described the discourse categories Steinberg identified in her research during workshops with Israeli Jewish and Arab students at the Ben-Gurion University of Beersheba: they began with "ethnocentric" discourse, went on to "opening a window" in a "double wall," to cognitively grasping how different the other is, and proceeded to moments of dialogue between the parties (Steinberg and Bar-On, 2002).[3] In addition, Rachel suggested that accommodating the dual-narrative approach demands long sequences of class time and cannot be achieved on a one-shot basis.

Another example of the intensity of this mourning process: the teachers went through thirteen workshops before one of them asked his colleague from the other side: "When I teach your text about the 1950s, what is important for you that I emphasize?" This is such a basic question regarding this learning process, yet it was not raised among the teachers earlier. Similarly, we saw how, only relatively late in the process of their work, some of the teachers developed mediating capacities and found ways of negotiating with members of the other group and of relating to their difficulties empathically, so that the process could continue to move ahead. This ability did not emerge among the teachers during the early phases of the project, and the mediating role had to be played by the authors of this introduction (Adwan and Bar-On, 2006).

To conclude this point we must note that learning the historical narrative of the other, in a real-world intractable conflict situation, is much more complex than simply cognitively managing more than one narrative in an experimental situation, as described by the literature cited above. Consider the experiences of the Israeli and Palestinian teachers compared with those of European teachers who attempted to test our dual-narrative approach; for the latter, sticking with a more "neutral" cognitive process may be more appropriate. In summertime seminars conducted between 2005 and 2007, for example, we could see that the European teachers who taught our two narratives had a different kind of task than that of the Israeli and Palestinian teachers. The first difference was that the Europeans were less affected emotionally by the feeling of loss. The second difference was in the effort put toward helping their pupils develop a more complex understanding of the Middle East conflict, since they had entered this learning experience with little previous knowledge about either narrative (no emotional involvement) and/or with a very one-sided view of the conflict (one-sided prior emotional involvement).[4]

THE TENSION BETWEEN THE ASYMMETRY OF POWER AND THE SYMMETRY OF THE NARRATIVES

In our teachers' seminars we observed that there was a constant tension between the fact that the two narratives were regarded equally, whereas outside the seminar room there was a continuous power of asymmetry between the parties to the conflict: Israel's dominance and occupation of the Palestinians in the occupied territories and the domination of the Palestinian minority by the Jewish majority within the State of Israel (Adwan and Bar-On, 2004; 2006). At the same time, most Israeli Jews tend to perceive themselves as a minority in a hostile Muslim Middle East and thereby construct an opposite asymmetry of feeling inferior. This tension between two contradictory asymmetries is well known to those of us who are experienced in working with small groups "under fire" (Maoz, 2004).

We assumed that the asymmetry of power between the parties could hinder the pupils from accepting our new approach as long as the occupation of the Palestinians and violence toward Israeli citizens continued (Adwan and Bar-On, 2004). Nonetheless we strongly hoped that once the pupils accepted our new approach, they would find their own ways of dealing with the transition from the relatively safe environment of the classroom to the more violent and less safe society in which they were still living. They needed to develop "reentry strategies" to permit them to hold on to what they learned in class about the two narratives, while readjusting themselves on returning to their hostile external environments (Steinberg and Bar-On, 2002).

THE TWO NARRATIVES REFLECT STAGES OF DEVELOPMENT OF NATIONHOOD AND CULTURAL VALUES

The Israeli and the Palestinian narratives are not symmetrical in their internal construction, and cannot be expected to be so at the current stage. The Palestinian narrative is much more monolithic in its internal structure, representing Palestinians' need to develop their independent statehood, similar to the way the Israeli Jewish narrative was framed when Israel struggled for its independence (Bar-On, 2008). The Israeli narrative, after fifty-five years of statehood, is a bit more self-reflective and self-critical concerning some of the traditional "Zionist" historical narratives. Since October 2000, however, the narrative incorporates a neo-monolithic turn. As a result it is no longer a radical or post-Zionist narrative, so that the majority of the Israeli Jewish pupils can feel comfortable with it (Adwan and Bar-On, 2004). In addition, the Israeli Jewish narrative reflects more of the Western cultural values of formal morality (Gilligan, 1982), while the Palestinian narrative reflects more Eastern values of interpersonal morality.

SUMMARY: AN EXPERIMENTAL APPROACH

We hope the single reader will enter the experimental mood of our approach to educational reform: our teachers are creators of knowledge rather than its consumers, developing their own "teacher's guide" on the PRIME website[5] and evaluating their new classroom experiences by visiting each other's classrooms. It is important to state that we are at the beginning, not the end, of this learning process. There is nothing final about the narratives presented in this book. These are the narratives that our teachers wrote at a violent stage of our conflict in 2002–2007. We suggest that this effort be repeated in ten years. We are sure that the texts will change, as historical narratives are always influenced by what happens in the reality of the given time. We hope that by 2012 or 2017, the political climate between our two peoples will have improved so greatly that the historical account of our bloody past will change accordingly.

REFERENCES

Ackerman, B. P. (1988). Reason inferences in the story comprehension of children and adults. *Child Development* 59:1426–42.

Adwan, S., and Bar-On, D. (2004a). Peace building under fire, *Palestinian/Israel Wye River Projects*. Beit Jala, PRIME.

Adwan, S., and Bar-On, D. (2004b). Shared history project: A PRIME example of peace building under fire. *International Journal of Politics*, Culture and Society 17:3, 513–23.

Adwan, S., and Bar-On, D. (2006). Educating toward a culture of peace. International Conference on Education Toward a Culture of Peace, Dec. 1–3, 2003, Bar Ilan University, Ramat Gan, Israel.

Bargh, J. A., and Chartrand, T. L. (1999). The unbearable automaticity of being. *American Psychologist* 54:462–79.

Bar-On, D. (2008). *The "other" within us: Changes in the Israeli identity from a psychosocial perspective*. New York, Cambridge University Press.

Bar-Tal (2000). Shared beliefs in a society: Social psychological analysis. Thousand Oaks, CA, Sage Publications.

Bonitatibus, G. J., and Beal, C. R. (1996). Finding new meanings: Children's recognition of interpretive ambiguity in text. *Journal of Experimental Child Psychology* 62:131–50.

Casteel, M. A. (1997). Resolving interpretive ambiguity in text: Children's generation of multiple interpretations. *Journal of Experimental Child Psychology* 64:396–424.

Coleman, P. T., and Lowe, J. K. (2005). Conflict, identity, and adaptation: Negotiating collective identities in the context of a protracted ethno-political conflict. Under review with *Political Psychology*.

Freud, S. (1930). Further recommendations on the technique of psycho-analysis, II (Remembering, repeating and working through). In *Standard Edition of the Complete Psychological Works*. Hogarth.

Fu, G., Lee, K., Cameron, C. A., and Xu, F. (2001). Chinese and Canadian adults' categorization and evaluation of lie- and truth-telling about pro- and anti-social behaviors. *Journal of Cross-Cultural Psychology* 32:740–47.

Gilligan, C. (1982). *In a Different Voice*. Cambridge, MA: Harvard University Press.

Harris, P. L., and Giménez, M. (2005). Children's acceptance of conflicting testimony: The case of death. *Journal of Cognition and Culture* 5:143–62.

Klausmeier, H. J. (1979). *Cognitive learning and development: Information-processing and Piagetian perspectives.* Cambridge, MA: Ballinger.

Maoz, I. (2004). Coexistence is in the eye of the beholder: Evaluating intergroup encounter interventions between Jews and Arabs in Israel. *Journal of Social Issues* 60:2, 437–52.

Morris, B. J., and Sloutsky, V. M. (2001). Children's solutions of logical vs. empirical problems: What's missing and what develops? *Cognitive Development* 16(4):907–28.

Opotow, S. (1990). Moral exclusion and injustice. *Journal of Social Issues* 46(1):1–20.

Peng, K., and Nisbett, R. E. (1999). Culture, dialecticism, and reasoning about contradiction. *American Psychologist* 54:741–54.

Piaget, J., and Inhelder, B. (1948/1956). *The child's conception of space.* London: Routledge and Kegan Paul.

Steele, C. M., Spencer, S. J., and Lynch, M. (1993). Self-image resilience and dissonance: The role of affirmational resources. *Journal of Personality and Social Psychology* 64:885–96.

Steinberg, S., and Bar-On, D. (2002). An analysis of the group process in encounters between Jews and Palestinians using a typology for discourse classification. *International Journal of Intercultural Relations* 26:2, 199–214.

Tajfel, H. (1982). *Social identity and intergroup relations.* London: Cambridge University Press.

NOTE TO READERS ON THE FORMATTING OF *SIDE BY SIDE*

Side by Side is designed to present, on facing pages, two parallel historical narratives. Given the complexity of balancing varying amounts of material from both sides of the conflict, there are several chapters in the book of uneven length. In these cases, a series of gray arrows has been placed on blank pages at the end of such chapters to advise the reader to move forward to find the start of the next chapter of a given narrative.

I

FROM THE BALFOUR DECLARATION TO
THE BRITISH MANDATE IN PALESTINE /
ERETZ YISRAEL[1]

BIRTH OF THE ZIONIST MOVEMENT

Until the nineteenth century, most Jews lived in the Diaspora. There were approximately 8 million Jews at that time, the majority of them in Eastern Europe. There were only some 24,000 Jews living in the Land of Israel. Ever since they were exiled by the Romans in the first and second centuries, the Jews had kept alive the hope of returning to their land, although we cannot point to any significant actions taken to realize that dream. The change began in the nineteenth century with the birth of the Zionist movement, which aspired to return the Jewish people to its homeland.

The Jewish national movement, Zionism, was born in the nineteenth century, during a period when contemporary ideas of nationalism and the Enlightenment[2] were reaching the Jewish communities of Europe. The Jews began to see themselves as a nation, desiring and deserving of a country of their own. What were the origins of the Zionist movement?

One was the growing power of Enlightenment ideas, which, thanks to public schooling, were gaining an ever-increasing audience. Society was becoming more secular and the idea that people control their own destiny and

THE BALFOUR DECLARATION, 2 NOVEMBER 1917

HISTORICAL PREFACE

Napoleon Bonaparte's plan in April 1799 for a Jewish state in Palestine may be considered as the first post-Renaissance attempt of cooperation between a colonialist power and the Jewish people before the birth of the Zionist movement. This was evident in Napoleon's effort during the siege of Acre to enlist Jewish support in return for his promise to build the Temple. However, Napoleon's defeat at Acre and Abu-Qir marked the end of this short-lived plan.

It was not until 1840 that Lord Palmerston came up with a proposal that eventually led to the establishment of a Jewish state in Palestine in 1948. In 1840–1841, Lord Palmerston, British foreign secretary, proposed the establishment of a regional zone within the Ottoman Empire which would be under British protection and which would constitute a human buffer zone to prevent the establishment of a political entity among the various Arab regions.

Britain launched a new policy supporting the settlement of the Jews in Palestine as Jews lived under poor conditions and suffered from cruel persecution particularly in some Eastern European countries and Czarist Russia.

can act to create change on the personal and social level was taking root. The Enlightenment and the French Revolution ushered in the era of nationalism. This concept swept through Europe in the nineteenth century and led, among other things, to struggles for national autonomy and the establishment of new nation-states.

Some of Europe's Jews, exposed to the Enlightenment and the idea of nationalism, felt that they had found the answer to their problems, just as other ethnic groups aspired to create their own sovereign national states. This approach required active intervention to resolve the problem of Jewish exile, rather than waiting patiently for salvation via heavenly intercession.

Another factor that led to the birth of Zionism was the disappointment with emancipation and equal rights. Following the French Revolution, Jews were formally emancipated in many European countries. The Jews now hoped to live as equals with others, but they often found that equality had arrived only in a formal sense, while discrimination against them continued both on the street and in public and private institutions. Meanwhile, in places with full formal equality, circumstances still posed significant challenges in the quest for cultural autonomy—something deemed important by a considerable proportion of the Jews—involving issues such as the freedom not to work on Jewish holidays.

During the second half of the nineteenth century, anti-Semitism intensified. Alongside the traditional, religion-based hatred, an extreme form of racism had arisen. This form of anti-Semitism defined Jews as an inferior and destructive race of people whom it was permissible to kill. There was anti-Semitism on the street, in the media, and within the platforms of various political parties. During 1881–1882, Jews living in the Russian empire were prey to severe pogroms. Many chose to immigrate, mostly to the United States, while a small proportion went to the Land of Israel.

Jewish nationalism was also tied to the yearning for Zion, an inseparable part of the religious and national identity of the Jewish people throughout its entire history. The longing for Zion rested on the biblical promise that the Land of Israel was given to the people of Israel by the God of Israel; on the historical periods during which the people of Israel had lived on the land and enjoyed political autonomy; and on the continuity of the presence of Jews, albeit in small numbers, in the Land of Israel.

This idea was expressed in *Hatikva*, the Jewish national anthem written at the time:

ISRAELI TEXT / טקסט ישראלי

Consequently, the establishment of the Zionist movement appeared as a radical international solution to the Jewish problem. Zionism embodied the transformation of Judaism as a religion into a nationalist bond which would be realized in a Jewish homeland and an exclusive Jewish state. A very important factor under which the Zionist movement was born, developed, and prospered was the increasingly competitive interests of the European world colonialist movement in Africa and Asia, and the Zionist movement's colonial interest in Palestine.

British imperialism found in Zionism a perfect tool for attaining its own interests in the Arab East, which was strategically and economically important for the empire. Similarly, Zionism found in colonialism an international support and the economic resources to realize its plan to colonize Palestine.

The alliance of British imperialism and Zionism gave rise to what is known in history books as the Balfour Declaration on 2 November 1917. The declaration was a culmination of a British foreign policy of unlawfully seizing another nation's land and resources and wiping out its identity in addition to aggression, expansion, and suppression of any attempts toward national liberation.

For the Palestinians, 1917 was the first of many years (1920, 1921, 1929, 1936, 1948, 1967) that were marked by tragedy, war, misfortune, death, destruction, homelessness, and catastrophes.

PARTITIONING OF THE ARAB EAST

In light of the strong European colonial competition, Britain called for the formation of a high committee of seven European countries. The committee submitted its report in 1907 to British Prime Minister Sir Henry Campbell-Bannerman. The report asserted that the Arab countries and the Muslim-Arab people living in the Ottoman Empire presented a very real threat to the colonial countries. The report made the following recommendations:

1. To promote a state of disintegration, division and separation in the region.

2. To establish puppet political entities under the aegis of the European imperialist countries.

3. To combat all kinds of unity (intellectual, spiritual, religious, or

As long as deep in the heart
the soul of a Jew still yearns
and onward toward the East
toward Zion, the eyes still gaze
our hope will not be lost
the hope of two thousand years
to be a free nation in our own land
the land of Zion and Jerusalem.

The Zionist movement was born among the large concentrations of Jews in Europe with the aim of restoring the Jewish people to its homeland and changing its anomalous status as a people dispersed among other nations without a home of its own. In 1882, a small wave of immigration of Jews to the Land of Israel began within the *Hovevei Zion* movement in Russia, the first of several waves of immigration that came to be known as *Aliyot* (singular: *Aliyah*—literally, "ascension"). The goal of Zionist Aliyah was to create a national Jewish society in the Land of Israel where Jews would work the land as free people. During the first Aliyah, some 60,000 Jews from Eastern Europe arrived, of whom about half remained, establishing agricultural villages (*moshavot*).

Theodor (Binyamin Ze'ev) Herzl, a Jewish journalist from central Europe, is considered the founder of the Zionist movement, as he envisioned the future State of Israel and was able to transform the national dream of a few believers into an organized and established political movement. In 1897, Herzl convened the First Zionist Congress in Basel, Switzerland, where the institutions of the Zionist movement were created and its goals carefully formulated.

The Basel Program declared:

Zionism aims to establish for the Jewish people a publicly, legally assured home in Palestine. To this end, the Congress intends to employ the following means:

1. Practical development of Palestine through the settlement of Jewish agriculturists, artisans . . .

2. Organizing and uniting all Jews in effective local economic enterprises . . .

ISRAELI TEXT / טקסט ישראלי ▼

historical) and find practical means to divide the region and in-habitants from each other.

4. To ensure the implementation of the previous recommendations, to create in Palestine a "buffer state" which would be populated by a strong, foreign human presence hostile to its neighbors and friendly to European countries and their interests.

It could be strongly concluded, beyond any doubt, that the recommendations of the Campbell-Bannerman High Committee did in fact pave the way to Palestine for the Jews. They also gave British foreign policy and the Zionist movement the green light to annex Palestine from the other Arab lands and thereby create the nucleus of a colonial entity that would ensure the colonialists' influence in the region.

There were several other Jewish colonialist projects for Palestine which followed in quick succession. The First World War (1914–1918) further emphasized the importance of Palestine to British and Zionist colonialism. During wartime, a secret exchange of letters went on between Sharif Hussein of Mecca and Sir Henry McMahon, British high commissioner in Egypt. In the first letter (14 July 1915), Sharif Hussein indicated to McMahon the boundaries of the Arab countries to which Britain would grant independence: the Arabian Peninsula, Iraq, and Syria in addition to certain parts of present-day Turkey. He excluded Aden because it was already a British military base. McMahon's response to Hussein on 24 October 1915 designated areas to be excluded from the future independent Arab state: the Syrian coastal areas west of the Damascus, Homs, Hama, and

The Sykes-Picot Agreement of 1916 for the partition of the Middle East

3. Preparatory steps to obtain the agreement of governments.[3]

The Zionist movement worked on two levels: "practical Zionism" and "political Zionism." Practical Zionism focused on expanding Aliyah, purchasing land and settling Jews in the Land of Israel, and resulted in the second Aliyah, in which some 35,000 new immigrants arrived, mainly from Russia. Impelled by a strong socialist and nationalist ideology, they founded unique agricultural communities (including a form of collective called the *kvutza*) and also expanded urban Jewish settlement. Their goal was to heal the alienation of the Jewish people and create a productive people working its own land with its own hands. The second Aliyah also included a few hundred families from Yemen, and by 1914 there were approximately 80,000 Jews in the Land of Israel.

Political Zionism focused on diplomatic efforts to promote support for Zionism among the powerful nations, and sought to obtain a charter for extensive settlement in Palestine. Despite his efforts, Herzl was unable to garner the support he needed, and the cherished charter was not forthcoming. It was not until a decade after Herzl's death, in the shadow of World War I, that Chaim Weizmann, then the leading figure in the Zionist movement, was able to persuade Britain to issue a declaration of support for Zionist aims, that became known as the Balfour Declaration.

THE BALFOUR DECLARATION

In a letter from British Foreign Secretary Lord Balfour to Lord Rothschild, a leader of the Jewish community in England, Balfour announced that the British government had decided to support the establishment of a national home for the Jews in the Land of Israel. This document was made public on November 2, 1917, toward the end of World War I, as the result of long years of diplomatic effort:

Dear Lord Rothschild,

I have much pleasure in conveying to you, on behalf of His Majesty's Government, the following declaration of sympathy with Jewish Zionist aspirations which has been submitted to, and approved by, the Cabinet.

Aleppo provinces, and the two regions of Alexandretta and Mersin. The exclusions, however, did not include Palestine.

At the same time that Britain was exchanging letters with Sharif Hussein which involved recognition of the independence of the Arab East, Britain and France concluded a secret agreement (the Sykes-Picot Agreement) in May 1916, in which the two colonial powers agreed to divide the Arab East under the Ottoman Empire as follows:

1. The Lebanese and Syrian coasts were given to France (Blue Zone)

2. South and central Iraq were given to Britain (Red Zone)

3. An international administration in Palestine excluding the ports of Haifa and Acre (Red Zone)

4. A French zone of influence, including eastern Syria and the Mosul province (Zone A)

5. Transjordan and the northern part of Baghdad province would be a British zone of influence (Zone B)

THE BALFOUR DECLARATION

The Balfour Declaration (2 November 1917) opened a new chapter in the history of the Arab and Muslim East and created a deep change in the map of the world. In fact, the Balfour Declaration was the cornerstone and basic pretext for the British mandate over Palestine. It was also the source of all the events that were to take place in Palestine later and was the excuse which Britain used to justify its policies in Palestine. It had the most dangerous consequences and deepest impact not only on Palestine but also on the future of the whole region.

The unholy marriage between Britain and Zionism was expressed in a letter that Lord Balfour, British foreign secretary, who had been working zealously for the interests of Zionism, sent to the well-known Jewish millionaire Lord Rothschild:

His Majesty's Government views with favour the establishment in Palestine of a national home for the Jewish people and will use their best

Theodore (Binyamin Ze'ev) Herzl—leader of the Zionist movement, 1897–1904

endeavours to facilitate the achievement of this object, it being clearly understood that nothing shall be done which may prejudice the civil and religious rights of existing non-Jewish communities in Palestine or the rights and political status enjoyed by Jews in any other country.[1]

Arthur James Balfour

This unholy relationship between British colonialism and the colonialist Zionist movement came at the expense of the people of Palestine and the future of the entire Arab nation. It was the culmination of the efforts of the Zionist-British team under the leadership of Chaim Weizmann whereby Britain granted a land it did not possess (Palestine) to a group who did not own it (the Zionists) at the expense of those who possessed and had the right to it. Ironically, Britain committed this crime even before its armies touched the land of Palestine.

The infamous Balfour Declaration can unequivocally be considered a blatant aggression against the right of the Palestinian people to its dependence on its own land. It was an unjust, illegitimate, and illegal promise made by Britain through its foreign secretary to grant Palestine, a land it neither owned nor had the right to bequeath to whoever it chose to. Britain also did not have the right to discuss the future of a state it did not control.[2]

The declaration was unjust because it ignored the rights of the Palestinians, who comprised the majority of the population, as if they were non existent. By stipulating that "nothing shall be done which may prejudice the civil and religious rights of existing non-Jewish communities in Palestine," the declaration clearly implied that the Arabs were a minority in Palestine, at a time when the Jewish population was the minority and comprised less than

"His Majesty's Government views with favour the establishment in Palestine of a national home for the Jewish people, and will use their best endeavours to facilitate the achievement of this object, it being clearly understood that nothing shall be done which may prejudice the civil and religious rights of existing non-Jewish communities in Palestine, or the rights and political status enjoyed by Jews in any other country."

I should be grateful if you would bring this declaration to the knowledge of the Zionist Federation.

Yours sincerely,
Arthur James Balfour

What had led the British to publicize such a declaration?

The British prime minister at the time, Lloyd George, and the foreign secretary, Balfour, were devout Christians who supported the return of the people of Israel to its homeland, in the spirit of the Bible on which they had been raised. Britain's commitment to the Jews was in line with this view, as expressed in Balfour's speech to the House of Lords:

It is our purpose to be able to send the tidings to each of the countries where this race [the Jews] resides, informing the Jews that Christendom is not ignoring their faith, is not turning a blind eye to the services they have performed for the world's major religions [. . .] and that we greatly desire to provide them, to the best of our ability, a suitable time to develop in peace and tranquility under the auspices of British rule, those same great talents which until the present time have had to be realized in countries not knowing their language or belonging to their race. This is the aspiration that I should like to see realized.[4]

The diplomatic efforts of Chaim Weizmann, who was among the most prominent of the Zionist leaders and who was well connected to people in the British government, contributed a great deal to the wording of the Balfour Declaration. Weizmann succeeded in inserting the Zionist idea into the political discourse and he presented it as furthering Britain's interests. At the time, Britain was deeply involved in World War I and hoped, with the Balfour Declaration, to secure the support of the Jews. British leaders believed that the

10 percent of the total population (60,000 Jews compared to over 650,000 Arabs).

A closer examination of the declaration would indicate that it made no mention of the inalienable political rights of the Palestinians. Instead it merely mentioned the civil and religious rights of Palestinians, which is evidence enough that Britain had no intention of developing the country so as to establish an Arab Palestinian government.[3]

ARRIVAL OF THE ZIONIST MISSION IN PALESTINE AND ARAB REACTION

In April 1918, Chaim Weizmann, accompanied by a Zionist mission, was sent by the British government to lay the groundwork for the establishment of the Jewish home in an attempt to implement the Balfour Declaration and at the same time, to lay at rest the suspicions of the Arabs concerning the real intentions of Zionism.

Near the end of 1918, several Muslim-Christian societies headed by leading figures and merchants from the main cities of Palestine were established. The main objective of these societies was to stand in the face of Jewish and Zionist organizations.

At this juncture, it would be worthy to mention a particular incident that had serious implications on the relations among the Arabs, the British, and the Zionists in Palestine. While paying a visit to Ismail Al-Husseini and his cousin, Mufti Kamel Al-Husseini, Weizmann attempted to calm down the fears of his hosts regarding the various problems that caused much alarm among the Palestinians. Then he touched on the problem of land, which most distressed the Arab leaders. He assured his hosts that seizing lands from the landowners and Arab peasants or forcing them out of Palestine by economic measures was the last thing he wished to do. Ormsby-Gore, the European intermediary accompanying Weizmann, noted that the two Arab leaders were suspicious about Weizmann's position and showed great reserve in their answers. However, Ormsby-Gore's report ignored this important incident which reflected the public political mood in Palestine at the time.

The popular political mood of the time was reflected in a theatrical production entitled *Adnan's Girl and Arab Chivalry*, which was performed in

Jewish community could influence policy makers all over the world, particularly in the United States, which had just entered the war alongside England and France. The wording of the declaration was also prompted by the knowledge that Germany, Britain's enemy, was about to publish a similar declaration, which Britain wanted to preempt.

One of Britain's central interests was its desire to solidify its presence in the Middle East, particularly in Palestine with its religious significance, both on account of the holy places there and on account of its geopolitical importance, meaning securing routes to the East and closeness to sources of oil. France was interested in the Middle East for the same reasons, and the British believed that support for Zionism would earn them priority.

The Balfour Declaration was received with great joy among Zionists all over the world. Herzl's vision had come to pass, only twenty years after it had been formulated at the First Zionist Congress in Basel, and the precious charter had been achieved. The declaration had tremendous importance since Britain, a world power, was seen by many as the probable ruler of Palestine after the war's end.

Nevertheless, by the end of 1917 the war was still in progress, and the declaration was worded somewhat vaguely, without a commitment to any specific, practical action. There was a stated commitment, on the other hand, not to violate the rights of the non-Jewish communities in Palestine, and this was liable to impede any action on behalf of a national home for the Jews. Nor was the actual territory to be allotted for the Jewish national home delineated; the declaration said it would be "in Palestine," i.e., in some part of it. Weizmann related, in that regard:

> When the Cabinet was meeting to approve the final wording, I was waiting outside, this time quite nearby. Sykes brought out the document, crying: "Dr. Weizmann, it's a boy!" And indeed the boy did not please me. This was not the young man I had prayed for. Still I knew that we were embarking on a great journey [. . .] a new chapter had opened before us, full of new obstacles, but not without its important moments.[5]

At the end of World War I, the Ottomans withdrew from the Land of Israel and Syria, and in 1920 the victorious powers, with the agreement of the international community, decided to create a British mandate in the Land

Jerusalem in April 1918 at the Al-Rashidiyyah Forum. In the vestibule of the forum and under the spotlights was a large relief map of Palestine. At the bottom of the map, the following verses were carved:

Oh blessed land of Palestine
Oh auspicious land of the children of the Arab nation,
Oh God's best land, don't despair!
I have no choice but love you.
We will sacrifice our souls for you
And travel the road of travail
Until you become as radiant as the sun
And shine from east to west.[4]

The theatrical production reflected the dissatisfaction of all the Arabs with the unjust British policy, the Balfour Declaration, as well as their distrust of Zionist plans and attitudes. The British policy and Zionist practices on the ground in Palestine comprised a clear violation of the rights of the Palestinian people to self-determination.

The issuance of the Balfour Declaration and the unremitting attempts to implement it by all means contradicted everything that Britain and its World War I allies had always stood and called for, namely, the right to self-determination. When the United States of America attempted to implement the principle of self-determination in Palestine by holding a referendum, Britain and France paid lip service to the United States but refused to send delegates to the commission that was supposed to oversee the popular vote. Consequently, the United States had to send an all-American commission, which later came to be known as the King-Crane Commission.

The results of the referendum revealed that the Palestinian Arabs were totally opposed to the establishment of a home for the Jews and Zionists in Palestine. They also indicated the desire of the Palestinians to preserve their country's historical and geographical unity with Syria. The results of the referendum, however, were never publicized, thus enabling Britain and its partners to ensure that the Zionist plans in Palestine would materialize, even if it were at the expense of its legitimate Arab inhabitants who constituted 90 percent of the total population.

The Arab demands, which had been formulated at the General Syrian

of Israel. In fact, only once the Balfour Declaration was formalized in the Mandatory Charter, which set forth the terms of British rule in Palestine before the League of Nations, did the political Zionism reach its peak.

In the Mandatory Charter (May 1922), Britain committed to the League of Nations as follows:

> Whereas the Principal Allied Powers have also agreed that the Mandatory should be responsible for putting into effect the declaration originally made on November 2nd, 1917, by the Government of His Britannic Majesty, and adopted by the said Powers, in favor of the establishment in Palestine of a national home for the Jewish people, it being clearly understood that nothing should be done which might prejudice the civil and religious rights of existing non-Jewish communities in Palestine, or the rights and political status enjoyed by Jews in any other country;
>
> And whereas recognition has thereby been given to the historical connection of the Jewish people with Palestine and to the grounds for reconstituting their national home in that country; [. . .] [The Council of the League of Nations] [. . .] confirming the said Mandate, defines its terms as follows: [. . .]
>
> Article 2: The Mandatory shall be responsible for placing the country under such political, administrative and economic conditions as will secure the establishment of the Jewish national home [. . .] and the development of self-governing institutions, and also for safeguarding the civil and religious rights of all the inhabitants of Palestine [. . .]
>
> Article 4: An appropriate Jewish agency shall be recognized as a public body for the purpose of advising and co-operating with the Administration of Palestine in such economic, social and other matters as may affect the establishment of the Jewish national home [. . .]
>
> Article 6: The Administration of Palestine, while ensuring that the rights and position of other sections of the population are not prejudiced, shall facilitate Jewish immigration under suitable conditions and shall encourage, in co-operation with the Jewish agency referred to in Article 4, close settlement by Jews on the land, including State lands and waste lands not required for public purposes.[6]

ISRAELI TEXT / ישראלי טקסט

Congress in Damascus in July 1919, were presented to the King-Crane Commission. They included the following:

1. Preserving the unity of Great Syria, including Palestine, which formed the southern part of Syria.

2. Refusal of the partition of Great Syria.

3. Calling for a constitutional monarchy in Great Syria.

4. Rejection of the British Mandate.

5. Calling for the right of self-determination for all peoples.

6. Rejection of the Balfour Declaration and the establishment of the Jewish national homeland.

7. Abolishing all secret treaties in accordance with the right to self-determination.[5]

The close cooperation between Britain and the Zionist movement from 1917 to 1948 provided the basic components for that state: land, people, and sovereignty. It was done by purchasing land, enacting land laws, immigration, implementing plans to drive the Arab Palestinians away from their homeland, controlling the Palestinian economy, and Judaizing the administration of the country.

REALIZATION AND IMPLEMENTATION OF THE BALFOUR DECLARATION

By issuing the Balfour Declaration, the British government was committed to its implementation, which could not have been possible without imposing its control over Palestine. It is quite likely that it was specifically for that purpose that the declaration was issued in the first place; that is to say, to pave the way to put Palestine under British mandate and to keep Palestine out of international rivalry. When the British army entered Jerusalem on 9 December 1917, Palestine, Syria, and Iraq had already broken away from the Ottoman Empire thereby ending four centuries of Ottoman rule, which had started in 1516.[6]

In fact imperialist Britain applied its full weight to make the idea of a national homeland for the Jews see the light. The British welcomed Weizmann,

CLASHES BETWEEN ARABS AND JEWS: THE 1920 RIOTS

The Jewish settlers did not come to an empty land. Around the end of the nineteenth century and the beginning of the twentieth, Arabs lived in both urban concentrations and rural communities in Palestine, and some felt threatened by the waves of Jewish immigration. Nonetheless, many of the Arab residents worked on Jewish farms, and relationships based on common interests were created between the two communities. However, in 1920 the first violent clashes between Jews and Arabs in the Land of Israel erupted, later to be known as the 1920 riots. The clashes were concentrated in two main locations: Tel Hai and Jerusalem.

Tel Hai was an isolated community in the northeastern region of the Galilee, near Metulla. It was founded in 1918 by a group of *Hashomer* members, aspiring to "conquer" the guarding of the Jewish settlements and the work within them from Arab hands. The story of the events that unfolded there became one of the important early Zionist myths. Late in December of 1919, Joseph Trumpeldor, who became a legend in his own time, arrived with a group of *Shomrim* (guards) to defend Tel Hai, splendidly isolated in the no-man's-land between the area under French control and the area under British control (prior to the final decision on the mandatory boundaries). Trumpeldor was something of a heroic figure, having lost his left arm in the Russo-Japanese war while serving as a Russian officer. He was among the founders of the first Jewish self-defense forces, a tiller of the soil, an ideologue, and a Socialist-Zionist leader with a significant following among the young people of the third Aliyah.

Because Tel Hai endured many attacks from Arabs in the area and was completely isolated in the Upper Galilee, its people requested help in defending it, but the leadership of the *Yishuv* (Jewish settlement) was divided as to whether Tel Hai should be defended or evacuated. Labor movement leaders argued that it should be defended even at the cost of human lives, the rationale being that the future boundaries of the new Jewish state would be based on the map of Jewish settlements. One laborer, Mr. Aharonovich, stated, "If we are afraid of a force greater than our own, we will have to leave Metulla today, Tiberias tomorrow and after that other places."[7]

On March 1, Arabs sought to enter the grounds of Tel Hai to ascertain whether there were armed French forces there. The defenders of Tel Hai

the Zionist leader who headed the Zionist mission that arrived in Palestine on 4 April 1918. The mission was accompanied by Ormsby-Gore, the British liaison officer, who later became minister of the colonies in 1939. For the first time in history, Weizmann established an office for the Zionist movement in Jerusalem in August 1918. The mission toured Palestine freely and demanded to be involved in the administration of Palestine so as to be able to establish the Jewish national home. In the meantime, the mission worked at calming down the suspicions of the Arabs regarding the true intentions of Zionism.[7]

Weizmann strongly believed that "the lands of the Palestinians could be redeemed for money and the Palestinians could be subdued with a little determination as they did not constitute a national movement of purport." He further believed that the Palestinians did not represent a serious obstacle to the Zionist and British schemes. In a letter to his son, Weizmann described the Palestinian people as "the rocks of Judea [. . .] that should be cleared from the rugged path."

Weizmann's opinions became the cornerstone of the Zionist strategy. He further denied the existence of an independent Palestinian nationality. His view concerning the expulsion of the Palestinians from the Jewish state to Arab lands, where they could find a substitute homeland became the basis for "population transfer" schemes that were popular in the 1930s and 1940s.[8]

In a complementary step of the British colonialist policy which supported the Jews and Zionist schemes in Palestine, Britain canceled its military administration in Palestine and replaced it with a civil administration. In July 1920, the British government appointed the Jewish British ex-minister, Sir Herbert Samuel, author of the famous memorandum headed "The Future of Palestine: A Scheme for a State of 3–4 Million Jews," as the first

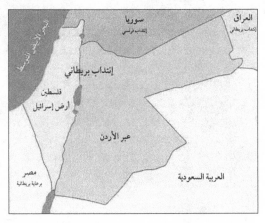

Map of the British Mandate (1922): the British divided the territory into the "Land of Israel" (Palestine) and the "Emirate of Transjordan"

The Roaring Lion statue that stands in Tel-Hai, created by Avraham Melnikov in 1932

permitted them access and then, for reasons not clear, shots were fired and a shootout developed. Some of the Tel Hai defenders were wounded and killed,

high commissioner of Palestine. Nobody was happier with this appointment than Chaim Weizmann, who stated, "We have put him in this position because he is our Samuel—he is the product of our Jewishness."[9]

The British mandate of Palestine was not an unplanned event. It was preceded by years of preparation to create the suitable circumstances under which the British declaration could become public and which would eventually become an official resolution issued by the League of Nations. Consequently any opposition to that resolution would be taken not only as an opposition to Britain but also to the international consensus and legitimacy and to all countries of the world.[10]

At the Peace Treaty Conference on 28 June 1919, Britain and France agreed to amend the Sykes-Picot Agreement whereby France conceded Mosul to Britain and agreed that Palestine should come under British rule in return for having a free hand in Syria and Lebanon. On 25 April 1920, the representatives of the Allies convening in San Remo passed several important and serious resolutions that totally ignored the rights and lawful demands of the Arabs. Lebanon and Syria were put under French mandate, Palestine under British mandate, in accordance with the desire of the Zionist Society on the condition that Britain would implement the Balfour Declaration. The mandate was formally approved by the League of Nations on 24 July 1922 after the colonialist powers had settled all the undecided issues among them. The mandate for Palestine came into force on 29 September 1923.

ONSET OF PALESTINIAN STRUGGLE AND POPULAR UPRISINGS

On 20 February 1920, General Bols, the British military governor of Palestine, made the first public statement about the British-Zionist policy in Palestine. He stated clearly that the mandate of Palestine was based on the Balfour Declaration and the establishment of a Jewish national home in Palestine.[11]

The Arabs' fears that Palestine would be transformed into a home for the Jews were now confirmed. So the Palestinians rose up to defend their country. Several Muslim-Christian societies came to the fore in response to the British policy and in expression of solidarity and unity against what the country was facing. These societies filed complaints to the Council of the

including Trumpeldor himself, who was injured during the evacuation. His last words were: "Never mind, it is good to die for our country." This sentence, whether actually uttered or not, became an educational slogan embodying the ethos of early Zionist settlement in the Land of Israel. The statue of the roaring lion erected at Tel Hai became a pilgrimage site for young people and the date of the battle became Tel Hai Day, marked with due ceremony in the nation's schools.

About a month after the incident at Tel Hai, riots grounded in national and religious feeling broke out in Jerusalem. Arab residents participating in the Nabi Moussa holiday celebrations were incited by groundless propaganda suggesting that Jews were trying to take over the Muslim holy places in Jerusalem. A crowd that began attacking Jews in the Jewish Quarter soon became a mob that went on a rampage through Jewish neighborhoods outside the Old City walls. The rioting then spread to the northern part of the country.

A personal impression of the rioting in the Old City of Jerusalem was given at the time by Zvi Nadav, who tried to defend the Jewish residents:

> I went down with Nehemia [Rabin] to David Street, leading to the Jewish Quarter. It was a terrifying scene—feathers flying through the air, shops broken open and looted—a picture very familiar to me from the rioting in Russia [. . .] an atmosphere like a pogrom. The [British] army and police were not restraining the rioters.[8]

The numbers killed, the sense of helplessness in the *Yishuv*, the inaction of the British police and its tolerant attitude toward the rioters suggested to many in the *Yishuv* that the Jews needed their own independent defense force. The workers' organizations decided to set up such a force, to be called the *Haganah* (Defense), and over time the *Haganah* became the fighting force of the Jewish community in the *Yishuv*.[9]

CONCLUSION

The British era in the Land of Israel opened with great hopes on the part of the Zionist movement, due to the Balfour Declaration of 1917, which expressed Britain's support for the establishment of a national home for the Jewish people in the Land of Israel. This hope was reinforced by the Mandatory Charter,

Allies to declare their rejection of the Balfour Declaration, Jewish immigration to Palestine, and the separation of Palestine from Syria.[12]

At that time, a newspaper called *Southern Syria* owned by 'Aref Al-'Aref led a campaign against Bols's offensive declaration. Al-'Aref, a well-known Palestinian historian, wrote a series of editorials denouncing the policies and practices of the British in Palestine.

The protests continued. On 27 February 1920 a large demonstration took place with the full knowledge of the British authority. Forty thousand demonstrators participated in the demonstration, which was the first political demonstration after the British occupation of Palestine. The demonstrators expressed their fears and dissatisfaction about the future of Palestine under British rule. They also protested against the Peace Conference which made Palestine a national home for the Jews.[13]

Several events followed. In March 1920, the Arabs clashed with settlers from Matullah, Tel Hai, in the Galilee. During the clashes, Joseph Trumpeldor, a Jewish soldier, was killed.

APRIL UPRISING

In April of every year, Palestinians celebrate what is known as the Season of Al-Nabi Moussa (Feast of Prophet Moses). During this festival, people from all the various parts of Palestine come together in Jerusalem before the procession heads to Jericho. The traditional celebrations on 4–8 April 1920 turned into bloody clashes between the Arabs and the Jews as a result of the tension building up from the highly charged political atmosphere prevailing at the time.

The people of Jerusalem were busy welcoming their guests from Nablus and Hebron and other cities. Speeches that were made by famous leaders like Kathem Al-Hussaini and 'Aref Al-'Aref, among others, moved the nationalistic sentiments of the audience.[14]

In the meantime, a group of Jews happened to be passing by in a rather challenging manner. This increased the tension and so clashes broke out between the two sides. The events spread throughout Palestine and a general atmosphere of explosive tension prevailed. The events resulted in the death of 5 Jews and injury of 211, and the death of 4 Arabs and injury of 32.[15]

At the end of these events, Britain sent an investigation committee headed by General Ballin. The committee report attributed the reasons for

which bestowed international legitimacy on the Balfour Declaration. But Arab violence toward Jews beginning as early as 1920 showed (for whomever wished to see) that there were two national movements competing for the land, one Jewish and of relatively long standing, and the other Palestinian and gaining in power.

disturbances to the disappointment of Arabs after the failure of Britain to fulfill its promise to grant them independence. The report also referred to the strong belief among Arabs that the Balfour Declaration represented an aggression against their right to self-determination and to Arabs' fears that the establishment of a Jewish state would lead to their subjugation by Jews in their own homeland as a result of the increasing Jewish immigration.[16]

Unfortunately, the British government, which was complacent with the Zionist conspiracies, chose to keep this report secret as it expressed some justice to the native inhabitants of the country.

CONCLUSION

The anxiety and fear of the Arabs concerning the Balfour Declaration was slightly set to rest by U.S. President Wilson's speech on 4 July 1918, in which he stated that the settlement after the war (World War I) would be based on the principle of the freedom of peoples to self-determination. The Arabs also felt much at rest after the publication of the official French-British statement on 7 November 1918, which made it clear that the purpose of the war was to liberate peoples from the Ottoman rule forever, and to form national governments which would take their power from the desire and free choice of the people.

Obviously, Wilson's principle of self-determination and a national government in Palestine according to the French-British statement were seen as the logical first steps for the establishment of a national Arab Palestinian government, particularly since the population majority was still Arab Palestinian. Sadly, all these dreams and aspirations were completely blown up by the project of British mandate over Palestine, which in fact had been based on the Balfour promise of a Jewish home in Palestine.

THE LAND OF ISRAEL AND THE *YISHUV* IN THE 1920S

The Middle East was divided, as previously noted, between France and Britain: France received a mandate over the areas that would become Syria and Lebanon, while Britain received a mandate over the areas that would become Israel, Jordan, and Iraq. The mandate system replaced the colonial system after World War I. The League of Nations gave the victorious powers control of conquered territories in the form of mandates for a limited period of time, the objective being the preparation of a physical and organizational infrastructure that would enable those territories to eventually become independent nations.

In 1920, the British mandate took effect in Palestine after hundreds of years of Muslim Ottoman rule. For the *Yishuv*—the Jewish community in Palestine—the 1920s were years of growth, although they began and ended with violent disturbances on the Arab side.

BRITISH POLICY IN PALESTINE: "BALANCED COMMITMENTS"

In July 1920, Herbert Samuel began his term as the first British high commissioner in Palestine. Upon arrival, Samuel, a British Jew who supported Zionist

BRITAIN AND THE JEWS

After the publication of the Balfour Declaration in 1917, Palestine was placed under British mandate. During their mandate of Palestine, the British provided all the conditions and facilitations necessary for the establishment of a national home for the Jews in Palestine.

Although the Jews claim to have historical rights to Palestine, though there had not been any Jewish sovereignty in Palestine for over 2,000 years, the Arabs strongly believe that these claims or rights are utterly groundless. At no stage in history did the Jews have full sovereignty over Palestine. The Palestinians insist that they are the true owners of Palestine.[1]

In order to give the Balfour Declaration a legal status, it was incorporated in the Mandate Document that was issued by the League of Nations. The Mandate Document consisted of a preamble and twenty-eight articles. The preamble made reference to the Balfour Declaration in addition to the consent of the Allied Powers to establish a national home for the Jews in Palestine. The document also made it the responsibility of the mandated

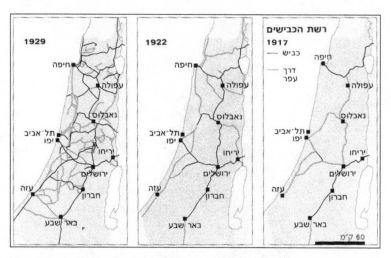

Map of the development of the road system in the 1920s[1]

The first high commissioner, Herbert Samuel, arrives in Palestine, 1920

aspirations, announced a policy of "balanced commitments" toward all its residents, both Jews and Arabs alike. He recognized and supported the institutions of Jewish self-rule, granted a generous Aliyah quota, and gave development projects to new immigrants. At the same time, the high commissioner gave state lands to the Arabs, established schools, and helped raise the literacy rate among the Arab population: the percentage of illiterates dropped from 90 percent to 70 percent.[2] (At the start of the mandatory era, approximately 20,000 students

country to ensure the execution of this promise. Following are some of the articles incorporated in the Mandate Document.

> Article 1: The Mandatory (Britain) shall have full powers of legislation and of administration.
>
> Article 2: The Mandatory shall be responsible for placing the country under such political, administrative and economic conditions as will secure the establishment of the Jewish national home.
>
> Article 4: The Jewish Agency shall be recognized as an overall body for the purpose of advising and co-operating with the Administration of Palestine in economic and social matters.
>
> Article 6: The Administration of Palestine shall facilitate Jewish immigration to Palestine with the consent of the Jewish Agency.
>
> Article 7: The Administration of Palestine shall facilitate the acquisition of Palestinian citizenship by Jews.[2]

The Mandate Document constituted a gross breach of the Hussein-McMahon Agreement in which Britain undertook to grant independence to Arab countries after the war. It also breached the League of Nations Convention, which granted the original inhabitants the choice of the mandatory power. The Arabs did not choose Britain; it was the World Zionist Organization that did.

The Mandate Document, which the British government itself had drafted, incorporated the contents of the Balfour Declaration in its preamble. The draft was met with strong opposition within the British government. One of its most prominent opponents was Foreign Secretary Lord Curzon. In commenting about the task of the mandatory "to prepare Palestine politically, administratively and economically for the establishment of a Jewish national home," Curzon made the following comments:

The Zionists, as well as many of those Britons who identify

"Two blows on the head is painful": cartoon critiquing the Sykes-Picot Agreement and the Balfour Declaration

Winston Churchill—British Minister of the Colonies, 1921–1922

with them, are working for the establishment of a Jewish state in which the Arabs will be "hewers of wood and drawers of water."

I have never been consulted as to this Mandate at an earlier stage, nor do I know from what negotiations it springs or on what undertakings it is based. . . . I think the entire concept wrong.

Curzon added cynically,

Five hundred eighty thousand Arabs and 30,000 Jews live in the country. . . . Acting upon the noble principles of self-determination and ending with a splendid appeal to the League of Nations, we then proceed to draw up a document which . . . is an avowed constitution for a Jewish State. Even the poor Arabs are only allowed to look through the keyhole as a non-Jewish community.[3]

Surprisingly, the Mandate Document of Palestine was different from the mandate in Syria, Lebanon, and Iraq, where the document stated that the responsibility of the mandate was to find ways to facilitate the development of these countries toward attaining their independence. In contrast, the first article in the mandate over Palestine granted the mandatory "full powers of legislation and of administration." This in fact amounted to turning Palestine into a British colony.[4]

After replacing the military administration with a civil administration in June 1920, Britain appointed Sir Herbert Samuel as its first high commissioner in Palestine. The British government saw in Samuel the ideal person to lay the foundations for implementing the Mandate Document and the special conditions therein together with the Balfour Declaration and the promise of a Jewish national home. After all, this was the same Jew who had published the well-known memorandum "The Future of Palestine: The Plan for a State Containing 3–4 Million Jews." The appointment of Samuel made no one happier than Chaim Weizmann, who announced, "We have appointed him to this position because he is our Samuel; he is the product of our Jewishness."[5]

During his term in office, Samuel first laid the foundations that were necessary for the development of all aspects of the Jewish society in Palestine. As a first step, Samuel enacted the first immigration law on 26 August 1920. This law permitted the entry of 15,079 Jewish immigrants to the country in

were attending Arab public schools; whereas in 1947, just before the British mandate had ended, 80,000 students were attending 504 public schools. A further 18,000 students attended Muslim schools and 22,000 were in Christian schools.)[3]

The occupation of the country by the British was a turning point in its modernization. The mandate regime invested heavily in the development of services and economic infrastructure, notably transportation: roads, railways, seaports, and airfields. The British established court systems, a tax authority, and a postal service. Education, health, and municipal government were generally left to the local people, while the British provided advice and assistance via government funding. The *Yishuv* was better able to take advantage of this than were the Arabs, due to their heightened organizational, diplomatic, and political awareness. The *Yishuv* operated autonomously in education, health, and employment, and even received important economic concessions. On the Palestinian side, however, no comparable developments emerged.[4]

In March 1921, Winston Churchill, the British minister of the colonies, visited Palestine to investigate the sources of tension between the Jews and Arabs. During his visit, Churchill reiterated England's support for the Balfour Declaration, despite Arab attempts to change his position, yet emphasized that the national rights of the Arabs were not to be harmed. Churchill's statements were among the principal factors contributing to the riots that broke out in 1921.

A group of immigrants that had organized a May Day procession was attacked by an Arab mob that moved on to the immigrants' house in the Ajami quarter of Jaffa, which for the Arabs symbolized Jewish immigration to Palestine. The unrest spread from there to the nearby Jewish neighborhoods: Neveh Shalom, Manshiya, and Abu Kabir. After the attacks in Jaffa, disturbances also broke out in the agricultural communities of Petach Tikvah, Hadera, and Rehovot, although there they were halted by organized groups of local residents. During the riots of 1921, a great deal of property was looted and forty-seven Jews were killed, among them author Yosef Haim Brenner.

After the rioting, Churchill published a British position paper regarding Palestine, the first White Paper (June 1922). In this document, the British government reiterated its commitment to the Balfour Declaration and even acknowledged the right of the Jewish people to establish a national home in

the first year. It was the green light that accelerated the Jewish immigration movement to Palestine.

Contributions were collected from Jews to pay for the immigration and acts of settlement through the Palestine Foundation Fund (*Keren Hayesod*). In the first British official population census conducted in 1922, there were 752,048 inhabitants in Palestine: 87.9 percent Arabs and 11.1 percent Jews. In order to execute Weizmann's plans to make Palestine as Jewish as England was English and France was French, more concessions were made to facilitate Jewish immigration to Palestine even further. From 1919 to 1923, Jewish immigration to Palestine totaled 36,761. From 1924 to 1928, the number came to 64,629, and in 1929, 5,249 Jewish immigrants arrived.

The following table shows the size of Jewish immigration to Palestine from 1919 to 1930:[6]

Year	Immigrants	Year	Immigrants
1919	1,643	1925	33,801
1920	15,079	1926	13,081
1921	4,784	1927	2,713
1922	7,834	1928	2,178
1923	7,421	1929	5,429
1924	12,856	1930	4,944

1921 UPRISING IN JAFFA

The uprising that broke out in Jaffa in 1921 followed large demonstrations held by Jewish communists marking Labor Day on May 1, which they had been in the habit of observing in Europe. At the same time, there was a counterdemonstration held by a group of anticommunist Jews. Clashes broke out between the two groups. When the police dispersed them, some marched on to the Arab neighborhood of Manshiyyeh, where they clashed with the Arabs who thought that the demonstration was directed against them. Information about the confrontation between the two groups reached the city of Jaffa and fighting broke out between the Arabs and the Jews in the city streets. Shops closed and looting occurred.[7]

Palestine. At the same time, the document set limits regarding the two promises given to the Jews: first, the territory promised for the national home was reduced, and the eastern bank of the Jordan River was to become a separate political entity ("Transjordan"); second, a precedent-setting limit was placed on the quota of Jewish immigrants, based on the capacity to absorb them economically in Palestine. Some in the Zionist movement saw this document as a renewed confirmation of Britain's commitment to Zionism, and believed that the limitation on Jewish immigrants according to the country's economic capacity to absorb them was appropriate, because it would prevent a dangerous influx of immigrants unable to support themselves. Others saw the White Paper as the first signs of the British withdrawal from the Balfour Declaration.

From the first White Paper:

> The tension which has prevailed from time to time in Palestine is mainly due to apprehensions, which are entertained both by sections of the Arab population and by sections of the Jewish population. These apprehensions, so far as the Arabs are concerned are partly based upon exaggerated interpretations of the meaning of the [Balfour] Declaration. [. . .] Unauthorized statements have been made to the effect that the purpose in view is to create a wholly Jewish Palestine. Phrases have been used such as that Palestine is to become "as Jewish as England is English." [. . .] His Majesty's Government regard any such expectation as impracticable and have no such aim in view. Nor have they at any time contemplated, as appears to be feared by the Arab delegation, the disappearance or the subordination of the Arabic population, language or culture in Palestine. They would draw attention to the fact that the terms of the Declaration referred to do not contemplate that Palestine as a whole should be converted into a Jewish National Home, but that such a Home should be founded "in Palestine."[5]

1922–1929: "THE SEVEN GOOD YEARS"

The period between the riots of 1921 and those of 1929 is termed, in some history books, "the seven good years," because there was relative quiet between Jews and Arabs, and the *Yishuv* enjoyed the support of the British.

Day after day, the disturbances expanded until they encompassed the whole Jaffa district. The Arabs attacked the Jewish settlements of Mulabbas (Petach Tikva), Hadira, Diran, and Tel Hai. The Arab revolutionaries also attacked the Zionist immigration center in Jaffa. British army and police forces stood at the side of the Jews and two British warships arrived in Jaffa port to scare the inhabitants.[8]

The disturbances lasted for fifteen days and eventually the British managed to bring matters under control. The events resulted in the deaths of 47 Jews and injury of 146; and the deaths of 48 Palestinians and injury of 75. Most of the Arab casualties were hit by fire from the British police and army. The government imposed large fines on the Arabs and the courts issued heavy sentences on them. The revolt in Jaffa was accompanied by demonstrations and unrest in the other cities of Palestine.[9]

Following the events in Jaffa, the British government set up a commission of inquiry chaired by Sir Thomas Haycraft, chief justice of Palestine. The commission interviewed Jews and Arabs and submitted its report in October 1921. The report was balanced and attributed the disturbances to the following:

1. The storm of emotions on the part of the Arabs was caused by the crass conduct of the young Jewish *halutsim* on the streets of Jaffa, both in regard to their inappropriate attire and stance, walking arm in arm, singing songs rowdily, and disturbing traffic.[10]

2. The opposition of the Palestinian Arabs to Zionism and to the policy of the British government, whose major goal was the establishment of a national home for the Jews. In the meantime, the government was not doing anything for the good of all Palestinians. The Haycraft Commission recommended that "It must be made clear to the [Jewish] migrants, regardless of their historical and religious claims, that they are seeking to establish a home in a country where the majority of inhabitants are Arab and so they [immigrants] have to adopt a fair attitude towards the people with whom they have to live in peace."[11]

3. The flow of foreign Jewish immigrants and the danger inherent therein for the Arabs of Palestine, particularly following the birth of political Zionism, which was not satisfied with limited legal immigration based on religious or charitable motives but encouraged mass Jewish immigration in order to settle in Palestine and then take control over it.

4. The report indicated that the Zionist leaders were planning to con-

"Work Battalion" pioneers building a road

If someone had left the Land of Israel at the start of the 1920s and returned at the end of that decade, he would have found a great change. Early in the decade, the country was still grappling with the shortages and hardships of the World War I period, but over the years it recovered, enjoying impressive economic growth. When World War I ended, there were only 56,000 Jews left in Palestine (as opposed to 80,000 before the war). With the end of the war came the third Aliyah (1919–1923), a wave of immigration of 35,000 immigrants, mostly Eastern European. These were generally young, ideologically motivated socialists, who came with the intention of creating an egalitarian and just society different from the Jewish-European one they had left behind. These pioneers set up communities of a new type, based on equality and partnership, and worked mainly in farming and road building.

The next wave of mass immigration, the fourth Aliyah (1924–1929), brought 70,000 immigrants mostly from Eastern Europe, following the economic crisis in Poland in the 1920s. The fourth Aliyah saw the arrival, alongside the pioneering youth, of many petit bourgeois families who brought along their small savings to invest in Palestine and strengthened the urban sector in the *Yishuv*. These new immigrants and the wealth they brought with them from Europe injected new blood into every sphere of life. In 1929, after the latest immigration, the *Yishuv* numbered 157,000 (compared with 900,000 Arabs).

DEVELOPMENT OF THE JEWISH ECONOMY AND HEBREW CULTURE

During the period of the first high commissioners (Herbert Samuel, 1920–1925; and Herbert Charles Onslow Plumer, Baron Plumer, 1925–1928), the country knew a reasonable degree of public order and security, and the *Yishuv* was able to take full advantage of this period to focus on economic development. Many of the third Aliyah pioneers were employed in

trol the whole of Palestine. It also gave testimony of an official in Palestine who said, "It is not possible to have more than one national home in Palestine and that is the Jewish home." The commission recommended protecting the rights of the Arabs and appeasing their fears.[12]

The British, however, ignored the report of the Haycraft Commission because it was not consistent with their policy of establishing a national home for the Jews. It was the first British commission of inquiry whose report was ignored by the British themselves.[13]

THE FIRST WHITE PAPER (CHURCHILL'S MEMORANDUM)

Following the bloody events in Jaffa, following the recommendations of the Haycraft Commission regarding the Arabs' rights and the reasons behind the events, following the activity of the Palestinian mission in London and the meetings it held with British figures, and after the Arabs had boycotted the legislative council that was proposed, Winston Churchill, minister of colonies, was convinced that there was no choice but to announce a promise that would please the Arabs. Accordingly, Churchill issued what came to be known as the White Paper on 22 June 1922.[14]

The White Paper stated that the British would not allow Palestine to become a state for the Jews and promised to help the inhabitants set up self-rule. The purpose of the White Paper was to mollify the fears of the Arabs concerning the goals of Zionism. The White Paper stressed the following:

1. The Balfour Declaration did not intend to turn the whole of Palestine into a national home for the Jews, but it meant that such a home would be established in Palestine.

2. A Jewish national home does not mean a Jewish state, and it does not have to be established instantly but gradually and with the passage of time.

3. Jewish immigration must continue though it must be restricted in accordance with the economic capacity of the country to absorb new immigrants.

4. A legislative council must be established as a step toward self-rule.

5. Palestine was excluded from the commitment for independence which Britain made in the Hussein-McMahon correspondence.[15]

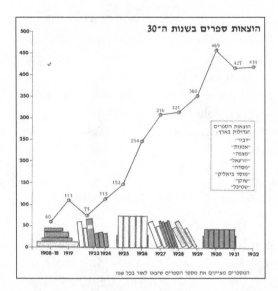

הוצאות ספרים בשנות ה־30׳

הוצאות הספרים
הגדולות בארץ:
"דביר"
"אמנות"
"מצפה"
"יזרעאל"
"מסדה"
"מוסד ביאליק"
"שוקן"
"שטיבל"

המוספרים מציינים את מיספר הסופרים שיצאו לאור בכל שנה

Hebrew-Language Publishing Houses in the 1930s

The largest publishing houses in Hebrew:
"Dvir"
"Amanut"
"Mitzpeh"
Jezreel
"Masada"
"Mosad Bialick"
"Schoken"
"Schtibel"

The numbers indicate number of books published each year.[6]

public works projects initiated by the first high commissioners, mainly road building.

In the fourth Aliyah, a notable impact was made by immigrants who came with their own capital and invested it in industry, infrastructure, and services in the new land. Two large factories were set up by Jews under an arrangement with the mandatory government: the power station in Naharayim built by Pinhas Rutenberg, and the Dead Sea Potash Works. The city that most benefited from this economic expansion was Tel Aviv; it absorbed more than half the immigrants from the fourth Aliyah and expanded in a single year to a population of 40,000. The influx of both population and capital was clearly evident in an unprecedented construction boom in Tel Aviv.

Dizengoff Circle in Tel Aviv, early 1930s

The construction industry now became a significant employment sector and attracted major investment. Tel Aviv, the new urban center, also acquired new prominence as the center of cultural and social life. In the evenings

Churchill's White Paper clearly ignored the demands of the Palestinians from the British to cancel the Jewish national home project, stop Jewish immigration, and establish an independent national entity for Palestinians. It was also evident that the purpose of associating Jewish immigration with the economic absorptive capacity of the country, to the disregard of the Palestinian national political considerations, was no more than a means to facilitate the continued flow of Jewish immigrants to Palestine.[16]

At the same time, several Palestinian conferences were held. The Fifth Palestinian Conference took place in Nablus on 20–25 August 1922. It called for:

1. The rejection of the constitution which the British had made for Palestine.

2. Boycotting of the elections to the legislative council in Palestine as the proposed formation of the council was designed to lead to British and Jewish control over it.

3. The rejection of the mandate over Palestine.

4. Boycotting of Jewish businesses.

5. Dispatching of a Palestinian mission to the Muslim East and another to America.

6. Protesting of the financial loan which the British had signed in the name of Palestine.

7. Refusal to participate in the Rutenberg project (electricity company).

8. Establishment of an Arab office in London.[17]

The conference announced a Palestinian national charter which the delegates swore to uphold. The charter read:

We, the representatives of the Palestinian Arab people at the Fifth Arab Palestinian Conference in Nablus, vow before Allah and before our nation and history to continue working for the independence of our country and to realize Arab unity through legitimate and legal means and to refuse the establishment of a Jewish national home and Zionist immigration.[18]

1925—the Hebrew University is founded

the city's residents sat in cafés, strolled along the attractive new boulevards, went to the theater, and attended the symphony orchestra's concerts. Book publishing flourished and there were several daily newspapers to choose from, many of them in Hebrew. The Hebrew language, virtually new to all the Jews in the country, enjoyed a renaissance and became the main spoken language in general conversation as well as the language of instruction in schools.

The mixed cities, Haifa and Jerusalem, also enjoyed economic and cultural growth. New Jewish neighborhoods were built, the first Hebrew University was founded in Jerusalem, and construction was under way of a new, modern port in Haifa. In the Ysrael Valley an entire new city was founded—Afula.

NEW COMMUNITIES, SOME OF A NEW KIND ALTOGETHER

A tour through the country at the end of the 1920s would have revealed about thirty new communities, all founded in the decade just ending, some of which were farming communities. They were established on lands purchased either by national institutions or private individuals, in the Ysrael Valley, the Zevulon Valley, and the Sharon region. Notable among them was a new and unique type of community: the *kibbutz*. The kibbutz offered a particular kind of socialist-style living based on ideas brought by immigrants from Eastern Europe and modified by the realities of life in the Land of Israel. It was a community of dozens or even hundreds of families, living a shared and

THE YEARS OF CALM AND STABILITY (1923–1929)

The period between 1923 and 1929 was considered to be one of relative quiet in comparison with previous years. The reason for that lies in the British deceitful maneuvering of the Palestinian leadership, which included declarations and calls not to touch the political and religious rights of the Arabs and not to turn all Palestine into a national home for the Jews. The Zionist program had come a long way in increasing the number of immigrants to Palestine. The number of Jewish immigrants during that period reached to 77,299 immigrants from Poland, Russia, Germany, Rumania, Britain, America, and Asia.

On their part, the Palestinian leadership failed to organize the Palestinian people into a true rebellion against the British-Zionist project due to the differences between the traditional powerful families and political parties on the Palestinian street. This stemmed from the British policy of "divide and rule."

At the same time, it cannot be claimed that this was a period of absolute peace. New means of struggle and opposition emerged especially in regard to preventing the sale of lands. In 1925 there was a general strike throughout Palestine to protest the visit of Balfour to Palestine to participate in the inauguration of the Hebrew University. The Palestinian press took a very firm stand against this visit. Khalil Al-Sakakini, the famous Palestinian educator and intellectual, gave a nationalist speech in Al-Aqsa Mosque, in which he asked Balfour to leave the country, which he had entered contrary to the desire of its inhabitants.[19] In June 1928, the Seventh Palestinian Conference was held and it called for forming a national parliamentary government.

THE POLITICAL CONDITIONS IN PALESTINE

In order to facilitate Jewish settlement and control over all spheres of life in Palestine, the British mandate recognized the Jewish Agency, which was set up in 1922. The functions of the agency, which were determined by its constitution in August 1929, were the following:

- To encourage and strengthen Jewish immigration.
- To provide for the Jews' religious needs.

PALESTINIAN TEXT / النص الفلسطيني

fully egalitarian life together. Members had no private property, all the assets belonged to the kibbutz, and the kibbutz took care of its members' needs and well-being: work according to one's abilities and receive according to one's needs. Decisions were made by all members in a democratic fashion, and daily life—meals, leisure activities, and child care—were handled collectively. Kibbutzim were built on land purchased with national resources, generally in outlying areas where life was hard, and they focused on tilling the land, industry, and contributing to the country's prosperity. At the same time, another group of workers' communities, *moshavim*, developed, practicing similar national and social ideas to those of the kibbutzim, but adopting a lesser degree of communal ownership. Each family had its own land to farm, and consumption and lifestyle were family based rather than collective based.

A famous poem of that era successfully conveys the spirit of the times, featuring the redemption and nurturing of the land:

Morning Song
by Nathan Alterman

Morning sun blazes on mountains
the valley yet wet with dew
We love you, our homeland,
in joy, in song and in work.

Clothe you in concrete,
cover you in gardens,
the grains on your rescued lands
will rejoice like bells.

from Lebanon's hills to the Dead Sea,
we will work you with ploughs,
we will plant you and build you,
make you beautiful indeed.

We'll carve a road through your desert,
and drain your swamps dry for you,
doing it all for your glory,
all of that and more.

- To develop the Hebrew language and nurture Jewish culture.
- To obtain ownership over land in order to expand the scope of Jewish settlement.
- To increase agricultural settlement.
- To establish armed terrorist Jewish bands (*hagana*) to protect the settlers and their property. (The Hagana Organization, under the leadership of Vladimir Jabotinsky, took charge of training Jews to fight.)[20]

In 1923, the High Commissioner Herbert Samuel tried to create an Arab agency like the Jewish Agency, but the Arabs refused to cooperate with the mandatory government because that project did not satisfy all their demands.

In contrast, Ze'ev Jabotinsky, who came out with the Iron Wall doctrine, and who was very active during Samuel's term of office, tried to establish an Arab-Jewish Brotherhood Society, but the name of this society belied its true intentions. The main purpose of this society was first to attack the Muslim-Christian Society and to tempt the weak Arabs to join the Brotherhood Society. Jabotinsky's plan failed due to the alertness of the Arabs.[21]

In addition, the British and the Zionists also applied the policy of "divide and rule." They set up Arab political parties to divide the Arabs. For example, they created the Agricultural Party, whose sole purpose was to sow suspicion and negative feelings among villagers toward city dwellers and vice versa. As a result, some animosity and dislike appeared between villagers and city dwellers. Fortunately, this party did not survive long; it was brought to an end by the villagers themselves. Some of the negative feelings sought by this party survived for a long time after the Agricultural Party had disappeared.[22]

The British played their divide-and-rule policy very smartly to divide the politically powerful Palestinian families. For example, following the death of the mufti of Jerusalem, Kamal Al-Husseini, in 1921, the Al-Nashashibi family tried to get their hands on that position so as to hold both it and the mayoralty of Jerusalem, then controlled by Ragheb Al-Nashashibi, who enjoyed the support of the British.

Public opinion, however, was in support of appointing Haj Amin Al-Husseini as mufti of Jerusalem, in place of his late brother. To circumvent this problem, Samuel decided to hold elections for the post of mufti instead

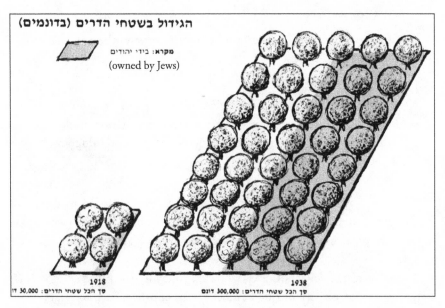

הגידול בשטחי הדרים (בדונמים)

מקרא: בידי יהודים
(owned by Jews)

1918
סך הכל שטחי הדרים: 30,000 דו׳

1938
סך הכל שטחי הדרים: 300,000 דונם

The development of the citrus areas (in dunams): 1918—30,000 dunams; 1938—300,000 dunams

The development of the citrus sector was the most important agricultural advance in the *Yishuv* during this period. The diagram above shows the impressive expansion in citrus farming during the 1920s and 1930s.[7]

INSTITUTIONAL LEADERSHIP AND POLITICAL PARTIES

Governmental-like institutions were established in the *Yishuv* from the beginning of the 1920s, based on general elections. These civil and governmental systems are frequently referred to as a "State in the Making."

The *Yishuv* was led by the *Va'ad Leumi* (national committee), which represented the autonomous Jewish community of Palestine in its dealings with the British mandatory authorities. The Jewish people overall were represented by the Jewish Agency.

The democratic character of its leadership and institutions was typical of the Zionist movement from its inception and was upheld in the Land of Israel. All members of the *Yishuv* enjoyed equal rights to the franchise, notably including women, before this was common in many developed nations. The old joke about the remote island with two Jews and three political parties

of using his authority to appoint Haj Amin Al-Husseini according to the wish of the people in Jerusalem.

Because the election results were fraudulent, Al-Husseini came in fourth, contrary to all expectations. The people and the Al-Husseini family protested against the result, and because of pressure exerted by some of the British officials who supported Al-Husseini, Samuel was eventually forced to appoint Al-Husseini to the position of mufti of Jerusalem. It was evident from the very start that the aim of this entire maneuver was to pit the Al-Husseini and Al-Nashashibi families against each another in order to engage the Palestinians with petty side disputes, such as family issues or differences over political parties, so as to weaken the national unity and resistance.

Haj Amin Al-Husseini played an important political and religious role during the entire period of the British mandate of Palestine by virtue of his appointment as mufti of the Holy Land on 8 May 1921. He contributed greatly to the establishment of the Supreme Islamic Council, which became so active in the defense of Arab rights and demands that the British viewed it as a "third government" in Palestine—the other two being the British government and the Jewish Agency. Haj Amin Al-Husseini began to lend support to the national schools both financially and morally, for example, Al-Najah School in Nablus and Rawdat Al-Ma'aref in Jerusalem. He safeguarded the lands of the *Waqf* (trust) and defended them against the greed of the British and the Jews.[23]

THE ECONOMIC CONDITIONS IN PALESTINE

The main aim of the British mandate was to do its utmost to facilitate the establishment of the Jewish national home in Palestine. This became evident through the facilitations provided for the establishment of Jewish economic projects and institutions, etc. This process was paralleled

The "Zionist Economy" (above) and "Arab Economy" (below)

was certainly applicable in the *Yishuv*. There were numerous political parties and organizations, each of which had its own settlement branch, economic arm, sports clubs, cultural institutions, and paramilitary organizations. By the spring of 1920, the Jewish residents of the Land of Israel (collectively known in Hebrew as *Knesset Yisrael)* went to the polls to vote in the first elections for the leadership of *Yishuv* institutions. At that time, there were 28,765 people eligible to vote, of whom 77 percent actually did so. Twenty different political parties succeeded in electing representatives to the elected assembly that would choose the members of the *Va'ad Leumi*. The data clearly attest to a vigorous and diversified political life in the earliest years of the *Yishuv*.

The largest and most prominent political camp was that of the workers, which adopted a socialist position: the Jewish state to be established would

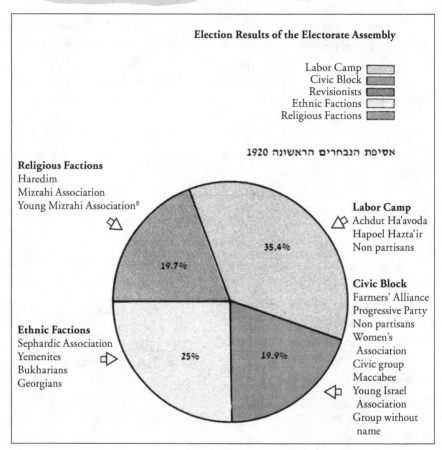

Election Results of the Electorate Assembly

Labor Camp
Civic Block
Revisionists
Ethnic Factions
Religious Factions

אסיפת הנבחרים הראשונה 1920

Religious Factions
Haredim
Mizrahi Association
Young Mizrahi Association[8]

Labor Camp
Achdut Ha'avoda
Hapoel Hazta'ir
Non partisans

Civic Block
Farmers' Alliance
Progressive Party
Non partisans
Women's
 Association
Civic group
Maccabee
Young Israel
 Association
Group without
 name

Ethnic Factions
Sephardic Association
Yemenites
Bukharians
Georgians

35.4%
19.7%
25%
19.9%

by a process of destruc-
tion of the Palestinian
entity and of dispossess-
ing the Palestinian people
of its land and natural
resources.

As high commis-
sioner, Samuel seized
extensive areas of state-
owned lands and closed
the Agricultural Bank
that had given loans to

The wheat harvest season in Palestine

Arab farmers during the Ottoman period. The mandate held the lands of
the farmers and impounded their livestock until they settled their loans and
exhausted the inhabitants by raising taxes to the point where they were forced
to sell their lands to pay off their taxes.

Samuel issued an order to establish a land registry and appointed Truman
Bentwich as its director. Being a Zionist, Bentwich's goal was to seize as much
Arab land as he could and give it to the Jews. The British government adopted
a variety of methods to impoverish the Palestinian farmer. For example, the
government would flood the market with imported wheat and oil just a few
weeks before the wheat harvest season or olive picking to force the local products to be sold at the lowest prices. This sometimes forced Palestinian farmers
to abandon their agricultural lands and migrate to the cities, where employment among laborers increased and wages dropped.[24]

Following is how a Palestinian peasant from the village of Sarsa' (district
of Safad) described the situation: "Just before a Palestinian farmer harvests his
wheat, the British would import cheaper wheat from Australia by sea and sell
it in Haifa at half-a-piaster per kilo. They are fully aware that the Palestinian
farmer cannot sell at this price."[25]

"The British Judaization policy knew no limits. It facilitated the Jews'
purchase of over 200,000 dunums in Marj Ibn Amar [Jezreel Valley] and this
led to the expulsion of nine hundred families of tenant farmers."[26]

Following all the concessions, Herbert Samuel passed the laws of transfer of ownership, registration, and arrangement in 1920. The purpose of these
laws was to speed up the pace of the Jewish takeover of Arab lands. One

David Ben-Gurion, one of the Labor Party leaders

have to be egalitarian and all the means of production and capital would be collectively owned. The most prominent party in this camp during the 1920s was United Labour, later to become Israel's Workers Party (popularly known as *Mapai*, its Hebrew acronym). This party led the *Yishuv* and the state for decades under David Ben-Gurion (who later, in 1935, was named chairman of the Jewish Agency). The dominance of the socialist worldview in the *Yishuv* was also evident in the economic sector. The largest economic organization in the country was a workers' organization established in 1920, the *Histadrut* Labor Federation. The *Histadrut*, led by Ben-Gurion until 1935, saw to the pay and working conditions of laborers and a great deal more; the *Histadrut* itself owned the largest construction and industrial organizations in the country, providing jobs for many workers. These companies, along with banks and the health organizations, were owned collectively by the *Histadrut* membership, so the workers enjoyed its profits in various forms, such as housing, medical, educational, and cultural services. The *Histadrut* strived for an egalitarian society guided by a strong mass of laborers, and essentially led the

of these laws was for the protection of the Arab farmers against expulsion by the landlord, since the overwhelming majority of estates belonged to absentee landlords who lived in Syria and Lebanon. Up to that time, the relationship between landlords and tenant farmers was excellent. But with the enactment of the new law, the tenants were under the impression that they did not have to pay lease fees anymore because the law granted them certain "leasing rights" which protected them from being expelled from the land. On the other hand, landlords found themselves in a difficult and unenviable situation—they hardly received any lease money from their lands, and in the meantime they were burdened by taxes and were left in a critical situation.

The policy of the British government was to send to court anybody who had outstanding taxes. Debtors received heavy fines or prison sentences. A special type of tax that farmers had to pay was the tithe, i.e., one-tenth of the produce. However, growers of American grapes were exempted from the tithe for ten years. The exemption was made in favor of the Jews, who were the only farmers who grew this grape cultivar; whereas the Palestinian farmers did not benefit from this exemption because they grew the traditional local grape cultivars that they had always grown.[27]

The role of Jewish middlemen in the transfer of Arab land to Jewish owners cannot be ignored. Jewish middlemen were very active in buying Palestinian lands and promoted their business by offering to buy the land and "relieve the owner of his troubles." In one single instance, 40,000 acres were sold, on which were 18 villages. As a result, 688 peasant families were expelled from their lands, while 309 families joined the ranks of the landless; others escaped to nearby towns and villages and became sharecroppers and laborers. Although this incident occurred in 1922, the problem of finding land for those who were expelled from their land as a result of the transfer remained at the door of the mandatory government until its final days in Palestine in 1947.[28]

A Palestinian farmer from Tulkarm describes the situation:

> I am selling my land and property after the government has forced me to pay taxes and tithes, at a time when I lack the means to support myself and my family. Under these conditions, I am forced to turn to a rich man for a loan. . . . Yet when the time comes for repayment I do not find a single piaster in my pocket to buy dinner that night. In effect, I am

Zionist enterprise in every sphere (immigration, absorption, security, promotion of the Hebrew language, education, culture, etc.).

The second camp was known as the civic (*ezrachi*) camp, comprising members of the middle class who supported the establishment of a state based on private capital and free economic competition. There were two main parties: the General Zionists Party, which was center oriented, and the Revisionist Zionists Party (known by its Hebrew acronym, *Tzahar*), which was a right-wing party led by Ze'ev Jabotinsky.

These two camps were distinguished from each other not only by social and economic issues but also by their attitudes toward the Arabs. The workers' camp believed that the conflict with the Arabs could be resolved through dialogue and cooperation, and in the spirit of socialist ideology tried to practice cooperation and even brotherhood between Jewish and Arab workers. The Fourth United Labour Convention (1924) adopted a resolution to create "a platform that would protect the interests of workers from both peoples, express international solidarity and serve to draw together, and create a dialogue between, the Zionist Labor movement and the authentic national movement of the Arab people."[9]

Meanwhile, the Revisionists did not believe that dialogue at this stage would alleviate Arab opposition to Zionism. Jabotinsky developed an "Iron Wall" philosophy, holding that only a strong show of force toward the Arabs would block their efforts to do away with Zionism, and eventually lead to dialogue and even reconciliation. Jabotinsky wrote:

> As to a voluntary agreement between us and the Arabs, such dreams are impossible. [. . .] There is no hope that the Arabs of Eretz Israel will agree to turn "Palestine" into a country with a Jewish majority. [. . .] They relate to Eretz Israel, at a minimum, with the same instinctive love and the same organic zeal which the Aztecs felt toward their Mexico. [. . .] Thus settlement can proceed under the aegis of strength [. . .] behind an iron wall which it will not be in the power of the local population to breach. [. . .] So long as the Arabs harbor a desire, with the slightest hope of success, of being rid of us, there are no pleasant words nor heartfelt promises that will persuade them to let go of this hope—and precisely because they are not rabble, but a living nation. [. . .] The only path to an agreement [. . .] is an iron wall; meaning, a powerful force in Eretz Israel that cannot be influenced one way or the

obliged to double the amount of the original debt hoping that I will be able to repay a month or two later . . . or years after. . . . This way I have to sell my land to pay off my debts, from which I have received only a small fraction.[29]

With respect to abandoned lands, the Abandoned/Dead Hand Lands Law was issued on 16 February 1921. According to this law, the state confiscated all abandoned lands from anyone who did not have a deed of ownership. The purpose of this law was to take the lands out of the hands of the peasants and put them under the control of the mandate so they could be easily transferred to the Jews. This law applied even to *Waqf* lands of the Al-Khatib family in Jerusalem in order to build the Hebrew University Hotel. Over 22,000 dunums were confiscated from the Orthodox Church and 40,000 dunums to the south of Jaffa were confiscated and then transferred to the Jewish colony of Rishon Lezion.[30]

Additionally, the British mandate granted extensive land privileges and natural resources to the Rutenberg electricity project, which was exempted from tax for seven years. Similar concessions were made to the Dead Sea project for extraction of salts, the Huleh Irrigation project, and the Himma Springs (sulfur springs).[31]

Jewish immigration and the various British economic policies enraged the Arabs and gave rise to great concern. Mr. Churchill publicized a report he had received from Symes, governor of the Haifa District, regarding the dismay and anger of the Arab residents. Following is an excerpt from Symes's report:

Economic conditions have a strong impact on political affairs. These conditions are particularly difficult and, therefore, the village inhabitants have responded well to the incitements against the Government. There are no jobs in Acre, Shfa 'Amr and Haifa; all businesses are quickly deteriorating. Additionally, the customs barriers with Syria are

other by the pressures of the Arabs. To put it another way: The only way to achieve an agreement in the future is to completely let go of any attempts to achieve an agreement now. (Z. Jabotinsky, On the Iron Wall (the Arabs and Us)[10]

Ze'ev Jabotinsky—leader of the Revisionist Party

destroying transit commerce. The situation of porters, laborers and others who do not have regular jobs has also worsened because the Jewish institutions and business owners are giving priority to new immigrant Jewish laborers. People from all social classes in cities are suffering from a rise in the cost of living and often have to choose between bankruptcy and emigration. The situation of landowners is not any better. They are burdened by heavy debts and are unlikely to find additional loans. The price of wheat and other grains is also low because foreign markets are closed. As for Bedouins, they are obliged to either become farmers or emigrate from the country.[32]

EDUCATION UNDER THE BRITISH MANDATE

Education during the Ottoman period was quite restricted. In 1914 there were 349 schools in Palestine. The situation under the British mandate was not much better. The British sought to keep the Palestinian Arabs uneducated and denied them their right to learn. Statistics indicate that the number of schools during the first years of the mandate (1917–1921) went down to 235 (1921); in other words, 114 schools were closed.

During the British mandate, there were three types of schools in Palestine, based on their ownership: state or public schools, owned by the mandatory government; private nationalist schools, owned by the private sector, both individuals and groups; and schools owned by foreign institutions, mostly ethnic schools.[33]

The mandatory government controlled the education sector. Humphrey Boman was appointed as the first director of education. The British director enacted and implemented all the educational regulations, appointed and dismissed teachers, and also had control over the curriculum. Teaching was largely theoretical with very few applied topics such as farming and life sciences. There was much emphasis on gymnastics and scouting. *Al-Karmel* newspaper noted that

Palestinian schoolchildren in front of their school

PALESTINIAN ARAB SOCIETY FORGES A NATIONAL IDENTITY

During the 1920s, the Arabs in Palestine began forging a national identity. Initially, they saw themselves as belonging to the greater Muslim Arab nation that replaced the Ottoman Empire. During British military rule (1918–1920), they announced their affiliation with "Greater Syria" and called the Land of Israel "southern Syria-Palestine." When the dream of Greater Syria was shattered and the League of Nations mandate was confirmed, a separate Palestinian national identity began to coalesce, calling for separate political self-determination.

During the 1920s, the Arabs of Palestine were politically weak and divided by internal conflicts in several ways:

1. There was a struggle for Palestinian leadership between two dominant clans in Jerusalem, the Husseinis and the Nashashibis.

2. The wealthy and mostly urban families, who owned most of the land in the country, were out of touch with the rural masses. This alienation was rooted in a quasi-feudal system of land ownership, and in educational and cultural disparities.

3. There was disagreement concerning the organizing principle for national identity, with one school led by the Mufti Haj Amin Al-Husseini, seeing it as religious and Islamic, and the other school seeing it as a national identity based on a modern national political awareness, as proposed by the *Istiqlal* (independence) party founded in the 1930s.

4. The British did not recognize the Arab community in Palestine as a separate national community, and during this period the British did not help the Arab community to develop its own governing institutions, as was happening in the neighboring Arab states.

The Palestinian national movement focused on the struggle against Jewish immigration and the acquisition of land by Jews, and devoted less effort to creating its own autonomous political community. In its struggle against Zionism, it set forth maximalist demands with no readiness for any sort of compromise.

"Palestine needs architects, civil, electrical, mechanical and agricultural engineers more than lawyers and physicians."[34]

Palestinian schoolteachers suffered from an atmosphere of fear and oppression. *Palestine* daily wrote:

> No one is likely to find himself in such a dilemma as our history schoolteacher. Supposing in one of his classes he came across a political situation similar to ours and he wanted to compare the two situations. He would be immediately accused of engaging in politics and would likely be sent behind the sun or under the ground. Soon the Education Administration would believe that story and take the appropriate measures to erase this criminal off the surface of the earth without any investigation. . . . We have heard of many cases in which students have been dismissed by the Education Administration because they went on strike on the day when the entire nation was on strike. Perhaps the Education Administration wants our students to be Greek or from the Land of Siberia.[35]

The Palestinian educator Amin Hafez el-Djani noted that the purpose of the school curriculum was "to erase the national and Arab identity, and to educate the new generation in English literature, and to keep them completely ignorant about Arab history, the geography of Arab countries and Arab heritage and culture. Palestinian students seem to know more about Britain and its history and literature than the English themselves."[36]

A review of the Palestinian press in the 1920s allows one to come to the following conclusions:

1. The British education administration totally controlled Palestinian schools while, at the same time, leaving the Jews free to run their schools by themselves.

2. The British occupation authorities did not open any new schools. In fact, their education policy resulted in the spread of ignorance and illiteracy.

3. The British administration restricted academic freedoms and arrested nationalist students. Eight students were expelled from the Arab College in Jerusalem after their participation in the 1930 general strike.

4. The efforts of the Arabs in 1922 to found an Arab university in

CONFRONTATION BETWEEN ARABS AND JEWS: THE 1929 RIOTS

The Friday prayers on the Temple Mount on August 23, 1929, were thronged by Muslim worshipers, many armed with sticks and knives following a long period of dispute around the arrangements for prayers at the Western Wall. At around eleven AM, shots were fired on the Temple Mount, intended to charge the atmosphere, whereupon hundreds of worshipers mobbed the alleys of the market area, attacking Jewish passersby. This was the start of a series of disturbances that broke out all across the country, from Yesod Hama'aleh in the north to Beer Tuvia in the south, during which 133 Jews and 87 Arabs were killed, with approximately 500 wounded on both sides. Dozens of Jewish settlements were attacked and many were emptied of their inhabitants; the riots marked the end of the ancient Jewish community in Hebron.

The background to these disturbances is tied to the development of the Jewish community in the Land of Israel, which was able to expand demographically and even overcome a severe economic crisis in 1928. The competition between Arab clans also contributed to the disturbances, by giving Haj Amin Al-Husseini an opportunity to bolster his national-religious leadership on a tide of Palestinian public opinion.

The immediate cause of this violent awakening was a conflict over the prayer arrangements at the Western Wall. The catalyst for the disruption in this highly charged location was a portable cloth barrier that the Jews set up at the wall plaza on Yom Kippur of 1929, intended to separate the men from the women during prayer. The British governor of Jerusalem treated this as an abrogation of the status quo in an area under the control of the *Waqf,* the Muslim religious authorities, and entered the wall plaza with his soldiers during the Yom Kippur prayers in order to remove the barrier by force. The mufti of Jerusalem, Haj Amin Al-Husseini, exploited this incident to incite the masses against the Jews and spoke in terms of "the boundless and avaricious aspirations of the Jews, who aim to lay their hands on the Al Aqsa mosque."[11]

Another factor in the disturbances was a procession arranged by members of *Betar,* the Revisionist youth movement, at the wall plaza one week before the outbreak of the riots, and an Arab counterdemonstration on the following day. A week later, on August 23, 1929, an Arab mob, inflamed by the Arab Higher Committee, attacked the Jewish quarter of Jerusalem and the rioting spread from there to Jewish settlements across the country. In Safed,

Jerusalem failed. At the same time, the Jews celebrated the inauguration of the Hebrew University in 1925.

5. The education administration did not have one single Palestinian official. According to *Al-Mir'aah* newspaper, the high-position officers of the education administration were the following:[37]

Director:	Sir Humphrey Boman (British)
Chief Inspector:	Antonius (Syrian)
Inspector:	Hussain Rawhi (Persian)
Inspector:	Kathol (Syrian)
Chief Writer:	Mr. Mansey Hannoush (Syrian)
Writer:	Blum (Jewish)
Accountant:	Sir Beale (British)

Despite all the attempts to tighten the grip around the Palestinians in all aspects of life, and despite all the British and Zionist intrigues and conspiracies to impoverish them and keep them ignorant and illiterate, the Palestinians were completely aware of what was going on around them. In response to such a situation, they held meetings and conferences, published articles about political and cultural matters, and resorted to popular uprisings, demonstrations, and strikes.

AL-BURAQ REVOLT, 1929

The Jews attempted several times and in several ways to put their hands on the courtyard in front of Al-Buraq Wall. They also tried to purchase this courtyard from the Muslims but were unsuccessful as that estate had been a *Waqf* since the rule of Mohammed Ali Pasha (1831–1840). They also tried to change the situation by bringing chairs and tables, and later by putting up a divide to separate men and women as is customary in synagogues. Haj Amin Al-Husseini, mufti of Jerusalem and chairman of the Supreme Islamic Council, filed a complaint with Keith-Roach, district commissioner of Jerusalem. The commissioner gave orders to the Jews to remove everything from the courtyard. This aroused the anger of the Jews and they started demonstrating near the wall.

Following these incidents, the Muslims held a conference in Jerusalem on 1 November 1929 to discuss the issue of Al-Buraq Wall. The participants

Haj Amin Al-Husseini, one of the Palestinian national leaders

despite good neighborly relations between the Jewish and Arab communities, eighteen Jews were murdered and some eighty wounded. Small Jewish communities in Beit She'an, Gaza, Jenin, and Tul Karem were abandoned, as were the small isolated Jewish settlements of Ramat Rachel, Atarot, and Beer Tuvia.

In Motza near Jerusalem, Arabs from Kolonia attacked the Maklef family home, murdering the father and mother, their sons, two of their daughters, and two guests. The attackers robbed the house and set it on fire. The lone survivor was an infant boy, Mordechai Maklef, who later became the third commander in chief of the Israel Defense Forces.

In Hebron, the attack hit hard at the veteran Jewish community of 700. Due to the good relations between Hebron's Jews and Arabs, the local Jews refused the military assistance offered by the *Haganah* (prestate militia). On

decided to set up in Jerusalem a society called Custodians of Al-Aqsa Mosque and Islamic Holy Places. In response to this, the Jews established the Association of Kotel [Western Wall] Loyalists. The Jews began to challenge the Arabs. Consequently, Britain issued the Second White Paper, which confirmed the ownership of the wall to the Muslims and gave the Jews permission to visit the site. The paper stated that it was necessary to preserve the status quo in regard to the holy places in Jerusalem.[38]

The Jews held a demonstration from Tel Aviv to Jerusalem on 15 August 1929. In this demonstration, the Zionist flag was raised; fiery speeches were given calling for control over Al-Buraq Wall. Slogans such as "The wall is ours" were shouted, and when the demonstrators reached the wall, they sang the Jewish anthem.

The following day, which coincided with the commemoration of the birth of Prophet Mohammed, the Muslims held a large demonstration protesting the Jewish demonstration on the previous day. When the demonstrators reached the wall, they overturned the table of the Jewish beadle and burned the supplicatory notes in the chinks in the wall. This increased the tension between the Arabs and the Jews and so began the Al-Buraq Revolt. There was great tension all over Palestine. In Hebron, the Arabs assaulted the Jews; as a result, more than sixty Jews were killed and many others wounded. Several people were injured in Nablus and the disturbances spread to Bissan, Haifa, Jaffa, and Acre.

The Jews broke into the home of Sheikh Abd Al-Ghani 'Awn in Jaffa and killed him and all members of his family. They cut open his stomach and crushed the skulls of his wife, young son, and nephew. In Jerusalem, the Jews attacked the tomb of Sidna Ukasha and desecrated the graves of the Companions of the Prophet Mohammed and smashed the whole place. In Safad, the Arabs attacked the Jews, killing and wounding more than fifty. According to official estimates, there were 133 dead and 339 injured Jews, and 116 dead and 232 injured Arabs. Most of the injuries among the Arabs were caused by the rifles of the British policemen. Because of the interference of the British and their siding with the Jews, demonstrations broke out in many Arab countries in support of the Palestinian people.

The Jews complained to the British that the people of Hebron had mutilated the bodies of the Jews who died in the incidents; the British government sent a commission of three Arab physicians, three Jewish physicians, and three British physicians. The dead bodies were exhumed on 12 September

The Baltimore News front page following the Hebron Massacre

Saturday, August 24, Arabs from surrounding villages formed a mob and perpetrated a cruel massacre on the Jewish residents, of whom sixty-eight were killed and fifty-eight wounded.

Lt. Colonel Frederick Kisch, of the Zionist Executive, testified as follows:

> On Friday, August 23rd, rioting began to spread. The murder of Jews began in Jerusalem around 12:30 in the afternoon, when Arab mobs wielding clubs and daggers went out of the Old City. Two hours passed until the police were given permission to shoot at the murderers. That day, the first victim fell in Hebron, a yeshiva student, and the next day on the Sabbath there was an attack in Hebron that can only be described as a "massacre," because the murderers did their best for two hours to exterminate the Jews of Hebron who had lived peaceably in that city since the olden days.[12]

Most of the Jews of Hebron were saved by Arabs who hid them in their own homes. The community's leaders wrote to the high commissioner that "were it not for the few Arab families who defended the Jews, none would have been left alive in Hebron." Four hundred thirty-five Jews were saved by their Arab neighbors; they found refuge in twenty-eight homes, some of

1929 and examined. The commission did not find any signs of mutilation or disfigurement of the bodies. The Jewish doctors asked that the examination be discontinued. On the other hand, it was the Jews who abused the bodies of the Arabs, as in the case of the Abu 'Awn family in Jaffa and elsewhere.[39]

The truth of the matter was that not all the residents of Hebron considered the Jews as part of the Zionist movement. This is evidenced by the fact that a number of Arab families protected and gave shelter to a large number of Jews (particularly Sephardic Jews). Similarly, the revolutionaries attacked only the houses and places in which there were new Jewish immigrants who had moved only recently to Hebron (mainly Ashkenazi Jews). Had the national movement in Hebron considered that all the Jews belonged to the Zionist movement, they would have killed them all.[40]

After the bloody incident, the city of Hebron was placed under day curfew for 140 days (from August 24, 1929, to January 13, 1930). The situation in the city was pitiful because of the deteriorating economic conditions and the acts of horror which the British police perpetrated against the Arabs. In many instances, police units went into villages near Hebron under the pretext of looking for articles stolen from the Jews. The police would ask the village notables to slaughter sheep in their honor and prepare meals for them, bring them tobacco to smoke, feed the horses, and then they would beat the notables with batons until their bodies bled.[41]

After the 1929 events, the British set up a military court to prosecute all Arabs and Jews who participated in the incidents. The court issued a death sentence against three Arab revolutionaries: Fu'ad Hijazi, Atta El-Zir, and Mohammed Jamjuum. More than 800 Arabs were sentenced to prison for varying periods. As for the Jews, only one Jew was sentenced to death. This was the Jewish policeman who perpetrated the massacre against the 'Awn family in Jaffa. However, the British changed the death sentence to ten years in prison, and eventually he was released before the end of his prison sentence.

The death sentence against the three Arab revolutionaries was carried out on Tuesday, 17 June 1930. The news about their execution was written in giant headlines in *Falastin* daily newspaper:

EXECUTION OF FU'AD HIJAZI, 'ATTA EL-ZIR AND

MOHAMMED JAMJUUM

A MANIFESTAION OF THE BALFOUR DECLARATION

which sheltered dozens of Jews. "There are Arabs who were injured while defending their neighbors," one Jew testified, and Dr. Abd el-Ael, an Egyptian doctor, provided care for the wounded and personally rescued an entire Jewish family.[13]

THE PASSFIELD WHITE PAPER:
THE BRITISH RENEGE ON THEIR COMMITMENTS

The riots of 1929 caused the British to reexamine their policy in the Land of Israel. Once again, a parliamentary commission of inquiry arrived in the country, this time headed by Judge Sir Walter Shaw. The commission heard testimonies from all sides. The Arabs argued that the Jews were evicting them from their lands and from their Muslim holy places, but the Jews argued that there was enough room in the country for both peoples. The commission found that the Arabs were responsible for the outbreak of the riots, although it evinced understanding of their motivation: the fear of Jewish control of their lands and their livelihoods. The commission recommended ending the Jewish immigration and land purchases by Jews. British minister of the colonies Lord Passfield adopted the commission's recommendations. In the second White Paper published in October of 1930, immigration was to be limited based on the level of employment among the Arab population, meaning that so long as there was unemployment in the Arab community, Jewish immigration would not be permitted. Land sales to Jews were also severely restricted. Settlement and demographic expansion, however, were the most important practical manifestations of the renascent Jewish nationalism, and the Passfield White Paper articulated for the first time Britain's backtracking from its commitments to Zionism. Jews in Palestine and abroad and public figures in Britain responded angrily to the White Paper. Chaim Weizmann, president of the Zionist Congress, resigned. The British prime minister, Ramsay MacDonald, thereupon published the MacDonald Letter, which annulled the decisions of the White Paper. The potential damage to the Zionist enterprise or British relations with Zionism had been prevented.

CONCLUSION

The British period in Palestine began with high hopes on the part of the

MAY THE BLOOD OF THESE MARTYR PALESTINIANS
WATER THE ROOTS OF THE TREE OF ARAB
INDEPENDENCE

REMEMBER THIS DAY EVERY YEAR

Several poets sang the praises of these three heroes in poems or songs to commemorate and immortalize them. A folk poet wrote:

> *Out of the prison in Akka, there was a funeral procession [for]*
> *Mohammed Jamjuum and Fu'ad Hijazi*
> *May Allah take revenge against the High Commissioner, his folks and all*
> *   those around him.*

The famous Palestinian poet Ibrahim Tukan eulogized the three martyrs in a poem entitled *The Red Tuesday*. Following is the last stanza of this poem.

> *Their bodies are in the soil of their homeland;*
> *Their souls in Paradise*
> *There they complain not about oppression*
> *There is an abundance of forgiveness and absolution.*
> *Ask for forgiveness from none but Him [Allah]*
> *He is the Lord of the world*
> *His hands grant fortune and prestige*
> *His mightiness is above those who are tempted by their mightiness on the*
> *   land or on the sea.*[42]

The British government appointed a committee of inquiry headed by Judge Shaw to investigate the factors that led to the bloody incidents. The Shaw Commission report (24 October 1929) made the following urgent recommendations:

1. The British should issue a statement about their future policy in Palestine.
2. The immigration of Jews should be restricted and supervised because of the fears of the Arabs.

Lord Passfield, British Minister of the Colonies, 1929–1931

3. Lands should be organized and should not be transferred or sold.

4. The British mandate should assist Palestinian peasants.

5. Autonomy should be granted to the Arabs in Palestine.

In addition, the Shaw Commission proved the Muslim ownership of Al-Buraq Wall.[43]

The events of 1929 weakened the weight of the moderates in the Palestinian National Movement. So new national political trends and movements appeared and started to call for a different way of dealing with the dangers surrounding Palestine. They believed that the British were the source of all evil and that armed struggle against both the Zionists and the British was the only way to extract that evil. In the light of such circumstances, armed groups started to surface, such as the Green Hand under the leadership of Ahmed Tafesh in October 1929. Its activities were concentrated in the northern area, between Safad and Acre.[44]

The precarious conditions prevailing in Palestine and the strong urgent feeling among the public that it was time to turn to violence became even more pronounced after the Al-Buraq Revolt. Yet this did not discourage the executive committee and the Palestinian notables from resuming their political activity and negotiations with the British in the hope of achieving some political gains for the Palestinian cause specifically in regard to the most critical issue, which was stopping Jewish immigration.

For this purpose, the Arab Executive Committee elected a delegation, headed by Mr. Musa Kathem Al-Husseini, to conduct negotiations with the British government in London in order to explain the explosive situation and the popular unrest and agitation in Palestine.[45]

Musa Kathem Al-Husseini, chairman of the Arab Executive Committee

The delegation arrived in London at the end of March 1930, and was received by the British prime minister, Sir Ramsay MacDonald, and Lord Passfield, minister of colonies. The Palestinian delegation presented a number of demands, the most important of which were:

Zionist movement, based on the Balfour Declaration and the mandatory charter. The 1920s were prosperous years during which the *Yishuv* was able to shape its "State in the Making," yet the violent response of the Arabs to Jewish immigration and settlement caused the British to gradually backtrack from their written commitments under the mandate. This process coalesced in the Passfield White Paper but was quickly curtailed, and the *Yishuv* then took advantage of the new window of opportunities opened by the British, with the publication of the MacDonald Letter. Aliyah and settlement continued and a self-defense capability was established during the 1930s.

1. Prohibiting the sale of lands.

2. Cessation of Jewish immigration to Palestine.

3. Reestablishment of the Ottoman Agricultural Bank.

4. Establishing a parliamentary government.

The British government replied by saying that it was bound to administer Palestine according to the Mandate Document and according to its commitment to the Jewish people and non-Jewish groups. His Majesty's government could not be coerced or intimidated. At the same time, MacDonald and Passfield promised to finalize their decision regarding the sale of lands and Jewish immigration after the land expert, John Hope-Simpson, had looked into the situation and submitted his report.[46]

Hope-Simpson reached Palestine on 30 May 1930, to investigate the land situation in Palestine and, in his report, he made the following conclusions:

1. About 29 percent of Palestinian families have become landless.

2. The Palestinian farmer does not receive any aid to improve his crops or the standard of his living while the Jewish farmer gets financial aid as well as assistance to improve his work and instruction in order to improve his produce.

3. Jewish immigration should be stopped and control over the borders increased so as to prevent secret immigration.[47]

On 24 October 1930, Lord Passfield issued the White Paper. The paper stated that the British were committed to the Mandate Document. It also noted the necessity to grant the Palestinians some autonomy. More important, the paper indicated that the British had decided to stop Jewish immigration to Palestine. But Prime Minister MacDonald immediately sent a letter to Weizmann overturning the White Paper, stating emphatically, "The statement of His Majesty's Government does not prevent Jews from obtaining additional lands. . . . His Majesty's Government does not even contemplate the discontinuation or prohibition of Jewish immigration." This letter, which came to be known among the Arabs as the "Black Paper," marked the beginning of a new era in Palestine.

3

THE LAND OF ISRAEL BETWEEN 1931 AND 1947

THE 1930S: PEAK YEARS FOR THE "STATE IN THE MAKING"

The 1930s featured unprecedented economic and demographic growth for the *Yishuv*, the Jewish community in the Land of Israel. During this period, the fifth Aliyah arrived, with more than 250,000 Jews. About 60,000 Jews came from Germany following Hitler's rise to power and the extreme anti-Semitic policies he promulgated; tens of thousands, many of them members of Zionist youth movements, came from Poland and other central European countries; families immigrated from Iraq and from Yemen. The Land of Israel had become a refuge for the Jewish people, practically the only one in the world. The British restricted Aliyah, mainly when it concerned immigrants with no financial means, thus began the phenomenon of illegal immigration (*ha'apala*) by Jews seeking to build their home in the Land of Israel.

During the 1930s, some 100,000 dunams (25,000 acres) of land were purchased, and the immigrants brought in nearly £30 million in capital. The agricultural and construction boom doubled the number of Jewish-owned enterprises in the country, with a 200 percent growth in production in the *Yishuv*. The power station in Naharayim was erected, the Dead Sea

3
THE PALESTINIAN-ISRAELI CONFLICT:
THE 1930S AND 1940S

BRITISH POLICY BETWEEN THE WHITE PAPER
AND THE BLACK PAPER

Following the Al-Buraq Revolt in 1929, Palestine witnessed a remarkable development in events. Prior to that date, events were generally a reaction to the actions of the Jews; however, in the 1930s, the Palestinians started to initiate actions. This change stemmed from a deep conviction on the part of the Palestinians, or most of them, that the oppressive policy of the British in Palestine and their complete bias toward the Jews would not change.[1]

At the end of 1930, High Commissioner John Chancellor sent a letter to the colonial secretary in which he indicated that the situation in Palestine would not be restored to the state before 1929, and that this was an indication of a crucial change in Palestinian policy and of a general feeling that it was no longer restricted to opposition to Jewish immigration and settlement but aspired to national independence, without British rule.[2]

At the same time, the official Palestinian policy toward the British rule until the end of 1933 was characterized by moderation. Palestinian distinguished figures felt that Palestine was going through a very special situation

Company and Mekorot water projects were built, and the port of Haifa was completed in 1936. Tel Aviv and Haifa tripled in size, and Jerusalem too grew substantially.

The early part of the decade saw an increase in tension between the Palestinians and the Jews, and between the Palestinians and the British. Several factors contributed to the Palestinians becoming more extreme in their position vis-à-vis British colonialism and Zionism:

Britain's weakness in the international arena: The 1930s marked a period of great prosperity for the three most powerful dictatorships in the world at the time (Japan, Italy, and Germany), in contrast to the weakness of the leading democratic powers (Britain and France). In 1931, Japan invaded Manchuria, and in 1935 Italy invaded Ethiopia without eliciting any significant response from the League of Nations. Nazi Germany crassly violated the Treaty of Versailles when it instigated compulsory conscription and established an air force and a navy, ignoring the restrictions stated in the treaty. Britain appeared to have passed its heyday, and it now seemed the right time to confront the British.

The British Parliament rejected a proposed law to set up a legislative council in the Land of Israel in 1935: During this same period, British-inspired parliaments were established in the neighboring Arab states, and from a Palestinian standpoint the creation of a legislature was the right action to take as it would reflect their majority status in the country. Rejection of this step by Britain strengthened the sense among the Palestinians that they were being discriminated against in favor of the Jews in the country and in comparison to other Arab territories on the road to independence. This perception of discrimination increased their determination to struggle for their rights.

Extremist trends in the Arab national movement: The new generation of Palestinian leadership was different from its predecessors: they were better educated and less bound by ties to families and clans; they were modern nationalists, intent on liberating Palestine from the British. The failure of the older generation to stop the development of the Jewish community in the Land of Israel and the aspirations of fascist Italy and Nazi Germany impelled the new nationalist entities (most notably, the *Istiqlal* party) to act more decisively. They called for a struggle against the British and against Zionism, and organized strikes and demonstrations in the larger cities. Grassroots

and that the most serious danger facing the Palestinians was the immigration of Jews and their settlement in the land of Palestine. There was therefore a great need to combine all efforts to fight this danger first and to delay the struggle against British colonialism until a later time.

British policy in Palestine was based on the subjugation of the Palestinians and their land in Palestine. This policy was carried out gradually, carefully, and according to a well-thought-out scheme. But it was contrary to the style adopted by the Jewish Agency, which demanded that the mandatory government pursue the Zionist plan by force. For this reason, there were frequent tensions in their relationship, particularly when there was some lull in the Arab resistance. Resistance would soon escalate whenever the two allies adopted new measures to Judaize the Palestinian land. With each escalation, the government would resort to a tactical withdrawal. The British government took giant strides in the service of Zionism, but only a small step to appease the Arabs.[3]

Under this policy, Britain published the Second White Paper at the end of 1930. In this paper, Britain explained its transitory policy in Palestine in light of the situation current then. The publication of the White Paper stemmed from a variety of factors and circumstances:

1. Various Palestinian protests and demands, and repercussions of the Al-Buraq Revolt locally and in Arab and Islamic countries;

2. The periodic reports sent by the high commissioner about the unstable conditions in the country;

3. The recommendations of the Shaw Commission and the report of the land expert John Hope-Simpson which pointed out the spreading unemployment among the Arab citizens and, consequently, the unfairness of allowing Jewish immigrants to fill job vacancies which could be filled by unemployed Arabs.[4]

Despite the weak formulation of the White Paper and though it did not satisfy the minimum expectations of the Arabs, the Zionist movement mobilized its forces to fight it by all means. They recruited the British and American press to combat it. Demonstrations against the paper were also staged in Europe and Britain. In addition, Chaim Weizmann resigned from his position as chairman of the Jewish Agency in protest against the White

extremist elements began operating and using terror (the Izz- Ad- Din al Qassam gang). Yet the most prominent Palestinian leader was the traditional nationalist leader Haj Amin Al-Husseini.

A stronger *Yishuv*, economically and demographically, following the fifth Aliyah: Zionist prosperity made clear to the Palestinians that the Zionist vision was about to be fulfilled.

THE ARAB REVOLT: THE RIOTS OF 1936–1939

THE RIOTS OF 1936 AND THE PEEL COMMISSION'S PARTITION PLAN

April 1936 saw an outbreak of Palestinian rioting that lasted three years and became known as "the Arab Revolt." Palestinian acts of resistance were wide-ranging and included frontal attacks on the *Yishuv* and on the British mandatory regime in the Land of Israel. The British had trouble suppressing this widespread wave of disturbances. The declared aims of the Palestinians were: to annul the Balfour Declaration and the mandate; to stop cooperation between Britain and the Zionist movement for the establishment of a national home for the Jews in the Land of Israel; to end Jewish immigration; and to prohibit the sale of land to Jews. The Palestinians demanded the establishment of one state in Palestine: an Arab state. The modus operandi of the Arab Revolt was varied and included confrontations with the British army and police, damaging Jewish vehicles on the roads, attacks on isolated rural settlements, and attempts to capture them. One such attack was an attempt to take over Kibbutz Tirat Zvi in February 1938. The Palestinians carried out acts of terror against Jews in the cities, such as the shooting attack on Jews in Jaffa in April 1936, in which nine Jews were killed and more than fifty wounded. They also burned fields, groves, and orchards in Jewish villages.

The Arabs also fought on the economic front. The Arab Higher Committee declared a general strike intended to bring pressure to bear on the British to change their policies. The strike lasted 175 days, but did not achieve its goal; Britain did not change its policies, and the *Yishuv* was not weakened, but in fact strengthened. Jewish workers replaced Arab workers in every sphere, and one outcome of the Jaffa port strike, for example, was that the British granted permission to open a port in Tel Aviv; this decision was not to the advantage of the Arabs who made their living as dockworkers at the Jaffa port. During the initial period of the rioting (April–October 1936),

Paper and announced his lack of willingness to carry on his cooperation with the British government.

In the light of these circumstances, the British government withdrew the White Paper with the speed of lightning, as though it had been expecting such reactions, and published another paper, which blew up the declarations in the previous paper. For this reason, the Palestinians called it the "Black Paper" or "MacDonald's Black Paper." The paper was actually a letter from British Prime Minister Ramsay MacDonald to Dr. Weizmann in which he stressed Britain's commitment to the Mandate Document and to the facilitation of the immigration of Jews to the country (Palestine). The Black Paper also emphasized the commitment of the British government to encourage the Jews to occupy additional lands and to employ Jewish hands on these lands. The paper clearly stated that Britain did not wish to stop or prevent Jewish immigration.[5]

The Palestinians protested against the Black Paper, which actually nullified the White Paper, but the British turned a deaf ear to the Palestinians' demands. In response to this negative reaction, underground groups formed to fight against the British and the Zionists; the General Islamic Conference was held in Jerusalem in 1931; and the Independence Party was established.[6]

THE 1933 UPRISING

The situation in Palestine continued to be very unstable. Several Palestinian or Palestinian-Arab meetings and conferences were held to discuss the situation in Palestine, most importantly the General Islamic Conference of Jerusalem in 1931. At this conference, the mufti, Haj Amin Al-Husseini emerged as a strong Palestinian leader recognized both locally and in the Arab and Islamic world. Several political parties were founded, such as the Young People's Conference Party and the Arab Independence Party, which was established in 1932 and called for fighting colonialism and Jewish immigration and for establishing Arab parliamentary rule. Izzat Darwaza and other founders of the Independence Party called on Haj Amin Al-Husseini to fight against the British policy and mandate.[7]

The different Palestinian political parties continued to oppose the British policy, particularly in view of the intensification of Jewish immigration to Palestine—from 4,075 immigrants in 1931 to 9,553 in 1932 and over 30,000 in 1933, in addition to illegal immigration. The parties were also

there were some 2,000 attacks on Jews and about 900 attacks on Jewish property. Some 80 Jews were killed and about 400 were wounded. About 200,000 trees and 17,000 dunams of crops were burned.

The atmosphere in the *Yishuv* following these attacks by Palestinians was described by Hillel Omer, who grew up at Mishmar Ha'emek (a kibbutz belonging to the Shomer Hatza'ir movement, which stressed the principal of brotherhood among nations):

> For a while now, since the "disturbances" broke out, shots have been heard every night. The [kibbutz] members find it hard to believe that the Arabs, our neighbors from Abu-Shousha and Rubiya, are such bad people. Maybe they simply refuse to believe. Suddenly a rumor broke out: Goldshlager was murdered! On the road from Joara, Arabs shot and killed him. All work was stopped and the members stood around in groups. They whispered for a minute, and then were quiet. And we children acted likewise. A British aircraft flew around over the mountains. People said it was looking for the murderers. At the funeral, when they buried Avraham Goldshlager, there was a tremendous silence and only the anemones and the cyclamens were flowering everywhere, as if no one had been killed. When the bull gored Chelnov and killed him, we knew that something like that could happen as it does in nature. But Goldshlager was murdered by people who surely also have a wife like Rosa, who is now a widow, and children, like Uzi and Zviko, who are now orphans. This was hard for us to understand and even harder to believe. But the Arabs wanted us to understand, so they burned our fields and our forest, and the sparks went up to the sky. But Goldshlager could not see them anymore. Not the burning fields and not the forest going up in flames. Because he was already dead.[1]

During the Arab Revolt, there was a wave of internal terror among Palestinians. Dozens of Palestinians were murdered by their fellow countrymen as suspected collaborators with the British or with the Jews, and sometimes this was used as an excuse to settle accounts or rivalries within Palestinian society.

THE BRITISH RESPONSE TO THE REVOLT

The mandatory authorities responded to the disturbances by hastening

quite aware of the unjust and harsh taxes imposed on the Palestinian citizens, which led to large amounts of Palestinian land being sold or taken over.[8]

For example, a Palestinian peasant from Tulkarm wrote to *Palestine*, a daily newspaper (24 August 1930) (See page 49).

Under these circumstances, the executive committee called for a meeting for the leaders of the different parties on 24 February 1933. The parties proposed various ideas, including civil rebellion and a boycott of British products. But the head of the committee, Musa Kathem Al-Husseini, persuaded the party leaders, contrary to the majority opinion, to select a delegation to meet with the high commissioner and present to him the issues that worried them, such as the heavy taxation, the accelerated Jewish immigration, and the loss of lands, in the hope that he might work on passing legislation that would protect the Arab inhabitants. However, the response of the high commissioner was a complete disappointment for the delegation.[9]

As the movement of youngsters and people calling for independence was growing stronger, the influence of the traditional leadership was shaken. So they addressed the high commissioner, saying, "So far, we have not resorted even to nonviolent demonstrations, but we find ourselves forced to turn to this means under pressure from the people. We had hoped that at such troublesome times, the government would help us rather than force us to lead the people in more grievous unrest."[10]

The members of the general council and the other parties met on 8 October and decided to hold mass demonstrations departing from Al-Aqsa Mosque on 13 October and led by members of the council. It was also decided that demonstrations be held in all the towns of Palestine.[11]

Although the demonstration in Jerusalem was quelled violently, that did not dissuade the Palestinians from continuing their protest. They held a

Musa Kathem Al-Husseini is beaten by British police

reinforcements to Palestine, by an uncompromising military response in the cities and villages, by the expulsion of the Arab leadership of the revolt, and by strengthening their ties and cooperation with the Jewish defense forces of the *Yishuv*. The British helped set up the *Notrim* (Guards), the Jewish Settlement Police to defend Jewish communities and property and British sites, and the Special Night Squads (SNS), a commando force under Orde Charles Wingate, specializing in ambush. Some 20,000 members of the *Yishuv*'s pre-state army, the *Haganah*, joined these special forces. The *Haganah* emerged significantly stronger from this cooperation, since thousands of its members were able to train openly with the British police forces. The *Haganah* also established units without British cooperation in which thousands of Jews served (the Field Companies, known by their Hebrew acronym as FOSH, and the Field Force, or HISH).

In October 1936, order was temporarily restored. In November, Britain sent a commission to Palestine, led by Lord Peel, to investigate the factors behind the uprising and to recommend a new policy. The Peel Commission traveled around the country hearing extensive testimony from both sides, in an attempt to understand the complexities of the situation.

Testifying before the commission, Zionist movement leader Chaim Weizmann said, "The devotion to the Land of Israel may bode ill for us but we are here; this is our destiny [. . .] the Commission is not obliged to determine on which side justice lies here but rather to decide between two kinds of justice." In describing the distress of Jews around the world and the need to create a national home for the Jews, he said, "Six million Jews are captive in places where they are not wanted. Six million people in whose eyes the world is divided into places where they live and places they cannot get into" (testimony before the Royal Commission, *Keren Hayesod*, 1937).

In July of 1937, the Peel Commission's report was published, recommending that two states be established side by side in the Land of Israel: a Jewish state and an Arab state, and that the region around Jerusalem remain under British control. The Jewish state was allocated 17 percent of the territory of the entire country. The introduction to the section recommending partition stated, in part:

> An irrepressible conflict has arisen between two national communities within the narrow bounds of one small country. There is no common ground between them. Their national aspirations are incompatible.

bigger demonstration in Jaffa. The British police faced the demonstration with severe brutality. As a result, twelve demonstrators were killed, seventy-eight wounded, and scores of demonstrators were arrested, including several Palestinian leaders. Among the injured was Musa Kathem Al-Husseini, chairman of the General Council, whose colleagues were unable to defend him against the batons and sticks of the British police.[12]

The 1933 intifada inflamed all Palestinians. Mahmud Abd Al-Raheem (1913–1948), a famous Palestinian poet, composed a poem entitled "Al-Shaheed" (The Martyr):

> I shall carry my soul in the palms of my hands,
> And throw it into the abyss of death!
> Let it be a life which brings joy to the heart of friends,
> Or a death which brings sorrow to the heart of foe!
> The spirit of a noble man has but two aims:
> To die nobly or attain its aspirations.
> What is life if I am not dreaded and
> If I cannot defend my homeland?
> When I open my mouth, the world hearkens
> And my words reverberate among all people.

Demonstrations and strikes spread out in most Palestinian cities in protest of the increasing number of casualties and the continued arrest of Palestinian leaders. Khalil Al-Sakakini (1887–1953), a well-known educator and man of letters, wrote, "Palestine became a battlefield today and yesterday; demonstrations everywhere; attacks on police and railway stations, hundreds of injured and dead. . . . There is no doubt that the results of this political revolt will not be in vain."

After their release, the Palestinian leaders immediately called for a licensed demonstration in early 1934. During the same year, Musa Kathem Al-Husseini, chairman of the general council, died of the injuries he had sustained during the demonstrations.

Following the 1933 intifada, High Commissioner Arthur Wauchope set up the Murison Trusted Commission of Enquiry. The appointment of the commission was a disappointment because its mission was restricted to reporting on the number of casualties of the uprising.

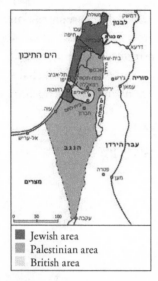

■ Jewish area
■ Palestinian area
□ British area

Map of the Peel Commission
Partition Plan

Neither of the two national ideals permits combination in the service of a single State. [. . .] In these circumstances peace can only be maintained in Palestine under the Mandate by repression. [. . .] The answer to the question which of them in the end will govern Palestine must be Neither. [. . .] But while neither race can fairly rule all Palestine, each race might justly rule part of it. [. . .] Partition offers a chance of ultimate peace. No other plan does.[2]

In the *Yishuv*, a heated argument ensued over the partition plan, with David Ben-Gurion and Chaim Weizmann leading the support for the idea. The Zionist movement agreed in principle to a partition of the country at the twentieth Zionist Congress, but expressed opposition to the proposed borders. The principle of partition was rejected absolutely by the Palestinian Arab leadership, and the revolt against the British was renewed. The British army acted aggressively to suppress the revolt, expelling prominent leaders from Palestine, among them Haj Amin Al-Husseini.

THE JEWISH RESPONSE TO THE RIOTS

The *Yishuv* responded to the Arab Revolt and the Peel plan with an accelerated settlement effort known as "tower and stockade," illegal immigration, and military action termed "restraint." Even prior to the publication of the Peel Commission report, the *Yishuv* had begun a broad settlement campaign. The main aim of this accelerated settlement was to expand Jewish areas in preparation for a future partition of the country, on the assumption that the location of settlements would determine the new borders. The settlement model was called "tower and stockade" because these settlements were set up and populated overnight, with a wall around them and a watchtower for defense. Between 1936 and 1939, about fifty such settlements were established, and they were not abandoned when attacked by Arabs.

Beginning in 1934, various parties expressed their opinions on the

AL-QASSAM REVOLT (1935)

The direct clashes with the Jewish immigrants did not undermine immigration or change British policy in the 1920s. The protests, strikes, and demonstrations against the British at the beginning of the 1930s did not bring about any change either. To the contrary, this period was characterized by exaggerated British efforts to please the Jews, particularly during the term of High Commissioner Arthur Wauchope. (In fact, in acknowledgment of his services to the Jews, Wauchope was described by David Ben-Gurion as the best high commissioner that Palestine had known.)

Not only did the average number of immigrants grow significantly during Wauchope's term in office, but he also acted intensively to raise the standards of the Jews over the Arabs in the educational, cultural, social, and economic fields. While the Arabs suffered unemployment and high taxation and lived in stifling economic conditions, the Jews obtained a lot of economic privileges which raised their standard of living in all respects. For example, the Jews were granted privileges for investment in the Dead Sea minerals, the Potash Company, and the electricity company. At the same time, Jewish provocations against the Arabs were on the increase, such as continued arms training and attacks on Arab villages by followers of Ze'ev Jabotinsky.

A particular shipment of arms which was smuggled to the Jews gave rise to great concern among the Arabs. In October 1935, Ibrahim Hussein Al-Liddawi, an Arab worker at Jaffa port, discovered by chance a large shipment of arms hidden in barrels of cement. The discovery caused great apprehension among the Arabs, particularly after realizing that it was not the first shipment. This incident substantiated the Arabs' belief that the Jews were planning for a serious confrontation with them.[13]

It was during this period that 'Izz Al-Din Al-Qassam, an Arab fighter of Syrian origin, gained widespread fame in Haifa and the towns around it. His job as a clerk in the Shari'a court and as a preacher in Al-Istiqlal Mosque in Haifa enabled him to move around the villages of north Palestine. He was able to arouse the feelings of the villagers and to inspire them to rid themselves of servitude to colonialism.[14]

Al-Qassam founded armed bands and regiments which began to strike against the British forces and cause a lot of unrest among them. He worked to enlarge his base both by recruiting more people and by providing them with arms in preparation for a rebellion against the British government.

circumventing of British quotas on Jewish immigration. New immigrants began arriving illegally, mainly by sea. Until the outbreak of World War II, some 20,000 illegal immigrants set out for the Land of Israel, but not all were actually able to enter the country.

From a defense standpoint, the question arose as to how to respond to Arab terror. Arguments over the policy toward Arab attacks had been going on since the 1929 disturbances. The official position of the *Yishuv* was called "the restraint policy," which meant that the *Haganah* would defend Jewish settlements without perpetrating acts of counterterrorism against the Palestinians in revenge, regardless of what they had done. Underlying this approach was the desire to avoid harming innocent people, and the belief that the *Yishuv* could unite only behind moral actions. The *Yishuv* also aspired to continue cooperation with the British based on a shared opposition to terror, and did not wish to exacerbate the conflict with the Arabs. The policy of restraint was later manifested in what was known as "going outside the fence," setting up ambushes outside the settlements and hitting back directly at the perpetrators of terror.

The *Irgun* (*Etzel*), an offshoot of the *Haganah*, which subjected itself to the authority of the Revisionist Party led by Ze'ev Jabotinsky, was notorious for responding to Arab terror with counterterror. Arguing that it was the only way to deter the Arabs from attacking Jews, the *Irgun* targeted Arab civilians in the marketplaces and on public transport. These actions totally contradicted the policy of the elected institutions of the *Yishuv*, and evoked revulsion in most of the Jewish community.

Meanwhile the disturbances continued, and the Arab Revolt during this period claimed 516 Jewish lives and more than 4,000 Palestinian lives (most of them victims of internal Palestinian warfare). Even if the Arabs did not achieve all their goals in the short term, in the longer term the British government did revise its policies to become completely pro-Arab. The reason for this reversal was the tense situation in Europe; in 1938–1939, war with Germany began to seem unavoidable, and under such circumstances Britain wished to have the Arabs as allies. As for the Jews, it was clear to the British that they would be on England's side, because Hitler and the Nazis were persecuting the Jews of Germany and Austria, and had labeled the Jewish people the enemy of mankind. From Britain's standpoint, its new policy was clearly justified, and during the war the majority of the *Yishuv* and most of the Arabs in the Land of Israel were loyal to the mandate.

ISRAELI TEXT / טקסט ישראלי

In November 1935, Al-Qassam left Haifa accompanied by twenty-five armed men, and was heading to Jenin to call upon the peasants in that area to take up arms against the British and Zionism. However, on the way, a small incident near the woods of Ya'bad alerted the British police to the presence of Al-Qassam and his men in that area and so they were surrounded.[15] Al-Qassam was determined to die as a martyr rather than surrender and urged his men to fight. After a fierce battle with the British army, Sheikh 'Izz Al-Din Al-Qassam and a number of his men were killed. The others hid in the woods and nearby mountains.

The death of Al-Qassam had a very deep impact on the Palestinians. Al-Qassam became a real hero and a symbol of self-sacrifice. Despite his death, Al-Qassam's followers remained true to his teachings and carried on the struggle. The Al-Qassam Revolt brought the Palestinian leadership closer to its ultimate goal.[16]

THE GREAT PALESTINIAN REVOLT (1936)

The course of events in Palestine in the early 1930s was a precursor of something far more serious: the Great Palestinian Revolt of 1936. The revolt lasted three years and passed through three stages.

First stage: 15 April 1936 to July 1937

Second stage: July 1937 to autumn of 1938

Third stage: 1938 until summer of 1939[17]

But how did the revolt begin? What were the underlying events and circumstances that gave it the momentum and determination to keep the struggle going? In order to answer these questions, we shall consider a lot of details and examine the factors and circumstances that led to the outbreak of this revolt.

1. In the two decades preceding the outbreak of the 1936 revolt, all British commissions of inquiry were in agreement that behind the events which had occurred in Palestine was the Palestinians' apprehension of losing their political aspirations for an independent state. There were also the Zionist practices: increasing immigration, purchase of lands, and job discrimination.

JEWS IN NAZI GERMANY, 1933–1939

Alongside what was taking place in Palestine, the Jews of Germany could feel the ground beneath their feet beginning to give way. In January of 1933, Hitler and the Nazis ascended to power and Germany became a totalitarian state based on racial statutes. The Nazis viewed the Jews as an inferior and dangerous race that could dilute the purity of the superior Aryan race. They adopted extreme anti-Semitic measures aimed at expelling the Jews from German society and making Germany *Judenrein* (free of Jews). During the first year of Nazi rule, various restrictions on Jews were implemented: they were fired from state and public jobs, removed from teaching posts, from positions in the arts, academia, the media, etc., and Jewish children were expelled from their schools.

Some months after the Nazis came to power, they organized a book-burning event in which books by Jewish authors were burned, including works by famous writers such as Sigmund Freud, Karl Marx, and Albert Einstein.

Next to come were the Nuremberg laws—racial laws annulling German citizenship held by Jews and prohibiting marriages between Jews and Germans (with a special addendum defining a Jew as anyone whose family had Jewish blood within the last three generations). The point of these racial laws was to rescind the civil rights of German Jews and preclude them from continuing to live in Germany as equal citizens. Unlike the longstanding hatred of Jews in Europe, which had a religious and social character and permitted Jews to convert to Christianity and thereby save themselves, the anti-Semitism of the Nazis was based on race and hence offered no way out. In 1938–1939 the situation of German Jews deteriorated; they were stripped of their jobs and businesses and left without the means of earning a living. Some 250,000 German Jews managed to emigrate (some to the Land of Israel in the fifth Aliyah).

The Evian Conference on Jewish Refugees convened in France in July of 1938 to examine what could be done about the Jews wishing to leave Germany who had no place to go, but the nations of the free world refused to open their doors to the Jews. This stance sent a clear message to Hitler that no one would lift a finger on behalf of the persecuted Jews. In November 1938, during a state-sponsored pogrom which came to be known as *Kristallnacht*, or the "Night of Broken Glass," German Jews and their property were attacked by soldiers of the S.S., joined by enraged mobs. Hundreds of synagogues were burned, Jewish businesses were destroyed or looted, Jews were beaten, tortured, and murdered, and the deportation of Jews to concentration camps

Yet, despite their unsatisfactory language, the recommendations of all commissions vanished in thin air as a result of the British policy, as their chief purpose was to put the Balfour Declaration into effect and to implement the mandate document. The Palestinians were weary of this policy and consequently their hidden and growing anger could readily be triggered by the least incident.[18]

"Jewish immigration to Palestine"

2. The ever-intensifying Jewish immigration to Palestine:[19] in a speech following the Balfour Declaration, Chaim Weizmann addressed the Jews: "A state cannot be established by a declaration or resolution. The Jews have to immigrate to Palestine and create the reality of a state by themselves."[20] David Ben-Gurion also said: "Britain will not make Palestine ours even though the declaration that it granted us was great; it is only the Hebrew people themselves, in their spirit and power of their capital, [who] can build their own homeland."[21]

However, perhaps the two Zionist leaders deliberately ignored the role of Britain in realizing what both of them (i.e., the Jews and Britain) were seeking. It was not a coincidence that the first high commissioner of Palestine, Herbert Samuel, was a Zionist. It was Samuel himself who proposed in 1915 a plan for setting up a Jewish state in Palestine as a British protectorate, which could accommodate three to four million Jews. It was also he who said in his first statement in office: "the policy of His Majesty's Government which I have come here to implement is to encourage the Jews to control the country and to enable them to set up a Jewish government."[22]

Commenting on the testimonies given in front of the British Commission of Enquiry in 1921, Ben Avi wrote in the Jewish daily *Davar Hayom*: "The Jews must purify their homeland Palestine of those who have usurped it. The Muslim inhabitants of Palestine must go to the Hijaz and the desert,

The Third White Paper, 1939

began. The bitter fate planned for the Jews of Europe under the Nazis was now obvious.

THE THIRD WHITE PAPER: BETRAYAL

Precisely at a time when European Jews were being increasingly persecuted and the world was refusing to take in Jewish refugees, Britain began backtracking from its promises to Zionism as set forth in the Balfour Declaration and the mandatory charter. The peak of Britain's new policy was the publication of the MacDonald White Paper (May 1939), a completely pro-Arab document. It stated that within ten years there would be an Arab state in Palestine with a Jewish minority, and that Jewish immigration would be limited to 75,000 over the next five years. This was followed in 1940 by the promulgation of new land-transfer regulations, reducing the ability of Jews to purchase lands to a minimum. The Third White Paper aimed to "freeze" Zionism and enable the establishment of an Arab state in the Land of Israel.

1939–1945: WORLD WAR II
AND THE HOLOCAUST OF EUROPE'S JEWS

With the outbreak of World War II, Nazi Germany invaded Poland, the home of more than three million Jews.[3] Nazi policy took shape as a planned

A synagogue in Berlin following the "Night of Broken Glass"

and systematic persecution. From this juncture, the Germans moved not only against the Jews of the Reich (within the borders of Nazi Germany itself), but also against Jews anywhere in the territories they conquered, foremost among them the Jews of Poland. Nazi policy,

and its Christian inhabitants must move to Lebanon."[23]

In 1918, the number of Jews was less than 56,000 while the Palestinians numbered 644,000. In 1922, the number of Jews rose to 83,790 while the number of Palestinians reached 668,258. The increase in the number of the Jews was due to immigration, whereas the increase in the Palestinian population was natural.[24]

Jewish illegal immigrants arriving to the land of Palestine

The immigration of Jews to Palestine continued despite popular opposition, and their numbers grew at a considerable rate until it reached 384,000 in 1934 compared to 983,000 Palestinians. The Jewish immigration was extremely disturbing to the Palestinians. They saw in it a catalyst that would cause the Palestinian people to "dissolve" in their own homeland, as it was expressed by many Palestinian leaders.

Besides the legal immigration approved by the British government, many immigrants entered Palestine through various illegal means. The increase in the number of Jewish illegal immigrants led to severe problems, and friction with these immigrants increased. The lack of trust in these immigrants and difficulty of understanding them together with their various practices in provoking the Arab citizens created a highly explosive situation that was about to go off any time.[25]

3. The problem of Arab lands and property: Hardly did a day pass without some Arab inhabitants losing some land or property, particularly due to the increasing number of immigrants and the variety of means and ways which the Jews adopted to put their hands on more Palestinian land and property. Palestinians of all denominations appealed continually to the British government to devise means that would permit the Arabs to hold onto their lands, either by passing legislation to prevent the sale of lands, by reviving the Ottoman Agricultural Bank or by establishing organizations that would assist farmers to maintain their ability to keep their lands and to move to modern methods of agriculture. Instead, the government worked to facilitate the transfer of lands to the Jews, so they were able to obtain much more land, often using various indirect and dishonest ways.[26]

4. Smuggling arms and arming the Jews: The Jews showed great creativity in finding ways and means of obtaining arms. The event in which an

which before the war had encouraged Jewish emigration, changed to one of confining Jews in ghettos. During the war, this persecution would evolve into the systematic murder of approximately six million of the Jewish people, including 1.5 million children. The history of the Jewish people in the twentieth century cannot be told without reference to the Shoah (Holocaust), as its influence on the Jews in the Land of Israel and around the world was and remains paramount.

JEWS ARE MOVED INTO THE GHETTOS

About three weeks into World War II, Poland had been divided between Germany and the Soviet Union. At that time, some two million Jews lived in the area under German occupation, which was partially annexed to the Third Reich (on the eve of the war, Jews in Poland numbered around 10 percent of the overall population). The Jews were required to attach a yellow patch in the shape of the Star of David to their clothing, and they were hounded both by the Nazis and their local collaborators. The beating of Jews, the forced shaving of their beards and side locks, and their subjection to various other humiliations—including being used as forced laborers—were routine occurrences during that period.

With the conquest of Poland complete, the Nazis began isolating Polish Jews by rounding them up into ghettos. As noted, Nazi ideology saw the Jews as a "culturally destructive racial group," hence the Germans wished to reduce contact with Jews to a minimum. A ghetto was an area within a city surrounded by walls or fences to prevent the entry or exit of its residents. Ghettos were set up in cities along the national railway network and housed Jews from the surrounding area, and later from all the territories conquered by the Nazis. A Jewish council (*Judenrat*) was appointed to manage each ghetto as dictated by the Germans. Living conditions in the ghettos were made extremely hard, so that members of the Jewish "race" would die as quickly as possible. While the daily food ration allotted to a German soldier in Poland was 2,800 calories, a Jewish resident of the ghetto received 180 calories.

Along with terrible hunger, the ghetto dwellers suffered from overcrowding and the bitter cold, and many were sent to exhausting forced labor sites. The harsh living conditions led to outbreaks of epidemics, with which the Jewish doctors were forced to deal with ever-dwindling resources. After a few months, the *Judenrat* organized teams to remove the corpses of those who had died across the ghetto. Tens of thousands died, yet despite the deaths and

A Jewish warehouse for smuggled weapons

Arab worker discovered smuggled arms at the port of Jaffa constitutes clear evidence of this. In this particular incident, various types of arms and weapons were concealed in barrels of cement. The event gave rise to suspicions on the part of the Arabs that the Jews were planning to attack them, particularly since this was not the first shipment they had received. It is worth noting that Britain acted publicly to arm the Jewish settlements, train them, and strengthen the *Haganah* organization in different ways.[27]

OUTBREAK OF THE REVOLT

Agreement between the Arabs and Jews became impossible for many reasons as previously noted. In February 1936, the British government signed a contract with a Jewish contractor to construct three schools in Jaffa. The contractor refused to employ any Arab workers. So Arab workers organized into a group

The termination of the Warsaw Ghetto, 1943

bereavement, the Jews in the ghettos managed to maintain a way of life that included a range of educational and cultural activities, conducted mostly underground. In the Warsaw ghetto, for example, which housed about half a million Jews, all the children had schooling. Theater groups performed plays and orchestras gave concerts on almost a daily basis. Several daily newspapers were published; articles described ghetto life, and the contributors included writers, artists, and poets. Youth movements gave children a home to replace that of their parents, offered them guidance, and lent meaning to their lives. A Jewish police force saw to public order, and there were even courts and jails.

"THE FINAL SOLUTION"

After the conquest of Western Europe, and with the German army's invasion of the Soviet Union in June of 1941, a systematic elimination of European Jewry was set in motion. The extermination of the Jews was code-named "the final solution of the Jewish problem." This mission was in the hands of special extermination units of the S.S., the *Einsatzgruppen* (mobile killing units), together with combat units of the German army. Initially the Jews were brought to huge pits dug in the middle of a forest or some camouflaged place; men, women, and children were forced to undress at gunpoint, after which they were gunned down and fell into the pit as they died. After the bodies were covered with dirt, another complement of Jews was brought, and so on and so forth; some 1.5 million Jews were massacred in this fashion. After some months, the Nazis began using another method of killing: gas trucks. A few dozen Jews would be crowded into the freight container of a truck, with the metal door shut and bolted behind them. The exhaust pipe of the truck was then diverted into the freight container, so the people inhaled the carbon monoxide and choked to death.

In January of 1942, a meeting of senior Nazi government and security

and surrounded one of the school construction sites and prevented the Jewish workers from reaching it. This incident was an early forerunner that warned of a potential explosion and an imminent revolt.[28]

Sheikh 'Izz Al-Din Al-Qassam carried arms against the British and the Jews in defense of Palestine and fell martyr. Yet his martyrdom did not stop his colleagues from following in his footsteps. On 15 April 1936, a group of Qassam followers, under the leadership of Farhan Al-Sa'di, killed

Al-Qassam, Sheikh Izz Al-Din

a Jew and seriously wounded two others. This event was the straw which broke the camel's back and heralded the revolt.[29]

The following night, a group of Jews killed two Arabs in their own homes near the village of Mlabbas (Petach Tikva) to avenge the killing of the Jews as was seen by the Arabs. The funeral procession of one of the Jews turned into a large demonstration during which Jews shouted antagonistic slogans. The demonstrators wanted to reach Jaffa, but when the British police tried to stop them, they clashed with the police. This incident was followed by several attacks on Arabs on the outskirts of Tel Aviv and on the Al-Manshiyya neighborhood in Jaffa. Word arrived that several Arabs had been killed during the clashes.[30] The Arabs gathered at Al-Saraya Square in Jaffa. Shops closed and life came to a standstill. The Jews and the Arabs clashed in the area between Jaffa and Tel Aviv, and several people from both sides were injured. Scores of Arabs were injured and many Arab houses in Jaffa were set on fire by the Jews.[31]

The British government hastened to impose curfew on Jaffa and Tel Aviv. Soon afterward it declared a state of emergency in the whole country

officials was held in Berlin. That meeting, named the Wannsee conference, was convened to step up the pace of the extermination of the Jews. At that point, the Nazis adopted a new method of killing: the gas chamber. This method had been used in Germany to kill the mentally retarded and terminally ill ("euthanasia") prior to the war, but was discontinued due to public criticism. To reinstate the same method against enemies of the Reich, six death camps were set up in Poland. The largest, Auschwitz, was constructed near a railway junction.

Jews were transported to the death camps from all over Europe by Germany's railway company. A few of them were kept alive to work in the camps and the rest were exterminated. Their belongings were taken to large warehouses for sorting, their hair was shaved off, their clothing was taken away, and they were forced into a sealed room. With the doors shut, poison gas was piped into the room and all died. In some camps, the gas was the exhaust from giant engines and in others it was Zyklon B, already in use as a pesticide. Any gold teeth were then removed from the corpses and the bodies were then cremated in large furnaces adjacent to the gas chambers. In these death camps, run like an assembly line, the death industry reached its peak. In Treblinka in eastern Poland, for example, the prisoner stepped down from a train and forty-five minutes later his body was burnt to ashes.

Toward the end of 1942, the Red Army began expelling the German army's invasion forces from Soviet territory, and during 1943–1945 the Soviets advanced westward toward Germany. As the Germans retreated, they took with them hundreds of thousands of Jews traveling on foot in what came to be known as the "death marches." The Jews were forced to march dozens of kilometers each day, generally in the cold and through snow, without food. Weakened after years in the ghetto, many

The entrance to the Auschwitz-Birkenau death camp

Confrontation between Palestinian demonstrators and the British police in 1936

in response to the establishment of an Arab national committee in Nablus which called for a general strike throughout all Palestine. The committee announced that the strike would continue until the British government had complied with the previous demands of the Palestinians, most importantly, the termination of Jewish immigration.[32]

Strikes and various kinds of protests spread out in all Palestinian towns and cities. In the meantime, the Arab political parties convened and set up a supreme committee, which was later known as the Arab Higher Committee. The grand mufti, Haj Amin Al-Husseini, was unanimously chosen as chairman of the committee.[33]

simply collapsed and were summarily shot by the Nazis. The murder of the Jewish people continued until Germany's final surrender in May of 1945.

By the second half of 1942, Western countries had begun receiving reliable information about the murder of the Jews of Europe. Leaders of the free world, in possession of countless reports on the subject, did nothing to stop it. Today it is hard to understand, for example, why the United States and Britain did not bomb Auschwitz and the roads leading to it, when their planes were flying over it anyway.

An important thing to remember is that even during this terrible period, thousands of Christians maintained their humanity and rescued Jews at the risk of their own lives and those of their families. These people were later referred to as "Righteous Gentiles" and the State of Israel made an effort to honor them.

The Shoah was the most devastating catastrophe in the history of the Jews, and many see it as an historical portent.

THE *YISHUV* DURING WWII: COOPERATION AND STRUGGLE

World War II and the knowledge of what was happening in Europe created a serious dilemma for the *Yishuv*. On the one hand, people were determined to struggle against Britain's pro-Arab policy so as to enable the maximum possible Jewish immigration, but on the other hand it was clear that Britain was the main obstacle to the Nazi war effort. Jewish Zionist leader David Ben-Gurion described the *Yishuv*'s position this way: "We will fight Hitler as if there were no White Paper, and we will fight the White Paper as if there were no Hitler." This meant that the *Yishuv* would support Britain in the war with Germany, while waging a nonviolent struggle against the British White Paper policy and bringing in as many immigrants as possible to settle the land.

COOPERATION

Cooperation between the British and the *Yishuv* was both economic and military. In the economic sphere, the *Yishuv* was a logistical home front for the British forces in North Africa and the Middle East. Numerous *Yishuv* factories produced food, uniforms, and equipment; Jewish contractors built buildings, performed maintenance work, and provided munitions for the British army. The resulting economic momentum for the *Yishuv* was tremendous. Militarily, there was broad cooperation as well. When World War II

The Arab Higher Committee assumed the responsibility of running the revolt and the unprecedented general strike which involved all facets of civil life. The British government attempted to break the strike and end the actions of the revolt using all means available to them, including the demolition of large parts of the old neighborhood in Jaffa, where they blew up more than 220 houses. The British also committed acts of killing, torture, and arrests with the aim of stopping the revolt and the strike.[34]

Notwithstanding, the British government ignited Palestinian Arab public feelings by initiating on 18 May 1936 the entry of 4,500 additional Jewish immigrants. This step inflamed the Arab revolt and turned it into a bloody armed rebellion.[35]

ARAB MEDIATION AND THE PEEL ROYAL COMMISSION

Besides the various violent methods the British government used to crush the revolt, it turned to diplomatic channels to end the popular revolt. It applied pressure on Arab governments to mediate with the Palestinians in order to end the strike and revolt in Palestine. The British government indicated to these governments its intention to send a commission of inquiry to look into the root causes of the basic complaints and concerns of the Arabs and the Jews in Palestine. The government further promised to look into the Arab demands as soon as calm was restored.

Arab kings and presidents managed to convince the Arab Supreme Committee to end the strike and revolt. The Palestinian leadership responded to this request despite their suspicions about the objectives of the proposed Peel Commission, especially that the British government had declared that the work of the Peel Commission would not prevent the government from acting according to the Mandate Document. The government also declared that it did not intend to discontinue Jewish immigration to Palestine while the Peel Commission was completing its work.[36]

The strike and revolt ended in November 1936 in response to the request of the Arab Supreme Committee under the leadership of Haj Amin Al-Husseini, which was characterized by moderation. However, the moderate policy of Haj Amin Al-Husseini throughout the previous period, even according to British testimonies, was completely undermined by the publication of the recommendations of His Majesty's commission to partition Palestine into two states, a Jewish state and an Arab state, leaving defined areas of strategic

began, Ze'ev Jabotinsky called on the *Irgun* to cooperate with the British; this included intelligence work (in Syria, Lebanon, and Iraq, where *Irgun* commander David Raziel was killed) and the establishment of regular combat units. Following this, some fighters left the organization and set up a new one, the *Lehi* (a Hebrew acronym meaning "Fighters for the Freedom of Israel"), headed by Avraham ("Yair") Stern. *Lehi* continued to attack the British during the war, and the British in response captured Yair and killed him, claiming he was trying to escape his arrest.

The *Haganah* cooperated with the British in training a defensive militia to counter any possible German invasion of the Land of Israel. This threat seemed most concrete in 1941–1942, when Syria and Lebanon were held by Vichy forces (the pro-Nazi regime in France), while in Iraq there was a revolt by pro-German forces and the German army in Egypt had reached El Alamein (100 kilometers from Alexandria), threatening to push on into Palestine. The *Yishuv* leadership conceived an emergency plan whereby the Jews would gather in the Carmel Mountains and confront the enemy from there, Masada-style. The imminent threat led to the establishment in the summer of 1941 of the *Palmach* ("strike force") as the combat arm of the *Haganah*, in a joint initiative of the *Haganah* and the British regime. The *Palmach* trained with British help and even went on joint missions with the British.

One of the famous instances of military cooperation was the paratrooper unit (thirty-two fighters) sent to Europe and dropped behind German lines on a dual mission: to gather intelligence and aid the Allies, while supporting Jewish resistance forces and helping to rescue Jews. Twelve of the paratroopers were captured, and seven of them, including Hannah Senesh, were executed. Despite its limited success, this was a heroic and important venture that became a symbol of Jewish heroism and solidarity.

The high point of military cooperation was the establishment of the Jewish Brigade in the British army, known in the *Yishuv* as the *Brigada* or *Hahail* (Hebrew acronym for "Jewish Infantry Brigade Group"). It included 5,500 combatants who were sent to Italy in October 1944 and fought under the blue-and-white Zionist flag. At the end of the war, the brigade soldiers were the first to encounter survivors of the concentration and death camps, and they aided Jews fleeing from Europe to Palestine. All told, some 30,000 Jewish men and women from the Land of Israel served with the British army during World War II.

importance under the rule of the British mandate.[37]

The Arabs rejected the partition plan because it meant the creation of a Jewish state on pure Arab land, whose owners only had the right to establish a modern state thereon and in which the Jews would be represented and their rights preserved. For that reason, the Arab reaction

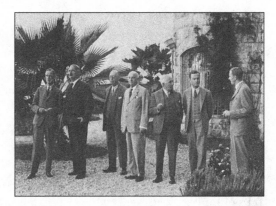

Members of the Peel Commission

was decisive and rapid, and so the revolt entered its second stage. Rebellious actions were renewed and took a variety of methods and means. The insurgency was no longer limited to sporadic clashes with the British and the Jews. Some groups specialized in attacking Jewish settlements and harassing the Jews by cutting down trees and plants. Other groups hit bridges, railway tracks, and oil pipelines.[38]

At this stage, the revolt achieved great success and spread its control over many areas despite the deportation of many leaders and the flight of others to neighboring countries. Among the leaders who left Palestine was Haj Amin Al-Husseini though he continued to run the revolt from Lebanon.[39]

Britain was determined to suppress the revolt, which had then entered its last stage. Britain adopted a variety of methods of violence, destruction, killing, and expulsion against the Palestinian people and their leadership, and brought in additional forces to the country in order to crush the revolt and disarm the revolutionaries. At the same time, it continued to support the Jewish organizations, supply them with arms, and provide them with training and organization.[40]

Eventually Britain managed to regain control over all areas that had been controlled by the Palestinian rebels. In fact, it seemed that a new military conquest of Palestine had started after more than five thousand people lost their lives, while thousands of others were wounded and many areas destroyed.[41]

OPPOSITION TO THE BRITISH

The rescue of as many Jews as possible from Europe was the main motive for the struggle with the British over immigration. After the Evian conference (1938), when the countries of the world closed their doors to Europe's Jews, their situation continued to deteriorate. As World War II went on, the need to rescue Jews became more and more urgent.

While the MacDonald White Paper permitted the immigration to the Land of Israel of 15,000 Jews a year, in practice the British did not fill the quota, to avoid a confrontation with the Arabs. The struggle over Aliyah during the war was both heroic and tragic: the *Yishuv* wanted to save the Jews of Europe, who were trying to flee, but the British did not permit them into Palestine. Twenty-four ships carrying illegal immigrants, vessels typically dilapidated and dangerously overloaded with would-be immigrants and a minimal quantity of food and water, embarked for the Land of Israel. Some 10,000 illegal immigrants managed to reach Palestine, but the British permitted them entry only after counting them against the immigration certificates issued to the Jews. More than 1,200 of these refugees drowned en route.

Despite the laws involving land purchase, the *Yishuv* found ways to buy land and settle it. During World War II, forty-five new settlements were established, among them Manarah in the north, Beit Ha'arava near the Dead Sea, and Nitzanim in the south. The new settlement activity created territorial continuity and enlarged the area of a future Jewish state in the event of a partition.

The Nazi policy of mass murder led the *Yishuv* in the Land of Israel to stand with the British during the war. Then, early in 1944, when it was clear that Germany was about to lose the war and the tremendous scale of murder began to emerge, the *Irgun* decided to join the *Lehi* in revolt against the British, hoping to force Britain to change its policy or get out of Palestine altogether. The military and terror campaign of these "dissident" organizations (so termed because they rejected the authority of the *Yishuv* leadership), and particularly the assassination of Lord Moyne (British minister of state for the Middle East) in Cairo in November 1944 by two *Lehi* members, completely contradicted the position taken by the elected leadership of the *Yishuv*. Thus began what was known as the *saison* (French for "season," i.e., hunting season), during which the members of the *Haganah* rounded up members of the dissident organizations, held them in improvised detention facilities, and even began handing some of them over to the British, with the idea of retaining

FROM THE WHITE PAPER (1939) TO *AL-NAKBAH* (1948)

A derailed train: Palestinian attacks after the decision of the Peel Commission

The increasing force and intensity of the revolt, especially following the publication of the recommendation of the Peel Royal Commission to partition Palestine, made Britain send a technical commission headed by Sir John Woodhead to Palestine to study the partition plan. Upon the arrival of the commission, there was a general consensus among the Palestinians to boycott it. At the same time, the revolt escalated in an unprecedented fashion and the rebels made many achievements on the ground.

The commission studied the conditions in Palestine and proposed three different partition plans. In the meantime, however, the commission itself contested all three plans in view of the political, geographical, economic, and demographic hardships prevailing in Palestine at the time.[42]

One of the members of the commission, Mr. Wood, denounced the partition plan, saying, "Partition is a drastic step that the custodians [of Palestine] should not experiment with or without the consent of the Palestinian people, who are neither naive and in need of a guardian, nor are they incapable of making a decision in this regard."

Accordingly, on 9 November 1938, the British government published a declaration abandoning the partition plan:

> After careful consideration and closer examination of the report of the partition commission and upon further examination of the proposal, His Majesty's Government sees that this additional investigation has pointed out that the political, administrative and financial difficulties implied by the plan which has proposed the establishment of an independent Arab state and an independent Jewish state are so great that the

Britain's cooperation after the war. The *saison* provoked a harsh response from the dissidents and a civil war in the *Yishuv* seemed imminent. Menachem Begin, head of the *Irgun*, prevented it, and the *Yishuv* leadership was able to exert its authority and put an end to the *saison*.

1945–1947: THE STRUGGLE TO ESTABLISH THE STATE

World War II ended with a victory of the Allies over the Axis powers. The war left widespread devastation in its wake. By conservative estimate, some 15 million soldiers were killed and another 20 million civilians died (other estimates range as high as 20 million soldiers and 40 million civilians dead). The losses in property and the economic price of the war are difficult to estimate, but wide swathes of Europe and Asia were laid in ruins. The Soviet Union and the United States were the big winners, but their respective situations were very different. The United States prospered during and after the war, while the Soviet Union suffered huge economic damage and some 20 million dead. Toward the end of the war, the two remaining superpowers began to compete for primacy, and what came to be known as the Cold War was under way.

Six million Jews, about 70 percent of the Jews in Europe, were murdered in the most devastating genocide in human history: the Holocaust, or Shoah. Hardest hit were the Jews of Poland, the Baltic States, and Russia in the areas conquered by Germany, where the German death machine killed about 90 percent of all Jews. Other badly hit areas were Western Europe, particularly France and the Netherlands, and central European countries like Yugoslavia and Greece, and of course, Germany, Austria, and Czechoslovakia. Genocide was also perpetrated in areas that came under Romanian control, where more than 400,000 Jews were murdered. The Shoah nearly ended the potential European Jewish participation in the Zionist enterprise, and within the Jewish people worldwide, the proportion of Jews from Muslim countries increased accordingly.

As the atrocities of the Holocaust were revealed to the entire world, sympathy was generated for the 200,000 surviving European Jews (known in Hebrew as *She'erit hapleitah*), languishing in displaced persons camps around Europe.

After the war, a Labour government took over in Britain, headed by Clement Attlee. During the Labour Party's time in the opposition it had

solution to this problem is quite impractical. Accordingly, His Majesty's Government will continue to bear its responsibility of ruling the whole of Palestine.[43]

In view of the international developments in 1939, Britain deemed it necessary to change its policy in the Arab region, particularly in Palestine through the use of a new diplomatic framework. This, however, seemed to be quite contradictory. Following the abandonment of the plan which called for the partition of Palestine into three areas of influence—Arab, Jewish, and British—Britain began to call for the establishment of a Palestinian state in several phases, which would end by the signing of a political agreement with Britain. To ensure the success of this state, the government stipulated the existence of firm cooperation between the Arabs and Jews.[44]

In the meantime, Britain invited the parties to a conference in London. The conference failed because of the deep contradictions in the positions of the participants on the one hand and Britain on the other. Malcolm MacDonald, head of the British delegation,

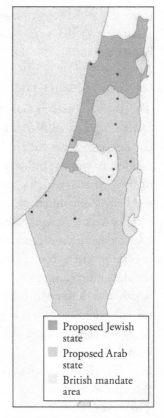

Proposed Jewish state

Proposed Arab state

British mandate area

The division plan of the Peel Commission in 1937

summarized the situation by saying, "The major purpose of this conference was to permit an honest exchange of ideas and, were it possible, to reach some mutual understanding. However, were this not possible, regrettably, His Majesty's Government would be able, at least, to construct a future policy with its full awareness of every aspect of the problem."[45]

While the conference was in session, rumors spread that Britain was planning to declare the independence of Palestine. The Jews started a terror campaign and threw grenades at Arab gatherings, killing four Arabs and injuring forty-five.[46]

The conference failed and the British government was given over totally to a discussion of the international situation and preparations for the world

drafted a pro-Zionist platform, but when it rose to power in the first few months after the war, it adopted the principles set forth in the White Paper of 1939.

UNITING TO FIGHT THE BRITISH

The British postwar policy was extremely frustrating for the *Yishuv*. The Jewish Resistance Movement was established in November of 1945 out of the desire to force the British to change that policy. Ben-Gurion decided to cooperate with the military organizations that had not accepted the authority of the *Yishuv* leadership thus far, in order to pursue a joint struggle against the British. Members of the *Haganah*, *Irgun*, and *Lehi* consolidated their efforts based on an agreement that the *Yishuv* leadership's authority would be respected. The resistance movement carried out diverse operations, attempting not to kill anyone in the process. They liberated illegal immigrants from the detention camp in Atlit, blew up the British radar station on the Carmel which was designed to detect incoming ships with illegal immigrants, blew up railway tracks, and in their boldest exploit, known as the "Night of the Bridges," they blew up eleven bridges connecting the Land of Israel with adjacent countries.

The British responded aggressively. Their campaign was known as the Broadside operation (culminating in "Black Sabbath" on June 29, 1946). They attempted to eliminate the armed resistance in the *Yishuv* and destroy the influence of its leaders. Field Marshal Montgomery, the famous hero of El Alamein and the Battle of Normandy, was appointed to head the campaign. Some 2,500 Jews from the *Yishuv* resistance movement were arrested, a great deal of weaponry was confiscated, and a huge cache of arms was discovered at Yagur.

The events of "Black Sabbath" rekindled the debate in the *Yishuv* about the value of the armed struggle against the British. Chaim Weizmann used his considerable influence to put a stop to it, and Ben-Gurion declared a cessation of resistance operations. The *Irgun* waited a few days and then blew up part of the King David Hotel in Jerusalem, which served as the British government headquarters in Palestine. This action killed ninety-one people—Arabs, British, and

Yagur weapons cache

war. The talks in London led to a proposal of the bases for the settlement of the Palestinian issue. Consequently, the 1939 White Paper was issued by the British government in which it expressed its desire for the establishment of a Palestinian state within ten years, "circumstances permitting," which would be run by both the Arabs and Jews together. It also called for the limitation of Jewish immigration to 75,000 a year for the five following years. The White Paper also called for the organization of the transfer of land to the Jews according to specified arrangements.[47]

King David Hotel in Jerusalem, destroyed by Jewish terrorist groups

Jews. The *Yishuv* was horrified—this was not its way. The resistance movement ceased to exist, and the *Yishuv* leadership decided on a different kind of struggle focusing on the foremost aims of Zionism: Aliyah and settlement, and the campaign to win favorable policies and positive public opinion from other nations.

The *Irgun* and *Lehi*, however, continued battling the British, becoming more and more extremist and increasingly taking on a terrorist cast. The elements that continued in this manner, remaining outside the authority of the *Yishuv* leadership, believed that only a war of attrition would make the British leave Palestine and permit the establishment of a Jewish state in the Land of Israel.

THE BATTLE OVER THE ALIYAH HEATS UP

One of the most effective methods the *Yishuv* had for opposing the mandatory regime was illegal immigration. Members of the *Haganah*, via *Hamosad l'Aliyah Bet* (an offshoot of the *Haganah* charged with this mission), hired ships in Europe and loaded them with thousands of would-be immigrants, survivors of the Holocaust, who had mostly gathered in coastal cities in Italy, Bulgaria, and France. Sixty-five ships carrying about 70,000 of these refugees attempted to reach a safe haven in Palestine. A few managed to reach the shore without being captured, but the great majority were caught by the British and sent to DP camps in Cyprus, where they remained until the establishment of the State of Israel. Before that, only some 4,000 of the illegal immigrants managed to reach Israel and remain there.

Illegal immigration became a powerful diplomatic tool against the British because official opposition to the arrival of these Jewish refugees to their home in the Land of Israel undermined the moral authority of the mandatory regime. The confrontations between British soldiers and the ragged immigrants, which were filmed and broadcast around the world, played very badly in the arena of public opinion. The most famous incident was the capture of the *Exodus* in July 1947 with 4,500 immigrants on board (most of them young people). During the ensuing struggle several immigrants were killed or wounded in plain view of the press cameras, and the ship was put back out to sea with the immigrants gathered on deck. The ship then anchored near the French coastline and its passengers declared a hunger strike. World public opinion railed against this abuse, whereby thousands of unfortunate refugees would be returned to DP camps in Germany. The *Yishuv*

ISRAELI TEXT / ישראלי טקסט מקבץ ▼

Although the Palestinians considered the White Paper a victory brought about by the 1936 revolt, they refused it for several reasons: (a) the uncertainty and haziness of its formulation, (b) the obvious desistance of the British government from working toward the independence of Palestine or to define the interim period, and (c) the British government's granting the high commissioner the authority to supervise the transfer of lands to the Jews and the organization of land sale and purchase.[48]

The Zionists wasted no time to denounce the White Paper and turned to violence and terror to express their opposition. Zionist organizations blew up the immigration and income tax offices and attacked High Commissioner Harold MacMichael and his wife in 1944. In 1945, they attacked Lord Moyne and blew up the King David Hotel in 1946. As a result of these Zionist terrorist attacks, 169 Britons were killed by Jews compared with 37 Zionist Jews killed by the British.

The death rates on both sides seem to be very strange when compared to the official figures of the casualties of the 1936 revolt: 211 Britons were killed and 500 wounded compared to 2,000 Arabs and thousands injured. Nevertheless, most Palestinian sources state that the number of dead among the Palestinian Arabs exceeded 5,000.[49]

With the outbreak of World War II, the Palestinian revolt began to gradually die down and finally came to a stop because of the state of war, the shortage of arms, the heavy losses, and the siege and tight grip imposed by the British and their French allies who persecuted the Palestinians in Syria and Lebanon. Britain outlawed the Arab Higher Committee, banned its activities and, for eight years, persecuted its leaders, who were arrested, or went into hiding or exile. In contrast, the Jewish leaders were released by the British government in October 1946 just four months after their arrest.[50]

At the Baltimore Conference in the United States in 1942, the Zionist leaders publicly declared their intention to take control of all Palestine and establish a Jewish state there. They also endorsed a plan calling for unlimited immigration to Palestine and the establishment of an approved military force there. The American Congress supported the plan and so Zionism started looking to the United States, particularly when it realized that the United States was very likely to emerge from the war as a giant world power.[51]

After the war, Britain withdrew the White Paper, supported the Zionist plans, and abandoned the issue of Palestine, by relaying it to the United Nations, knowing fully that the scales were in favor of Zionism considering

leadership understood that the crucial struggle was that for favorable public opinion in the democracies of the world.

THE UNITED NATIONS DEBATE

In February of 1947, British Foreign Secretary Ernest Bevin announced that the question of Palestine was being handed over to the United Nations. Some viewed this as evidence that Britain was sick and tired of its responsibility for Palestine and the consequences of the historic moves by the Labour government to reduce the size of the British Empire; others saw it as Britain's attempt to reinforce its position in Palestine by obtaining the support of the UN and of the United States for the continuation of the British mandate, albeit under more agreeable conditions. The UN decided to create a United Nations Special Committee on Palestine—UNSCOP—in May 1947. Committee members came from eleven nations, with no representation of Arab nations or the great powers. The committee visited DP camps in Germany and arrived in the Land of Israel in July 1947 (in time for some of its members to observe the battle over the *Exodus*). UNSCOP recommended to the UN that the country be partitioned into a Jewish state and an Arab state, and that Jerusalem remain an international zone.

The debate at the UN on the UNSCOP recommendations was very tense. The Zionist movement and the *Yishuv* felt that their destiny hung in the balance, and that this was the moment when the fate of the Jewish state would be decided. Dozens of attempts at persuasion were undertaken all over the world, among diplomats and governments, and until the last moment it was unclear how the vote would go. On November 29, 1947, UN Resolution No. 181 was passed, adopting (with minor modifications) the partition plan recommended by the UNSCOP, by a vote of thirty-three in favor, thirteen against, ten abstentions, and one absentee vote: the required two-thirds majority had been achieved. The United States supported the partition plan, but it was the Soviet Union that carried the vote. Andrei Gromyko, the Soviet ambassador to the UN, made a pro-Zionist speech to the General Assembly that featured the Jews' ties

Map of the Partition Plan, November 29, 1947

the unconditional support of the United States.

On 7 May 1947, the General Assembly of the United Nations resolved to set up an international committee of inquiry, which would be composed of representatives of governments, most of which were known to fall under the influence of the United States. The committee came up with two plans which required approval by a majority of the members. One of the plans called for the partitioning of Palestine into two states. The Jewish state would consist of the Eastern Galilee, Marj Ibn Amar (Jezreel Valley), most of the coastal plain, and Bir Al-Sabe' (Beersheba), including Al-Naqab (the Negev).[52]

Following the vote on the committee's plan on 29 November 1947, the United Nations recommended the partitioning of Palestine into two states, an Arab state and a Jewish state. The latter would comprise 56 percent of the area of Palestine, contrasted with only 7 percent of the area that the Jews held at the time, although the Jews constituted less than 35 percent of the population.[53]

The Palestinians were convinced that there was no reason for them to

The partition of Palestine in 1947

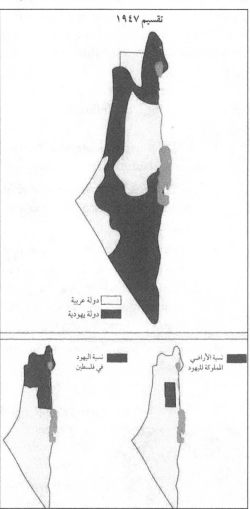

Left: percentage of Jews in Palestine; right: percentage of land owned by Jews in Palestine

to the Land of Israel, their suffering during the war, the problem of the displaced Jews of Europe, and the fact that the nations of Europe had failed in protecting the rights of the Jews. Gromyko argued that the solution to the problem was the establishment of a Jewish state as the Jewish people's national home.

The partition plan adopted by the UN on November 29, 1947, decreed, among other things, the following:

1. The Palestine mandate would end as soon as possible, in any case no later than August 1, 1948.

2. Two independent states, one Jewish and one Arab, would be established in the Land of Israel two months after the British withdrawal.

3. The two states would have an economic union, including: a joint currency and conversion rate, agreed-on management of traffic and communications (sea, air, post, telephone), joint economic development in matters of investment and infrastructure, equitable access to water sources.

4. The city of Jerusalem would be under a separate international regime.

The resolution for partition was greeted in the *Yishuv* with great rejoicing. People danced, prayed, and sang in the streets. The entire Arab world, and the Palestinians in particular, rejected the decision and declared a state of mourning. Two buses with Jewish passengers were attacked the very next day near Wilhelma (B'nei Atarot). Seven people were killed, and the War of Independence began.

The celebrations following the UN resolution for partition

pay for the tribulations and torture that the Jews suffered at the hands of the Christians in Europe, which in fact amounted to a serious crime against humanity. Furthermore, Zionism appeared before the Third Reich, which meant that the Zionist aspirations in Palestine preceded the great crime that befell them during World War II. It was quite baffling to the Palestinians why it wasn't fair for the Jews to be a minority in a Palestinian state, though it was deemed fair to transform half the Palestinian people, who comprised the majority of the original inhabitants living on the land of their fathers and forefathers, into a minority living under foreign rule in a Jewish state blessed by the partition plan.[54]

Many demonstrations were held against the partition plan. And immediately after the declaration of the partition plan, daily fighting broke out between the Arabs and the Jews. The fighting continued until May 15, 1948, the date on which Britain was scheduled to withdraw from Palestine.[55]

4

THE WAR OF INDEPENDENCE
AND THE FOUNDING OF THE STATE OF ISRAEL

On November 29, 1947, the United Nations General Assembly approved, by a two-thirds majority vote, a proposal to create two independent states in the Land of Israel—a Jewish state and a Palestinian state, side by side (Resolution 181). Arab attacks on Jewish residents began the next morning, as the Arabs did not accept the partition plan. The war that began on November 30, 1947, is known as the War of Independence because the Jewish *Yishuv* succeeded in gaining its independence after the Arabs in the Land of Israel and neighboring nations tried to prevent it. Jews also call this the War of Liberation.

This war is generally viewed in two parts: The first part was a civil war, which began with the UN vote for partition and ended when the British high commissioner left the country and the British mandate formally ended (November 29, 1947–May 14, 1948); the second period featured an international war against the Arab nations. This began with the invasion of the newly declared State of Israel by several Arab countries, and ended with the signing of an armistice between Israel and Syria (May 15, 1948–July 20, 1949). The civil war phase involved three principal forces: the British,

4

AL-NAKBAH, 1948

⁓

On 29 November 1947, the United Nations General Assembly passed Resolution 181, which called for the partitioning of Palestine into two states, an Arab state and a Jewish state. This was in fact the start of the countdown for the establishment of the State of Israel on 15 May 1948 and the 1948 *Nakbah*, which uprooted and dispersed the Palestinian people.

Al-Nakbah (Arabic for the "catastrophe") represents the defeat of the Arab armies in the 1948 Palestine War, the Arabs' acceptance of the truce, the displacement of most of the Palestinian people from their home cities and villages, and the emergence of the refugee problem and the Palestinian Diaspora.

The catastrophe which befell the Palestinians was first and foremost the result of the British policy during its mandate of Palestine, which was granted to it by the League of Nations. Since the beginning of its occupation of Palestine in 1917 until its evacuation of Palestine on 15 May 1948, Britain exerted its best effort to establish the foundations for a homeland for the Jews at the expense of the Palestinian people. And it spared no effort to suppress the Palestinian people and to arrest and deport their leaders. The British did not

the Jews, and the Arabs in Israel. When war broke out, the British were "masters" of the land, both in the legal sense and because of their military and diplomatic advantage. When the UN voted for partition, the British immediately began an orderly withdrawal of mandatory administrative personnel. Their troops were also gradually withdrawn, so that Britain's military capability in the country decreased as time went by. The remaining units were directed to maintain order, not to aid either side in achieving a decisive outcome. The British leadership wanted to get out of the Land of Israel without any British soldiers being harmed, and both sides also tried to avoid any confrontation with the British as their withdrawal neared its completion.

The Jewish population at that time was approximately 650,000, mostly living along the coastal plain between Haifa and Tel Aviv, and some 100,000 in Jerusalem. The combat forces of the *Yishuv* included the *Haganah*, with some tens of thousands of members, among them about 3,000 regular fighters of the *Palmach*; the *Irgun*, with about 3,000 members; and the *Lehi*, numbering a few hundred. The strength of the *Haganah* lay in the military training its members had undergone and in the unity of its command. It had a national headquarters and could move its units from one front to another as the need arose. The Jewish forces had another important advantage in the supply of weapons; a short time after the violence began, the United States and Britain had imposed an embargo on the shipment of weapons to the Land of Israel, but the *Yishuv* overcame that by signing an agreement with Czechoslovakia to supply it with arms. At the end of March 1948, the first arms shipment from Czechoslovakia arrived and the ordnance was immediately transferred to the Jewish fighters around Jerusalem. Additional shipments over the ensuing months allowed the Jewish forces to strengthen their military capacity and contributed very significantly to the outcome of the war.

The Arab population numbered about 1.3 million at that time, spread throughout the country and comprising the overwhelming majority in rural areas. Their main advantage was in having settlements all over the country and being able to cut off the isolated Jewish settlements and mount localized attacks. However, they had no military training, could not coordinate their forces, had no united leadership and no clear joint objectives. Some of the fighting was done by volunteers from outside who did not cooperate with the local Arab leadership, which was, in any case, splintered.

allow the Palestinian resistance to exercise its right to defend the Palestinian people and land against the Zionist expansionist movement. It suppressed the popular uprisings one after the other beginning in 1920 and then in 1921, 1929, 1930, 1935, and 1936. The British government considered all forms of Palestinian resistance

From the drawings of Naji Al-'Ali: the pain of Al-Nakbah and the waiting for the return

and defense of Palestinian rights as illegitimate acts of terrorism, extremism, and fanaticism. It also passed unjust laws against Palestinians carrying arms or ammunition. For example, the sentence for possession of a handgun was six years in prison, twelve years for possession of a grenade, five years of hard labor for possession of twelve bullets, and eighteen months for misleading soldiers.[1]

In contrast, Britain allowed free Zionist immigration to Palestine. The increasing number of immigrant Jews always led to a deterioration of the economic conditions. Britain also permitted the Zionist movement to build its military force, represented mainly by the *Haganah* and *Etzel* and others. Members of these organizations carried out bombings in Jerusalem, fired on British soldiers, and smuggled arms and immigrants.

More important, the British allowed an armed brigade of the Zionist movement to be attached to the British Army. This brigade took part in the events and battles of World War II, and thereby acquired field training and experience in the techniques of war. In 1939 ten detachments of Zionist settlement police were formed, each led by a British officer, totaling 14,411 men. There were 700 policemen in Tel-Aviv and 100 in Haifa, all of whom were members of the *Haganah*. By 1948 most Jews over fourteen had already received military training at the hands of these organizations. This gave the Zionists a great military advantage over the Palestinians during the 1948 war.[2]

In an interview with an American journalist in 1946, a British officer in Palestine declared: "If we withdraw British forces, the *Haganah* will

"CIVIL WAR" BETWEEN THE PALESTINIAN ARABS
AND THE JEWISH *YISHUV*

It was a difficult war, and in its early days, many people around the world did not believe that the Jews would be able to actualize their right to a state of their own. Britain, whose forces were still in place, was drawn into an inconsistent policy: some at the decision-making level wanted to leave as quickly as possible and instructed the British forces under their control to begin a military withdrawal, leaving the field open for battles between Arabs and Jews; while others argued that if things fell apart, the United Nations might rethink its decision and ask the British to remain, giving international legitimacy to an extension of the mandate. In the ensuing confusion, the British did not provide protection from attacks. Without a clear policy from above, the British in the field supported one side or the other according to their personal inclinations or interests.

Right after the UN decision and in the ensuing months, until March 1948, irregular and local Arab forces (including the volunteer Rescue Army under Fawzi al-Qawuqji) attacked isolated Jewish settlements and roads and mounted terror attacks in the mixed cities, which led to counterterrorism by the *Irgun*. Jerusalem and Haifa were the two cities most vulnerable to Arab and Jewish terror, and both sides suffered as a result.

During that period the *Haganah*, particularly the *Palmach* units, focused on defensive measures or on attacking specific targets. Roadblocks had cut off different parts of the *Yishuv* from the rest, and the *Haganah* did its best to bring arms, food, and reinforcements to the besieged communities. *Haganah* soldiers traveled on the more dangerous roads in convoys, which quickly became death traps. Particular efforts were made to bring supplies to embattled Jerusalem and its 100,000 Jewish inhabitants. The city became wholly dependent on the convoys for food, water, and arms.

In memory of the many victims who fell on the road to Jerusalem, Haim Guri wrote the famous poem "Bab el Wad," the Arab name for Sha'ar Hagai, about the route the conveys traveled from the coastal plain to Jerusalem.

> *Here I pass; I pause by this rock,*
> *The pitch-black road, the stones, the ridges,*
> *Night falls slowly, breezes from the sea,*
> *An early star shines over Bet-Machsir.*

take control of all Palestine tomorrow." When asked if the *Haganah* could maintain its control of Palestine under such circumstances, the officer replied: "Certainly, they could do so even if they had to confront the entire Arab world."[3]

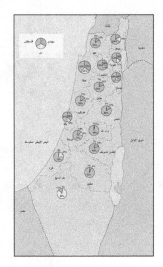

Distribution of land in Palestine until 1946

When the British pulled out of Palestine just before the outbreak of the war, they either turned a blind eye or actually conspired with the Zionists who seized British arms and equipment. This further strengthened the Zionist movement's military superiority over the Palestinians.

When Britain lifted its hand off the Palestinian question in front of the United Nations, it was in fact a very influential member of the international organization. The partition resolution 181 was merely a revival of the partition plan proposed by Britain in the aftermath of the 1936 revolution.[4]

On the other hand, the Arabs and their leaders had the lion's share in the responsibility for the 1948 defeat. Their participation in the war was like a drama whose director was a British military officer, Glubb Pasha, who commanded the Transjordan Arab troops in the war. The Arab armies did not actually participate in the war until the Palestinian people had already been totally exhausted by the war.

PALESTINE AND THE 1947 PARTITION PLAN

Before the 1947 partition plan, the population and land distribution in Palestine were as follows:

Palestinian population	1,364,330	69%
Jewish population	608,230	31%
Palestinian Arab land	25,100 km²	94.5%
Jewish land	1,470 km²	5.5%

Bab El Wad,

Remember our names forever
Convoys wind through on the road to the city.
By the roadside hang our dead,
Rusting iron wrecks as silent as my comrade.

Pitch and lead, roasted in the sun,
Nights passed with fire and knives,
Sorrow and glory side by side,
Scorched armor and some unknown name.

Bab el Wad . . .

Silently I walk by here
Remembering them one by one
Here the cliffs and rocky ground,
Where we fought, one family, together.

Bab el Wad . . .

Spring will come, the cyclamen will bloom,
Red anemones on hill and valley,
When you pass along the road we traveled,
Remember us, remember Bab el Wad.

Hagai Horvitz, a *Palmach* fighter and a historian, describes in an interview how he and his contemporaries viewed the goals of the Arabs at that time:

In 1947, the Arab National Movement made a radical change in its current objectives: no longer would it attempt to block the advance of the "Zionist entity," but would make a combined effort, Palestinian and overall-Arab, to conquer by force the Jewish-held areas and bring an end to the Jewish presence in the country. Indications of this already surfaced when the Grand Mufti befriended Hitler. But in 1947, the clear and immediate danger to our continued existence here became for the first time obvious to everyone. The certainty did not come from some imaginary

UN Resolution 181 called for division of the land as follows:

Palestinian land	42.88%
Jewish land	57.12%

Skirmishes and clashes between the Jews and Palestinians began immediately after the UN General Assembly passed Resolution 181 on 29 November 1947. The situation deteriorated into an unequal confrontation. Zionist forces were organized, armed, and trained. Not only were they superior to the Palestinians, who for over thirty years had been exhausted by unjust British policy and Zionist terrorism, but the Zionist gangs were also superior to the Arab armies which entered the war on 15 May 1948. The armed forces of five Arab countries totaled some 21,000 soldiers, plus 10,000 volunteers of the Rescue Army and the Holy Jihad, against 65,000 Jewish soldiers.

EVENTS UNTIL THE PERMANENT ARMISTICE

In February 1947, the British government declared its plan to end its mandate over Palestine as it had included many clashing promises, and so delegated the Palestinian question to the United Nations and declared 15 May 1948 as the deadline for pulling out from Palestine. The British government also declared that any interference from any Arab country would be taken as an attack on Britain. On the other hand, the Arab countries knew ahead that the withdrawal of the British would create a vacuum in Palestine and a state of chaos which would give the Jews the opportunity to take over the country due to their organizational and military superiority.

The Zionists' military strategy for the war was divided into two phases whose implementation would depend on the conditions prevailing at the time. The first phase (or Plan C) called for keeping pressure on the Palestinians in order to obtain a land free of its Arab inhabitants, with the possibility of keeping contact with the Jewish settlements situated in the land allocated to the Arab Palestinian state. By employing a variety of terrorist actions, mainly committing massacres against the Palestinians and spreading rumors, the Zionist forces succeeded in forcing over 250,000 Palestinians out of their homes from the issuance of the partition plan on 29 November until 15 May 1947.[5]

The second phase (or Plan D) called for waging a wide-scale attack in

Water distribution in bisieged Jerusalem

anxiety, historical or manipulated, but from a sober look at the Arabs' goals as they were expressly declared, in official decisions, and in passionate mass propaganda, and above all by their actions: the firm rejection of the UN partition; the Palestinian attacks and massacres of Jews that intensified toward the end of '47 all over the country; and, the crowning jewel—the invasion by regular armies of the Arab states with armored and tank corps, navy and air force, to eliminate Israel while still in its cradle![1]

The first months following the vote for partition were the hardest in the *Yishuv*, which did not seize the initiative during that period and was unable to fully organize its fighting forces. Some 50,000 *Haganah* and *Palmach* soldiers carried the major burden.

In March of 1948 ("Black March"), three convoys were trapped on their way to besieged communities and most of the fighters were killed. Jerusalem was blockaded, its Jewish neighborhoods cut off from one another, and other communities were also cut off (Gush Etzion near Jerusalem, Yechiam in the north, and settlements in the Negev). During that month, there were also signs that the United States was about to retract its agreement to the partition plan, and the survival prospects for the new Jewish state seemed more remote than ever. During the first phase of the war, the *Yishuv* lost about 1,200 civilians and fighters, and its very existence was in grave jeopardy.

PLAN DALET (PLAN D)

In April 1948, the *Yishuv* leadership went on the offensive with Plan Dalet. The goals included: gaining control of the roads (capturing Arab villages in strategic locations overlooking roadways), gaining control of Arab

order to seize Palestinian lands and keep them after the withdrawal of the British forces from Palestine. In this regard, Yigael Yadin, commander of the *Palmach*, declared: "Were it not for the entry of the Arab armies, there would not have been a way to stop the expansion of the *Haganah* forces, which would have been able to reach to the western natural borders of Israel, as most of the enemy forces were paralyzed at that time.[6]

As soon as the Arab armies entered Palestine, the Arab governments were pressured by the UN Security Council to accept the armistice based upon the request of the Jews. The Arabs were opposed because they were convinced that this would not stop the Jewish raids against the Palestinian towns and villages or stop the flow of Jewish immigrants to Palestine, especially those who were able to serve in the army. The Arabs were also afraid that the armistice would not prevent the smuggling of arms to the Jews.

The Arabs and the Jews agreed to the armistice in response to the request of the Security Council, which stipulated a number of conditions that in sum called on both sides to preserve the situation obtaining at the time of the armistice. Count Bernadotte was appointed as an international mediator to settle the conflict in Palestine.[7]

The Jews did not adhere to the conditions of the truce. They imported a great variety of arms and weapons such as warplanes, guns, tanks,

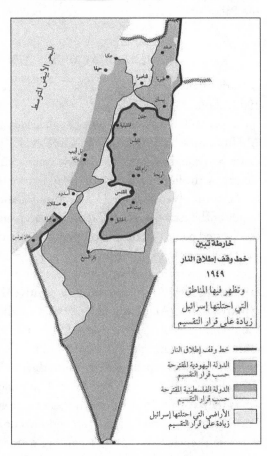

Map showing the line of the ceasefire in 1949 and the areas that were occupied beyond partition

neighborhoods in the mixed cities, and the conquest and evacuation of villages representing a threat to Jewish population. Via Plan Dalet, the *Yishuv* leaders intended to take control of the territory allocated to the Jewish state under the partition plan.

In the Nachshon campaign, prior to Plan Dalet, the *Haganah* fighters had taken control of three Arab villages on the route to Jerusalem. The road was opened temporarily, and three supply convoys were able to reach the embattled city. During the implementation of Plan Dalet, the mixed cities were also taken: Haifa, Jaffa, Acre, Tiberias, and Safed. This broke the grip of the Palestinian military resistance and accelerated the flight of Palestinians from their villages. During April, some 350,000 Palestinians left the country, and the Palestinian refugee problem was to become a main player in the conflict.

ARAB REFUGEES

As early as the initial stages of the war, between December 1947 and March 1948, about 75,000 Arabs had already left the country, mainly people from the upper and middle classes. The Arab leader in the Land of Israel, Haj Amin Al-Husseini, who at that time was in Egypt, did not denounce this trend because he thought that a temporary evacuation by civilians would facilitate victory by the fighting forces; the result, however, was a significant weakening of the entire Arab society. The Arab population also suffered greatly at the hands of the Arab irregular forces and the armies that came to their aid, who confiscated people's food and property. Sometimes the Palestinians were more afraid of them than of the Jews.

The political and military leadership of the *Yishuv*, for the most part, saw the flight of Arab residents as a positive thing, whether from a political standpoint (the Arabs would become a small minority) or from a military standpoint (distancing a hostile population from the areas where fighting was taking place). During the execution of Plan Dalet, the *Haganah* forces began, for the first time, expelling Arabs from their villages. There was no order from the political level to do so, but the military commanders had the freedom to act as they saw fit. In April 1948, there was a massacre at the Arab village of Deir Yassin, near Jerusalem; *Irgun* and *Lehi* units attacked the village, and by the time the battle was over, according to most updated historical research, 100 to 120 Arabs had been killed, including women, children, and the elderly. The *Yishuv* institutions and the Jewish public vehemently denounced

and ammunition. Immigration continued as before, and the attacks against the Palestinians never ceased. This in fact was a realization of the fears of the Arabs and led to an imbalance of power in the region in favor of the Jews.[8]

At this stage, Count Bernadotte proposed a solution for two states, an Arab state and a Jewish state. The proposal was directly refused by the political committee of the Arab League Council because it was based on the partitioning of the whole country. On the other hand, the Jews refused this project because it kept Jerusalem and the Negev in the hands of the Arabs.

At the end of the first armistice on 3 July 1947, fighting broke out and the superiority of the Zionist organizations was quite clear. They were able to occupy Lod and Ramlah after the withdrawal of the Jordanian army and succeeded in expelling 60,000 people from the two cities. They also made some achievements in the north and south of the country.[9]

On 18 July, fighting stopped as a result of the second armistice. Count Bernadotte started to implement his proposal. Yet he was assassinated by *Stern*, a Zionist gang, which deemed the Bernadotte proposal as a threat to the Zionist plans.[10]

While the Arabs honored the armistice, the Jews continued with their expansionist plans. They occupied the Negev in the south and the Galilee in the north and continued until they had occupied the greater part of Palestine, displacing 750,000 Palestinians in the process.

The Arabs complained about the Jewish aggression to the Security Council, but the council was not able to dissuade the Jews from their plans. The Jews did not agree to the resolutions of the council, which aimed at restoring the situation to the time before the Jewish aggression. After much vacillation, fighting stopped on 8 January 1949. Soon, negotiations began for permanent truce between Israel and the Arab countries that took part in the war.[11]

EVENTS OF THE 1948 *AL-NAKBAH*: EYEWITNESS REPORTS

The Palestinians are still suffering from the devastating results of *Al-Nakbah*. The word *Nakbah*, meaning "catastrophe," actually expresses what happened to this people. Many massacres were committed against the Palestinian people, about which very little is known. There are still many facts about these massacres which are so atrocious that nobody would dare to describe. What really happened to the Palestinian people in 1948 can be described as an as-the massacre, but this incident had more impact than any other on the flight of Palestinians during the conquest of the mixed cities and the villages.

The departure of the Arab residents thus came about for several different reasons: fear, the rough attitude of the Arab volunteer fighting forces, intimidation and violent warfare by Jewish forces, expulsions carried out by the Jewish army, and personal considerations on the part of families who wanted to get far away from the front until things calmed down. During the next phases and until the end of the War of Independence early in 1949, the systematic expulsions increased and hundreds of thousands more Arabs left the country.[2] The exact number of refugees who left the area of the State of Israel during the War of Independence is in dispute, with estimates ranging from 600,000 (according to Israel) to over 800,000 (according to the Arabs).

THE STATE OF ISRAEL IS ESTABLISHED

In April 1948, the political institutions of the *Yishuv* began preparing to take over governance from the British, and a temporary People's Council was established which included representatives from all the political parties, on a proportional basis. The People's Council chose a People's Administration (a provisional government) to be its operational arm. Thus the new state's democratic institutions were born and were prepared by consensus for an orderly takeover as soon as the British left. These were, as noted, temporary entities, pending a written constitution and elections for a legislative council to be carried out at a later stage.

The People's Administration was thus the body that decided on the Declaration of Independence on the 5th of Iyar, 5708 (May 14, 1948). This decision was not easy, and was adopted by a margin of only two votes, after long debate. What concerns made it difficult for the administration's members to decide?

The reality at that time was complicated, and while some factors functioned to encourage a declaration, others did the opposite. The situation at the front was terrible: The Jewish quarter in Jerusalem was in danger of being captured and the city was besieged. The fighting at Gush Etzion (which was captured on the eve of the decision) was at its fiercest, with surrender very near. And the Negev was cut off. The Arab states announced that their armed forces would invade the territory of the Jewish state the moment the Jews declared independence. The future seemed bleak indeed. At the same time, Plan

sassination of the right, a murder of the land, and an uprooting of human beings. None of these events was incidental.

Al-Nakbah was the result of frequent oppression, anger, killing, executions, arrests, exile, and international and Arab conspiracy against the Palestinians. It was the accumulation of ignorance, weakness, and chaos within the Palestinian society resulting from thirty years of British occupation. The Palestinian society had to contend with Zionist bands that were supported and organized by the British.

On 19 April 1948, upon attacking Zir'in, a Palestinian village north of Jenin, the *Palmach* forces issued the following command: "Upon the occupation of Zir'in, all houses should be destroyed; only some houses should be spared for our convenience." David Ben-Gurion also said: "We should destroy Arab pockets [in Jewish areas], such as Lod, Ramlah, Bisan and Zir'in, which will constitute a danger in case of invasion and may keep our forces engaged."[12]

The destruction of 418 Palestinian villages inside the green line (pre-1967 Israeli border), destroying all symbols of Palestinian life, and the massacres committed against the Palestinian people are the best evidence of the

Drawing of the Palestinian expulsion in 1948

Dalet created conditions conducive to the continuation of the fighting, given its results: the *Yishuv* forces were taking control of areas of land, roadways, and most of the mixed cities. Arms had begun arriving from Czechoslovakia for the Jewish troops, permitting a continuation of the fighting. The British announced that they intended to leave the country in mid-May—after which, conceivably, there would be anarchy. In the *Yishuv*, it seemed urgent to get organized as an independent state, equipped to face whatever would ensue. In addition, there was a will to establish an official state and by doing so end the internal divisions among the Jewish community and allow the *Yishuv* leadership to make the transition into an official, democratic authority with a national army, compulsory conscription, and the imposition of a central governing authority over both the army and the civilian population.

The main reason for declaring independence at that point, however, was evidently the insight shared by Ben-Gurion and his entire circle: this was a historic window of opportunity which might never recur. The United States was now working to annul the partition plan, and postponing a declaration might lead to a whole new debate in the United Nations, which in turn might lead to rescinding the UN decision of the previous November.

On May 14, 1948, at four o'clock in the afternoon, the *Yishuv*'s Jewish leadership gathered in Tel Aviv. David Ben-Gurion announced the establishment of the State of Israel and read a draft of the Declaration of Independence, signed by the members of the acting People's Council. It was the nation's finest hour, although the Jewish leadership clearly realized that the euphoria would be short-lived and that, in response to the declaration, Arab forces would invade Israel.

The Declaration of Independence states:

> The Land of Israel was the birthplace of the Jewish people. Here their spiritual, religious and political identity was shaped. Here they first attained to statehood, created cultural values of national and universal significance and gave to the world the eternal Book of Books.
>
> After being forcibly exiled from their land, the people remained faithful to it throughout their Dispersion and never ceased to pray and hope for their return to it and for the restoration in it of their political freedom. [. . .]
>
> On the 29th of November, 1947, the United Nations General Assembly passed a resolution calling for the establishment of a Jewish

ISRAELI TEXT / טקסט ישראלי

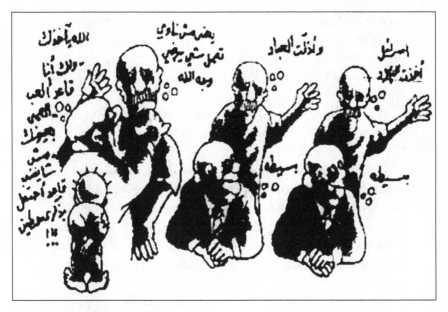

Pal: Israel took the land
AL: Never mind
Pal: It humiliated the people
AL: Never mind
Pal: Does this mean you don't intend to do anything about it:
AL: It's God's will
Pal: Then, may God would take you! [i.e. Then, go to hell!]
AL: What's the matter with you, you dope, can't you see I'm having fun? I'm celebrating the anniversary of the Hittin victory. [in which Saladin defeated the Crusaders]

brutality Palestinians were exposed to and which resulted in the dispersion of the Palestinians throughout the world.

One of the most notorious massacres perpetrated against the Palestinians took place in Deir Yassin on 9 April 1948. The Zionist forces killed more than 100 and wounded dozens more. The remaining inhabitants were forced to leave the village after being exposed to the most barbaric kinds of torture and immoral and inhuman practices.

The following story was recounted to a young Palestinian man by his mother, who had survived the massacre at Deir Yassin village:

My mother escaped with my two small brothers, who were one year old and two years old. My aunts and their small children were also with her. When the Jews met them on the road, they wanted to kill my small

State in the Land of Israel; the General Assembly required the inhabitants of the Land of Israel to take such steps as were necessary on their
part for the implementation of that resolution. This recognition by the
United Nations of the right of the Jewish people to establish their State
is irrevocable.

This right is the natural right of the Jewish people to be masters
of their own fate, like all other nations, in their own sovereign State.
[...]

The State of Israel will be open for Jewish immigration and for the
Ingathering of the Exiles. [...] It will ensure complete equality of social
and political rights to all its inhabitants irrespective of religion, race or
sex; it will guarantee freedom of religion, conscience, language, education and culture; it will safeguard the Holy Places of all religions; and it
will be faithful to the principles of the Charter of the United Nations.
[...]

We extend our hand to all neighboring states and their peoples in an
offer of peace and good neighborliness, and appeal to them to establish
bonds of cooperation and mutual help with the sovereign Jewish people
settled in its own land. The State of Israel is prepared to do its share in a
common effort for the advancement of the entire Middle East.

The Declaration of Independence became the foundational document in the
history of Israel. The declaration set forth the two guiding principles of the
state, as "a Jewish state" and "a democratic state," and the State of Israel has
been struggling with the integration of these two principles ever since.

THE ARAB ARMIES INVADE AND THE CONQUERORS ARE STOPPED

On the evening of the last day of the mandate, the British left the country
and the Arab armies invaded as expected. The Egyptian army invaded from
the south along two axes: a coastal invasion that got as far as Nitzanim,
and another toward Jerusalem that reached Ramat Rachel in the Jerusalem
foothills. The Syrian army invaded from the north and came down the
Jordan Valley to Tzemach and Masada, stopping at Kibbutz Degania. The
Lebanese army tried to invade the upper Galilee. The Iraqi army invaded
via Naharayim on the Jordan River, captured the power station there, and
stopped at Kibbutz Gesher, also taking Wadi Ara. The Jordanian army

brothers and my cousins. My mother and my aunts started to beg them and said: "We will give you all the gold and the money we have, but do not kill our children." The Jews did not listen to their pleas and killed my brothers and cousins in cold blood and told them: "Now, go away and tell everyone what you have seen."[13]

The behavior of the Zionist gangs was intended to spread terror among Arabs to force them to leave their villages—especially after the Deir Yassin massacre. When they attacked Zir'in on the night of 20 April 1948, they screamed as they were charging, *"Kadima, Kadima* [move ahead], *Deir Yassin, Deir Yassin."*[14] Such expressions were enough to evoke great terror in all Palestinian citizens and to make them flee their homes in fear for their honor, their children, and themselves. The Palestinians who left their homes did not have the least doubt that it would be for a few days, after which they would return: "We thought that we would return after one or two weeks. We locked the house and kept the key, waiting to return."

In 1948, Palestine had a population of 1.4 million people. After *Al-Nakbah* about 750,000 Palestinians were wandering about not knowing where to go. Families were separated, the elderly died, children carried younger children, nursing children died of thirst. Suddenly they found themselves expelled from their own homes and in an alien world that regarded them as a different kind of human being who evoked a feeling of fear and suspicion—they were "refugees"! All the international community did was provide some humanitarian assistance. They did not attempt to investigate the reasons for the refugees' forced migration and displacement.

Ghassan Kanafani depicts the flight of the Palestinian refugees in his story *The Land of Sad Oranges*:

When we left Jaffa for Acre there was no sense of tragedy. We were like those who go away every year to spend the holidays in another city. Our days in Acre passed—there was nothing unusual about them; quite the contrary, perhaps because I was young at the time, I enjoyed them because I didn't go to school. In any case, on the night of the big attack on Acre, the picture became clearer. . . . That harsh night was marked by the gloom of men and the supplications of women. . . . You and I, and all those of our generation, were too young to understand what the story meant from beginning to end. . . . However, that night the threads

fought in Jerusalem and its environs and blocked the road to the city, near Latrun.

The context for the war that developed in Jerusalem between the Kingdom of Transjordan and the State of Israel was that the major powers failed to implement the decision to internationalize the city. In the ensuing political vacuum, it gradually became clear that the fate of Jerusalem would be decided by what happened on the ground—by the Jordanian Legion and by the Israel Defense Forces. From Israel's standpoint, the struggle for Jerusalem, and especially the urgent need to break the siege on the city, was a top priority. During June of 1948, however, the attempts to take over the Latrun police station failed, while the blockade on Jerusalem was bypassed by the discovery of the "Burma Road" which was paved in early June. A water pipeline was also laid along the Burma Road route, which rescued the residents of Jerusalem from a severe water shortage.

The Israel Defense Forces (IDF) formally came into being on May 31, 1948—accepting thousands of young volunteers from abroad, including pilots and trained combatants, Holocaust refugees newly arrived from Europe, and would-be "illegal" immigrants freed from DP camps in Cyprus—and thereafter it was the IDF against the Arab armies.

Hagai Horvitz describes how residents of the *Yishuv* felt during that period:

> We saw clear as day what we were up against. Even now I fail to understand how people don't realize that we were confronting a continuation of the Holocaust in Europe. We, the Jews of the Land of Israel, were meant to be annihilated. This was the plan, and we heard it and saw it. In Israel there were riots and killings on the roads and in the Jewish settlements, and then came the invasion: They came across the Jordan River bridges, they came up from the south and inland through the Ephraim Mountains, right before our eyes. It was obvious that we were fighting for our very existence, for the lives of the children who had been born here. . . . The very clear-cut understanding that, if we did not win, we would be annihilated was one of the foundational experiences of that generation, and so we fought.[3]

After about a month of fighting, both sides were exhausted and accepted the suggestion by UN mediator Count Bernadotte to agree to a month's truce

began to become clear, and in the morning when the Jews withdrew, threatening and foaming with anger, a large truck was parked at the gate of our house. . . . Hurried, frantically—a simple collection of sleeping things was thrown into it from here and there. . . . I was leaning against the old wall of the house when I saw your mother climb into the truck, then your aunt and then the young ones. Your father started to throw you and your brothers into the car, on top of our belongings. Then he pulled me up, out of the corner, raised me above his head to the iron cage of the roof of the driver's cabin, where I saw my mother and Riad sitting quietly. Before I could seat myself properly, the truck moved. The beloved city of Acre was disappearing little by little in the curves of the road leading up to Ras Al-Naquora.

RESULTS OF *AL-NAKBAH*: EYEWITNESS REPORTS

Jewish villages were built on the remains of Arab villages. You don't even know the names of those Arab villages and I don't blame you because geography books no longer exist. And not only geography books don't exist anymore, but also the Arab villages themselves have disappeared. Nahalal was established on the site of Ma'lul, Kibbutz Giv'at on the site of Jebbata, Kibbutz Sarid in the place of Khneifes, and Kfar Yehoshua on the site of Tel Shoman. There is not a single place in this country that did not have a former Arab population. [Moshe Dayan, speech delivered at Technion (Israel Institute of Technology) in Haifa, *Ha'aretz*, 4 April 1969]

Because of the expulsion and forced migration of the Palestinians, their suffering increased and the Palestinian family system was shattered. A man from Nahr Al-Bared refugee camp in Lebanon recalls what happened to his small daughter:

I had a daughter—she was three and a half years old, and was separated from her mother during the fighting. Some people told me they had seen her going towards the Druze village of Yarka, so I went there to look for her. I searched until the morning but I couldn't find her. In the morning I went up to Yarka. Some children were playing in the courtyard. I saw

(June 11 to July 9, 1948). Count Bernadotte also submitted a draft of his plan for achieving order in the Land of Israel to the UN, in which he proposed changing the partition plan. Under the Bernadotte plan, another Arab nation would not be created, but rather Jordan would receive the areas that were to have constituted the Arab state in Palestine, along with the Negev and Jerusalem. Both parties to the conflict, however, unequivocally rejected this proposal.

It was during the first truce that the *Altalena* affair, which inflamed the *Yishuv*, occurred: the *Irgun*, most of whose fighters were already serving with the IDF, brought the *Altalena* ship loaded with weapons to Israel, intending to arm its own ranks, and refused to turn over the arms to the IDF. After negotiations to resolve the matter failed, David Ben-Gurion, prime minister of the new state, gave an order to prevent the unloading of the weapons at all costs, and the *Altalena* was fired upon. It blew up and sank off the shores of Tel Aviv; nineteen *Irgun* members and three IDF soldiers lost their lives. The *Altalena* was perceived as a turning point for Israeli democracy when, at the risk of sparking a civil war, the legitimate government headed by Ben-Gurion quelled a rebellion.

VICTORY IN WAR: FROM THE TEN DAYS BATTLES TO THE ARMISTICE

On the 8th of July, 1948, the fighting was renewed for another ten days, until a second truce was implemented. The trend was now different, with the IDF taking the initiative and going on the offensive; its forces captured Lod and Ramla (the Danny campaign) and Nazareth (the Dekel campaign). The IDF was unable to capture the Old City of Jerusalem, and there was a hard battle with the Jordanian Legion for control of the city, with both sides attempting to capture neighborhoods. Houses were taken and retaken in the Mea She'arim, but in the end the sides were unable to appreciably alter the situation at the front. The IDF did not succeed in capturing the area near Latrun and to reconnect the Negev to the rest of the State of Israel. The tremendous effort invested in the defense of Jerusalem tapered off at the end of July with the start of the second truce on July 18th. Fighting in Jerusalem ended, and Transjordan and Israel agreed on a boundary, in line with the reality on the ground. The Old City remained under Jordanian control. Israel and Jordan abolished the internationalization of Jerusalem by dividing the city between

my daughter standing in front of a boy who was eating a piece of bread. She was hungry and asked the boy to give her a piece. The boy did not pay any attention to her. I came up from behind and hugged and cradled her in my arms. I couldn't utter a single word because I was in tears. In just twelve hours our condition changed from a position of honor to a position of humiliation.[15]

Another man from the Nahr Al-Bared camp in Lebanon recalls the suffering in the first years of Diaspora: "I had a seven-year-old brother, who died at Al-Qar'oun at the beginning of the winter. Many other children died as well. They put us in barracks with 20 or 30 families in each. One night a child went out to relieve himself; the next morning he was found frozen."[16]

Palestinians describe their first days in the camps using expressions such as "death," "paralysis," "we don't exist," "we lost the way," "we lost all we had," "we lost the dearest things in life."

The following poem by an Iraqi poet, written in colloquial Arabic, describes Palestinian deprivation:

He who has lost gold
Will find it in the gold market
And he who has parted with a loved one
May forget him after a while
But he who has lost a homeland
Where will he find it?

Article 11 of UN Resolution 194 (December 1948) stipulated that refugees "wishing to return to their homes and live peacefully should be allowed to do so as soon as possible and that compensation should be paid for the property of those who decide not to return." According to international law and justice, the responsible government and/or authorities must pay compensation for loss and damage.

However, despite these recommendations, the Palestinian refugees continued to suffer in their camps in Lebanon, Jordan, Syria, and everywhere in exile. In the part of Palestine occupied in 1948, where 900,000 inhabitants used to live, most of these inhabitants were expelled, and some were killed. Only 160,000 remained there under the yoke of Israeli military rule until 1967.

them. After the ten days of renewed fighting, the second truce took effect and continued until October of 1948.

In October 1948, the IDF launched another offensive. The Yoav campaign was intended to thwart, once and for all, the Bernadotte program to remove the Negev from the Jewish state, as well as to eject the Egyptian army from the Negev. Bernadotte meantime had had second thoughts concerning parts of his original plan, but not with regard to the Negev. On September 16, Bernadotte was assassinated by *Lehi* fighters in Jerusalem; it was the last act of terror by that group.

The Yoav campaign succeeded in creating a bridge to the isolated and besieged settlements in the Negev and incorporating them into the territory of Israel, and Beersheba was also taken. While the IDF was unable to get the Egyptian army out of the Negev, they remained surrounded and besieged in the Fallujah area (along the Ashkelon–Beit Govrin axis). The Yoav campaign was followed by the Hiram campaign, which aimed to expel Qawuqji's volunteer Army of Liberation from the north and to create a line of defense along the borders of mandatory Israel. The Hiram campaign was the last one in the Galilee, during which time the IDF moved into Lebanon and conquered territory there; this land was subsequently returned under the armistice agreements.

Raising the Ink Flag in Eilat, 1949

The Horev campaign (December 1948–January 1949) aimed for a decisive victory over the Egyptian army. The IDF forces were able to breach the Egyptian lines in the eastern front and to break through via Sinai, but they were unable to achieve a victory over the

Destroyed homes and deserted houses
in Jizmo (Rammlah), Al-Mansourah
(Ako), Kufer Lam (Haifa), and
Khaldeh (Rammlah)

The West Bank fell under Jordanian rule, and Palestinians were not allowed to mention the name Palestine and were banned from exercising their national rights or keeping their national identity. In contrast, the Palestinians in Gaza Strip enjoyed more freedom to build their personality and identity because the Egyptians did not have any plans to control the Palestinians there, unlike the Jordanians who were always looking forward to annexing the West Bank.

The period after *Al-Nakbah* was characterized by a political vacuum due to the absence of a Palestinian leadership, which would be in charge of all the affairs of the Palestinians and would organize their struggle for their right to return and would fend for their rights. This period witnessed the emergence of Palestinian nationalism, which soon led to the rise of the PLO as the sole and legitimate representative of the Palestinian people in 1964. However, it seemed that some Arab leaders were not up to the challenge and responsibility. Perhaps some of them were conspiring about what was left of Palestine.

The armies of three Arab countries were not able to stand in the face of the Israeli occupation army for more than six days in the June 1967 war. As a result, the last part of Palestine was lost together with Sinai and the Golan.

Egyptian forces in the Gaza Strip. Under pressure from England and the United States, Israel withdrew from Sinai and returned to the mandatory border in the Nitzana area.

The last campaign of the War of Independence was the Uvda campaign in March 1949. The objective was to gain control of the southern Negev and reach the apex of the triangle affording access to the Red Sea. During that campaign, the conquest of the Negev was completed and the village of Umm Rash-Rash (later Eilat) was taken.

THE END OF THE WAR

In January 1949, the first elections to the Knesset were held, and February saw this first-ever legislative assembly convened in the State of Israel. The state was launched as an independent, sovereign, and democratic state. With UN mediation, armistice agreements were signed between Israel and the Arab countries, except for Iraq, which refused to sign. These agreements brought an end to the war, but did not herald peace between Israel, the Palestinian people, and the Arab nations. In December 1949, on the eve of the debate in the UN which would attempt to renew the process of internationalizing the city, west Jerusalem was declared the capital of the State of Israel.

Israel attained its independence thanks to its organizational ability, both political and military, a visionary leadership grounded in reality, and the massive enlistment of the *Yishuv* and Jews abroad. The combat forces fought valiantly and were prepared to give their lives for their homeland, with a powerful spirit of comradeship in arms to support them in the fiercest fighting. The *Yishuv* paid a heavy price, with 6,000 combined civilian and military casualties—about 1 percent of the Jewish population on the eve of the war.

A Palestinian state was not established, and the Palestinian people were obliged to live under the sovereignty of Israel, Egypt, Lebanon, and Jordan. Hundreds of thousands of Palestinian Arabs in Israel became refugees, living in appalling conditions in camps set up for them by the Arab states. Israel's borders were not peaceful, and the dynamic of the conflict continued.

Notwithstanding, the refugee problem will forever remain the danger signal that is ticking away in the Arab and international arena, especially in view of the natural increase among Palestinian refugees, whose number has reached around 6.5 million.

The plight and suffering of the refugees has been depicted by Mahmoud Mufleh, a Palestinian refugee poet, in a poem titled "Palestine: Thyme and Bullets":

Once we were young and had tender shoots
Then our green stems turned dry
We are as old as the Nakba which came upon us
Karbalaa compares not to our agony
Scorching thirst and stubborn patience
And aspirations, then stumbling,
and awesome adversity;
And standing on the embankments
And an eye staring into the horizon
Oh, if only Acre knew!
And old men stunned by disaster
And women unlike no other women!
Worry begets worry
And misery follows misery![17]

5

THE STATE OF ISRAEL: THE FIRST DECADES,
1950S AND 1960S

The State of Israel was founded with the War of Independence (May 14, 1948). After the war, two processes occurred that led to a significant change in Israel's demographic balance: the first was the emigration and deportation of hundreds of thousands of Arabs from Israeli territory, following which they became refugees in several Arab countries; the second was the granting of citizenship to hundreds of thousands of Jews, most of them refugees from the Holocaust, who immigrated to the State of Israel during this same period.

The war ended with the signing of armistice agreements rather than inclusive peace treaties. The Arab countries refused to recognize the existence of the State of Israel, and Israel refused to relinquish the territories it had conquered during the war (territories not included in the partition plan), and did not permit the Arab refugees to return. Golda Meir expressed this sentiment in the 24th Zionist Congress (1956):

> I readily concede: I am afraid not only of war. I am terrified when, in certain places in the world, they begin speaking about peace in Israel and in the Middle East. What peace? At what price? Compromises at

5

YEARS OF HOMELESSNESS AND DESPAIR:
THE 1950S AND 1960S

PALESTINE AFTER *AL-NAKBAH*

The 1948 war led to the establishment of Israel in a large part of Palestine. It also resulted in the displacement of over 750,000 Palestinians from their own homeland. They took shelter in the remaining areas of Palestine and in neighboring Arab countries. As soon as the war ended, Israel started to impose a fait accompli policy exploiting the truce agreements, which afforded the new state a good opportunity to apply the partition plan. Through further aggression, Israel managed to seize a total of 77 percent of Palestine, although the partition plan had allocated only 55 percent to the Jewish state.

The catastrophe of 1948, which later came to be known as *Al-Nakbah*, turned the Palestinians' lives around, from a life full of hope and stability to one of devastation, dispossession, homelessness, and despair. The war destroyed the Palestinian society and put an end to the Palestinian people's hopes and dreams. The people were dispersed; and the social, political, and economic structures of the Palestinian society collapsed. The principal elements of the society, people, and land, were completely ruined.

The land of Palestine was divided into three parts. The first was the part

whose expense? Making compromises and concessions is usually a fine quality, but our opinion is that it is a fine quality for the wealthy, and not for beggars. And I want to know: this beggar, the Jewish State, with the tiny area of land it stands on—what compromise is being asked of it? What concessions will it have to make?[1]

The State of Israel may have won the War of Independence, but the economic, security, and social issues it now faced were daunting. Some 6,000 members of the *Yishuv* were killed in the fighting (1 percent of the Jewish population). The long war exhausted the economy of the young country, while the threat posed by the Arab countries and the Palestinians to the security of the fledgling state did not abate.

This chapter will deal with various aspects of Israeli reality during the country's initial years as a state: the relationship with Israel's neighbors; internal processes that occurred in the realms of economy, society, and mass immigration; and the young country's relationship with its Arab citizens.

BORDERS OF THE STATE AND ARMISTICE AGREEMENTS

With the end of the war, the IDF discharged most of the troops who had been called up, leaving just three regular brigades on active duty: two infantry brigades and one tank brigade. The air force included a number of old piston airplanes. Prime Minister David Ben-Gurion then charged Chief of Staff Yigael Yadin with the task of reducing the military budget by 20 percent, but the latter refused and resigned. Mordechai Maklef, appointed chief of staff in his stead, disbanded an additional infantry battalion, which contributed to the weakening of the IDF. At the same time, Israel was beset both by infiltrations from Arab countries and Syrian attempts to change the border. These and other events were to a large extent the result of diverse interpretations of the armistice agreements.

The State of Israel believed that the agreements gave them three inalienable rights:

1. A complete end to the violence between both sides—not just between the regular armies, but also between irregular forces and civilians.

on which Israel was established and it covered 77 percent of Palestine (20,770 km²). The second part, covering 20.3 percent of Palestine (5,878 km²), was later known as the West Bank. This part received a considerable number of refugees who were driven out of their land, and was later annexed to the Hashemite Kingdom of Jordan. The third part was the Gaza Strip, and it covered an area of 365 km² (2.3 percent of the area of Palestine). The population of the Gaza Strip literally increased overnight from 80,000 to 300,000 people and was later annexed to the Egyptian administration.[1]

As for the Palestinian people themselves, they were dispersed in different countries and could be classified into three categories:

UN partition decision of Palestine in 1947

1. Palestinians who remained in their homes under Israeli control;

2. Palestinians living in the West Bank and Gaza Strip and who remained there;

3. Palestinian refugees who became homeless during or after *Al-Nakbah* because they fled their homes or were driven out as a result of the terrorist activities and atrocities committed by the Jews against the Palestinians and who took shelter in areas of Palestine that had not been occupied until that time.

PALESTINIANS IN THE AFTERMATH OF *AL-NAKBAH*

PALESTINIANS IN THE OCCUPIED TERRITORIES

Palestinians in the occupied territories were those who stayed in their homes in those areas of Palestine that fell under the control of the Zionist armed

Map of the Armistice Borders,
1949

2. Recognition that the armistice borders
   were final, and that the state could do
   as it pleased within them.

3. The right to settle Jews on the land
   and develop the country's economic
   infrastructure without considering the
   ownership of the Palestinian residents
   who had either left or been deported
   from their lands.

The Arab countries understood the
agreements differently, believing that they
had been granted three rights:

1. The right to continue the confrontation in any manner as long as it did
   not include the use of arms, e.g., by
   blocking waterways, economic boycott, and hostile propaganda.

2. Rejection of the idea that the armistice
   lines determined the borders of the
   State of Israel, and consequently refusing to accept that the State of Israel
   could make use of the demilitarized
   areas as it pleased. For example: Syria claimed that the State of
   Israel did not have the right to make use of the water sources
   within its demilitarized borders, as determined by the armistice
   agreement.

3. Recognition of the right of Palestinian refugees to return to their
   homes, and the right to continue the struggle as long as they
   were not permitted to return to their homes and did not have
   their property restored to them. The Arab states believed they
   had a right—indeed, an obligation—to assist in the Palestinian
   struggle.

The broad discrepancies in the way the armistice agreements were

forces in 1948. They were the first to suffer from occupation and the first to feel a great sense of alienation on their own land. How did all this happen? And what were their living conditions under occupation? And how were they treated by the occupiers?

While hundreds of thousands of Palestinians fled, were expelled, or were forced to leave their homes, more than 160,000 Palestinians remained in their lands and had to confront an unknown future. In fact, the Zionists would not have preferred to have such a number of Palestinians in the areas they controlled, because they had always wanted a land without people.

This stance was reflected by Abraham Sharon, a Zionist Jew, who made his racist views public in a bulletin entitled "Racist Remarks About the Arabs": "Coexistence [with Arabs] is impossible and runs against human nature, for harmony exists only between an individual and his fellow people. Therefore, and for the sake of maintaining the purity of the Zionist state, the remaining Arabs must be expelled to Arab countries."[2]

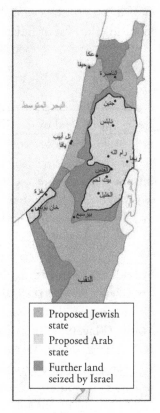

Proposed Jewish state

Proposed Arab state

Further land seized by Israel

Map of the armistice in 1949

Within the Palestinian territories that were occupied in 1948, 60 percent of the Palestinians lived in the Galilee area in the north, 30 percent in the triangle area (the midland), and 10 percent in Al-Naqab (the Negev) and Bir Al-Sabe' (Beersheba). These communities survived long years of seclusion imposed by the occupation. They were not allowed to contact members of their own families or relatives in the other parts of Palestine, i.e., in the West Bank or Gaza, or in the neighboring Arab countries where the relatives had taken shelter.[3]

The Palestinians in the occupied lands, who were once the majority in their native land, became an undesired and oppressed minority and were under the mercy of military decrees and emergency laws that remained in effect until 1966. Military courts were the only body in charge of looking into all

viewed by both sides contributed to the unrest at Israel's borders in the years following the War of Independence.

RETALIATORY OPERATIONS

Infiltration by refugees from 1947–1949 into Israeli territory began immediately with the end of the War of Independence. The reasons for the infiltrations were primarily economic: theft of working animals, irrigation pipes, equipment, and crops (some from lands that had belonged to the refugees in the past); and a desire to visit relatives or reassume residence in the places from which they had fled or been deported. There were also infiltrators who came to set mines, vandalize, and commit murder based on nationalist motives.

From 1949–1956 there were shooting incidents between the IDF and the Arab armies. The confrontations resulted mainly from activities initiated by both sides in areas that had been demilitarized as a result of the armistice agreements. At first, the IDF emerged as the weaker party to the conflict. One of the activities that detracted from the IDF's image was its maneuver at Tel Mutila (May 1951) near Moshav Almagor, north of the Sea of Galilee. An IDF unit was sent to Tel Mutila to remove the Syrian forces that had captured it. A three-day battle ensued, during which forty IDF fighters were killed and seventy-two wounded. Following the battle, the erosion of self-confidence among Israeli citizens and the army was palpable, and moreover, the IDF was unsuccessful at stopping the infiltrations into Israeli territory.

IDF commanders deliberated about how to restore the fighting spirit that had characterized the IDF during the War of Independence, and one of the resolutions was the establishment of Unit 101, headed by Ariel Sharon. This unit comprised skilled fighters, young men from kibbutzim and moshavim, who specialized in commando combat techniques. The unit was sent on combat missions against infiltrators and carried out many "retaliatory actions" (in response to hostile Arab activities) that took place across the border.

In 1953, there were many incidents in which Israeli soldiers and civilians were attacked near the Jordanian border. Forty-six Israelis were killed during a period of approximately six months. In October, infiltrators from Jordan threw a hand grenade at a home on the outskirts of Yehud, killing a mother and two of her children. Israel decided not to let the matter go, and two days later, Unit 101 and a paratrooper force crossed the Jordanian border. Unit 101 blew up forty houses in the village of Qibya, one of the villages being used as a

kinds of cases. The military governor exercised unlimited arbitrary powers. For instance, Palestinians would be expelled from one area to another or prohibited to enter certain areas for alleged security reasons or under some other pretexts. People who dared to complain about the bad conditions or discrimination would often face exile.

Personal freedoms suffered enormously and movement was highly restricted. Palestinians could not leave their areas of residence for other areas without special permits. These permits not only specified the length of time they were allowed to stay outside their own areas but also specified the routes on which they had to travel. As most farms were often far from residential areas, Palestinians had to secure daily permits to get to their own farms.[4]

In his memoirs, which were published in 1940, Yosef Weitz, manager of the Jewish National Fund, wrote:

> What goes on amongst us has to be made public. It is impossible for two peoples to coexist in this land; the presence of Arabs among us will not help us achieve our goals. The only solution lies in turning the land into the land of Israel (Eretz Yisrael), or at least the Arab land of Israel without Arabs. This can only be achieved if all Arabs are transferred to neighboring countries, and if not even a single [Arab] village continues to exist.[5]

The fact that a number of Palestinians remained in the emerging Jewish state was against the wishes of the Zionist pioneers, who wanted to establish a purely Jewish uninational state. Consequently, the Israeli authorities sought to push the Palestinians out of their land through the harsh measures they imposed on them, or by directly expelling them out of Palestine. This happened to the Negev bedouins. For instance, the Al Sane' tribe was deported to the south of Hebron, and the tribe of Abu Samahdana to Egypt. The two villages of Iqrit and Kufur Bur'um were other examples of deliberate expulsion of Palestinians from their own homelands. In place of these two villages, Kibbutz Bar'am and Moshav Doviv were established, though the Arab inhabitants of the two villages were told they would be allowed to go back to their homes within a fortnight.[6]

The Palestinians living in the occupied part of Palestine remained without a leadership, particularly since the Palestinian national leadership itself, like all Palestinians, had been dispersed. However, the harsh living conditions

base by the infiltrators, and it was later learned that village residents had been hiding in some of the houses. Although the commander of Unit 101, Ariel Sharon, claimed that his fighters had evacuated the houses before bombing them, sixty-nine residents of the village were killed in that action.

The Israeli media did not critique the incident and aligned itself with Ben-Gurion's mendacious claim that it was not IDF soldiers who had carried out the action, but rather angry residents of Israel's outlying communities. One of the few voices that condemned the operation was expressed in a letter sent to *Ha'aretz* newspaper, which railed against the collective punishment inflicted by the IDF in this maneuver: "Even in our gloomy world, the world of the jungle, one recoils from the indiscriminate murder of women, children and non-combatants."[2]

Ariel Sharon, in a lecture at Sapir College in March 2003, responded thus to the various accusations leveled against IDF retaliatory raids during the 1950s:

> I would like to go back in time to the first years after the War of Independence and to the context of the policy of retaliatory action. The Jewish *Yishuv* in Israel numbered about one and a half million people in total, and faced a wave of harsh terrorist acts that originated mainly in Judea and Samaria [which were under Jordanian occupation] and in the Gaza Strip [that was under Egyptian occupation]. After the War of Independence, the IDF, which had conquered the armies of seven countries, stood helpless in the face of the situation that had arisen.
>
> I founded Unit 101 in August 1953, and immediately upon its establishment, its soldiers began carrying out operations. Within a short time, we proved that there is no task that we cannot successfully complete. Two prominent operations were the Qibya raid and the Hebron raid. These two raids had an immediate effect on the enemy. The Lod area, where there had been many losses over the years, became quiet, and remained so for many years, and a similar gain was achieved in Jerusalem.
>
> The people who for years were charged with carrying out the retaliatory raids were not as bloodthirsty as they are being described today. They were young people who cared. The IDF's retaliatory raids during the period preceding the Sinai Campaign—seventy in number—reduced the scale of Arab terrorist activity and turned it from disorganized but

made it necessary for a Palestinian body that would fend for them, and so the Arab Popular Front (APF) appeared in June 1958 to fight against the Israeli policy aimed at destroying the national identity of the Palestinians. The APF also called for the termination of military rule. Shortly after, the Land Movement, or Land Group, was founded in 1959 to fight against the confiscation of Palestinian lands and to protect the rights of more than 30,000 Palestinians who had remained in the occupied part of Palestine, but who had become refugees in villages away from their own hometowns and villages, like the people of Iqrit and Kufur Bur'um.[7]

Map showing the movement of refugees and refugee camps in different places and under different authorities

PALESTINIANS IN THE WEST BANK AND GAZA STRIP

A quick look at the map of Palestine and the surrounding areas reveals the extent of dispersion that was inflicted upon the Palestinian people in the aftermath of the 1948 war. In addition, Palestinians found themselves without an efficient leadership due to various external and internal reasons. The external reasons were as different as the forces that ruled over Palestine. Internally, the results of the war caused the old differences between the national movement and the opposition to come to the forefront anew. This further deepened the division and dispersion which had befallen the Palestinians.

Following the war in 1948, the Gaza Strip was put under Egyptian military rule, as the Egyptian forces had been positioned there during the

Motta Gur and combatants prior to carrying out a raid on Qalqiliya

very high-volume activity to fewer actions organized by Arab governments. This is the reason that over time, our response targets gradually became governmental targets—that is, an attack on the government responsible for the terror.[3]

The Qibya raid had a number of immediate repercussions: the Jordanian Legion stationed its troops along the border with Israel and retaliatory actions in the area decreased. The nature of these actions also changed: the IDF switched from retaliatory actions against villages to actions against army and police camps in Arab countries. These actions greatly increased the tension between Israel and the Arab countries, tension that accumulated over the years and became one of the causes of the outbreak of the Sinai War.

The IDF carried out other retaliatory raids that were much greater in scope than the Qibya raid. Among them were the actions in Gaza, Khan-Yunis, northeast of the Sea of Galilee, and Qalqiliya. The combination of the establishment of Unit 101, the paratrooper battalion, and the retaliatory raids created a new ethos of Israeli bravado. The paratrooper commanders were seen as strong and brave, and many young Israelis looked upon them as role models.

THE SINAI WAR (1956)

BACKGROUND AND CAUSES

In the years 1954–1956, the tension between the State of Israel and its neighbors grew, and the possibility of a new war became more and more of a reality. Reasons for this war included:

1. Border tensions: as stated, the quiet along the borders was disrupted many times by terror activities of Palestinian infiltrators (Arab countries did

war. The military administration was later replaced by an Egyptian civil administration.

On the eve of the war, Gaza had a population of 80,000. Yet, as a result of the war, large numbers of refugees flowed into the strip. By the end of the war, the number had risen to over 300,000. They lived on an area of 365 square kilometers, making the Gaza Strip the most densely populated area in the world. The new living conditions led to great social and economic hardships. Consequently, many Palestinians emigrated to the Arab Gulf countries to secure the basic necessities of life for themselves and their families. This automatically meant further dispersion of the Palestinians, who had already been suffering from dispersion as a result of the war.

Haj Ameen Al-Husseini and Ahmad Hlimi Abdel Bagi in a group of Palestinian men

During the second truce agreement and on 28 September 1948, Haj Amin Al-Husseini, head of the National Movement, moved to Gaza. He started to plan for the establishment of a civil administration for Palestine. On 1 October 1948 the Palestinian National Conference was held, which announced the establishment of an all-Palestine government. The head of the Arab Supreme Board was selected as head of the National Council while Mr. Ahmed Hilmi Abd Al-Baqi was selected as head of the government.[8]

Jordan refused to recognize the new Palestinian government and asked the Arab League to withdraw its recognition. But the Arab League refused to do so. In the meantime, Britain declared that an Arab government could not be established in the remaining parts of Palestine and believed that a merger with Jordan would be a better option.

Due to pressure from different sources, the all-Palestinian government was limited to the head of government and a couple of aides. Under pressure from the British, Haj Amin Al-Husseini was summoned to Egypt and this had a detrimental effect on the new government. Admittedly, the government

not prevent them from entering Israeli territory, and sometimes even encouraged them) and military actions by Arab countries. Despite their retaliatory actions, the IDF's deterrent power continued to decline. The actions taken against Israel included shooting attacks against Israelis in demilitarized areas, and Syria's struggle for control of water sources in the north. Increasing numbers of people in Israel, foremost among them Chief of Staff Moshe Dayan, believed in the need for a broader operation in order to ensure quiet along the borders.

2. Establishment of the Baghdad Pact (officially: Central Treaty Organization—CENTO) and establishment of ties between Egypt and the Soviet Union (1955). The formation of the Baghdad Pact came with the breaking off of relations between Iraq and the Soviet Union, and the signing of a defense treaty between Iraq and Turkey. Britain, Pakistan, and Iran later joined the agreement, the objective of which was to halt the spread of the USSR from North Asia. Egypt, however, viewed this pact as an erosion of its status as the leader of the Arab world, and began strengthening its ties with the USSR. The main expression of this mutual rapprochement was the Czechoslovakian arms deal, in which Egypt received modern Soviet arms from Czechoslovakia, a Soviet satellite state. This deal reinforced the sense of threat felt by the Israeli population and its leadership.

3. Nationalization of the Suez Canal by Egypt in June 1956: during that year, Egyptian President Gamal Abdul Nasser decided to nationalize the canal, which was under partial ownership of Britain and France. The nationalization of the canal prevented Israeli ships from passing through it, and in so doing cut off the sea connection between Israel and Asia, the East, and South Africa. In October 1956, a secret committee was convened between representatives of Britain, France, and Israel in the city of Sèvres, near Paris, which decided that the three countries would join forces in a war against Egypt. The role of the State of Israel in the war was to conquer the Sinai Desert and reach the Suez Canal, in order to force Nasser to change his policy. Israel signed an arms deal with France that included modern planes and tanks.

THE WAR

The Sinai Campaign began on October 29, 1956, at 17:00, when sixteen Dakota planes dropped some 400 Israeli paratroopers near the Mitle and Gidi passes, some thirty kilometers from the Suez Canal. The paratroopers

was born weak due to the internal differences between Haj Amin Al-Husseini and his opponents as well as the international conditions which were supportive of Israel but opposed to the establishment of any form of Palestinian government. As expected, the All-Palestine government did not survive its first few months, and the Gaza Strip remained under Egyptian administration until the 1967 war.[9]

The West Bank fell directly under the control of the Jordanian army. Ragheb Al-Nashashibi, who was a chief opponent of Haj Amin Al-Husseini, was appointed general military governor. Jordan, under the leadership of King Abdullah, sought to annex the West Bank but needed to guarantee the support of the Palestinians themselves. So several conferences were held for that purpose. The first conference, which was held in Amman on 1 November 1948, called for the unification of Jordan and the West Bank. On 1 December, another conference was held in Jericho and the participants endorsed the unification with Jordan. The Jericho Conference decisions were approved by the Jordanian ministers' council. A unified National Assembly was formed and King Abdullah was sworn in as king of the West Bank and the East Bank. However, King Abdullah was assassinated on 20 July 1951 during a visit to Jerusalem.[10]

Through unification, the West Bank was put under the full control of Jordanian rule. As a result, the Palestinian political decision and national entity disappeared, and the Palestinians were deprived of their right to exercise self-determination even in the Gaza Strip and the West Bank. The 1950s witnessed the loss of the Palestinian national identity.

One of the major goals of the Zionist immigration to Palestine was to ensure the superiority of the Jews in Palestine, which would bring about the desired demographic change. The aim of the 1948 war was to not only take control of the land and populate it with Jews, but also to empty the land of its Arab population by

Palestinian reugees on boats after they were expelled

were ambushed in the Mitle pass and thirty-eight fighters were killed. Additional fierce battles took place at the Ruafa Dam (near Nitzana) and at the Rafah Junction. Two days following the outbreak of the war, the French and the British bombed Egypt's airports in the Suez Canal area, and the Egyptian chief of staff decided to retreat in the direction of the canal to prevent its conquest. Within a few days, Israel succeeded in taking the Gaza Strip and most of the Sinai Peninsula, and was able to ensure free passage for Israeli ships on the Suez Canal and in the Straits of Tiran. This victory resulted in heightened public confidence in the IDF and great admiration for its fighters.

At the international level, the war caused great anger on the part of the two superpowers, the USSR and the United States, toward Britain, France, and Israel. Although the two superpowers were at the height of their estrangement in the Cold War, they jointly condemned the war against Egypt and made an unequivocal demand of Israel and her allies to withdraw from the territories that had been occupied. This pressure forced Britain, France, and Israel to withdraw. Following a UN decision to evacuate Israeli forces from Sinai, Israeli Prime Minister David Ben-Gurion ordered Israeli troops to leave Sinai. Israel thus returned to the international border, and UN forces were positioned in Sinai and the Gaza Strip in order to guard the border and maintain the peace. An important achievement gained by Israel as a result of the war was that the Straits of Tiran were reopened to Israeli ships.

The war and the Israeli military achievement were not reflected in diplomatic terms. Nasser claimed victory in having successfully forced Israel and its allies to withdraw, while Israel had demonstrated its military power both to itself and the rest of the world, and its self-confidence grew.

Yechiel Mohar wrote the song "Standing at Mt. Sinai" immediately after the victory in the war, and the song was well loved by most of the Israeli public:

> It is no legend, friends, and not a dream to spurn;
> Behold at Mount Sinai
> Right here at Mount Sinai the sneh—the bush—does burn.
> It burns inflamed in song,
> the soldier boys in chorus
> The city gates in the hands of Samson's mighty force

all possible means. To this end, the Jews perpetrated several massacres in many villages to frighten the Palestinian population, spread terror, and force them to flee from their lands. The most terrifying massacre took place in Deir Yassin. The news about what happened there spread fast. The Jews used the Deir Yassin massacre to scare off Palestinians in other villages by threatening them with the same fate.[11]

In view of Jewish military superiority, the only way for Palestinians to avoid being massacred was to flee from their homes and lands. More than 750,000 Palestinians fled under tragic conditions, leaving behind their dearest belongings and property, albeit, hoping to return soon. An endless number of stories and anecdotes accompanied the Palestinian people as they fled their homes. Some of these stories were recorded in *A Palestinian Without Identity* by Salah Khalaf (Abu Iyad):

The 13th of May [1948] will be carved in my memory forever. On that particular day, my family fled from Jaffa to take refuge in Gaza. We were besieged and the only way to save ourselves was by sea. We set off in what looked like a boat, and came under a barrage of gunfire from neighboring Jewish gathering places including Tel Aviv. . . . For a boy of about fifteen, the day of departure seemed like doomsday. I was overwhelmed by the scene of masses of men, women, elderly and young who were swaggering under the heavy weight of their bags or bundles heading toward the piers at the port of Jaffa in a saddening clatter. Screams, wailing and sobbing were interrupted only by deafening explosions.

As the boat was about to set sail, we heard a woman crying frantically; she had just realized that one of her four sons was not on the boat, and wanted the boat to return to port to fetch her missing son. But it was almost impossible to turn back under heavy gunfire endangering the lives of two to three hundred people, including lots of children, packed on the small boat. The brave woman's pleas fell on deaf ears and so she broke down in tears. Then losing control of herself, she went over the handrails and threw herself overboard. Her husband failed to grab her and he too dived in the sea. Neither knew how to swim and to the shock of the passengers who felt paralyzed, they were both swallowed by the sturdy waves.[12]

Oh Divine fires—in the eyes of the corps,
Oh Divine fires—in the engines' roar
This day will yet be told, dear men
The nation's come to stand at Sinai again

It is no legend, friends, and no illusion vain
From back then to this day the bush is burning still
The burning bush, in flame
It burns in passionate song
In hearts in unison,
of God, of chariots bearing
young men of Zion

Oh Divine fires . . .

THE MASSACRE IN KAFR QASSEM

One of the gravest and most tragic events in Israeli history—the massacre at Kafr Qassem—took place on the eve of the Sinai Campaign. The story of the massacre must be seen in the context of the prevailing atmosphere in Israel during the 1950s. The fledgling state, which had been in conflict with the Arab world since its inception, was now poised before a "second round." The Jewish public felt threatened by the Arab countries headed by Nasser, and viewed the Israeli Arabs as constantly "suspect." The fear of Israeli Arabs volunteering to help their brothers in neighboring countries became even greater during wartime. Here it is important to note the date and time of the massacre: October 29, 1956, at 17:00, i.e., exactly the same time that Israel launched the Sinai Campaign.

In the days before the Sinai Campaign, the IDF leadership created an emergency plan for combined military activity against Egypt and Jordan. The political echelon decided not to implement the plan, and most of the IDF's activity was planned for the Egyptian area. On the morning of October 29, 1956, the Central Command announced to his officers that the plan to go to war against Jordan had been canceled, and dictated a policy that emphasized maintaining the daily routine in the Arab villages. At 13:00 IDF Brigade Commander Issachar Shadmi ordered Major Shmuel Malinki of the Border Police to declare a 17:00 curfew on the area between Kafr Qassem and Taibe

The plight of Palestinian refugeees in the summer of 1948

British and American reports indicated that 70 percent of the Palestinian citizens were driven out of their land from the outbreak of the war on 15 May until its end in June 1948. This was due to the killings and terrorizing operations committed by the different armed Zionist organizations, chiefly the *Haganah*, the Israeli army, in various Palestinian cities and villages.[13]

The fleeing Palestinians took shelter in neighboring Arab countries—Jordan, Syria, and Lebanon, and in what later came to be known as the West Bank and Gaza Strip. Very few settled in Iraq and Egypt. The Palestinian refugees in these countries lived near the border areas, hoping to return at the end of the war. They found themselves homeless, wandering aimlessly, dispersed in every direction, and without any protection. These living conditions created a real human crisis that necessitated a quick solution. The United Nations provided tents for the refugees. On 11 December 1948 the United Nations Conciliation Commission for Palestine (UNCCP) came into being "to take steps to assist the parties concerned to achieve a final comprehensive peace settlement of all questions outstanding between them and to facilitate the repatriation or resettlement with compensation of the Palestinian refugees."

The UNCCP repatriation attempts failed, and so it confined its efforts

Monument in memory of the victims of Kafr Qassem

(until this debriefing, the village had generally been put under a 21:00 curfew, but it was decided to make the curfew earlier in order to ensure quiet during the war). Malinki asked how curfew violators should be dealt with, and Shadmi responded with the Arabic expression *Allah yirhamo* (which can either be translated as "may God have mercy on him" or as the English expression "may he rest in peace"). In Malinki's 13:20 debriefing to his officers, he said that anyone who violated the curfew was to be shot. One of the officers (Aryeh Manshas) asked how women, children, and people on their way home from working in the fields should be dealt with. Malinki responded that they were to be treated like the others, repeating the phrase *Allah yirhamo*. In effect, each commander operated independently; one company commander (Frankenthal) decided to delay the beginning of the curfew in the area for which he was responsible to 17:30, and forbade his soldiers to open fire until the late night hours. The commander of the other company (Haim Levi) ordered his officers to operate in accordance with the instructions of battalion commander Malinki.

At 16:30, the men of Haim Levi's company told the mukhtar of Kafr Qassem that the curfew was going to begin earlier. The mukhtar sent a man to spread the word around the village, and asked the border police to update those returning from work in the fields that the time for beginning the curfew had been moved up. The information did not reach those working outside of the village, and soldiers from Haim Levi's company shot forty-nine people to death: men, women, and children.

On the day after the massacre, the Central Command established an investigations committee, and a few days later a number of those involved were arrested. In January 1957, their trials began and the incident became a central issue in Israeli public discourse. The battalion commander, Malinki,

to dealing with the Palestinian refugee problem. A year later, UNRWA (United Nations Relief and Works Agency for Palestine Refugees in the Near East) was established to provide relief and work for the refugees in the West Bank, Gaza Strip, Jordan, Syria, and Lebanon.[14]

CONDITIONS OF THE REFUGEES

At the beginning, the Palestinian refugees stayed in tents provided by the United Nations and the Arab League as a temporary measure until they could return to their homes. The camps lacked the simplest elements of a decent life, even after the tents were replaced by houses made of mud bricks and corrugated tin roofs in certain areas in the hosting countries.

The refugees suffered very harsh living conditions. Camps were extremely overcrowded; there were severe shortages in health and educational services. Simply put, there was no infrastructure—running water, electricity, and sewage systems were mere figments of the imagination.

Although a total of 750,000 Palestinian refugees settled in different places, they lived under the same inhumane conditions. They led a life of misery, deprivation, and desperation. They suffered from being deprived of the right to go back to their own homes and lands. The vast majority couldn't even find enough to feed their families.

Away from their villages, cities, orchards, and farms, dispossessed and facing homelessness and dispersion, the masters of yesterday became a group of unemployed people who lived off the hands of charity. All that deepened their misery, suffering, and despair much further. A large number of refugees sought employment and opportunity in other parts of the world, especially in the Arab Gulf countries, and that contributed to their dispersal and pain even further.

A refugee camp

was demoted to the rank of private and sentenced to seventeen years imprisonment. Others involved in the affair were also similarly demoted and given prison sentences of 7–15 years. Approximately one year after the sentences were given, in December 1958, a *sulha* (traditional reconciliation ceremony) was conducted with representatives of the state, and many saw this as an artificial attempt to clear the conscience of Jewish society. After the *sulha*, a presidential clemency was granted to those who had carried out the massacre and they were released from jail. This sequence of events—the harsh punishment on the one hand, and the quick clemency on the other—illustrates the different attitudes to the massacre at Kafr Qassem among the Jewish public. While the judiciary system was trying to bring those responsible to justice, and in so doing to clearly demarcate the boundaries between what was permissible and what was not, the political and military system, on the other hand, stepped in and minimized the punishments, conveying the reverse message.

To this day, the massacre at Kafr Qassem is viewed as a blemish on the history of the State of Israel, illustrating that it does not reflect the way the state operates (even though there are exceptions). The rulings against those accused in the affair gave rise to the term "a clearly illegal order"—meaning an order that runs counter to human ethics, which IDF soldiers and commanders must avoid carrying out in any situation.

A number of important processes occurred in the Middle East from the middle of the 1950s: the influence of the Soviet Union in the area grew, mainly in Egypt, Syria, and Iraq. The lack of political stability in the Arab countries continued, with the exception of Egypt, where Nasser's stature increased. The struggle against the Syrians over water escalated: the IDF foiled Syria's plan to divert the waters of the Jordan, while the Syrians attacked fishermen on the Sea of Galilee and shelled communities in the Hula and Jordan Valleys. The border with Egypt grew quiet, but clashes and retaliatory action in Jordan and Syria continued, and the dynamic of conflict between Israel and the Arab states remained.

In 1959, Fatah was established by Yasser Arafat, who had become the leader of the Palestinians, and an organizational and ideological change took place in the terror activities of the Palestinians against the State of Israel.

ISRAELI SOCIETY

The establishment of the State of Israel was a longed-for moment for which

A photo of a refugee camp after it was developed

the Jews had waited for many years, but it did not complete the fulfillment of the Zionist vision. The state's first years were devoted to helping as many Jews as possible to immigrate to Israel. Between 1949 and 1955, the Jewish population in Israel increased two and a half fold. Over one million immigrants from many different countries and cultures, speaking different languages and comprising both the secular and religious, were taken in by Israel's 650,000 residents. In a wave of immigration unprecedented in human history, Jews from around the world moved to a country that had just been established, with a weak and impoverished economic and housing infrastructure, and a tough security situation along its borders. This was an extraordinary undertaking by the society and its institutions, which made tremendous efforts to establish the State of Israel as the state of the Jewish people, as a "safe sanctuary" for world Jewry and as a democratic state with a Jewish majority. The demographic balance in the young state changed dramatically: the Arabs went from being a majority to a minority, considerably impacting on majority-minority relations in the state to this day.

DIFFICULTIES IN ABSORPTION
AND CONSOLIDATION OF A NEW IDENTITY

The mass immigrations brought together many Jews from diverse countries and cultures; some of the immigrants were Holocaust survivors who arrived from Europe after the war (e.g., Romania, Poland, and Bulgaria), and the majority were immigrants from the Islamic countries (e.g., Yemen, Iraq, and Libya). The immigrants were housed in makeshift camps, on abandoned

British army bases, and in the homes of Palestinians who had not been permitted to return to Israel after the War of Independence. The conditions in the camps were horrific as the fledgling state found it difficult to provide sufficient food, clothing, and housing for the newcomers. No less difficult was

Immigrants' Ma'abara in the 1950s

This situation was depicted by Ghassan Kanafani, the Palestinian novelist, writer, and journalist, in his novel *Men in the Sun*. The novel describes the journey of three men whose miserable conditions in Palestinian refugee camps bring them together in Basra, Iraq, on their way to Kuwait, where they hope to find work and opportunity. The desert road to Kuwait is long and tiring, and the only way to get there is by being smuggled across the border. A fourth Palestinian, Abul Khaizuran, agrees to smuggle them in a water tank. To implement the smuggling plan, and despite the very hot weather, the three men enter the water tank just before the last crossing point. At the border, the car has to wait longer than necessary due to the silly behavior of the officials. Upon finishing the procedures, Abul Khaizuran drives away and soon discovers that all three men have died.

> The weakened small world struggled its way through the desert like a heavy oil drop on a warm tin container. The glaring shiny round sun was rising above their heads, and none of them bothered to dry up his sweat. As'ad put his shirt on his head, folded his legs to his hips allowing the sun to grill him over without resistance. Marwan dropped his head on Abu Qais's shoulder and shut his eyes. Abu Qais was looking intently at the road with his lips quite shut up under his grey bushy moustache. None of the four felt the desire to talk any more not just because of their exhaustion but because each of them dived deeply in his thoughts. The huge car, which was struggling its way through, was carrying them, their dreams, families, ambitions, hopes, hopelessness, desperation, weakness, powerfulness, present and past, as if it was storming the mighty door to an unknown destiny. All the eyes were fixed to that door as if they were tied to it with invisible ropes.[15]

The novel concludes with the following lines:

> An idea slipped from his head and rolled over his tongue: Why didn't they knock on the sides of the tank? He went around in a circle afraid that he might fall and dropped his head on the driving wheel: Why didn't you knock on the sides of the tank? Why? Suddenly the desert echoed his words: Why didn't you knock on the sides of the tank? Why? Why?[16]

providing them with income and a sense of dignity, and very few were lucky enough to find work, usually at initiated jobs. Later, the government began constructing *maabarot*—miserable, makeshift neighborhoods comprising shanties and tents put up near cities. Here too, the plight of the immigrants did not improve, and they felt neglected and resentful when exposed to the relatively superior situation of the more veteran residents.

The State of Israel did much to bring Jews from around the world, and representatives of the Jewish Agency were sent to the ends of the earth to find Jews and facilitate their immigration to Israel. In certain countries, this required bribing governments, arms deals, and great financial undertakings. At the beginning of the 1950s, the young country almost collapsed due to the tremendous waves of immigration, but demands to limit the scale of immigration were vehemently rejected by Prime Minister Ben-Gurion, who deemed the creation of a significant Jewish majority in the State of Israel a goal of primary importance. In 1951, Ben-Gurion capitulated to the pressure, and immigration was restricted: only immigrants who were at risk in their country of origin or who could arrive at their own expense were allowed in. For a certain period, the state preferred young, healthy people and those with a trade, and this "selective immigration" was harshly criticized and stirred up great controversy. It appears in retrospect that this was an almost unavoidable strategy that enabled the state to focus on the crucial tasks of organization and formation.

The process of accelerated, wide-scale absorption that took place in Israel in the 1950s could not have proceeded without difficulty. The established veteran immigrants had arrived mostly from Europe, and they helped their relatives and others who came from a similar background, while there was no one to help the Jews from the Islamic countries. In addition, the establishment and the main strongholds of power in the state were managed by immigrants from Western cultures, which made it very difficult for the immigrants from the Islamic nations to integrate into various realms of life in the State of Israel. The absorption authorities tried, sometimes forcibly, to impose the new Israeli culture and identity onto the immigrants, while rejecting their cultural heritage and religious norms. The education and absorption systems quickly tried to establish a new image of Israel—the image of the proud, strong, rough, brave, nature-loving "Sabra," disassociated from the Diaspora ethos of his parents and now identified with the heroes of the Bible and the resurgence of nationalism. The guiding ideology was that of the "melting pot,"

THE REFUGEES' RIGHT OF RETURN

On 11 December 1948, the General Assembly of the United Nations issued Resolution No. 194 stating

> that the refugees wishing to return to their homes and live at peace with their neighbours should be permitted to do so at the earliest practicable date, and that compensation should be paid for the property of those choosing not to return and for loss of or damage to property which, under principles of international law or in equity, should be made good by the Governments or authorities responsible.

The Palestinians felt that they were not in need of a UN resolution or permission to return to their homes—their right of return was indisputable and not forfeitable. In the meantime, Israel was absolutely opposed to the idea of allowing the refugees to go back to their homes, not even with an international resolution.

The refugee problem thus became the most complicated and dangerous problem following *Al-Nakbah*. Several proposals were put forward to solve the problem. Yet most of these proposals called for resettling Palestinian refugees in the countries they had fled to or in some other parts of the world. Apparently these proposals aimed in the first place at appeasing Israel. Club's Committee and UNRWA director John Blandford's 1951 project for resettling 250,000 Palestinian refugees were among the pioneering projects in this regard.[17]

The refugees held fast to their right of return. They insisted on the implementation of UN Resolution 194, which called for their return and compensation to those who lost property. They preferred the life of misery and deprivation they were leading over any resettlement project. For

An old Palestinian refugee holding the key to his home (from which he was expelled in 1948) as a sign of his insistence on returning to it

which tried to forge a new and original culture from the diversity of cultures that had arrived in Israel: "Israeli culture."

However, in effect, the diverse cultures did not blend: the European-Sabra culture dominated the educational perspective and its implementation nationwide, and the immigrants were expected to adjust. The price they paid was dear, and still is for many to this day: immigrants from Yemen were forced to cut off their side locks, the secular educational system desisted from passing on Jewish tradition, and immigrant children studied in Hebrew while their mother tongues—mainly Arabic and Yiddish—were ignored. The glorious past of the immigrants in their countries of origin was forgotten and not mentioned in the textbooks of the educational system. No less difficult was the treatment of Holocaust survivors, who more than once were blamed for being led like sheep to slaughter. Young Israeli society developed an attitude of derision toward the "Diaspora Jews" and felt itself superior to the new immigrants.

An additional process occurred in the realm of family, which in many cases suffered from acute disruption. In the case of immigrants from Islamic countries, the pain of disruption was especially acute: these Jews hailed from a patriarchal culture, in which the father signified authority, power, and knowledge. Upon arriving in Israel with its new culture, language, and customs, parents often lost their authority, their ability to earn a living, and their dominance. In *The Dove Flyer*, a novel by Eli Amir, who came to Israel from Iraq, a son describes the difficult reality encountered by his father in the immigrant transit camp:

> Now, standing on the stinking pile of garbage, I remembered him standing and dreaming the dream of his fragrant return, and he became a flame of happiness. And here I see him dragging his feet and walking along slowly, looking neglected, his eyes dim, his gaunt face, head hanging and shoulders slumped, his hands hanging limply at his sides, and mumbling to himself without pause. When I walked along behind him I tried to prevent him from noticing me. I feared for him.[4]

The tremendous financial cost of the absorption efforts led the government already in April 1949 to declare an emergency economic plan: "the regime of austerity" (in Hebrew, *tzena*). All residents of Israel—new immigrants and veteran Israelis alike—were given coupons, the only means of

Four Jewish female settlers taking over furniture from a Palestinian home in Ein Karim, 1948

them, resettlement entailed loss of their national identity and further injustice. Rarely since the war did a day pass without some refugee making an attempt to go back to his home, where they might feel tranquil and safe.

The Israeli historian Ben Morris relates that Palestinian infiltrators most often returned to their homes in order to satisfy their hunger. Most of them were unarmed and did not pose a security threat to Israel. However, Israel devised a plan to hunt them down, often leaving their bodies as a trap to kill those who would attempt to retrieve them. According to Morris, until 1956 more than 6,000 people were killed in this manner.[18]

The relentless attempts of the refugees to go back to their homes continued and Israel always foiled them. Such attempts were sometimes motivated by a feeling of injustice which they constantly felt or because of the wretchedness and frustration they were enduring after losing their homeland. Other attempts were driven by the desire to avenge their beloved ones who were killed while trying to return to their homeland.

Later, Israel formed Brigade 101, which was put under the command of Ariel Sharon. Its task was to comb the areas behind the Arab lines to prevent infiltration and to deter the refugees from merely thinking about going back. Brigade 101 carried out several operations and killed many people. On 14

acquiring basic foodstuffs and items of clothing. All renounced personal interests for the sake of immigrant absorption and creating a sound basis for
the country. Over time, the austerity regime gave rise to a black market—an
illegal trade in goods—and generated resentment and criticism against the
government. In 1952 the regime of austerity was called off, mainly thanks to
aid from American Jewry and the signing of the reparations agreement with
Germany. The improvement of the economic situation made it possible to lift
the restrictions on immigration, and in 1954 a large wave of immigration was
taken in, mainly from North Africa (Morocco). In the context of the new immigration policy, immigrants were sent to development towns and moshavim,
mainly in border zones; at the root of this policy lay the idea of decentralizing
the population and strengthening the borders. This was a difficult experience
for the immigrants, some of whom refused to settle in the places to which
they were assigned. Many immigrants grew increasingly embittered and angry in light of the difficulties of absorption and discrimination on the part of
the veteran establishment.

WADI SALIB INCIDENTS (1959)

Particularly difficult were the feelings of frustration experienced by North
African Jews, which were expressed in the Wadi Salib events of 1959. Wadi
Salib was a poor neighborhood with a high unemployment rate located on the
slopes of Mt. Carmel in Haifa, whose residents were mainly North African Jews
(the neighborhood was inhabited by Arabs until the War of Independence).
The veteran, well-established Ashkenazi Israelis lived above them at the top of
the mountain. Feelings of anger and deprivation came to a head when police
tried to arrest an drunk resident who was disturbing the peace. During the
attempted arrest, he was shot and wounded, causing a wave of spontaneous
and organized demonstrations to erupt across the country. North African immigrants protested the neglectful and patronizing attitude of the Ashkenazi
establishment. The demonstrations were dispersed with great force, but the
negative feelings experienced by the "other Israel"—the Sephardic Jews who
lived lives of hardship—lingered on. This was an important turning point in
Israeli society: for the first time, the protest of the immigrants from Islamic
countries entered the Israeli consciousness, exposing the social gaps between
citizens from Western countries (the Ashkenazim) and those originating from
North Africa (the Sephardim), and the feelings of alienation and marginaliza-
tion experienced by the "other Israel."

October 1953, it attacked Qibya, a border village near Ramallah. The brigade opened gunfire at the village and later blew up most of the village houses, killing more than seventy people and injuring dozens of women and children. Similar bloody operations were launched against other border villages, such as Budrus and Nahhalin.[19]

Moshe Dayan, then chief of staff, described these operations as being vital to the security of Israel.[20] On the other hand, Moshe Sharett, then minister of foreign affairs, condemned the bloodshed in Qibya as an act of unjustified retaliation for a small border incident. At a meeting of the ministers' council, Sharett warned that "the world would look at us as bloodsucking gangsters who are ready to commit mass killings regardless of whether such killings would lead to war or not."[21]

JEWS AND THE NEW SITUATION FOLLOWING THE WAR

The 1948 war had two immediate results. On the one hand, the war resulted in the dispossession and dispersion of the Palestinians all over the world, while their dreams for an independent state vanished into thin air. On the other, the war resulted in the establishment of the State of Israel on the occupied part of Palestine, which meant the opportunity for bringing together the Jews from all over the world in one place.

At the end of the war, the structure of the Jewish Zionist institutions remained intact. The British mandate had laid the foundations for all the main institutions of the Israeli society. Mandatory legislations maintained the separation between the Palestinian society and the Jewish one. It was due to these legislations that the Jewish society together with the Zionist institutions retained its integrity. What was needed after the war was just the adaptation of the Zionist institutions to the new reality in a way that would help to develop the new Jewish state.

The Jews controlled more than three-quarters of the land of Palestine, although before the war they were in control of only 6.5 percent. Before the war, the Jews numbered 650,000 compared to a million and a half Palestinians. The refugees left behind them entire cities where they had been the only or the majority of inhabitants. There were over 700 villages where the Palestinians were the sole owners of the land, wealth, goods, and furniture.[22]

In regard to what the Palestinians left behind, the Jewish state passed a number of legislations aimed at putting their hand on all forms of Arab

Demonstration in Wadi Salib

In retrospect, there is no doubt that the Ashkenazi establishment did tend to patronize and denigrate North African Jews, and they were often discriminated against relative to the veterans and European immigrants (for example, in the job market). Feelings of neglect and alienation on the part of Sephardic Jews are evident in the State of Israel to this day, and to a large extent shapes politics, the public atmosphere, and social and economic relations in the country. However, despite criticism of the lack of sensitivity, condescension, and disregard directed toward these immigrants, the impressive and unprecedented achievements of immigrant absorption in the 1950s cannot be ignored. The *Yishuv* operated out of the belief that all the diverse cultures and traditions that arrived in the newly founded state should be combined into a single national culture which would be able to deal with its future as a unified country. It succeeded in absorbing about one and a half million immigrants, providing most of them with housing, and created a new Israeli culture from the great mix of languages and cultures—all of which was achieved under difficult conditions of economic hardship, security threats, organizational glitches, and problems of absorption and integration natural for an immigrant nation and newly conceived state.

INTERNAL POLITICS

The dominant element in Israeli politics in the 1950s and '60s was the *Mapai* party, led by David Ben-Gurion, a strong and charismatic leader. Until 1977, *Mapai*, in its various incarnations (the Labor Party, "*Maarakh*") controlled Israeli politics; *Mapai* determined and shaped the state's socialist policies, running a centralized economy in which broad segments of society were based on a "welfare state" model. In opposition was the *Herut* party, led by Menachem

property and at erasing the Palestinian identity of those Palestinians who remained in the occupied lands. These laws included:

1. 1949 Law of Emergency: this law gave automatic control of absentee property to the Custodian of Absentee Property.

2. 1950 Law of Return: according to this law, any Jew regardless of his/her indigenous homeland or nationality has the right to immigrate to Israel. In contrast, Israel banned the refugees from returning to their cities and villages by force. It destroyed more than 500 Arab villages and built hundreds of settlements on the lands of the destroyed villages.

3. 1952 Nationality Law: according to this law, all immigrant Jews were immediately granted Israeli nationality to enhance the Jewish character of the state and to wipe out the Palestinian identity.

Through these laws and regulations, the Jews gave themselves a free hand to deal with Arab property, allowing immigrants to live in Palestinian homes and villages and to use their lands and farms.

The new Israeli laws and regulations regarded those Palestinians who remained in the occupied part of Palestine as second-class citizens and also regarded them as worthless and held them in contempt. This can be exemplified by the following incident which took place in Kafr Qassem on 29 October 1956. A curfew was imposed on the village, and the villagers were given thirty minutes to get to their homes. But this time was insufficient for people working in the farms to get back home. So, on their way back, farmers were indiscriminately shot at by the Israeli soldiers who killed forty-seven villagers. Later, it became clear that soldiers were given shoot-to-kill orders. To show contempt to Arabs and their valueless lives, a military court ordered the officer who had issued the order to shoot the Palestinians to pay a fine of one piaster.[23]

ECONOMIC, SOCIAL, AND CULTURAL CONDITIONS (1948–1967)

Up to *Al-Nakbah*, the Palestinian economy had always been based on agriculture, though there were very small and light industries such as glass, tobacco,

Begin, former commander of *Etzel*, which had a right-wing ideological, economic, and national orientation.

In 1952, a heated political crisis erupted between the two parties around the topic of the "reparations payments." The Israeli and German governments were due to sign an agreement whereby Germany would make payments to the State of Israel and to Holocaust survivors as compensation for what the Jews had suffered during the Holocaust: genocide, property theft, deportations, immeasurable human suffering, and more. Weeks of demonstrations, protests, and political storms preceded the agreement. Opponents of the agreement, headed by Menachem Begin and the *Herut* party, accused Ben-Gurion of selling the traumatic memories of the Holocaust victims for material gain. Moreover, it was claimed that receiving payments would be tantamount to forgiving Germany and reducing its culpability for the Holocaust. The opponents of the agreement held stormy and sometimes violent demonstrations, and at a certain point the government even considered declaring the *Herut* party illegal and the army was placed on alert for a civilian uprising. Ultimately, the agreement was approved in the Knesset by a narrow margin.

The funds from Germany were essential for the young state, and helped it to "get on its feet" and establish itself. Many immigrants who had arrived from Europe also received reparations from the Germans, and were thus able to establish themselves financially. Ben-Gurion, the leader who had guided the "state in the making" through the first decade of an independent Israel, later retired from politics following "the mishap," which came to be known as the Lavon Affair: Israeli intelligence operated a cell of Egyptian Jews who sabotaged British and American installations in Egypt. Their intention was to create the impression that the actions were being carried out by an Egyptian underground organization, and in so doing to influence the West's policy regarding Egypt. Members of the cell were caught and the defense minister, Pinchas Lavon, resigned, albeit claiming that it was not he who had initiated the operation. The question then arose as to "who had given the order." The affair took on broad proportions, causing a serious crisis in *Mapai*, and ultimately, the resignation of Ben-Gurion from his position as prime minister and defense minister, and his replacement by Levi Eshkol in 1963.

EICHMANN TRIAL (1961)

One of the events that took the country by storm at the beginning of the 1960s was the trial of Adolf Eichmann, who to a large extent was responsible

soap, and leather, in addition to some food processing industries which met the needs of the local market. In order to talk about the Palestinian economy during the 1950s, it is important to distinguish between the economy of the Palestinians under Israeli occupation, on the one hand, and the economy of the West Bank and Gaza Strip, on the other hand.

The war had severe destructive effects on the Palestinian economy in the occupied lands; yet it goes without saying that Israeli policies contributed to the deliberate destruction of what was left.

1. Israel destroyed entire Arab villages and confiscated the agricultural land, denying Palestinian owners the right to use the land or the water resources on it.

2. Palestinian farmers were continually pressured into abandoning their farms and so had to work under bad conditions and with little pay.

3. Palestinians were excluded from official and important positions (in the private sector, or civil service) for alleged national security reasons.[24]

The population density in the West Bank, the relative weakness of its economic resources, the lack of farming lands and water resources, and the absence of any developed industries made it difficult to build an efficient economy in it. Before the war, the West Bank economy was dependent on other parts of Palestine, especially the coastal cities.

Al-Nakbah had many destructive effects on the West Bank economy due to the following factors:

1. The sudden population increase due to the great flow of refugees into the West Bank strained the available services and increased competition over job opportunities and created social, economic, and health problems.

2. As job opportunities decreased, unemployment increased, wages went down, and the purchasing power became weaker.

3. Due to the miserable conditions, some industrialists and skilled labor left for the East Bank of Jordan.

4. The West Bank was isolated from the more developed coastal areas.

Adolf Eichmann during his trial in Jerusalem

for carrying out the "final solution"—the murder of European Jewry in the Holocaust. Eichmann was kidnapped from his hideout in Argentina by the Mossad—Israel's intelligence agency. He was flown to Israel and brought to trial for his crimes against the Jewish people. In his opening speech, Gideon Hausner, the attorney general serving as legal prosecutor, said:

When I stand before you, oh judges of Israel, to lead the prosecution of Adolf Eichmann, I do not stand alone. With me here are six million accusers. But they cannot rise to their feet and point their finger at the man in the dock with the cry "J'accuse!" on their lips. For they are now only ashes—ashes piled high on the hills of Auschwitz and the fields of Treblinka and strewn in the forests of Poland. Their graves are scattered throughout Europe. Their blood cries out, but their voice is stilled. Therefore will I be their spokesman. In their name will I unfold this terrible indictment.

During the trial, Holocaust survivors gave chilling testimonies that described in great detail the hell they had endured. The testimonies gave rise to a discussion of the Holocaust in schools and Israeli society in general that had never before taken place. Since the trial, the preoccupation with Holocaust memory and trauma has continued to expand, and the second and third generations have begun to develop a new awareness regarding this period in Jewish history. The trial went on for some eight months, and when it ended, Eichmann was given the death sentence, the first and only such sentence in the history of the State of Israel. The Eichmann trial rocked Israel to

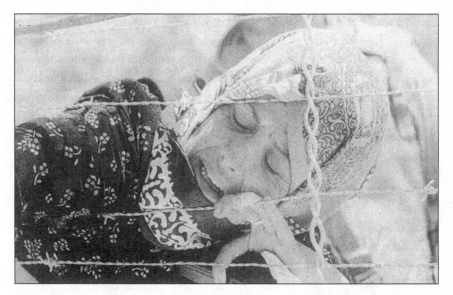

A Palestinian refugee woman extends her arm across the border to shake hands with her relatives

5. The loss of a large area of Palestinian land to the Israeli occupation.[25]

The bad conditions to which the Palestinian economy had fallen were the result of a strategy that was carefully designed by the Zionist leadership, first, to empty the land of its inhabitants, and second, to subordinate the already failing Palestinian economy to the Israeli economy. To achieve this, Ben-Gurion's aides closed down Arab stores and prevented materials from reaching Palestinian factories and plants. Yigael Yadin, head of the operations unit in the Israeli army, made an official proposal to stop all traffic in and out of Arab villages and towns in order to drain the economic resources of Arab Palestinian villages. Ben-Gurion also asked Sharett to concentrate on economic matters, saying, "The difference between these days and 1937 lies in the fact that the Arab Palestinian economy is more vulnerable as Haifa and Yafa are now under our mercy. We can make them starve to death. Motor vehicles, which play an important part in their lives, are at our mercy."

Sasson called for destroying the Palestinian economy, even if that resulted in destroying the Zionist economy. He justified this by saying, "We can recover from any economic disaster, but the Palestinians cannot."[26]

the core and fascinated the public. It carried an important statement regarding the obligation of the State of Israel to protect Jews all over the world and reinforced its historical role as the state of the Jews, responsible for the fate of world Jewry. This statement also expressed the position that the State of Israel would not rest until it had brought to justice—wherever possible—all those guilty of wrongdoing in the Holocaust.

ISRAELI ARABS IN THE 1950S

In 1950, the Jewish population of Israel numbered some 1.2 million, while the number of Arabs was approximately 167,000 (about 14 percent of the population). Due to the mass immigration in the 1950s and 1960s, and despite the rapid natural population growth among Israeli Arabs, their proportionate representation in the Israeli population declined, and in 1965 stood at 11.2 percent.

With the founding of the State of Israel, the leadership struggled with the question of how to relate to the Arab minority in its midst. The Israeli Declaration of Independence guarantees civil equality and democratic rights, but it also states that Israel is a "Jewish state." The combination of these two values has proved very problematic, since the State of Israel was first and foremost a Jewish state (in terms of investments, establishment of communities, immigration and absorption, etc.). In addition, the Arabs of Israel belong to a nation that is in conflict with Israel, and among the Jewish population and its leadership there were many who were skeptical regarding the desire of Israeli Arabs to become loyal citizens. Expressions such as "dual loyalty" and "fifth column" were often heard in the public discourse. Consequently, it was decided to grant citizenship to those Arabs physically present in the country on the day of its establishment, but to place areas with a concentrated Arab population under military rule.

MILITARY RULE (1948–1966)

The military rule went into effect during the War of Independence, and in 1950 was officially approved by the Knesset. In the areas under military rule—the Galilee, Wadi Ara, the Sharon, and the northern Negev—the IDF operated under the Emergency Regulations, which gave broad authority to the military governor. Among other things, military rule led to limited freedom of movement for Israeli Arabs, appropriation of land and buildings, administrative

The war resulted in the displacement and dispersal of thousands of Palestinians in different places and under basically the same circumstances. This in turn caused the destruction of the political, social, and economic entities of the Palestinian people. Social communication among the Palestinians was almost nonexistent due to the dispersion of families as well as the refusal of the Jews to repatriate refugees. Under such circumstances, it was not unexpected that severe psychological trauma would find fertile ground to survive. Feelings of frustration, dispossession, repression, injustice, being uprooted, alienation, social isolation, and disrespect had a heavy toll on the Palestinians.[27]

The destruction of all forms of Palestinian life (political, economic, and social) brought about by the war imposed an overwhelming sense of tragedy and disaster. Even though the Palestinians could do very little to change these frustrating feelings, they had to adapt themselves to cope with the new realities. The cultural life was affected deeply. The oral and written literature of this period reflected the sense of suffering, dispossession, frustration, and defeat, and highlighted national awareness.

One of the literary forms of the period was popular poetry; it spread very quickly and reached a large audience as it reflected popular feelings and concerns.[28] The following example of popular poetry expresses the theme of homesickness and yearning to the homeland:

> *My homeland!*
> *How kind and compassionate*
> *Oh Mother, when I die,*
> *Bury me in my homeland under the shadow of an olive tree.*

The following verses describe the Zionist atrocities:

> *Oh Arab brethren,*
> *I am talking about the wounds of my homeland*
> *Listen to me and do not wonder about my condition*
> *First came Balfour's declaration,*
> *It took us by surprise*
> *Oh, Palestine*
> *God has witnessed the killing of our folks*
> *in Deir Yassin and Qibya.*

detentions, regular night curfews, and the requirement that citizens obtain permission every time they left their villages. This created a situation in which the Jewish residents of Israel enjoyed a progressive democratic government, while the Arab residents were subject to the army. This reality made it difficult for Arabs to earn a living, study, and come into contact with the Jewish majority, and significantly delayed many aspects of their integration process.

At the end of the 1950s, restrictions imposed by the military government were eased, and at the beginning of the 1960s, the restrictions on movement for the Druze were lifted entirely. During these years, opposition to the military rule grew in the Knesset, including by MKs from both the right and the left, but it was only in November 1966 that Prime Minister Eshkol announced its final annulment.

IDENTITY PROBLEMS AMONG ISRAELI ARABS

In contrast to the Palestinians who remained outside the territory of the State of Israel in 1948, the Palestinians who remained within Israel's borders (whom the state called "Israeli Arabs") were influenced by two conflicting trends: on the one hand, they viewed themselves as part of the Arab nation hostile to the newborn state, but on the other hand, they were interested in rehabilitating their lives and integrating into the society that was coming into being in the State of Israel. These two contrasting trends grew stronger during the 1950s and 1960s. In the Arab world, hostility toward Israel grew; Nasser, who had taken control of the Egyptian government and sought to unite the Arab world under his leadership, saw the Palestinian tragedy as a focal point of identification and cohesion for the Arab nation. A substantial percentage of the Palestinian refugees of 1948 were still living in deportation camps during these years, and Israel was held accountable. The Palestinian problem was a central topic in Nasser's speeches, to which Palestinian citizens of Israel listened intently and with great longing.

If generalized Arab enmity were not enough, the Israeli Arabs had additional reasons for their hostility, as the State of Israel had turned them from a majority into a minority, imposed a military government upon them, and had annexed a substantial percentage of their lands (which greatly impinged on their basic right of ownership and on one of the most important values in Arab society). The Jewish majority viewed them with suspicion and discriminated against them, making them feel like strangers in their own land.

This nationalistic theme appeared in the 1950s with the appearance of the Nationalistic Unity Movement led by the Egyptian President Jamal Abdul Nasser, who campaigned for unity among the Arab countries. In his speeches, he emphasized the Palestinian refugees' right to return, unity, and the fame of old days. Representative verse of this era includes:

Hey Israeli!
Go and treat your wounds
Arab drums have become louder
Zionists—down with your state!
And long live unity among the Arabs
Our enemy cares not about our amassing arms
They care more about our unity and the strong arm.[29]

ARAB NATIONAL MOVEMENT AND RESISTANCE

The intensification of Palestinian nationalistic awareness in the early 1950s opened new venues for struggle against Israel, including guerrilla work. Until that time, deliberations at the United Nations about the Palestine question had reduced it to an issue of refugees rather than an issue of a dispossessed people driven out of their land. This was also accompanied by a hostile atmosphere toward the Palestinians.

In the early 1950s, small guerrilla groups started to attack Israeli targets inside the occupied territories. Palestinian guerrilla groups and organizations received the support of the Egyptian government led by Jamal Abdul Nasser. In early 1954, guerrilla operations inside Israel, which were supported by the Egyptian army, increased and caused a lot of damage. In an attempt to stop or deter the guerrilla operations, Israel responded by launching several offensive attacks inside the Palestinian and Egyptian territories and committed massacres in the West Bank and Gaza. The most atrocious attacks were in Al-'Arish in 1956 and in Gaza in 1955 and 1956. These attacks aimed essentially to terrify the inhabitants and frighten them off their new places of residence and to pressure the guerrilla groups to discontinue their attacks against Israel. In 1956, Israel would start preparation for a great offensive against Egypt to hit the guerrilla groups and to expand its territories.[30]

Despite the increase in hostility, a slow but steady process of integration and increasing closeness to the Jewish population was nevertheless under way. The Israeli Arabs learned Hebrew and established economic ties with the Jews, and the local leadership collaborated with the Zionist parties. A serious attempt to integrate Arab citizens into Israeli society took place in 1954. During that year, the Knesset approved the recruitment of Israeli Arabs into the IDF, in exchange for full civil rights. Tens of thousands of Arabs answered this call, but many were afraid of such a large number of armed Arabs and the topic was taken off the agenda. In 1956, the state recognized the Druze population as a separate ethnic group, and Druze men, as well as many Bedouin, were included in the mandatory draft to the IDF. The trend toward integration strengthened with the termination of the military rule, but as the Arabs became more integrated into Israeli society, they increasingly found themselves growing apart from their brethren in neighboring countries.

In the political realm, Arab candidates ran for Knesset seats, most of them through the Labor party, and most Arab voters cast their votes for this ruling party. Thus Israel's Arab minority became devoid of political influence as far as its own interests were concerned. The political impotence of Israel's Arab citizens was clearly illustrated in 1963, when the *Mapam* movement, most of whose members are Jewish, presented a proposal in the Knesset to put an end to the military rule. Rather ironically, the three Arab Knesset members voted against the proposal and it was removed from the agenda. In an effort to deal with the complexities of their reality, Israel's Arabs developed a worldview that helped them integrate into Israeli society. Many of them made a distinction between daily life and ideology: in their daily lives (work, studies, etc.) they did everything possible to facilitate swift integration into the Israeli economy. They set out en masse to work as salaried employees in the Jewish workforce, encouraged their children to integrate into the public school system and to learn Hebrew, and the leadership took intensive measures to stifle expressions of extremism that might endanger the entire Arab public. At the ideological level, however, Israeli Arab support for the Arab countries and the struggle of their Palestinian brothers was widespread. As part of this conception, various steps were taken against those who openly supported the Israeli side or who committed acts considered harmful to the integrity of the society.

From the end of the 1950s, and particularly during the 1960s, Arab society began undergoing new processes of modernization, organization, and

THE TRIPARTITE AGGRESSION AGAINST EGYPT IN 1956

Soon after Egypt and Britain concluded the Evacuation Agreement in 1954 which ended the British occupation of Egypt, Israel started to prepare for a new aggression against the Arab countries to occupy more Arab land as a step to realize the Zionist plan. In his memoirs, Moshe Sharett described a meeting he had had with Ben Zvi, the Israeli president, on 11 October 1953. At that meeting, Ben Zvi raised a number of perplexing queries. Would it be possible to occupy Sinai? Wouldn't it be wonderful if the Egyptians launched an offensive against Israel? Israel would be able to stop it easily and then it would advance to occupy that desert.[31]

Israel had always planned to have freedom of passage through the Red Sea and the Aqaba Gulf as it was the only passage connecting Israel and the continents of Asia and Africa. This was very vital both militarily and economically.

The period that preceded the 1956 war witnessed the emergence of new Arab leaderships and regimes. In Egypt, Jamal Abdul Nasser came to rule and headed the Arab National Movement. He fought against colonialism politically, culturally, and militarily. He assisted liberation movements in Africa and Asia to release themselves of colonial rule. He offered great military and financial assistance to Algeria in its fight against French colonization.

In the meantime, Egypt stood against the policy of military alliances, especially those supported by Western countries. As a result, the United States withdrew its offer to finance the construction of the High Dam. In return, Egypt nationalized the Suez Canal, which was controlled by British and French companies, which had in fact deprived Egypt of any revenues for a very long time.[32]

In addition, each of the three assailant countries had its own reasons for waging a war against Egypt.

1. England wanted to take revenge on Nasser for nationalizing the Suez Canal. It also wanted to regain its position as a colonial power, particularly after evacuating its troops from Egypt.

2. France aimed to avenge itself on Nasser for supporting the Algerian revolution.

3. Israel aspired to destroy Egyptian military power, expand its

awareness. Broad exposure to education led to the weakening of the influence of religion and to a decline in the traditional status of the extended clan. In many traditional societies, the clan, which includes second- and third-degree familial relationships, is extremely important. However, the Israeli Arabs were at the height of a transition from a traditional to a modern society, and more than once, members of the same clan voted for different parties in elections, thus disregarding the clan leader's authority to determine who to vote for. The Israeli Arabs knew that in many senses their situation was much better than that of their Palestinian brothers, who lived under Jordanian and Egyptian rule. This situation led to a weakening of the pan-Arab trend, and the increasing prevalence of the view that promoted integration into Israeli society. On the other hand, the increase in education and daily contact with Jewish society fortified the political awareness of Israeli Arabs. Harsh criticism was directed at politicians serving the Zionist parties, and new parties were established that opposed Zionism and were designed to serve the interests of the Israeli Arabs. The most prominent among them was the Israeli Communist Party, which mainly comprised Israeli Arabs. Among the Arabs, voices were heard demanding civil equality and the development of new identity symbols that would enable them to live as equal citizens in the State of Israel.

The 1950s in Israeli society were stormy and eventful. The young state tried to establish its identity as a Jewish democratic state, and during the 1950s an unprecedented wave of immigration arrived, establishing the Jewish majority. Despite the impressive absorption of this wave of immigration, fissures and tensions developed in Israeli society. An additional challenge confronting the young state was the continued conflict with the Arab world, which reached its peak in the Sinai operation. During that operation, the Kafr Qassem massacre took place, forcefully bringing home the problematic status of the Palestinian citizens of Israel and their complex relations with Jewish society and the Jewish state.

territories to the Suez Canal, occupy more Arab land, and end the guerrilla attacks which were launched from the Egyptian territories and with the support of the Egyptian government.

In light of these circumstances, the "Sinai Campaign" or "Tripartite Aggression" started on 29 October 1956 and ended on 7 November 1956. Egypt and the Arabs fought against the aggressors. The Soviet Union and the pressure exerted by the international community on the aggressors forced France and England to stop the war. Israel was forced to pull back its forces to the lines of the 1949 Truce Agreement.

From a political and military viewpoint, the aggressors failed to achieve their goals. Due to strong international pressure, Britain, France, and Israel were forced to accept a ceasefire. Britain suffered heavy material losses, and more important, it lost its leading position as a world power; with the emergence of the United States and the Soviet Union, it receded to the third position among the world's giant powers. And while Israel could not maintain its hold on the Gaza Strip and Sharm al Sheikh, it gained free passage for its ships through the Aqaba Gulf to the port of Eilat.[33]

Egypt, on the other hand, benefited politically from the war despite its military loss. It gave a big boost to Nasser's popularity in the Arab and nonaligned countries. The war was also a direct factor in nurturing nationalist Arab awareness and in highlighting the importance of achieving Arab unity.

ARAB SUMMIT CONFERENCES AND THE EMERGENCE OF THE PALESTINE LIBERATION ORGANIZATION

The period between 1957 and 1962 was characterized by a freeze in the Arab-Israeli conflict, even though each side retained its principles of the conflict. The Arabs continued to refuse to recognize the existence of Israel and still hoped to liberate Palestine; Israel, on the other hand, continued to develop its military capability and expand its settlements in order to secure its borders.

This five-year period was also distinguished by its calm. It witnessed a number of Arab summit conferences. During these conferences, Nasser used different styles of address to reach all parties concerned. He addressed the emotions of the Arab masses to call for the liberation of Palestine to reinforce

his popularity. He used a balanced language in dealing with foreign diplomats, who described him as a moderate and realistic leader. With the Soviet Union, he used yet a third language and managed to emphasize his leading role as a supporter of liberation movements in Africa and Asia.

When Israel diverted the Jordan River and drained Al-Hula Lake, the Arab countries called for an Arab League conference. The conference was held on 16 January 1964 and was devoted to a discussion of the diversion of the Jordan River. At the conference, Ahmed Al-Shukayri, representative of Palestine in the Arab League, was authorized to resume contact with the Arab countries and the Palestinians in order to set up an organization for the Palestinian people that would organize and prepare them to be able to participate in the struggle for regaining Palestine. On 28 May 1964, the Palestinian Liberation Organization (PLO) was born.[34]

The second conference of the Arab League was held in Alexandria on 5 September 1964. In this conference, an annual budget was approved for the PLO. The PLO was guaranteed the Arab countries' financial and political support that was necessary for the new organization to come into being. It was in this conference too that the Arabs made the liberation of Palestine from Zionist colonialism their national goal, and so approved the establishment of the Palestine Liberation Army.

The third conference of the Arab League was held in Morocco in 1965 and it endorsed the Arab Solidarity Charter. All Arab countries promised to work toward the achievement of pan-Arab solidarity, especially by fulfilling their financial obligations toward the PLO and the Palestine Liberation Army.[35]

Due to this support, Palestinian resistance started to materialize on the ground. During the First Palestinian Conference of Jerusalem (1964), it was agreed to establish the various apparatuses of the Palestine Liberation Organization:

1. A military apparatus: to train able-bodied Palestinians to carry arms.

2. An organizational apparatus: to form committees and unions.

3. A political apparatus: to promote the Palestinian cause both locally and internationally.

4. A financial apparatus: to raise funds to support the Palestinian issue through the Palestinian National Fund.[36]

EMERGENCE OF A PALESTINIAN NATIONAL IDENTITY

With the rise and spread of nationalistic awareness and increasing cultural openness in the Arab East, there were calls at universities, cultural clubs, and forums for establishing a forum that would bring all Palestinians together and be their spokesman. There were several factors that contributed to the emergence of a Palestinian national identity: first, the inability of the Arab states to liberate Palestine because of the conflicts among them and the connections that some had with the colonial powers; second, the ever-increasing military power of Israel and the unlimited support European countries were providing to Israel.

At the end of the 1950s, Palestinian political life witnessed the beginnings of a new movement in different fields to reorganize the Palestinian people, and revive their national entity, and create new institutions to organize Palestinian action. So Fatah (Palestine Liberation Movement) was the first such organization to appear on the political scene in the late 1950s.[37]

On the intellectual side, the emergence of a monthly magazine called *Falastinuna* ("Our Palestine") played a vital role in reviving the Palestinian national identity. From 1959 to 1964, *Falastinuna* worked diligently toward the revival of the Palestinian identity and for the reorganization of the Palestinian people. It appealed to the Palestinian youth as an integral element in the revival of the Palestinian people; otherwise, the magazine cautioned, "there would be no liberation."[38]

The general atmosphere prevailing in the early 1960s contributed to the appearance of several Palestinian parties and movements. Leading these movements was Fatah, which surfaced only after very long preparations by a group of young people led by Yasser Arafat and Khalil Al-Wazir. The latter was able to transfer the experience of the Algerian revolution to the Palestinian revolution.

As for Yasser Arafat, he was able to move the center of his group's activities in the early 1960s from Egypt to Kuwait, where he was allowed to open training camps. He used the donations offered by the rich Gulf countries to organize the newly established movement. The armed struggle for the liberation of Palestine started officially on 1 January 1965. On that day, a Fatah

armed group launched its first military action against Israel. It also issued a statement appealing to Palestinians to be unified as there would be no liberation without unity. This military action marked the start of a new stage in the struggle against Israel.[39]

6

THE SIX-DAY WAR OF JUNE 5–10, 1967

During the years that preceded the Six-Day War, Israel was busy addressing serious problems that had confronted the nation since its founding. It suffered infiltration of terrorists from Arab states and the murder of civilians, shelling from Syria and a military threat from Egypt, and responded to attacks on its citizens with retaliatory action. At that time, Israel was armed mainly with French weapons and only in the latter half of the 1960s did it begin to buy small quantities of arms from the United States.

The newness of the country and the mass immigration of the 1950s and 1960s (totalling more than 1.5 million immigrants) created substantial challenges; the state had to supply housing, education, and health services to hundreds of thousands of recent arrivals. Jobs had to be created for all the newcomers in the quest for economic self-sufficiency, and all this demanded tremendous effort and capital. There were no easy solutions, and conditions worsened. In 1966–1967, Israel suffered a severe economic recession, which resulted in serious unemployment levels, despair, and emigration. A popular joke at that time stated: "Will the last one to leave the country please turn out the lights at Lod airport." There was a sense that the administration of

6

ISRAELI AGGRESSION AGAINST ARAB AND PALESTINIAN LANDS: JUNE 1967 WAR

The war which Israel waged against the Arab countries in 1967 is known in Arab world as the "Aggression of June the Fifth," because it was Israel that first declared and started the war. By definition, aggression is an unprovoked initiation of the use of power by one country to attack or invade the lands of another country and to take control of them by force of arms. According to the 1933 Armistice Conference, an aggressor is "the party which declares war on another country and invades its lands through its military power." Aggression is also defined as "an attack which opposes the right and which aims at invading demilitarized zones as defined in an international agreement while prejudicing the integrity and independence of neighboring countries."

Israel had always been preparing for an attack on the Palestinian lands. It was always "on the alert" and closely followed international and Arabic conditions to find the right moment to wage an attack against the Arab countries.

In December 1948, Ben-Gurion declared, "Our military victories are only introductions to the long-term goals of Israel." In a graduation ceremony of Jewish officers in 1949, he said, "We have not yet realized our goal, namely, absolute victory. So far, we have fully liberated only one part of our homeland.

Levi Eshkol, Israeli Prime Minister, in a visit to the United States

Levi Eshkol was failing to govern the country properly, and the government lost credibility.

International diplomacy had a decisive influence on events in the Middle East and the world in general. The two superpowers of that era, the United States and the Soviet Union, were engaged in a Cold War for hegemonic supremacy and control of world affairs while avoiding direct military confrontation. The Six-Day War was part of this struggle; the major powers, under the guise of cultural, economic, and military aid, were extending the maximum possible control over many other nations, which in turn fell under their sphere of influence and were "identified with" one power or the other. Thus evolved the "Eastern bloc," which identified with the (communist) Soviet Union, and the "Western bloc," which identified with the (democratic) United States. In exchange for aid and support, the smaller countries were required—at times against their own best interests—to serve the interests of one or the other of the two superpowers.

Egypt, Syria, and Iraq joined the "Eastern bloc," while Jordan and Israel joined the "Western bloc." The Cold War led to what was termed an "arms race," with both superpowers stockpiling nuclear weapons in a quest for a "balance of threat." The United States and the USSR at times seemed on

The fate of the other parts will be as the fate of this part, which our brave troops now control."[1]

DEVELOPMENTS DURING THE THREE YEARS PRECEDING THE WAR

In 1964, the first Arab summit conference was held in Cairo. The main item on the conference agenda was a discussion of "the measures that should be taken by the Arab countries after Israel started pumping water from the Jordan River to the Negev." At the conference, the Arab states decided to divert the path of the Jordan River from its sources so that it would flow directly into the Yarmuk River. The plan was to dig a canal to divert the waters of the Hasbani in Lebanon and the Banias in Syria. This would enable the Arab countries to utilize 60 percent of the Jordan River. The summit allocated £400 million for this operation.

According to the 1953 Johnston plan, 60 percent of the Jordan River water was to be allocated to Syria, Lebanon, and Jordan, and 40 percent to Israel, but the plan was rejected by the Arabs. Later, Israel diverted the water from the south of Lake Hula and left nothing for the Arabs.[2] Ironically, the 1964 Arab summit adopted the Johnston plan, albeit indirectly, and called for getting 60 percent of the river water. Subsequently, as will be shown later, Israel prevented the Arabs by force from achieving their plan. In fact, the water issue was one of the main reasons for the outbreak of the war.[3]

When work on the Hasbani/Banias diversion canal started in November 1964, Israeli artillery and tanks began a nonstop shelling of the work sites; planes bombed those sites that were out of its artillery range. As a result, work on the diversion canal stopped as the Arab countries felt they were not prepared to go to war with Israel over water. Israel continued to take all the water of the Jordan to provide its settlements in the Negev, while the Arabs received nothing.

Sporadic clashes on the Syrian-Israeli border created serious tension. The frontline Syrian forces fired on Israelis who were trying to farm lands in the demilitarized zone and on fishing boats that repeatedly crossed the armistice line in Tiberias. Syrian artillery on the Golan Heights occasionally shelled Israeli settlements in reaction to shelling of Syrian military positions and villages by Israeli artillery.

Several groups of Palestinian fedayeen (guerrilla fighters) were able to cross the border with Jordan at various points and attacked many Israeli military

the brink of a nuclear war that would imperil the very existence of the entire world.

BACKGROUND TO THE WAR

The Six-Day War began on June 5, 1967, and ended six days later, on June 10, 1967. Israel fought in three Arab countries—Egypt, Syria, and Jordan—and won a victory that proved to be a pivotal turning point in Zionist history. The outbreak of the war must be viewed in the context of the relations between Israel and the Arab countries in the 1960s.

Beginning in 1964, tensions between Syria and Israel increased when Syria began construction designed to divert water from the sources of the Jordan River to cut off the flow into the Sea of Galilee. It is important to note that the Sea of Galilee is Israel's only freshwater reservoir, and it feeds the national aqueduct that supplies water to all the towns and villages in the Negev desert. Because of the Sea of Galilee's existential importance to the nation, Israel decided to sabotage the Syrian water diversion project by bombing the earth-moving equipment being used. The Syrians retaliated with intensive shelling of fishermen on the Sea of Galilee and civilian communities in the vicinity, including Haon and Ein Gev, causing extensive damage. Known as "the water war," these hostilities reached a peak in April 1967, when Israeli air force planes knocked six Syrian MiG aircraft out of the sky in one day. Syria demanded that Egypt do something about all this, pursuant to a military treaty in force between the two countries.

Between 1965 and 1967, encouraged by Syria, Palestinian incursions from Jordan into Israel became more frequent. The Jordanian government did not stop the terrorists who used its territory as a base from which to launch strikes at Israeli soldiers and civilians, injuring many. Israel retaliated by attacking the areas where the attacks originated, hoping to put

The IDF retaliation attacks in the village of Samua

targets. In most cases, the Israeli forces managed to stop the Palestinian fighters, kill some of them, and detain others. On 13 November 1966, and under the pretense that the Palestinian fighters had infiltrated into Israel from the Jordanian territories, Israel launched an extensive attack on Al-Samu', a village that lies at the southernmost part of the Hebron area, about four kilometers away from the cease-fire line. The Israelis chose to target this village because of its close location to the Israeli military positions, which meant the Israelis could easily retreat to their position after completing their mission. At the same time, being at the southernmost part of Hebron, the village was very far from the main Jordanian army bases to the north. This meant that the operation would be completed before any help or reinforcement could make it to the village.

The Israeli attack forces were supported by tanks and aircraft and successfully destroyed many houses in the village, killing and wounding many of its inhabitants. During the operation, the villagers were thrown out of their houses; their houses were blown up later. A small Jordanian force from the Hebron area was sent for the rescue but was caught in an ambush that the Israelis had set to the north of the village. The Israelis had also set up land mines on the route of the vehicles that would attempt to bring any rescue forces. The Israeli operation against Al-Samu' resulted in the deaths of twenty-one Arab soldiers and the injury of thirty-seven.[4]

A long time before the war, Israel had decided to start the war by attacking the Egyptian forces at this particular period of time, as inter-Arab relations were highly strained. It therefore assumed Arab forces would not unite to fight together according to one unified defense plan. Preparations for the war started by calling the Israeli reserve forces, while escalations on the front lines helped to bring about the situation that Israel had been waiting for in order to attack the Arab armies one after the other.

MAIN MOTIVES BEHIND THE ISRAELI AGGRESSION IN 1967

Israel had planned to wage a preemptive war against the Arab armies, particularly before the Egyptian army could be trained to use the modern arms it had obtained from the Soviet Union a short time before the war. Israel exploited the steps announced by Egyptian President Jamal Abdul Nasser as an excuse to show public opinion in the United States and in the world that Israel was not always the aggressor but was waging a preemptive war forced upon it in

a stop to the aggression. After a series of terror incidents in the Mt. Hebron area, the IDF retaliated very harshly against the village of Samua. During this action, forty-one homes were destroyed and twenty-six people were killed, half of them soldiers of the Jordanian Legion and the rest civilians. King Hussein's stature in the Arab world and Jordan was greatly diminished by the Samua raid. Although Jordanian Legionnaires had fought bravely, King Hussein was blamed for not opposing Israel strongly enough. The Egyptians and Syrians called for overthrowing Hussein's regime, and in Jordan there were stormy demonstrations against him. Hussein meanwhile attacked Egyptian President Gamal Abdel Nasser, arguing that he only talked but did not actually take any action against Israel.

In May of 1967, following Syria's demand that Egypt take action against Israel, Egyptian President Nasser took the following steps:

1. He declared a full military alert and sent massive troops and weapons to the Sinai Desert.

2. He then demanded that the United Nations remove its forces from the Egyptian-Israeli border. To Israel's amazement, not only did the UN secretary-general move the UN troops away from the border, he removed them from Sinai altogether.

Gamal Abdel Nasser, Egyptian president during the Six-Day War

3. On May 22, Egypt blocked the Straits of Tiran (at the southern end of the Red Sea) to Eilat-bound Israeli shipping, effectively cutting Israel off from Asia and East Africa.

4. On the same day, at a widely publicized meeting with Egyptian pilots in Sinai, Nasser called for war, declaring,

order to defend its very existence, which was being gravely threatened by the Arab armies. At the same time, this was an attempt on the part of Israel to take over new Arab lands in a quick war, and consequently would enable it to establish additional settlements and absorb a large number of Jewish immigrants. This in turn would create a stronger bargaining position that would force the Arabs to sit for negotiations according to Israel's own terms.[5]

At this juncture, it might be worthwhile to refer to a report published by the American Combined Forces Command almost twenty years before the 1967 war. The report was about Zionist strategic planning, which was being realized in 1967.

> The Zionist strategy aspires to drag the United States into a lengthy series of warring actions the purpose of which is to realize maximalist Zionist goals, which can be summarized as follows:
>
> 1. Acceptance by the powers of the right of the Jews to unlimited immigration to Palestine.
>
> 2. Realization of Jewish sovereignty over the whole of Palestine.
>
> 3. Enlarging the territory of the Land of Israel such that it will include East Jordan and parts of Syria and Lebanon.
>
> 4. Placement of a leading Jewish role, militarily and economically, in all the countries of the Middle East.[6]

The actual planning for the 1967 aggression started upon conclusion of the tripartite aggression against Egypt in 1956, particularly since Israel was forced to withdraw from the Egyptian lands and the Gaza Strip, which it had occupied in 1956.

How did Israel plan for the 1967 war? After it had succeeded in creating suitable conditions for war, Israel initiated the aggression by striking each of the Arab armies separately, and one after the other.[7] All the Israeli forces operated as a single combat unit under a single command, fighting according to one strategic plan. Israel controlled the initiative and so it started a comprehensive attack on the Arab forces on all fronts in accordance with its preset war plan.

The Israeli military aggression against Egypt, Jordan, and Syria aimed to achieve the following goals:

Hakim Omar, Egyptian Chief of Staff and Vice President during the Six-Day War

> "The Jews believe in war, and we are telling them, *Ahlan wa'sahlan* [Welcome!]—we are prepared for war!"[1]

5. On May 26, 1967, Nasser made public and explicit threats against Israel, saying: "The closing of the Straits means total war

1. To occupy Sinai and keep it as a buffer zone between it and the Egyptian forces.

2. To open the Suez Canal to Israeli navigation, expel Egyptian forces from Sharm El-Sheikh, and open the Straits of Tiran to ensure the freedom of navigation through the Red Sea to the port of Eilat.

3. To occupy the Golan Heights to ensure adequate defense of Israeli settlements in the area of the Sea of Galilee.

4. To occupy the West Bank and Jerusalem. Capturing the whole of Jerusalem was a dream Israel had looked to since its establishment of the state. Israel aimed to achieve this as quickly as possible before being forced to stop the fighting in case the United Nations Security Council took a resolution to stop the fighting.

Israel succeeded at achieving its goals as it had planned.

Israel's plan for the war was as follows:

1. Destruction of the Egyptian air force at its bases in a decisive lightning strike which would grant Israel full control of the air over Egypt at the outset of the war.[8]

2. A rapid land assault in order to break through Sinai and thus ensure access to the Suez Canal.

3. Destruction of the Jordanian army and the occupation of Jerusalem and the West Bank after gaining complete air control.

4. Redeployment of all land and air forces from the Egyptian and Jordanian fronts to occupy the Golan Heights as rapidly as possible.

OUTBREAK OF THE WAR

Israel initiated the war with a major air strike against the airfields and bases of the Egyptian air force. At exactly 7:45 on the morning of Monday, 5 June 1967, the Israeli air force waged a comprehensive and massive attack on all

with Israel. This required preparation. When we felt ready, we did this. [. . .] If we are attacked, there will be war, and our fundamental goal will be to destroy Israel."[2]

6. On May 29, 1967, Nasser added: "There is no doubt that God will help us return to the situation prior to 1948."[3]

With these political and military moves, Nasser abrogated the existing agreement between Israel and Egypt signed after the Sinai operation (1956). His public statements created an extremely volatile anti-Israel atmosphere. Nasser's aggressive approach was evidently due to pressure from Jordan and Syria, to his desire to preserve his status as leader of the Arab world, and to a great extent also to the influence of the Soviet Union.

On May 30, Jordan joined the defense pact between Egypt and Syria, and Iraq then followed suit. Thus Israel found itself surrounded by enemy states calling for war, disseminating aggressive propaganda, and denying Israel's right to exist. The Israeli public felt tremendous anxiety at the steps taken by Nasser as the Arab world rallied around him, and many felt threatened by annihilation. The trauma of the Holocaust was still present in the Israeli psyche. A young officer who fought in that war said, "People believed that if we did not win, we would be exterminated . . . they were afraid. . . . The legacy of the Shoah was this concept ('extermination'). This is a very concrete term for anyone who grew up in Israel, even if he did not go through the Holocaust but only heard and read about it. . . . That was the lesson of the Shoah."[4]

People in Tel Aviv digging defensive trenches against possible air raids

The government of Israel understood the danger, and considered its options. The generals, led by chief of staff Yitzhak Rabin, pushed for a preemptive strike to prevent a disaster, but the cabinet ministers were worried.

Egyptian air bases in Sinai, the Delta, and Cairo. The first raid covered nineteen Egyptian air bases. The Israeli warplanes were not detected by Egyptian radars because they flew too low. The choice of an early morning attack was based on Israeli intelligence information about the daily routine of Egyptian pilots, who would be returning home from their bases at exactly the time when the raid was scheduled. It was evident that the Israelis had traced the daily routine of the Egyptian pilots and had also obtained significant information from its agents in Egypt.

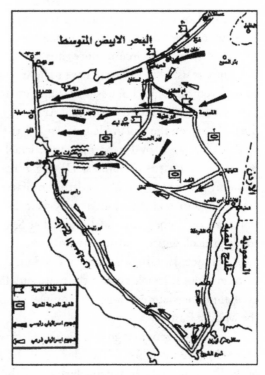

A map of the Eygptian front, June 1967

On the other hand the Jordanian and Iraqi air forces succeeded in attacking some Israeli air bases and other vital targets. Jordanian planes bombed an Israeli military airfield near Moshava Kfar Syrkin. Iraqi planes, taking off from Base H3 in Jordan, bombed the town of Naharia on the Mediterranean. On the Syrian front, the Syrian artillery shelled the oil refinery installations in Haifa and a military airfield near Megiddo.

After totally destroying the Egyptian air force, the Israeli air force turned its attacks against other Arab air forces. It managed to destroy all the planes of the Jordanian air force, most of the planes of the Syrian air force, and a large number of Iraqi planes at Base H3 in Jordan. Although the Israeli air force did lose a total of 26 planes in some air clashes, by the end of the first day it had destroyed a total of 416 Arab planes, of which 393 were destroyed on the ground while 23 were downed in air battles. With all the Arab air force destroyed or disabled, Israel achieved total air control, and so Arab air space was exclusively open to the Israeli air force.

At the end of the security cabinet meeting on the eve of the war, Interior Minister Moshe Chaim Shapira turned to Rabin and said, "How dare you go to war when all the circumstances are against us? None of the world powers will support us. [. . .] We will have to fight on at least two fronts and possibly three. Even the United States is not supporting us."[5]

Israel faced great danger. The Arab states assembled their forces in the Sinai Desert, on the Golan Heights, and on the Jordanian border. Responding to the steps taken by Egypt and Syria, Israel called up its military reserves personnel to guard its borders. During three weeks of waiting, the Israeli economy came to a virtual standstill; insofar as possible, women and teenagers replaced men at their jobs as they were called up for reserve duty, a situation that could not go on indefinitely. The Soviet Union encouraged the Arab states to declare war and sent them a steady supply of weaponry, while the West (France, Britain, and the United States) did not declare their commitment to support Israel. France, the main supplier of the Israel Defense Forces, even announced an embargo—a complete cessation in the supply of arms to the Middle East.

Israel's citizens and government were left on their own to face an unprecedented existential threat. The closing of the Straits of Tiran; the expulsion of the UN forces; the heavy involvement of the Soviet Union; a multinational Arab military accord with the declared intention of eliminating the State of Israel; the inability of the West to rein in Nasser's aggression; the French arms embargo; the call-up of the reserves, and the economic paralysis in Israel—all these contributed to anxiety on the Israeli street, while adults and young people enlisted to defend their homes. The Israeli government organized thousands of beds for the wounded and prepared space for mass burials.

THE SIX-DAY WAR

Israel felt isolated and its situation seemed to deteriorate by the day. The fear of a combined Arab strike against the borders of its narrow territory was intolerable. Given the circumstances, the Israeli government decided on a preemptive strike to reduce the risk.

On June 5, 1967, at dawn, the Israeli air force attacked Egypt's airfields and destroyed most of Egypt's fighter planes on the ground. Control of the air helped facilitate movement by ground forces, and despite fierce battles across half of the Sinai Peninsula and in the Gaza Strip, the IDF overwhelmed the

There were several serious ground battles, but Arab land forces were an easy and open target for Israeli warplanes, particularly since they did not have ground defense against Israeli airstrikes. So, from the first hours of the battle, Arab land forces found themselves in a difficult situation; in view of the air superiority of the Israeli air force, they had no reasonable hope of winning the battle.[9]

THE EGYPTIAN FRONT

The overall strategic plan of the Israeli army for the Egyptian front relied on a breakthrough operation of three divisions to be carried out at three stages:

Stage One: Opening of the northern axis along the coast from Khan Yunis to Al-'Arish and the opening of a central axis from Nitzana to Um Qutuf and Abu Aqila.

Stage Two: Advancing deep into the Sinai Peninsula.

Stage Three: Controlling the Mitleh and Gidi mountain passes, which overlook the road to the Suez Canal.

The most difficult battles on the Egyptian front took place deep in the Sinai Desert and in the Gaza Strip. A paratrooper brigade, assisted by tanks, advanced parallel to the coast toward Gaza, when the Israeli army broke through the area of Khan Yunis. Fierce battles also broke out in the villages and refugee camps throughout the Gaza Strip. During most of the next day, bitter fighting took place in Khan Yunis and Gaza. Despite the fierce defense put up by the Arab forces, the Israeli forces managed to take both cities by the evening of the third day of fighting. With the fall of Khan Yunis and Gaza, the Israelis were in control of the whole Gaza Strip. The Egyptian and Palestinian forces incurred terrible losses in the battles of Sinai and the Gaza Strip. Human loss was estimated at ten thousand dead and wounded and about five thousand prisoners, including five hundred officers.

THE SYRIAN FRONT

On June 9, after the cease-fire came into effect on the Egyptian and Jordanian fronts and after it had been ascertained that the Jordanian and Egyptian forces were out of the struggle, Israel started its attack on the Golan Heights. The Israelis managed to carry out their plan with total success.

Yitzhak Rabin, IDF Chief of Staff during the war

Egyptian army and came to a halt at the edge of the Suez Canal on June 8.

After the outbreak of fighting in the south, the Foreign Ministry dispatched a message, signed by Prime Minister Levi Eshkol, to King Hussein. Hussein was asked not to enter the war and Israel promised in exchange not to attack Jordan. Hussein did not accept this suggestion and the Jordanian Legion began heavy shelling of the Jewish sections of Jerusalem and other areas. After Jordanian aircraft took off to attack targets in Israel, the Jordanian air force was also routed. The battles on the Jordanian front were hard-fought and the war for Jerusalem especially so, with heavy losses. As the fighting went on, the entire West Bank was captured and the IDF stopped on the banks of the Jordan River.

On the northern front, the war too began on June 5. The Syrian air force attacked targets in northern Israel and Syrian artillery shelled the Jordan Valley communities and those along the Sea of Galilee. In response, the Israeli air force destroyed most of the Syrian aircraft on the first day of the war. In the ensuing days, Syria and Israel fought an artillery duel. Only toward the end of the war, under heavy pressure from the residents of the Upper Galilee and the Jordan Valley, who had suffered from Syrian shelling throughout the 1960s, did the IDF move to conquer the Golan Heights. The Golan Heights were taken on June 10, and the Six-Day War ended.

Israel gained a brilliant victory that changed its history and that of the entire Middle East. The Old City of Jerusalem was captured by Israel, as were

The IDF during the Six-Day War

cities and biblical sites in the West Bank, the Sinai Desert, and the Golan Heights. The Israeli public was euphoric to the point of intoxication, and some Israelis perceived the victory as a messianic religious experience.

The accompanying map shows the territories

The Israeli air force directed an intensive attack on all Syrian positions. The main attack targeted the northern section of the Golan Heights, in the area of Tel Azizat. The goal was to open the Banias road and the slopes of Mount Hermon, connecting to the Massada-Kuneitra road to the north.

As fierce battles were taking place in Kuneitra, Israeli infantry and armored forces moved on June 10 and attacked the southern part of the Golan Heights, bordering on the Sea of Galilee from the east in the area of Tawafiq. After heavy artillery shelling and bombing from the air, the Israeli forces managed to take the township of Tawafiq[10] and soon after the townships of Piq and ʿAlʾal to the east. They occupied Bteiha and Rafida and the whole of the Golan Heights, overlooking the plains of Damascus from Massada in the north to Kuneitra and Rafida in the south in the direction where the Jordan and Yarmuk meet. A cease-fire was declared at 2:00 PM, 10 June 1967, and thus ended the Golan battle.

THE JORDANIAN FRONT

The war on the Jordanian front began at about eleven o'clock on Monday, 5 June 1967. Timing was very important for the course of the war. After destroying the Egyptian air force, the Israeli air force turned its attention to the Jordanian and Syrian fronts. Israeli ground forces had already broken through the Egyptian front defensive lines in Sinai and had begun to widen their activity and penetrate deep into Sinai.

Regarding the Jordanian forces, General Abed El-Munʾem Riad, the commander in chief of the allied Arab forces, issued an order to the commander of the western front to take Jabal Al-Mukabber in the south of Jerusalem and the area of Mount Scopus on which were Hadassah and the Hebrew University to the north. But, in the final resort, the focus was on the conquest of Jabal Al-Mukabber. The battle started at about eleven o'clock in the morning when the Jordanian artillery started to shell Jerusalem and other Israeli targets within its range. Later, one regiment moved and took Jabal Al-Mukabber, but Mount Scopus was left in the hands of the enemy and the Jordanian army was satisfied by shelling the area.

This, however, was a bitter mistake. Jabal Al-Mukabber had no strategic value and had no impact on the battle of Jerusalem as the area of Mount Scopus and the nearby Mount of Olives did. This was a vital area, overlooking the whole area and from which it was possible to surround Jerusalem from the east and north. Had the Jordanian army taken control of this area it would

This cartoon by the famed Israeli artist Dosh embodied the feelings of ordinary Israelis after the Six-Day War

Map of the new borders of Israel following the war

added to Israel at the end of the war. The boundaries of the state at war's end provided a new sense of security. Control of the Golan Heights secured the sources of water most important to Israel (the Jordan River and the Sea of Galilee). Control of the Sinai created a buffer zone, both on the ground and in the air, and added a wealth of tourism sites and land-based resources (oil). Control of Judea and Samaria provided a broad defensive barrier between Israel and Jordan, access to Jewish holy places like Rachel's Tomb and the Machpelah Cave, and control of mountain aquifers.

The conquest of Jerusalem made it possible to unify the city and provided access to the Western Wall, the holiest site in Judaism.

have had contact from the north and west with the Nabi Samwil ridge, Bab Al-Wad, and Latrun, and from that vantage point it would have been possible for the Jordanians to control the whole of Jerusalem, or would at least have secured a better defense of its positions against the Israeli attack and held on for a longer time.

THE BATTLE FOR JERUSALEM

The battle for Jerusalem began with a heavy artillery bombardment on all parts of the city at the same time. At this time, an infantry regiment from the Hittin Brigade began

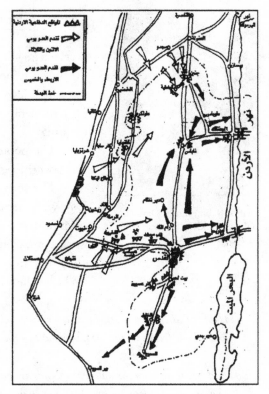

A map of the Jordanian front (West Bank and Arab Jerusalem), June 1967

its attack on Jabal Al-Mukabber. The regiment had just completed the conquest of the area, when it was met by a counterattack of an Israeli infantry division. As a result of this battle, the regiment withdrew completely from Jabal Al-Mukabber, and the Israeli division turned its attention to the township of Sour Baher, occupied it, and blocked the road leading south to Hebron, which now had become completely isolated. Apart from a small number of roads through mountainous rocky terrain, the Jordanian army had no open transport lines to send reinforcements to Hebron.

The goal of the Israeli army was to occupy the entire West Bank in order to ensure taking Jerusalem. In the first stage of the operation, Jerusalem was surrounded from the west and north, with a breakthrough to the positions of the Jordanian army on the hills overlooking the Tel Aviv–Jerusalem road near Bab Al-Wad and the settlement of Ma'ale Hachamishah. Subsequently, the

Yitzhak Rabin, Moshe Dayan, and Uzi Narkis at the gates of Jerusalem

Capturing East Jerusalem and the Western Wall evoked an emotional response in Jews everywhere—as the realization of an ancient dream over thousands of years of exile, during which Jews prayed daily, "If I forget thee, O Jerusalem, may my right hand lose its cunning."

The population of the conquered areas was now the responsibility of Israel.

The song most identified with the Six-Day War, "Jerusalem of Gold," composed by Naomi Shemer about three weeks before the war began, eloquently expressed the yearning of the Jewish people for Jerusalem (Lyrics written before the war:):

How the cisterns have dried out, the market-place is empty,
and no one frequents the Temple Mount in the Old City.

And in the caves on the mountain winds are howling
and no one goes down to the Dead Sea by way of Jericho.

Jerusalem of gold, and of copper and of light
Behold I am a violin for all your songs.

(Lyrics added by Shemer after the war:)

We have returned to the cisterns and to the market-place
a ram's horn sounds on the Temple Mount in the Old City.

And in the caves on the mountain thousands of suns shine—
We will go down again to the Dead Sea by way of Jericho!

Jerusalem of gold, and of copper and of light
Behold I am a violin for all your songs.

Israeli forces blocked the road between Jerusalem and Ramallah. On the morning of June the sixth, the Israeli forces took over the hills to the north of the village of Beit Hanina, opposite Tel Al-Ful, and Nabi Ya'kub camp to the north of Jerusalem and took control of the Jerusalem-Ramallah road and the surrounding hills, cutting it off from Nablus. This was a key area for the occupation of Jerusalem, and the roads leading to it from the north and east had throughout history been an objective for armies advancing to take the city.[11]

On 28 June 1967, the Israeli authorities approved a law annexing Jerusalem to the State of Israel. Based on this law

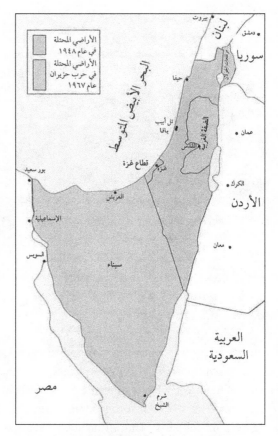

A map of the Israeli occupation of the west bank, Arab Jerusalem, the Gaza Strip, Sinai, and the Golan, June 1967

Arab Jerusalem and its Arab residents were governed by Israeli legislation. The annexation of Jerusalem was met with unanimous opposition of all the countries of the world and was considered an illegal step that was against international law and conventions. The rest of the West Bank was not formally annexed to Israel. The Israeli occupation authorities kept the Jordanian laws and regulations in the West Bank and the Egyptian laws and regulations in the Gaza Strip, though they introduced several basic amendments to these laws to best serve the interests of Israel.[12]

Settlers from Elon Moreh

ISRAEL'S STANDPOINT
AFTER THE WAR

The Six-Day War represents a turning point in many aspects of the Israeli experience. It was a significant military, economic, and political achievement which had a tremendous impact on the national mood. The military echelon enjoyed great prestige following the victory, and its influence on Israeli politics increased. Israel, which had taken control of territories and populations in three countries, asked itself: "What should we do with this great victory?"

Within Israel, a major public debate ensued over the future of the conquered territories, featuring two opposing trends:

1. Supporters of "Greater Israel" did not want to concede an inch of land. The Greater Israel movement had two subgroups, the religious and the secular. With nationalist-messianic characteristics, the religious group (later to become the Gush Emunim movement) saw the war's outcome as divine intervention and a sign that the Messiah was soon to arrive; for these people, settling the entire Land of Israel was a huge *mitzvah* (fulfillment of a holy commandment). In a broadsheet to his followers, Rabbi Tzvi Yehudah Kook said, "This land is ours, there are no Arab territories or Arab lands, only Israeli lands, the lands of our fathers forever, and everything within Biblical boundaries belongs to Israel."[6] Devotees of Greater Israel linked the victory with a vision of a new future for the people of Israel and with the approach of redemption: "The choice before us is: to withdraw into the old ghetto [. . .] or to follow the Messiah, whose coming echoes now in the sounds of our aircraft and the noise of our tanks."[7]

The secular group believed that, in the wake of the difficult experience of the Six-Day War, the new map of the State of Israel gave it more security with defensible borders. They also felt that the historic tie of the Jewish people to the Land of Israel justified retaining the territories conquered.

"Is this justice? We are replacing Arabs with Jews."

RESULTS OF THE JUNE 1967 AGGRESSION

The Arab forces took heavy human and material losses. The greatest and most serious loss, however, was the occupation of the Holy City of Jerusalem and the entire West Bank. For all the Arabs, the only compensation for this loss is to recapture all the occupied Arab lands, including first and foremost Jerusalem.

The Sinai Peninsula was occupied by the Israeli forces. After the 1967 war, the Israelis started to build front defense lines along the entire eastern bank of the Suez Canal. This meant that Egypt was no longer able to control the movement of shipping in the Suez Canal and stop Israeli navigation. Egypt also lost its crucial oil and other natural resources. From a military point of view, with the loss of Sinai, Egypt lost its strategic depth, which had granted it a unique advantage in previous wars with Israel.

The Syrians lost the strategic Golan Heights, which had always granted Syria superiority and control over the roads to the Galilee, Lake Hula, and the Jewish settlements between them. With the loss of the Golan Heights, Syria lost control over the sources of the Jordan River near Banias, and the possibility of diverting water from the Jordan River to the Negev was now lost forever. The plan to divert the Jordan River water was one of the factors contributing to the build-up of tension along the Arab-Israeli borders and eventually the outbreak of the war.

Israel occupied very important positions on the summit of Mount Hermon and set up electronic observation centers, which enabled it to have

Cabinet Minister Yigal Alon,
who formulated the Alon Plan

2. Supporters of compromises based on "land for peace" thought that the outcome of the war provided a good opportunity to negotiate for peace. A combat veteran of fierce fighting during that war said, after it ended: "Regarding the defense of the previous border, you can go back there once, twice, even three times—if necessary. But if now you would have to defend Nablus or Ramallah . . . you wouldn't do it. . . . And that means making sure that we educate people about the things we went there to defend . . . and that we don't turn into an army of occupation with all that implies."[8]

When the 1967 war ended, Israelis were concerned about the fate of the hundreds of thousands of refugees who had fled during the War of Independence and now lived in refugee camps in the territories that were conquered in 1967. The Israelis began discussing potential resolutions involving the Kingdom of Jordan. About two weeks after the war (June 19, 1967), the Israeli government decided that it ought to withdraw from Egypt and Syria to new and more secure borders. Egypt and Syria responded negatively to this proposal:

"Egypt: Israel is proposing to abrogate a peace agreement based on the internationally recognized boundary (from the British mandate era) and on the needs of Israel. According to the international boundary, the Gaza Strip is within Israeli territory. Syria: Israel is proposing to abrogate the peace agreement based on the international boundary (as above) and Israel's security needs."[9]

The government made no decision concerning Judea and Samaria (the West Bank), and there was strident disagreement between proponents of Greater Israel and the land-for-peace supporters. Cabinet minister Yigal Alon argued in the Alon plan (formulated in 1967–1968) that Israel should conclude a peace treaty with Jordan based on "defensible borders." Alon thought that Israel should give back the densely populated Palestinian parts of Judea and Samaria (the high ground that included Nablus, Jenin, Ramallah, Bethlehem, and Hebron), but should retain the Jordan Valley and southern Hebron Hills, which have few Arab residents but were important from the

A cartoon of an Arab summit in Khartoum: men sleep while the leader says, "No peace with the enemy"

control over all the neighboring Arab countries. In general, the achievements that Israel made as a result of the 1967 aggression against the Arabs far exceeded what it had ever hoped for. The most important achievements are the following:

1. Destruction of the military powers of Egypt, Jordan, and Syria. This resulted in a serious imbalance of military power in favor of Israel. The 1967 defeat caused a deep crisis in the Arab world, which soon turned into civil wars as in Jordan, Lebanon, and Syria.

2. The Israelis occupied large areas of Arab lands, far exceeding the area which Israel took over as a result of the 1948 war. The new occupied lands included: the West Bank (including Arab Jerusalem), the Gaza Strip, Sinai, and the Golan Heights.

3. Israel opened the Straits of Tiran to shipping and took control over Sharm El-Sheikh and consequently ensured freedom of navigation to the port of Eilat.

4. Israel occupied oil sources in Sinai and was now able to guarantee the needs of its local market.

5. Israel gained strong, natural defense lines: the Suez Canal, the Jordan River, the Golan Heights, and Mount Hermon. As a result, Israel now enjoyed a wide range of maneuverability.

6. Large Arab lands and their inhabitants were now held hostage by

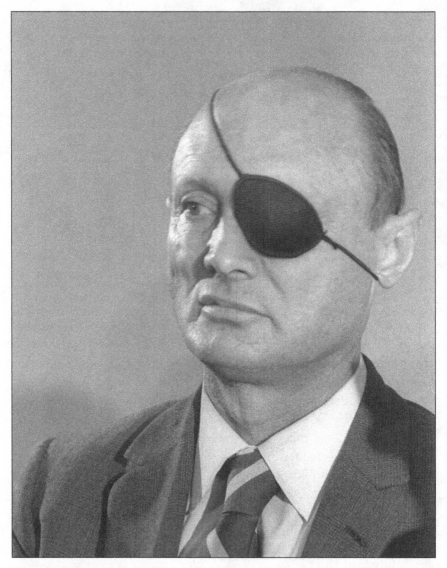

Defense Minister Moshe Dayan

standpoint of Israel's security as a defensible border between Israel and the Jordanian army. Alon called for <u>massive Jewish settlement along the length</u> of the <u>Jordan Valley</u>, and many people answered the call. About his plan, Alon said, "Yes [. . .] we are arriving at the possibility of a resolution that takes into account the basic interests of the parties to the conflict, based on territorial

Israel, guaranteeing it a better bargaining position which could be exploited to force the Arab countries to come to peace with Israel according to its own terms.[13]

7. The 1967 war pushed the Palestinians to organize independently of the other Arab countries and to take their cause in their own hands. They succeeded in creating a moral and political challenge and they initiated their struggle against Israel. The Palestine Liberation Organization was soon recognized as the sole and legitimate representative of the Palestinians and took hold of the reins of resistance.[14]

8. The war helped Israel to come out of a serious economic crisis of recession and unemployment.

9. It also gave new momentum to immigration to Israel, which had reached the lowest level before 1967. (A witty and cynical joke common in the press and cultural salons at the time said, "The last person to leave the airport is requested to turn off the lights and leave the key under the doormat.")[15]

10. The war resulted in the expulsion or displacement of more than 250,000 Palestinians to Egypt, Jordan, Syria, and Lebanon. In addition, 150,000 Syrian citizens were expelled from Kuneitra and the Golan Heights to Syria.

11. The war enabled Israel to confiscate Palestinian lands and to build settlements on them.

12. Israel took control of all Palestinian property. It also destroyed, albeit gradually, more than 347 Palestinian villages and towns, wiping them off the face of the earth, and establishing Israeli settlements in their place. It put its hand on 20,500,000 dunums out of 26,305,000 dunums, the total area of Palestine.[16]

13. In the Arab world: Two months after the war, leaders of the Arab countries held a summit conference in Khartoum. The conference concluded with a resolution that came to be known as the "Three No's of Khartoum":

- No peace with Israel

- No recognition of Israel

- No negotiations with Israel.[17]

14. Internationally: On 22 November 1967, the Security Council published its famous Resolution 242, which advocated:

compromise."[10] The uniqueness of the Alon plan lay in the fact that it was the only proposal offering a peace agreement as the resolution of the conflict with Jordan and the Palestinians.

Defense minister Moshe Dayan, meantime, argued in the Dayan plan (formulated in 1967–1968) that conquest of the entire area of Judea and Samaria should become permanent; five army bases should be created to control the area, and Jewish urban settlement should spread across the occupied areas. Dayan wrote, "We have to create an organized presence on the ground so that, over time, we can 'digest' Judea and Samaria and merge them to 'smaller' Israel."[11] Dayan argued that the Palestinians should have limited social and political autonomy under Israeli rule. Note that, under Jordanian rule, the Palestinians did not enjoy national autonomy. Over time, the Palestinians began to demand recognition as a separate national entity.

Eventually, the Israeli government did not approve any of the plans, although its subsequent actions were in accordance with the Dayan plan.

THE UN POSITION AFTER THE WAR

After the Six-Day War, the UN debated the implications and conditions for reaching peace in the Middle East. In UN Resolution 242, adopted in November 1967 (and reaffirmed in Resolution 338 following the Yom Kippur War), a framework was laid out for a peace agreement based on the following principles: "Withdrawal of Israeli armed forces from territories conquered during the last conflict; an end to the claim or situation of war; and recognition of the sovereignty, territorial integrity and political independence of every state in the region."[12]

Israel supported the decision and so did the Arab countries, except for Syria and the Palestinian Liberation Organization (PLO). A disagreement took shape around the interpretation of Resolution 242: Israel's version is that "withdrawal from territories" does not mean what the Palestinians argue it means: "withdrawal from [all] the territories."

THE ARAB WORLD'S POSITION AFTER THE WAR

After the war, the Arab world spoke with one voice and one orientation; at the Khartoum Conference convened by the Arab nations (September 1967), they

a. The withdrawal of Israeli forces from the territories occupied in the recent conflict.

b. The right of every one of the states in the region to live in peace within secure and recognized boundaries.

c. A just settlement of the refugee problem.

It is important to note that the wording of the resolution was intentionally vague and thus allowed different interpretations. In contrast with the English version which referred to "withdrawal from territories," the French version referred to "withdrawal from *the* territories." Arab governments (Egypt, Jordan, and Syria) based their acceptance of the resolution on the French interpretation. On the other hand, the English text, which did not include the definite article, allowed such interpretations as "withdrawal from some of the occupied territories but not all of them." It was this interpretation that encouraged Israel to accept the resolution.

The core issue in this resolution was not the presence or absence of the definite article "the" from the text but the implied recognition of Israel's right to exist as all the other countries of the region. The resolution, however, did not recognize the Palestinian people as a people with certain inalienable rights, but it referred to the Palestinian issue as a refugee problem only. The acceptance of Resolution 242 by the Arabs led to the automatic rescinding of the No's of Khartoum.[18]

ACHIEVEMENTS OF ISRAEL FROM THE AGGRESSION ON THE ARAB LANDS IN 1967

For the first time since its establishment, Israel achieved a strategic defensive depth on the Egyptian front—the Sinai Desert in the south represented a buffer zone against any possible Egyptian attack. With the occupation of the entire West Bank, Israel succeeded in establishing a defensive line along the Jordan River. It was now free of the danger of any direct attack from the east against the center of the country and around Jerusalem. With control over the Golan Heights, Israeli armored forces were positioned in the area and became a direct threat against the Syrian capital, Damascus, and the plains surrounding it.

united around the "three no's": no negotiations with Israel, no recognition of Israel, no peace with Israel.

THE PALESTINIAN POSITION AFTER THE WAR

In 1964, the National Council of the Palestine Liberation Organization wrote a charter denying Israel's right to exist. This was revised in 1968 and included, inter alia, the following articles:

1. "The Balfour Declaration and the Mandatory Charter shall be considered null and void. [. . .] Judaism, being a religion, is not an independent nationality. Nor do Jews constitute a single nation [. . .]" (Article 20).

2. "The Palestinian Arab people possess the legal right to their homeland and have the right to determine their destiny after achieving the liberation of their country [. . .]" (Article 3).

3. "The Arab Palestinian people, expressing themselves by the armed Palestinian revolution, reject all solutions which are substitutes for the total liberation of Palestine [. . .]" (Article 21).

4. "Armed struggle is the only way to liberate Palestine. This is the overall strategy, not merely a tactical phase [. . .]" (Article 9).[13]

In 1974, the "Staged Plan" was added to the charter; there is disagreement as to its meaning. Following are articles 3 and 4:

1. "The PLO will struggle against any plan for a Palestinian entity the price of which requires recognition, acceptance, and (setting) secure borders (for Israel) [. . .] and negation of our people's right of return and of self-determination in its national homeland" (Article 3).

2. "Any step toward liberation is a link in the continued strategic realization by the PLO of a democratic Palestinian state" (Article 4).[14]

According to the "Staged Plan," the Palestinians must obtain their goal: founding a Palestinian state on the whole territory of the Land of Israel, by

The 1967 war boosted Israeli morale beyond limits. Israel's defeat of the Arab armies created a feeling of greatness among the Israeli leadership. They started to behave arrogantly and haughtily, and bragged about defeating all the Arab armies in an unprecedented short time. However, they overlooked the fact that their defeat of the Arab armies was not due to the invincibility of the Israeli army, as the Israelis always depicted it, but was a result of the absence of unity among the Arabs and their inability to unite and combine forces and resources properly.[19]

The policy of Israel in the occupied territories was based on two major principles: Judaization of the land and displacement of the people. This oppressive, colonialist, and racist policy was carried out against 1.5 million Palestinians who had to face a policy of confiscation and Judaization of Palestinian lands by various means. To implement their policies, the Israelis resorted to the following tactics:

1. Taking over state-owned lands and property.
2. Taking over absentee lands and property.
3. Confiscating lands and enclosing them under the pretense of national security.
4. Forcing farmers to exchange their lands with lands located elsewhere.
5. Purchasing lands from their owners using deceptive methods or by way of financial temptation.

With these means and methods, Israel succeeded in controlling extensive areas of Arab lands in Jerusalem, Hebron, the Jordan Valley, Rafah, and the Golan. Thousands of dunams were confiscated and whole villages were erased, such as Yalo, Emwas, and Beit Nuba. Whole neighborhoods were leveled, such as the Magharba Quarter in Jerusalem; Jewish neighborhoods were built on the same land. The annexation of East Jerusalem was the first action implementing the policy of Judaization. Israel announced the unification of Jerusalem and declared it to be the unified and eternal capital of Israel.

At the same time, Israel built many settlements on the Palestinian lands it had occupied by force and created new realities on the ground in order to block any international attempts to force Israel to withdraw from these territories to allow for the establishment of a Palestinian state. Several weeks after

progressing in stages, according to what is possible to maintain at a given time, until the goal is achieved. Israel sensed there was no partner on the Arab side and thus encouraged the trends wishing to maintain the war's achievements and weakened the forces willing to compromise.

CONCLUSION

The Six-Day War was a watershed event in the history of the State of Israel and its neighbors and in the history of the Palestinian people. Even if the reasons for the war have not been fully clarified, its dramatic results are clear.

Israel won a huge victory in a war it did not initiate or intend, and conquered territories that were not within its borders in 1948. These territories belonged to Arab nations but most of the residents were Palestinians. At that point, Israel, the Arab nations, and the Palestinians needed to join forces in creative thinking and mutual concessions in order to arrive at a mutually secure and shared existence in the Middle East. Instead, the mutual violence and nonrecognition continued.

the occupation, Labor minister Yigal Alon proposed a plan that outlined the Israeli settlement policy in the occupied Palestinian territories. The Alon Plan reflected the position of the Israeli government regarding the Jewish state, its secure borders, and the future of the Palestinian problem, and it refused to recognize the existence of the Palestinian people and their national rights. The plan called for the right of Israel to keep the large area of Arab land occupied in 1967 but without the inhabitants. Successive Israeli governments implemented the plan, and by 1970 more than twenty-eight Jewish settlements were constructed on these lands.

IMPACT OF THE ISRAELI OCCUPATION POLICY
ON THE WEST BANK AND GAZA STRIP

From the first day it occupied the West Bank and the Gaza Strip, Israel worked to subjugate the economy of these areas to the Israeli economy. It started by luring the Palestinian workforce to Israeli employers. The Israeli policy disallowed a development policy that would result in the absorption of the Palestinian workforce in the West Bank and Gaza Strip or the development of a Palestinian economy independent of the Israeli economy.

To achieve this goal, Israel adopted a number of economic measures. The most prominent of these measures were closing all Arab banks in operation in the occupied territory until the eve of the war, imposing heavy taxes on Palestinian products and property, creating obstacles for the development of a local Palestinian industry, and granting concessions to businesses that were tied to the Israeli economy. Israel simply aimed to keep the economy of the occupied areas totally dependent on the Israeli economy and to transform these territories into a consumer market for its products. Accordingly, industry in the West Bank did not develop; it remained the same as it was in 1967.

As for agriculture, due to the confiscation of Palestinian lands by Israel, the farmlands diminished and a great number of farmers abandoned their lands and went to work in Israeli factories and farms. They were tempted by the relatively high salaries, especially as they had to face the difficult living conditions the occupation had enforced upon the land and the people.

Meanwhile, Israeli legislation prevented the marketing of Arab agricultural produce within Israel at a time when agricultural produce from the occupied lands faced stiff and unbalanced competition with Israeli produce,

which profited from government subsidies. This resulted in Palestinian agricultural produce being referred for export to the East Bank, and it remained hostage to the changing policies of the Israeli and Jordanian governments.[20]

Israel's measures after the aggression were not confined just to this realm. They touched on the fields of education, culture, and society. The military censorship laws were applied to school textbooks, the press, magazines, and books. The Israelis resorted to a variety of pretenses to confiscate newspapers and magazines or close their offices. Even more seriously, the Israelis attempted to the take over Palestinian heritage and to restrict the activities of cultural, charitable, and social societies.[21]

EFFECTS OF THE JUNE 1967 AGGRESSION
ON PALESTINIAN CULTURE

The June war exposed the backwardness of the fragile Arab regimes and caused the average Arab citizen to reexamine his aspirations and philosophy. Citizens called for the restructuring of these regimes. Arab intellectuals, writers, and poets began to produce symbolic literature exposing the depth of the suffering and pain agitating in the heart of every Palestinian who had been uprooted from his land. The sense of pain and loss is depicted by the Palestinian poet Khalil Tuma's poem "Songs of the Last Nights":

Letters are born,
They grow, bear leaves and
Climb up your arms like ivy
But do not reach up to your forehead
Because faces that become stretched in the darkness of the morn
When they take in the drops of dew
With the sad oranges
Get lost like a path that rises
From the depth of the massacres to the banks of the sun
Jerusalem has become a prisoner
A body that engages all prayers
What else?
On a very hot day
The flocks of swallows were on the other bank
Recounting the story of a body lying on the sidewalk

Extending a shaking hand to passersby
Though he wouldn't accept alms
He would stare at the bodies of young people
At their arms and at their legs
And through the running tears
In front of him appear columns of fire.

CONCLUSION

As result of the 1967 aggression, all Palestine fell into the hands of the Israelis. The Palestinian people are still suffering from occupation and aggression. Since 1967, the Palestinian people have been living a life of humility. They have not been able to move around their homeland freely and securely. For over four decades, Israel has worked to impose a new reality on the ground and on the people through an occupation policy based on oppression and deprivation of the Palestinians of their homeland. Palestinian refugees are still outside their homeland. In the meantime, Israel continues with its policy of land confiscation and the construction and expansion of settlements.

The aspirations of the Palestinians to lead a dignified life of peace and security like all the other nations of the world will continue until they have ensured a glorious future for their children to live as the other children of the world in freedom and security. We are certain of the day when the occupation will be gone forever and when all Palestinians will live in freedom, security, and dignity on their own land.

7

FROM THE SIX-DAY WAR TO THE FIRST INTIFADA: ISRAEL IN THE 1970S AND 1980S

The 1970s and 1980s in Israel saw revolutionary transitions in the life of the country along three parallel axes. The first axis represents the relations between Israel and the Arab countries, at the center of which was the progression from the Six-Day War to the earth-shattering Yom Kippur War, which ultimately led to a peace agreement with Egypt. The second axis is internal, and represents the State of Israel's transition from the exclusive hegemony of the Labor Party to the political "upheaval" in 1977 and the rise of the Likud Party. The third axis represents the relations between the State of Israel and the Palestinians in the territories it occupied in 1967, which underwent a radical transformation: from Palestinian deference and obedience to rebelliousness and attempts to free themselves from the yoke of occupation.

ISRAEL AND THE ARAB STATES: FROM "NEVER BEEN BETTER" TO "EARTHQUAKE"

The Six-Day War dramatically changed the balance of power in the Middle East; Israel's military superiority had been proven, and the aspiration of the

7

PALESTINE AND THE PALESTINIANS, 1967–1987

❧

The 1967 June war, or *Al-Naksa*, created a new reality for the Palestinian people. The Israeli occupation was beginning to have a great impact on all aspects of Palestinian life. The Palestinian resistance against the occupation was also starting to acquire an identifiable reality. The role of the PLO as the sole and legitimate representative of the Palestinian people was becoming more pronounced. The relations of Palestinians with the neighboring Arab countries were taking a new turn. The economic, social, and religious aspects of Palestinian life were undergoing deep changes.

Following the 1967 war, the UN issued Resolution 242 in November of the same year. The Palestinians refused the resolution forthrightly because it addressed the Palestinian issue simply as a refugee question and failed to address the rights of the Palestinians as a people. The Palestinians were thus determined to fight the occupation by all means. Israel attempted to crush the Palestinian resistance violently.

Al-Karama battle in 1968, the war of attrition in 1969, the October war in 1973, Land Day in 1976, the Litany battle in 1978, and the Lebanon war in

Soldier overlooking the Suez Canal

The Bar-Lev line

Arab countries to oust Israel from the region had failed. Israel enjoyed a measure of economic prosperity following the war, the broad support of world Jewry, and a large wave of immigration. Their overwhelming victory gave the Israelis a sense of extraordinary power, and the general atmosphere was almost euphoric (complacence and enthusiasm). During these years, a new expression entered the Hebrew language: "Our situation has never been better." This feeling diminished somewhat following the renewal of terror and the intensification of the war of attrition.

THE WAR OF ATTRITION

Immediately following the Six-Day War, Egyptian President Nasser said, "I can't conquer Sinai, but I can tire Israel out and break her spirit." In the field, this was translated into the development of a sniper war, with shelling and infiltrations along

1982 were milestones in the resistance and struggle against the Israeli enemy, who had acquired new lands as a result of the 1967 war.

AL-KARAMA BATTLE, 1968

Israel initiated the fighting on 21 March 1968 in order to liquidate the Palestinian resistance in the Jordanian town of Al-Karama in the Jordan Valley. It pushed a reinforced contingent consisting of two armored battalions, a paratrooper brigade, an infantry brigade, an engineering regiment, and five artillery field brigades. The Palestinian fighters, who numbered 500, stood against the Israeli forces from 5:30 AM to 9:00 PM and stopped the Israeli army from achieving its goal. At the end of the battle, Israel incurred the following losses: twenty soldiers killed, three missing in action, ninety injured, four tanks, two armored vehicles, and one airplane. In contrast, the Palestinian resistance movement showed a much higher competence in organized warfare and grew more self-confident. This battle moved the Palestine Liberation Movement to an organized stage of struggle. In the meantime, it gave a great boost to the position and role of the PLO.[1]

PALESTINIAN RESISTANCE AND THE EMERGENCE OF THE ROLE OF THE PLO

Following the 1967 war, the UN Security Council issued Resolution 242. The resolution called for the withdrawal of the Israeli army from the territories it had occupied in the war. More important, it emphasized the need for a just solution to the Palestinian refugee problem. The PLO refused the resolution because it did not meet the aspirations of the Palestinian people. It was Ahmed Al-Shukayri, head of the PLO then, who played an outstanding role in promoting the Palestinian question in the international arena. For this reason, Zionists accused him of calling for throwing the Jews into the sea.[2]

In the early 1970s, the Arab region witnessed some calm. The Palestinian issue was almost removed from the international agenda. The resistance movement thought that it could bring the issue back to the international attention by hijacking airplanes. (Incidentally, Israel was the first country in the Middle East to hijack an airplane. On 14 December 1954, Israeli fighter airplanes intercepted a civilian Syrian airplane that had taken off from Damascus and

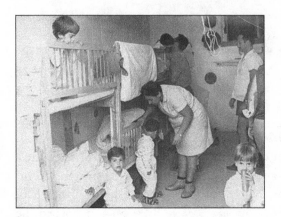

Residents in bomb shelters

the Suez Canal that also spread to the Jordanian and Syrian fronts.

Israeli response to shelling from Egypt was two-pronged: defensive and aggressive. Its defensive response was to establish a fortification line along the canal (named the Bar-Lev Line after the chief of staff at the time), and at the same time it responded aggressively, mainly by using the air force to carry out aerial attacks on cities along the canal and targets deeper inside Egypt. The Egyptians conducted a static war, which robbed the IDF of its advantage of maneuverability. The cost in human life was high: every day, pictures of the fallen—whose numbers were in the hundreds—were published in the newspapers. Israelis became increasingly despondent with the growing realization that no signs of imminent victory were in sight. The need to deploy large forces and tremendous resources along the front line also served to erode Israeli morale.

Exchanges of fire began at the Jordanian border as early as the end of 1967. The communities of the Jordan Valley and Beth-Shean Valley suffered shelling throughout the war, and residents began sleeping in bomb shelters on a regular basis. Shells even hit communities on the Lebanese border. Along with the confrontations on the borders, the Israelis suffered from ongoing terror activities throughout Israel and abroad. The conflict increased Soviet and American involvement in the region, and undermined Israel's international diplomacy. Under pressure from the superpowers, Israel and Egypt agreed on a cease-fire in August 1970, and after efforts to achieve peace failed, it was extended a number of times until the Yom Kippur War.

YOM KIPPUR WAR

The dramatic turning point in Israel's relations with the Arab countries began late in the afternoon of Yom Kippur, 1973. On that day, October 6, Israelis were startled to discover that they were under full attack from the Egyptian

forced it to land in Lod airport. The passengers were taken hostage for forty-eight hours until the Israeli prime minister ordered their release.)[3]

The Popular Front for the Liberation of Palestine (PFLP) hijacked three airplanes and forced them to land in Zarqa airport in Jordan. Three days later a fourth airplane was hijacked. The 450 Israeli passengers were taken hostage for six days. They were given a statement about the Palestinian issue and were then released.[4] This proved that the PFLP did not aim to kill the Israeli hostages but to turn the international attention to the Palestinian cause.

After the Palestinian resistance movement was forced out of Jordan, and moved to Lebanon under severe restrictions, the Palestinian question was again marginalized at the international level. Consequently, the liberation movement decided to change its battleground. On 8 May 1972, a Palestinian organization called Black September hijacked a Belgian airplane and demanded the release of Palestinian prisoners in Israeli jails. On 5 September 1972, the same organization carried out the Munich operation which targeted members of the Israeli Olympic team. The organization took eleven members of the Israeli team hostage and demanded the release of 200 Palestinians from Israeli prisons. Israeli Prime Minister Golda Meir refused the Palestinian hijackers' demand and ordered an attack against them. All the kidnappers and hostages were killed during the attack.

As usual, the Israeli retaliation after the Munich operation was violent. Two days later, Israel attacked ten Palestinian refugee camps in Lebanon and Syria, leaving behind 200 injured refugees.

On 15 May 1974, ninety Israeli students from Ma'alot school in the north Galilee were taken hostage by three members of the Democratic Front for the Liberation of Palestine. The kidnappers demanded the release of twenty-three Palestinian prisoners. Israeli forces stormed the school, killing all the kidnappers and sixteen students. In retaliation, Israel bombarded refugee camps in Lebanon, killing 40 Palestinians and injuring 208, most of whom were civilians, including a large number children.[5]

Israel continued to target the Palestinian resistance movement and leaders in Arab countries and around the world in different ways. On 19 July 1972, booby-trapped mail was sent to Dr. Anis al Sayigh, head of the Palestinian Research Institution in Beirut; his fingers were cut off. On 25 July 1972, similar mail was sent to Bassam Abu Sharif. On 25 October 1972, booby-trapped mail was sent to the PLO offices in Algeria and Libya. On 10 April 1973, Israel assassinated a number of Palestinian leaders in Lebanon,

and Syrian armies. Israel was taken completely by surprise. There had, however, been many indications of the intention to attack, had Israel but taken note: Egypt and Syria had concentrated troops along the border; thousands of Russians who had served as military experts in the region had been precipitously evacuated and Egypt had closed Cairo International Airport; and according to various sources, King Hussein had also come to warn Prime Minister Golda Meir. Israel's military and political leadership, however, insisted on seeing all of these as mere maneuvers.

As it turned out, Israel was imprisoned in a flawed paradigm later referred to as the "conception." One underlying assumption in this conception was that Egypt would only initiate an all-out war with the goal of conquering the entire Sinai Peninsula and vanquishing the IDF, and Israeli intelligence did not take into account the possibility of going to war for partial goals. Locked within this conceptual framework, Israel's leaders assumed that Egypt would not enter into war as long as it did not have long-range fighter jets that would enable it to reach deep into Israel. The Egyptians, however, decided to enter into a war of limited scope in response to the diplomatic freeze in the region, an undertaking for which their planes and the enormous quantity of Soviet arms and antiaircraft missiles in their possession were sufficient.

The IDF was caught unprepared, with its forces scattered sparsely along the border. Because Israel's security strategy relies—in cases of acute danger—on preemptive strike and reserve duty call-up (due to the small size of its regular army), the absolute surprise made it impossible for the IDF to act according to plan. Emergency supply stores also fell short, including, for example, tanks whose engines could not be started. Most alarming were the shortcomings in the reserve corps, which needed to compensate for the limited regular army and step in to deal with the multitudinous forces attacking them. Indeed, the Egyptian and Syrian forces advanced quickly, protected by heavy fire. In the south, the Egyptian army, advancing with 70,000 soldiers and some 1,000 tanks, succeeded in crossing the Suez Canal and conquering the Israeli deployment lines along the canal. The Israeli soldiers were trapped, many were killed, and others were taken captive. The counterattack in the south, launched some two days later, failed, and there were many casualties as well as IDF air force jets damaged by Egyptian antiaircraft artillery. The IDF fought with all its might to hold Egypt back.

In the north, some 40,000 Syrian soldiers and 800 tanks flooded the

most notably Kamal Nasser, Kamal Adwan, and Muhammad Yousef Najjar and his wife.[6]

Israel's assassination operations of Palestinian leaders were also carried out in European countries. For instance, Wael Al-Z'eiter, PLO representative in Italy, was assassinated in Rome on 17 October 1972, and Mahmoud Al-Hamshari, PLO representative in France, was assassinated in Cannes on 9 January 1973.[7]

Israel continued to bombard Palestinian refugee camps. On 2 December 1975, Israeli fighter airplanes attacked the Nabatiya camp in Lebanon, killing 100 women and children and injuring 140. Amid such events, the General Assembly of the United Nations adopted Resolution 3379 on 10 November 1975, which determined that Zionism is a form of racism and racial discrimination.[8]

FORMATION OF THE PALESTINIAN NATIONAL IDENTITY

One of the most important results of the 1967 war was the emergence of Fatah as the most popular movement among the Palestinians and Arab masses and the most influential at the international scene. Fatah was also to play an important role in the future of the PLO. At that time, the PLO was headed by Ahmed al Shukayri. He resigned in 1969 and was succeeded by Yasser Arafat.[9]

In the early 1970s Jordan wanted to bring the Palestinians back into its fold. However, the Palestinians insisted on taking control of their own affairs. Consequently, the Arab countries endorsed a vitally important resolution at the Rabat Summit in 1974. The resolution emphasized the right of the Palestinian people to return to their homeland under the leadership of the PLO as the sole and legitimate representative of the Palestinian people on any liberated part of Palestine. Jordan accepted the resolution.[10]

At the international level, from 1964 to 1974 the United States continued to talk about the interests of the Palestinians and their problem as refugees but never talked about the Palestinians as a people with inalienable rights. It therefore continued to base its position on UN Resolution 242, which considered the Palestinians as a group of refugees.[11] Notwithstanding, on 13 October 1974, Yasser Arafat was invited to address the 29th session of the UN General Assembly. In his speech at the UN, Arafat held an olive branch as a symbol of peace and appealed to the peoples of the world to support the olive branch.[12]

Golda Meir, Israeli prime minister

Golan Heights. The IDF regular forces, with a total of just 177 tanks, struggled to halt the attack and suffered heavy losses, while the Syrians continued to stream in fresh troops. All of the Israeli communities in the Golan were evacuated and some were even temporarily captured by the Syrians. Syrian commando forces conquered the Israeli Hermon and its crucial lookout position (known as "the eyes of the State"). Israeli citizens who had grown accustomed to announcements of IDF victories in previous wars were filled with terror and a feeling of existential danger. The feeling in the leadership was similar. On the third day of the fighting, Defense Minister Moshe Dayan said that Israel was poised before the "destruction of the Third Temple."

During Yom Kippur itself, a day of fasting and atonement, Israel began rapidly recruiting its reserve forces, which reached the front within seventy-two hours and helped halt the advancement of the Egyptian and Syrian armies. An air convoy from the United States, which began arriving a week after the war started, delivered 23,000 tons of equipment and weapons in 670 flights. After a considerable number of days of combat, the Israeli forces in Sinai succeeded in breaking through the Egyptian lines and crossing the Suez Canal to its western side. Inside Sinai, the IDF surrounded the Third Army

Bridge built by the IDF over the Suez Canal

and trapped its thousands of soldiers. In the north, the IDF regained the Golan Heights and the Hermon, and even occupied part of Syrian Golan. The IDF managed to recover from the shock of surprise and the heavy blows it was dealt in the first days, and to end the war with a military victory at a distance of 101

On 22 November 1974, the UN General Assembly adopted two resolutions relating to the Palestinian question. UN Resolution 3236 recognized the Palestinian people's inalienable rights, including the right to self-determination and the right to return. The resolution was passed by a vote of 289 to 7. Not surprisingly, the United States was among those countries which voted against Resolution 3236.[13] The second was UN Resolution 3237, which granted the PLO observer status at the UN General Assembly. The resolution was passed by a vote of 91 to 17.[14]

War of attrition in the late 1960s and early 1970s: "Whoever gets tired first loses"

On 29 November 1974, the UN General Assembly adopted Resolution 3246, which stated:

> The General Assembly strongly condemns those governments that do not recognize the right of peoples under colonial domination . . . , and in particular the African peoples and the Palestinian people, to self-determination and independence. . . . [The General Assembly] reaffirms the legitimacy of peoples' struggle for liberation from colonial and foreign domination by all available means, including armed struggle.[15]

These UN resolutions marked an important decade in the life of the PLO, characterized by a clear vision at the Arab and international levels and an international recognition of the Palestinians' legitimate right to fight against the colonial rule of the Israelis.

THE WAR OF ATTRITION, 1969

Following the 1967 war, the Soviet Union started to provide Syria and Egypt with arms, while the United States continued to support Israel in every way. Israel started to launch sporadic attacks along the borders with Egypt. In response, Egyptian President Jamal Abdul Nasser declared "a war of attrition"

Moshe Dayan, Israeli Defense Minister

Israeli soldier standing by the
milestone marking thirty-six
kilometers from Ismaelia

kilometers from Cairo and 35 kilometers from Damascus. However, the price in casualties, morale, and military equipment was very high.

On October 24, eighteen days after the war began, Israel stopped fighting in response to pressure from the superpowers, and began disengagement negotiations. During 1974, with the United States serving as mediator, disengagement agreements were signed whereby Israel returned the territories it had occupied in this war and prisoners on both sides were returned home.

Although from a military standpoint the Yom Kippur War was an Israeli victory, it constituted a fault line in Israeli history, led to an undermining of faith in the political leadership, and was a reminder of Israel's extreme vulnerability, which had been forgotten due to the swift victory of the Six-Day War. In addition, Israel paid a heavy toll: 2,365 dead and 6,400 wounded, and for the first time, hundreds of soldiers were captured. In addition, it became clear how dependent Israel was on the United States for weapons, and how weak it was in the face of the weapon of Arab oil: the oil-producing nations instituted an economic ban through which they exerted international pressure forcing Israel to withdraw from all the territories it had occupied and to release the encircled Third Army.

PEACE WITH EGYPT—CAMP DAVID AGREEMENT (1979)

Four years after the Yom Kippur War, in November 1977, Egyptian President Anwar Sadat declared before the Egyptian National Assembly, "In order to

on 8 March 1969. Nasser made his famous statement: "What was taken by force can only be restored by force." The war of attrition at the Israeli-Egyptian front was initiated by Egypt and lasted eighty days.[16] (In a war of attrition, each of the warring sides aims to inflict on the other side the heaviest losses in terms of soldiers, arms, or installations. Successive attacks last over a long period of time and aim to exhaust the other side as much as possible.)

During the war of attrition, Israel attacked Abu Za'bal in February 1970, killing eighty workers in a steel factory. In April 1970, Israel raided a children's school in Bahr Al-Baqar and killed forty-six schoolboys. The war of attrition between Israel and Egypt and Syria continued through 1970 and ended with the intervention of the United States.[17]

POSITION OF ARAB COUNTRIES REGARDING PALESTINIAN RESISTANCE

Palestinian guerrilla work grew in the Arab countries that have borders with Israel, namely, Egypt, Jordan, and Lebanon. Each of these countries had its own vision about how the Palestinian question could be solved. The different positions of these countries sometimes slowed down the resistance or at times brought it to a halt.[18] The following section is a review of the attitudes of Egypt, Jordan, and Lebanon toward the Palestinian resistance movement.

EGYPTIAN-PALESTINIAN RELATIONS

Egyptian-Palestinian relations were generally satisfactory. Egypt stood by the Palestinians and the PLO since its establishment. In 1972 Egypt supported the PLO by rejecting King Hussein's project for the United Arab Kingdom.[19] Egypt also waged the 1973 October war in order to attract the world's attention to the Palestinian cause, which was suffering from political stagnation at that time. Unfortunately, the Camp David Accords excluded Egypt from the center of Arab-Israeli struggle.

JORDANIAN-PALESTINIAN RELATIONS

Jordan viewed the acceptance of UN Resolution 242 as a key to the solution of the Palestinian problem. The resolution proposed a number of projects for solving the Palestinian problem. However, the different Jordanian projects completely disregarded the role of the Palestinian leadership and called for

achieve peace and to save the life of one Egyptian soldier, I am prepared to go to the ends of the earth and even to the Knesset in Jerusalem." That very month, Sadat landed in Israel, visited Jerusalem, and even gave a speech in the Knesset. This dramatic gesture amazed Israelis; the fact that the head of the largest and most important Arab country recognized the existence of the State of Israel disproved the entrenched claim that "there's no one to talk to."

How did such a dramatic turnabout take place such a short time after the bloody Yom Kippur War? In effect, Sadat, who was appointed president of Egypt after Nasser's death in 1970, had looked for ways to make peace even before the war: he had already expressed willingness for peace in 1971, in exchange for the return of all of the territories occupied in the Six-Day War. The Israeli government, headed by Golda Meir, ignored this offer due to the ingrained suspicion in Israel toward the Arab countries, but mainly due to the underlying assumption that a complete return of the territories would pose a serious security risk to Israel. Moshe Dayan once said that he "preferred Sharm el-Sheikh without peace to a peace without Sharm el-Sheikh." The United States, on its part, also misunderstood Sadat's desire to strengthen ties and benefit from U.S. sponsorship.

In addition, Sadat encountered difficulties at home due to social and political disquiet. The situation of "neither peace nor war" was insufferable

Anwar Sadat, Egyptian president from 1970 to 1981

the annexation of the West Bank to Jordan. An example of this was the six-point proposal that King Hussein discussed during his visit to the United States in 1969.[20]

The Palestinians, however, insisted on regaining and holding on to their identity. They were determined to fight any attempt to exclude them from any discussion of their issue. This created tension with Jordan, often calling for some Arab mediation. The first armed confrontation between the Jordanians and the Palestinians broke out in 1970 following the formation of a temporary military Jordanian government. The military government issued a statement of eleven items banning, among other things, the carrying of arms, demonstrations, and the distribution of bulletins.

Fighting round the Palestinian camps began on 1 September 1970. Arafat sent a memo to the Arab League secretary general calling for ending the conspiracy of liquidating the Palestinian resistance. On 15 September Arafat sent another memo to all Arab leaders requesting their assistance but to no avail. The confrontation spread to all Palestinian military locations in and outside the Jordanian capital. The fighting lasted nine days despite the resolution issued by the Arab League on 17 September, which called on the two parties to discontinue the armed confrontation.

Upon the request of Egyptian President Jamal Abdul Nasser, an emergency Arab summit was held on 26 September. It was agreed that all guerrilla factions should pull out of all Jordanian cities and move to certain forested areas outside Irbid and Ajloun. But Jordan insisted on expelling the Palestinian resistance from its land. Despite several agreements that Jordan signed, the confrontation between the two sides broke out again on 13 July 1971, when Jordan attacked some guerrilla bases. The confrontation lasted seven days.[21]

On 14 March 1972, Jordan announced a project for the United Arab Kingdom as a solution to the Palestinian problem. The proposal called for a federation between the West Bank, Gaza Strip, and Jordan. The Palestinians rejected the proposal since it ignored the PLO, the legitimate and sole representative of the Palestinians.[22] The proposal was also rejected by some Arab countries since it was seen as an attempt to abort the revolution and liquidate the Palestinian cause.[23] In its turn, Israel refused the plan as being inappropriate as a basis for peace. Menachem Begin, head of the Likud party, said, "Non-Israelis have no right to talk about the land of Israel."[24]

The refusal of King Hussein's plan for the United Arab Kingdom

Anwar Sadat, Menachem Begin, and Uri Avneri

Menachem Begin, Jimmy Carter, and Anwar Sadat

increased the estrangement between the Palestinians and Jordanians. Palestinian forces were thus not allowed to enter Jordan to participate in the 1973 October war against Israel. At Arab summit conferences, Jordan refused to recognize the PLO as the sole representative of the Palestinian people, even at the Rabat Summit. Yet the resolution of the Rabat Summit forced Jordan to recognize, albeit grudgingly, the PLO as the sole representative of the Palestinian people.[25]

LEBANESE-PALESTINIAN RELATIONS

After 1967, the PLO and the resistance movement in Lebanon were stationed in the south along the borders with Israel and around the refugee camps. Some differences arose between the PLO and some Lebanese factions.[26] This led to the ratification of the Cairo Agreement on 2 November 1969, which aimed at a Lebanese-Palestinian understanding. The agreement consisted of nineteen points, four of which called for the organization of the Palestinian presence in Lebanon. The other points related to the need to facilitate the work of the resistance movement in Lebanon.[27] After the departure of the resistance movement from Jordan in 1971, there was an intense transfer of Palestinian fighters to Lebanon. The concern this caused led Israel to launch a number of attacks against the Palestinian refugee camps in Lebanon.[28]

OCTOBER 1973 WAR AND UN RESOLUTION 338

Jamal Abdul Nasser died on 28 September 1970 and was succeeded by Anwar Al-Sadat as president of Egypt. The region was thrust into a difficult and inflexible situation—a period of no-war and no-peace. To end the stagnation and to oblige the big powers to implement UN Resolution 242, Sadat decided to wage a limited war, whose objective was to create some political movement rather than to liberate land. This was evident in his orders to the Egyptian army not to advance more than twenty kilometers east of the Suez Canal after crossing the canal.[29]

After mobilizing their armies, and at 2:00 PM on 6 October 1973, Egypt and Syria launched a simultaneous offensive against Israel along the Egyptian and Syrian fronts. The Egyptian forces managed to cross the Suez Canal and destroy the fortified Bar-Lev Line, which Israel had always boasted was impenetrable. The forces started to liberate Sinai. On the Syrian front,

Menachem Begin and Yitzhak Rabin

for him. He decided to take the path of war with a sure victory, even if it was partial, and thus shatter the diplomatic freeze that functioned to Israel's advantage. Sadat wanted to force the Americans to promote peace negotiations following the international tension that would ensue, and hoped in this manner to strengthen Egypt's status. And indeed, the Yom Kippur War, which to this day is perceived by the Egyptians as a tremendous military victory, is what enabled Sadat to embark on the peace initiative from a position of strength, without appearing to have surrendered to Israeli dictates.

It took a year and a half of diplomatic contacts to reach an agreement. Disagreements centered on the depth of the Israeli withdrawal and the fate of the Palestinians. Sadat demanded, as he had in the past, a complete withdrawal from the territories occupied during the Six-Day War and self-determination for the Palestinians. On the Israeli side, Prime Minister Menachem Begin, who touted the idea of a Greater Israel, would not easily relinquish territory. At this stage, the Americans, led by President Jimmy Carter, decided to join in the process in order to advance the vision of peace in the Middle East. They were also motivated by the fear that failure would undermine the international standing of the United States. At the peak of the process, the three leaders closed themselves off from the world at the presidential vacation site of Camp David for thirteen days, until they reached an agreement and signed

the Syrian army was forced to retreat after proceeding twenty kilometers in-side the Golan Heights until they reached the environs of Tiberias.[30]

The war was a great surprise to the Israelis. Some Israeli leaders were about to order the use of nuclear weapons against certain Arab strategic tar-gets. Prime Minister Golda Meir thought of committing suicide; Moshe Dayan, then defense minister, had a nervous breakdown.[31] It was the first time that the Arabs had succeeded at using their petrol as a weapon. Ten days after the war (16 October 1973), Sadat announced his peace initiative. It called for implementing of UN Resolution 242 and holding an international conference in which the Palestinians were supposed to participate.[32] On 22 October 1973, the UN Security Council adopted Resolution 338 based on a Soviet proposal. The resolution called for settling the Middle East conflict by implementing Resolution 242 and for a cease-fire and initiating negotiations among the parties concerned.[33]

For the Palestinians, the 1973 war was a highly significant event because it disproved three Israeli theories: Israel's security, secure borders, and military supremacy. The war was important also because it put an end to the political stagnation in the region on the eve of the war. There was also the emergence of the Palestinian initiative on 8 June 1974.[34] The initiative included a phased political program consisting of ten points and called for the establishment of a Palestinian state on any part of Palestine that is liberated or from which Israel withdraws.[35] The concept of a Palestinian national authority appeared then for the first time. This became a reality when Arafat and the Palestinian forces arrived in Gaza in July 1994.

LAND DAY (30 MARCH 1976)

On Saturday, 30 March 1976, and after twenty-eight years of curfew rule, se-vere travel restrictions, oppression, injustice, racial discrimination, land con-fiscation, demolition of entire villages, and deprivation of the expression of thought and organization, and in view of the increase in immigration from the Soviet Union—which had reached record numbers in 1972 and 1973 (40,000 per year)—the Arab Palestinians in all cities, towns, and villages in 1948 occupied areas rose up against the Zionist occupation. A general strike was staged and there were massive demonstrations. The Israeli army opened fire at the demonstrators and killed six Palestinians.

The martyrs were: Khadija Shawahna, Raja Abu Raya, Khader Khalayla

two documents: one was a framework for peace between Israel and Egypt, while the second constituted the basis for a comprehensive solution in the Middle East, including the Palestinian problem.

The Camp David Agreement between the countries was signed in a festive ceremony on March 26, 1979, whereby Israel committed to return the Sinai Peninsula, with the exception of the Gaza Strip, to Egypt for a period of three years. Egypt committed to complete peace and normalization of neighborly relations. Demilitarization of some regions of the Sinai and limitations on military deployment and weapons were agreed on. A decisive achievement had been gained regarding Israel's aspirations to integrate into the region.

SOCIAL AND POLITICAL TENSIONS IN ISRAEL— FROM HEGEMONY TO UPHEAVAL

This is how journalist Aryeh Avineri described the fateful broadcasting moment of what became known as the "upheaval," the change of government in the Knesset elections in May 1977:

> Chief television news announcer, Haim Yavin, seemed relatively calm pictured on the small screen. Beside him sat the experienced statistician Hanoch Smith, who had acquired for himself a reputation as a "diviner" of election results of astounding accuracy. Smith could not conceal the mysterious smile stretching across his face. It was still hard to guess what the significance of this smile was. Yavin kept thousands of viewers in suspense: "We're about to release the forecast of the Israeli Television [. . .] we are taking a certain risk, but this is our forecast [. . .]." From a blackboard positioned across from him, Yavin began reading the results that led to general stupefaction: "The Likud is in first place, 43–44 mandates—the Maarakh takes second place, with 32–33 mandates, Dash 14–15 mandates." At Metzudat Ze'ev (Likud headquarters), those present could barely believe their ears and eyes. Had the grand dream really come true: overnight, a tremendous wave of joy hitherto unbeknownst at Likud headquarters burst forth.[1]

Why was it called the "upheaval"? Ostensibly, there was a change of government through elections, as sometimes occurs in democracies. But in effect, this change signaled the end of the exclusive hegemony of the Labor

(from Sakhnin), Kheir Yassin (from Arraba), Muhsin Taha (from Kufr Kanna), and Ra'fat Ali Zuhdi (from Nur Shams who fell in the village of al Tayba). Scores of people were injured and over 300 were arrested.[36]

The direct reason behind the Land Day uprising was the confiscation of 21,000 dunams belonging to the Arab villages: Arraba, Sakhnin, Deir Hanna, and Arab al Sawa'id. The confiscated land was to be allocated

Lefthand page, top: "Diaspora Government, passport." Lefthand page, bottom: "Abdel Ghani Basim, profession: unemployed—UN Resolution 242-338." Righthand page: "Passport—restrictions of using this passport: valid to all Arab countries except Palestine."

to Jewish settlements within the context of Judaizing the Galilee area. It is worth mentioning that from 1948 to 1972 the Israeli authorities confiscated more than a million dunams from the land of the Arab villages in the Galilee and Al-Muthallath on top of the millions of dunams that were seized by the Zionist authorities following the massacres committed by the occupation army and the forceful expulsion of the Palestinians in 1948.[37]

Following is the account of Qassim Shawahna, the father of Khadija Shawahna, who was martyred on Land Day:

In the morning hours of 30 March 1976, I was at home when I heard a loudspeaker announcing a curfew, so I asked all members of my family to stay inside. At 7:30 A.M. I heard someone screaming outside. Khaled, one of my sons, nine years, ran in the direction of the rising sounds. My wife asked our daughter Khadija to bring her brother Khaled back home and followed her to see what was happening. They ran into some soldiers. One of them ordered Khadija to go home. When she turned her back, he shot her and she fell down just fifty meters away from the house. Khadija died as a martyr at the age of twenty-three; she was unmarried.

movement on politics and on most realms of Israeli public life. This hege-mony had not only spanned over thirty years of the state's existence, but had also reigned in the days of the "state in the making." Already at the beginning of the twentieth century, when the Jewish *Yishuv* began organizing itself into select institutions, this movement led the *Yishuv* in all areas and gave rise to its leadership.

Revolutions tend to take society by surprise, but a closer look reveals the preliminary indications of change, whether manifest or hidden. In this chapter, we will try to describe the central factors that led to this dramatic turnabout.

PROTEST AGAINST THE YOM KIPPUR WAR

The crisis of faith caused by the Yom Kippur War following the complete surprise and the steep price that had been paid in fatalities and injuries, led to an outburst of protest, initially led by few individuals. The protest later gained momentum and became a call to bring those guilty for the oversight to justice. The movement started as a one-man protest by Motti Ashkenazi, a reserve captain and commander of the northern outpost along the Bar-Lev Line during the war, who was subsequently joined by other fighters. A na-tional commission of inquiry, the Agranat Commission, was established to investigate what had gone wrong, but did not succeed in quieting the protest since its accusations were confined to the military. While the Labor Party lost

The Agranat Commission

Khader Khalayla was shot as he was helping Amna Ammar, a school teacher, who was ordered by some Israeli soldiers to go home. But when she turned her back, she was shot.[38] Khader was shot in the head and arm and died on the spot.

Land Day martyrs killed by Israeli police in 1976

The Land Day uprising was not accidental; it was the outcome of a long suffering that started the day the Zionist entity was established. The Palestinian people in the occupied West Bank took part in the events of the day. Land Day became a national occasion for Arabs and Palestinians, and a symbol of unity against oppression and injustice, and it is an anniversary for solidarity of all the Palestinian people all over the world.[39]

CAMP DAVID AGREEMENT, 1978

Following the October 1973 war, U.S. Secretary of State Henry Kissinger was very persistent in his mediation efforts between Israel and Egypt. Eventually, he succeeded in persuading Anwar Al-Sadat to visit Israel. In his speech to the Israeli Knesset (parliament), Sadat officially recognized Israel and welcomed coexistence with it. Kissinger's efforts were crowned with the signing of the two Camp David agreements by Anwar Al-Sadat, Menachem Begin, and U.S. President Jimmy Carter. The accord included two documents. The first document was about peace in the Middle East and called for the establishment of autonomy in the West Bank and the Gaza Strip for five years, at the end of which the final status would be discussed. The second was a peace treaty between Israel and Egypt. Despite the refusal of all Arabs, Sadat signed the treaty on 26 March 1979, which included an official recognition of Israel, ending hostilities between the two countries, and the withdrawal of Israel from Sinai in three years.[40]

The Palestinians and all Arab countries rejected the accord, severed their diplomatic ties with Egypt, and suspended Egypt's membership in the

a number of seats in the Knesset in the elections held at the end of that same year, it still retained control of the government. Thousands protested in front of the Knesset demanding that the politicians be brought to justice, and this civil protest led to the resignation of Prime Minister Golda Meir and to the appointment of Yitzhak Rabin, Israeli ambassador to the United States and chief of staff during the Six-Day War, as prime minister (this was the first Rabin government, 1974–1977).

PROTEST OF THE SEPHARDIC JEWS

The public outrage following the Yom Kippur War can only partially account for the upheaval. One of the central factors, if not the central factor, was the strong feeling of the Sephardic Jews that they had neither representation in the government nor influence in the State of Israel, since these were passed on "by inheritance" within a closed circle of Ashkenazim. This feeling mingled with a strong sense of neglect and deprivation that was born out of the difficult absorption of the Sephardic Jews during the first years of the state.

A resident of the immigrant town of Beit Shemesh described his feeling of neglect and anger to Amos Oz several years after the upheaval:

> Really, think about this: When I was a little kid, my kindergarten teacher was white and her assistant was dark-skinned. In school, my teacher was Iraqi and the principal was Polish. On the construction site where I worked, my supervisor was some redhead from Solel Boneh. At the clinic the nurse is Egyptian and the doctor Ashkenazi. In the army, we Moroccans are the corporals and the officers are from the kibbutz. All my life I've been at the bottom and you've been on top.[2]

The economic hardships suffered by Sephardic Jews and their cultural-social deprivation were particularly accentuated after the Six-Day War, with the increased wealth of the Israeli middle class in light of the benefits granted to immigrants from the Soviet Union. The Black Panther movement emerged in the underprivileged neighborhood of Musrara in Jerusalem as a social protest group focused on fighting discrimination. In May 1971, violent clashes erupted between protesters and the police, and seventy-four members of the organization were arrested. Golda Meir, prime minister at the time, expressed a deep disgust at the violence of Jews against Jews in the capital. She coined the expression "they're not nice" after her meeting with members of

Arab League.[41] The accord resulted in a division of the Arab position on the Arab-Israeli conflict. The accord terminated the military option for Egypt and so excluded Egypt from any future military confrontation with Israel.[42]

On the other hand, the accord increased Israel's hegemony and freed its hand regarding Jewish immigration and the confiscation of Palestinian land.[43] In contrast, Egypt could not spread its full sovereignty on its entire land as it was not allowed to deploy armored forces in Sinai.

Caricature illustratig the Israeli government's attempts to uproot Palestinians from their lands

Sadat, Carter, and Begin at Camp David after signing the Camp David Acorrd

LITANY BATTLE, 1978: PRELUDE TO THE EVICTION OF PALESTINIANS FROM LEBANON

The presence of the Palestinians in Lebanon was a source of worry for the residential areas in the north of Israel. (These settlements were built on properties the Palestinians had been forced to leave in 1948.)[44] On 15 March 1978, Israel launched a ground attack against the Palestinians in the south of Lebanon hoping to stop the resistance attacks from the south. It also aimed to force Lebanon to annul the 1969 Cairo Agreement.[45] The Palestinian fighters together with fighters from the Lebanese National Movement succeeded in driving back the Israeli attackers and prevented Israel from achieving its goals.[46] However, Israel was

Demonstration by the Black Panthers

the Black Panther group. This statement summed up the Labor Party leaders' utter incomprehension of the feelings of the Sephardic Jewish public.

Menachem Begin, the opposition leader, exploited these feelings to advance his own political struggle. He succeeded in winning over the Sephardic community by relating to them as Israelis of equal worth. He accepted them as they were, and did not try to turn them into new Israelis. Since he had been a leader of the opposition since the establishment of the state, he was also perceived as a victim of Ashkenazi hegemony and as representing those exploited and oppressed by the *Mapai* establishment. This is how he was seen by the public, and this is what gave the Likud party its source of mass

Menachem Begin, Israel's Prime Minister from 1977 to 1983

able to establish a security zone in the area that was previously known as Fatah Land. The security zone was put under the control of a Lebanese major called Sa'd Haddad.[47]

ISRAELI INCURSION AND EVICTION OF PALESTINIAN RESISTANCE FROM LEBANON IN 1982

The continued presence of the Palestinian resistance in the south of Lebanon caused unrest for Israel, especially following its failure to evict the resistance from Lebanon in 1978. On June 4, 1982, Israel used the failed attempt on its ambassador's life in London as a pretext to launch a military operation into Lebanon, which was called "Safety of the Galilee." Israeli forces besieged Beirut and shelled the city from the sea and the air using internationally prohibited weapons. Tens of thousands of shells fell on Beirut every day. The assault on the city resulted in large-scale destruction and in the death of many people. After eighty-eight days of fighting, the Palestinian resistance was forced to leave Beirut for Tunisia. There was much suspense and anticipation.[48]

The Palestinians departed from Lebanon under international coverage and with an agreement with the Lebanese that Palestinian civilians would be protected.[49] However, contrary to the agreement and with the support and complacency of the Israeli defense minister Ariel Sharon and Chief of Staff Rafael Eitan, the Lebanese Christian Phalangist militia attacked the Palestinian twin refugee camps of Sabra and Shatila on the morning of 16 September 1982 and committed atrocious massacres against the unarmed inhabitants of the two camps. According to some accounts three thousand people were killed in cold blood and a larger number of people were considered missing.[50]

After the Israeli incursion into Lebanon, Israel had one more hurdle to overcome: gaining Arab recognition of its right to exist as an ordinary country, and ending all Arab boycotts. In the mid-eighties, Israel believed that it was possible to sign peace agreements

Cartoon commemorating the martyrs of Sabra and Shatila: "If there is no way to escape death, it is pointless to die cowardly"

support. During the 1970s, the party managed to promote local politicians who were Sephardic Jews, a strategy that ultimately enabled it to form a government in 1977. This government continued to be dominant more or less throughout the 1980s.

This phenomenon was explained to author Amos Oz by a resident of Beit Shemesh:

> I'll tell you something about the hatred. But write it in good Hebrew. You want the hatred between us to end? First of all, come and apologize, properly. We have sinned, we are guilty, we have dealt treacherously—that's what you should say. Like in the prayers of Yom Kippur. That's what you should say in Beit Shemesh and in front of Begin's house. Hold another giant demonstration—four hundred thousand—in the Kings of Israel square—with posters saying "We've sinned" instead of "Begin and Sharon Are Murderers." Say you're sorry for the thirty years when you were in power, and say you're sorry for the five years you've been slinging mud at the opposition. After that—welcome. Please. Come into the government, and we'll work together.[3]

PUBLIC SUPPORT FOR A "GREATER ISRAEL"

In the 1970s and 1980s, many Israelis saw the occupation of the territories as "liberation" and claimed that Israel must administer over them forever and annex them to the state, out of religious and security concerns. The fact that the land over the Green Line was inexpensive also led to the broadening of support for keeping the territories in Israeli hands. The Likud Party had always included Greater Israel (from the Jordan to the Mediterranean) as part of its platform, and this ideological line won it public support and helped it gain ascendancy.

THE STATE OF ISRAEL AND THE PALESTINIANS—
FROM CONTROL TO SHIRKING MODERATE
MILITARY RULE IN THE OCCUPIED TERRITORIES

After the Six-Day War, no practical progress was made regarding Israel's occupation of the West Bank and Gaza Strip. The diplomatic stalemate that formed after the war regarding the fate of the territories was broken by Defense Minister Moshe Dayan. He established a military government in the West

with the Arab countries by sidestepping the PLO in order to ensure its security, without giving rights back to their legitimate owners. Yet, Israel was in for a surprise when it found itself fighting against unarmed people using small stones, who were defending themselves and their right to a decent life. On December 8, 1987, Israel found itself face-to-face with the first Palestinian intifada (uprising).[51]

STATUS OF RELIGIOUS PLACES UNDER OCCUPATION AND ISRAELI PRACTICES TO JUDAIZE JERUSALEM (1967–1987)

After occupying the West Bank in 1967, Israel seized the Buraq Wall (or what is known as the Western Wall to Al-Haram Al-Sharif). In 1984, Israel put the wall under the jurisdiction of the Israeli ministry of religions, thus ending any authority of the Islamic Awqaf on the location. This was contradictory to a resolution issued by the League of Nations in 1930, which considered the location part of Al-Aqsa Mosque and under the control of the Islamic Awqaf.[52]

Israel started its excavations under Al-Aqsa Mosque immediately after the occupation of Jerusalem. In fact, one Jewish group built a synagogue in one of the tunnels as early as 1968. In its eighteenth general conference, the UNESCO issued Resolution No. 427/3 of 1974, condemning Israel's continued excavations. But these excavations went on, resulting in the collapse of the Shar'iyya Islamic court, Al-Khalidiyya library, the floor of the Ottoman School, and thirty-five Arab houses.[53]

In addition, fifteen Jewish organizations were set up whose main aim was to destroy Al-Aqsa Mosque, build the temple, and empty Jerusalem of its Arab inhabitants.

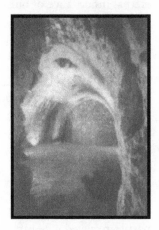

Photographs of the tunnels that Israel dug under Al-aqsa Mosque

Bank and the Gaza Strip, and attempted to persuade the local population of its advantages. Israel granted a large measure of self-governance to the municipalities and a largely free movement of goods, and sometimes of people, between Jordan and the West Bank. When the demand for university studies arose, the establishment of the first Palestinian universities were approved (Bir Zeit in 1972, a-Najah in 1977, and the Islamic University in Gaza in 1978), a move that the Jordanian and Egyptian authorities had refrained from making. Israel viewed this policy as "enlightened occupation" and it changed the way of life for residents of the territories in most areas. The Palestinians became integrated into the Israeli economy: some 40 percent of the workforce from the territories was employed in Israel, leading to a rise in the standard of living both in Israel and in the territories.[4]

ISRAELI SETTLEMENT POLICY

As we have seen above, the diverse opinions regarding the fate of the territories led to the lack of a clear and consolidated settlement policy in both the left-wing (Maarakh) government and the right-wing (Likud) government. It might be said as a generalization that all the various governments were influenced by a small political group by the name of Gush Emunim. The Gush Emunim movement was established in 1974 and adopted its ideas from the school of Rabbi Tzvi Yehudah Kook, who said: "This land is ours, there are no Arab territories and Arab lands here, but rather the lands of Israel, the eternal inheritance of our forefathers, located in all of its biblical borders and belonging to the authority of Israel."[5]

The movement, infused with a messianic ideology, succeeded in taking advantage of the lack of a clear policy to establish facts on the ground. It enjoyed the active support of the right-wing parties and the passive support of most of the other parties. The movement began its settlement project in the mountains of Samaria: it tried seven times to establish a settlement on the site of the ancient town of Sebastia, east of Nablus, but each time was forcibly removed by the IDF. Ultimately, it received permission for a temporary settlement, and later was allowed to establish the permanent settlement of Elon Moreh.

The settlement effort of members of Gush Emunim and the right-wing parties received a significant push with the election of the Likud, and most of this effort was now focused on the areas of Gav Hahar (on the eastern edge of Samaria) and the western margins of the West Bank, with the goal of

These organizations in-
cluded: Ateiret Cahanim,
the Temple's Trustees, the
Temple's Fund Society,
Kahana Hai Movement,
and the Movement for
Seizing Al-Aqsa.[54]

The Israeli viola-
tions against Muslim
religious places contin-
ued. On 15 August 1967,
Shlomo Gore, head of the
Israeli army rabbis, ac-
companied by a number
of officers, performed re-
ligious rites in Al-Aqsa compound. On 21 August 1969, an Australian Jew
named Dennis Michael set Al-Aqsa Mosque on fire. As a result, the southern
part of the mosque was burned, including the famous minbar (pulpit), which
was brought by Salah El-Din from Damascus in 1188.[55] The fire lasted for

In 1969, an Australian set a fire in Al-Aqsa Mosque: an interior and an exterior view of the burning mosque

The Settlement of Elon Moreh (Sebastia), one of the earliest settlements in the West Bank

preventing any possibility of territorial compromise. By 2005, 230,000 settlers were living in the "territories" in 145 settlements—seventeen of them were in the Gaza Strip, but these were evacuated in August 2005.

At the other end of the political spectrum, an additional nongovernmental movement, Peace Now, was established in 1978. This movement was established following the request submitted by 350 reserve officers to Prime Minister Menachem Begin to continue on the path of peace forged by Anwar Sadat. Peace Now was established with the aim of

"Peace Now" activists demonstration

a number of hours as the Israeli police prevented fire engines from coming from Ramallah and Hebron. The United Nations Security Council adopted Resolution 271, which unanimously condemned the attempt to burn Al-Aqsa Mosque.[56]

Israeli soldiers with their girlfriends posing for a photo in front of the Dome of the Rock

Violation incidents against Al-Aqsa Mosque did not stop after the fire. On 5 January 1976, the Israeli court of Jerusalem issued a ruling allowing Jews to pray in the mosque compound.[57] On 8 April 1982 and 2 March 1983, explosives were discovered in the mosque compound.[58] On 11 April 1982, Harry Goldman, an Israeli army reservist, accompanied by other soldiers, stormed the compound and opened fire at the people who were praying. Two were killed and sixty were injured. The mosque structure incurred some damage.[59] On 17 October 1986, an Israeli air force pilot flew off in a warplane armed with missiles in the direction of Al-Aqsa Mosque, but fortunately, he was stopped by other Israeli air force planes.[60]

Al-Ibrahimi Mosque in Hebron did not fare any better. From 1975 to 1987, there were scores of violations. It was desecrated several times. Wine was consumed and spilled inside the mosque, dancing parties were held, and circumcision rites were performed in it. Dogs were used to sniff the Muslim worshippers' clothes, and the ablution water was polluted with unknown chemical substances.[61]

The desecration of religious places was not the only means to hurt the feelings of Muslims in the occupied territories. The Israeli media took an active part in that. On 24 April 1970, the Israeli daily *Yediot Ahronot* published an article entitled "A Prophet in His Own Country." The article described Prophet Mohammed (peace be upon him) as a bandit and claimed that he suffered from epilepsy.[62]

Abie Natan and the "Voice of Peace" ship

convincing the public and policy makers of the need and possibility of achieving a historic peace and reconciliation with the Palestinians and the Arab nations in exchange for territorial compromise, based on the principle of "land for peace."

In 1975 Abie Natan operated a pirate broadcasting station called the Voice of Peace, broadcast from beyond the Israeli coastline in English and in Hebrew. The station featured music, advertising, and Jewish-Arab dialogue, a rare phenomenon during those years, as well as the promotion of humanitarian operations, such as the collection of donations and money for hospitals in neglected areas. The station was closed in 1992 but is considered to have heralded Israel's willingness to make concessions in exchange for the hope of peace.

PLO TERROR OPERATIONS

The Palestinian Liberation Organization underwent changes in the 1970s.

Yasser Arafat, chairman of the PLO

During the 1960s, Fatah had controlled the PLO, and Yasser Arafat, leader of Fatah, became the president of the PLO in 1969. The Fatah movement promoted the idea of armed struggle and guerrilla warfare against Israel. Indeed, during the 1970s, the PLO carried out terror attacks against Israeli and Jewish targets both in Israel and abroad.

In the territories of Judea, Samaria, and Gaza, however, there was almost no such violence. The population in the territories had enjoyed a certain improvement in their standard of living following the Israeli occupation. This, in combination with military

On the same day that Jerusalem was occupied (7 June 1967), Israeli defense minister Moshe Dayan stood in front of Al-Buraq Wall and declared, "We have reunited the city. . . . We have returned to the city, and we will never leave it."[63] Upon his orders, Al-Magharba Quarter was demolished and its inhabitants were moved to other places. Hundreds of Arab families were forced to leave their city. They were simply put on buses or trucks and transferred to Jericho. All crossing points between the two parts of the city were removed; a "no-man's land" sign was also removed.

The Israeli authorities set out on a gradual Judaization process of Jerusalem. By early 1980, Israel had confiscated 24,000 dunams of land within the district of Jerusalem. It also seized property registered under the name of the Jordanian government, thus bringing the total area of confiscated lands to 70,000 dunams. On 30 July 1980, the Knesset approved the basic law, which stated: "Jerusalem, complete and united, is the capital city of Israel; it is the seat of the President of the State, the Knesset, the Government and the Supreme Court."[64]

At this juncture, it is worth mentioning that by 1985 Israel controlled 52 percent of the West Bank.[65] By 1984, Israel had built 154 settlements in the West Bank. From 1967 to 1977, the Ma'rakh party set up 34 settlements and the Likud erected 120 settlements in the seven years of its rule. In 1986, the number of settlers in the West Bank was 80,000; in Gaza Strip there were 1,500 settlers in 16 settlements.[66]

CULTURAL AND ECONOMIC LIFE IN PALESTINE

In the occupied Palestinian territories, agriculture represents the basic economic resource for Palestinians. Israel, therefore, tried to hinder the development of this sector in a number of ways. By 1974, Israel had confiscated 800,000 dunams and by 1984 the number had risen to 1,800,000.[67]

In 1973, Israel passed a special land law, which made it easier for Israel to confiscate more lands. Consequently, at the end of 1981 Israel had confiscated 250,000 dunams under the pretext of the preservation of nature.[68] To further hinder the development of the Palestinian agriculture sector, Israel placed restrictions on Palestinian agriculture; for example, it banned the planting of certain fruitful trees. It also banned marketing Palestinian produce in Israeli markets. Exportation to Jordan was permitted only through Israeli private companies.

supervision and control and a strong intelligence network, forced the various opposition organizations to establish their bases outside Israel, and a considerable percentage of their attacks were carried out against Israeli and Jewish targets overseas.

Under these conditions, it was more convenient for Fatah to operate from Jordan, where they established their own power base. Terrorist (guerrilla) infiltrations into Israel continued to increase, and terror attacks became routine. On March 21, 1968, in response to an attack on a student bus, IDF units invaded the eastern Jordan Valley near the village of Karameh, where Fatah headquarters were located. Despite the superiority of the Israeli air force, the IDF encountered serious difficulties from the outset of the attack due to a topographical disadvantage, advance intelligence warnings to the enemy from the Jordanian Legion, and the difficult terrain. During the battle there was fierce fighting between IDF troops, the Jordanian Legion, and PLO fighters. The PLO and the Jordanians fought against the IDF with surprising intensity, and Israel did not complete its mission and was forced into a premature retreat. The fighting ended with 33 IDF soldiers dead and 161 wounded, 27 Israeli tanks damaged and 4 abandoned. The PLO lost 156 combatants, and 141 were taken prisoner. On the Jordanian side, 84 soldiers were killed and 250 wounded. The significance of the Battle of Karameh lay in the Palestinian myth that emerged from it: it became a symbol of Palestinian combat and resistance and was viewed as the first victory over the Israeli army. It increased the number of recruits to Fatah and renewed the flow of funds to the organization.

PLO activity from Jordan ceased in 1970. After one of the branches of the PLO hijacked and blew up four western planes, the king of Jordan took aggressive military action against the Fatah base in Jordan. The action, which came to be known as "Black September," was a cruel and massive crackdown during which 3,000 Palestinians were killed and the organization's institutions closed, leading to diplomatic and operational changes in the PLO. The organization established its base in South Lebanon (until it was pushed out by the IDF during the first Lebanon war), and in operational terms, switched to terror activity abroad against Israeli targets as well as within Israel from Lebanon and the sea.

Included in the PLO's terrorist activity was the murder of eleven Israeli athletes during the Munich Olympics by members of Black September in

More significantly, Israel controlled 95 percent of the water resources in the West Bank and restricted water consumption inside the occupied territories. It also passed a number of laws about water, including a law forbidding Palestinians to dig wells.[69]

"Only 7 percent of the Arab Palestinian lands are left for them after Israel's confiscation"

The commercial sector was greatly affected by the policies adopted by the Israeli occupation from 1967 to 1987. Through closures, blockades, and flooding the Palestinian market with Israeli products, Israel succeeded in subordinating the Palestinian economy to its economy. Eighty percent of Palestinian foreign trade was conducted through the Israelis. The commercial deficit from

"Palestine is drowning by settlements" [The peace dove flies with a sign saying "a new round of negotiations."]

1970 to 1980 increased drastically. The West Bank and Gaza Strip became a consumers' market for Israeli products.[70]

In the 1970s there were only traditional industries, mainly handicraft. The Israeli policy aimed at marginalizing the Palestinian industry and taking over its markets.[71] In 1974, the Israeli authorities closed down factories in Hebron and Nablus for alleged security reasons. It banned food industries and the exporting or importing of raw materials. It also opened its labor market behind the Green Line to Palestinian laborers at very low wages in contrast to the Israeli workers.[72] This significantly reduced the contribution of the industrial

Welcoming home the Israelis highjacked in Entebbe

September 1972, the massacre at Rome Airport in 1973, and letter bombs sent to Israeli diplomats and leaders of Jewish communities. In June 1976, an Air France plane en route from Tel Aviv to Paris was hijacked. The hijackers landed the plane in Entebbe (Uganda). In a daring military operation (Operation Entebbe, or Operation Yonatan), the IDF freed over 100 Israeli hostages.

In Israel itself, the terror attacks became more vicious. In May 1970, a bus full of children was attacked; two years later, an attack was carried out at Lod Airport by three Japanese terrorists acting as agents of the Popular Front (the most famous of whom was Kozo Okamoto); additional attacks took place in Kiryat Shmoneh and Nahariyah in which civilians were killed; in Ma'alot, students and teachers were killed in an attack on a school; in March 1978, a devastating attack was carried out on an Egged bus traveling along the coastal road, which triggered an intensive military response by Israel against terrorist bases in Lebanon—the Litani Operation (March 11, 1978).

The leadership of the Arab public in Israel changed during the 1960s and 1970s, transitioning to the nationalist Arab parties that had stopped cooperating with the Zionist parties. These leaders found their political home in the Communist Party, Rakach, that became in effect an Arab party. This party unified antigovernment protest in the Arab sector. On the 30th of

Violent clashes with the security forces in Nazareth, 1976

sector to the gross national income before 1978 to 7.65 percent in the West Bank and 12.5 percent in the Gaza Strip.[73] The most outstanding Palestinian traditional handicraft industries include: wood-carving, pottery, textiles, handmade rugs, skin dyeing, glass, embroidery, and ceramics.

After occupying the West Bank and Gaza Strip, Israel retained the Jordanian and Egyptian laws and curricula that were used in the West Bank and in the Gaza Strip. However, it interfered with the curricula in a way that served its interests and policies. The occupation also pursued university and school students and teachers.[74]

Among a total of 1,100 military orders that Israel issued before 1987, many orders concerned school curricula. On 9 August 1967, for instance, Israel issued an order that banned 78 out of 121 school textbooks produced by the Jordanian ministry of education that

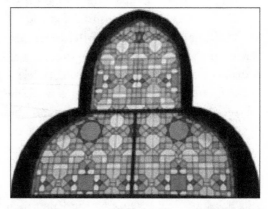

Palestinian crafts: wood carving, pottery, and stained glass

March 1976, a massive demonstration was held in the Galilee against the government's intention to confiscate 20,000 dunams in the Sakhnin area toward the goal of "Judaization of the Galilee." The leaders of the Arab parties such as *Rakach* and the heads of the local councils called for a general strike day and protest demonstrations. During the demonstrations, police forces killed six demonstrators, three of them in Sakhnin. Land Day is marked to this day as a day of protest against the neglect of Israel's Arab citizens in the area of lands and in other realms.

THE LEBANON WAR

The PLO's continued base in South Lebanon, together with the terror attacks and shelling of the northern settlements, constituted an intolerable situation from Israel's perspective. Local or medium-sized operations, such as the Litani Operation (1978) and the shelling of the PLO headquarters in Beirut (1981), did not bring about a change in the power balance. Ariel Sharon, defense minister in Menachem Begin's second government (1981), formulated a broad strategy aiming to bring about the establishment of a strong Lebanese state headed by the Christians, while removing the PLO and the Syrians from Lebanon. An assassination attempt on the Israeli ambassador to London by a competing arm of Fatah served as Israel's pretext to invade Lebanon. Most of the government ministers, who knew nothing of Sharon's master plan, approved a limited incursion after the fashion of Operation Litani, whose goal was to keep the rain of rocket fire away from the Galilee communities.

This was the mandate that the government gave to the IDF and to the heads of the security establishment at the beginning of Operation Peace for the Galilee on June 6, 1982. After a number of days of fighting, it began to dawn on the Israelis that Israel did not intend simply to push the PLO to a distance of forty kilometers from Israel's northern border (the Katyusha rockets' range) as declared, but to create a new order in the area. IDF forces advanced northwards, reached Beirut, and besieged it. At this stage, the consensus that had characterized Israeli society in all of its previous wars was ruptured, and a heated and earnest debate was unleashed regarding the goals of the war and the extent to which it was necessary.

Following diplomatic efforts on the part of the United States, a plan was developed for evacuating the Palestinian forces from Lebanon, and on September 1, 1982, Arafat left Beirut for Tunisia, accompanied by the armed

were used in the West Bank. On the other hand, books that were not banned were modified. To cite some examples, the term "Arab homeland" was replaced by "Arab countries," and the statement "Nationalism means to do, not just to say" was replaced by "Determination means to do, not just to say." All texts relating to Salah Al-Din Al-Ayyoubi's defense of Palestine and Jerusalem were deleted.[75] Besides school textbooks, from 18 January 1977 to 4 August 1982, Israeli military authorities banned the circulation of a total of 1,215 books and periodicals.[76]

Because Palestinians had always valued the role of education in their life, they established a number of local universities: Bethlehem University in 1973, Bir Zeit University in 1975, An-Najah National University in 1977, the Islamic University in Gaza and Al-Quds University in 1978, and Hebron University in 1980. Seventeen community colleges were also established. (It is worth mentioning here that in 1948 Palestine did not have a single Arab higher education institution.)[77]

Palestinian institutions of higher education suffered all kinds of Israeli harassments and closures. In July 1980, the Israeli occupation authorities issued order no. 854. The order placed Palestinian universities, like schools and community colleges, under the authority of the Israeli education officer. This meant, among other things, universities were subject to the same regulations that applied to primary and secondary schools, including control and supervision of student admission, faculty recruitment, curricula, and textbooks.[78]

Professor Menahem Milson, professor of Arab literature at the Hebrew University in Jerusalem, was appointed in 1981 as the first civil governor of the West Bank. With the appointment of civil governors, there was a remarkable increase in closures of Palestinian universities. In the academic year 1981/82, Bir Zeit University was closed for six months; An-Najah National University was closed from 4 June to 1 September 1983. On another occasion, An-Najah was closed for four months (30 November 1984 to 1 April 1985). In July 1983, an Israeli settler fired at students in Hebron University, killing three and injuring many others.[79]

Israeli policies did not spare Palestinian students. In 1983, Israel arrested thirty-four students who were sitting for their Tawjihi exams (the school leaving exams) for a whole week.[80]

Due to the aggressive policy against universities and because local Palestinian universities could not cope with the increasing number of students,

Israeli APC in the Lebanon War

Palestinian forces. This was a fatal blow for the PLO, which lost both its prestige and its territorial base, and was forced into exile outside the region, in Africa.

THE MASSACRE AT THE SABRA AND SHATILA REFUGEE CAMP

On September 14, 1982, several months after the beginning of the Lebanon war and after the evacuation of Palestinian forces from Beirut, Bashir Jemayal, leader of the Lebanese Christians, and recognized by Israel as the leader of Lebanon, was assassinated. Fearing that chaos would ensue in the aftermath of the assassination, the IDF entered Beirut to search for Palestinian terrorists. The mission of eliminating opposition in the Sabra and Shatila refugee camps was delegated to the Christian Phalanges militants. The Phalange embarked on a "purification" operation in the camps, in which hundreds of Palestinians, including women and children, were murdered. The IDF and the State of Israel were accused of being responsible for the massacre. In Israel, public opinion mobilized to demand that those guilty of the grave oversight be brought to justice. A wave of protest, together with mass demonstrations

a proposal to establish Al-Quds Open University was made in 1976, but it did not materialize until 1985.[81]

LITERATURE OF RESISTANCE UNDER OCCUPATION

POETRY

After the 1967 war, Palestinian poetry underwent certain fundamental changes. It became more "revolutionary" and more realistic.[82] It depicted the reality of the Palestinian people and started to embody feelings of expulsion, exile, homelessness, and homesickness. In addition, poets started to exploit symbolic images.[83] In the 1970s, Mahmoud Darwish, Muin Bseiso, Abdelkarim Al-Karmi (Abu Salma), and Yousef Al-Khatib became prominent Palestinian poets in the diaspora, whereas Samih Al-Qassim, Ziyad Zayyad, and Fadwa Tuqan were the leading poets under the Israeli occupation.[84]

Representing this period is "I Love You More," a poem written by Mahmoud Darwish in 1967, from his collection, *The End of the Night*:

> *Your hands are like a thicket*
> *But I do not sing*

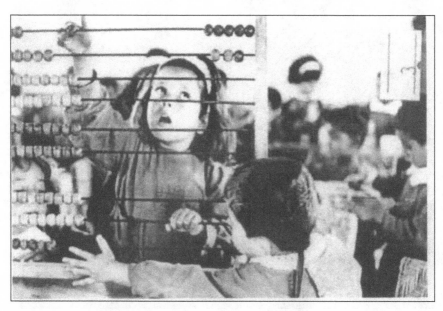

Palestinian girls in a Palestinian school

The 400,000-strong demonstration at the Kings of Israel Square in Tel Aviv following the massacre at the Sabra and Shatila refugee camps

Ariel Sharon testifying before the Kahan committee established to investigate the massacre

As other birds do
My chains have taught me how to fight,
fight, fight.[85]

In another poem, he says:

We are in the flesh of our country
It's inside us
Before June, we were not like nestling pigeons
So our grains did not vanish in the midst of land terraces
We do not write verse
We fight.[86]

FICTION

Palestinian fiction between 1967–1987 was characterized by themes revolving around the 1967 defeat, the factors leading to it, and the setbacks resulting from it, as well as the crisis of war and the crisis of leadership. Ghassan Kanafani's novella *Returning to Haifa* (1968) is a good representative of the fiction of this period. In this work Kanafani deplores the delusion of return under the Israeli occupation and calls for the real return to Palestine after liberation. Sa'id, a Palestinian refugee returning to Haifa with his wife after 1967 as visitors, is blamed for leaving his son Khaldoun behind when he fled his homeland in 1948 and for not allowing his other son Khaled to join the fedayeen (guerrilla fighters) after the 1967 defeat. For the first time in any of his works, Kanafani uses Israeli characters who voice their own problems and concerns, and allows a Palestinian character and a Zionist character to meet under the same roof away from the battlefield.[87]

In *The Days of Love and Death*, Rasha Abu Shawar depicts the problems and sacrifices of rural Palestine before and after *Al-Nakbah*. This novel also discusses the problems and concerns of the Arab society at large. In her novel *The Cactus*, Sahar Khalifeh depicts the reality of the different classes and sectors of the Palestinian society, all of whom look forward to liberation from the Israeli occupation.[88]

The Adversary (1978) by Afnan Darwazah describes a meeting in Paris between a Palestinian in exile and an old Jewish neighbor who used to live next door to him in Palestine before the establishment of the State of Israel, the event that turned them into adversaries. Darwazah exploits this setting to

at the Kings of Israel Square in Tel Aviv, spurred the establishment of a commission of inquiry regarding the massacre. The commission established that responsibility for the massacre fell entirely on the Phalanges, and not on the State of Israel, but at the same time, it pointed out a series of errors and recommended, among other things, that Ariel Sharon be removed from his post as defense minister. This recommendation was indeed carried out.

FREEZE AND THE OUTBREAK OF THE INTIFADA

On September 17, 1978, Egypt and Israel signed two documents. One related to Israeli-Egyptian relations, and the second was entitled "A Framework for Peace in the Middle East"; this second document dealt with the Palestinian problem and promised an independent Palestinian government for the population of the West Bank and Gaza Strip. For the first time, the Israeli government recognized that resolution of the conflict was contingent upon upholding the rights of the Palestinians. Many topics were vaguely defined, such as responsibility for security in the territories, the status of Jordan in the West Bank, the limits of the autonomy that would ultimately be granted the Palestinians, and of course, the fate of the Jewish residents of Judea and Samaria and the Gaza Strip. In effect, nothing was actually achieved; on the contrary, the settlement enterprise grew stronger, leading to the eruption of the first intifada at the end of the 1980s.

present the Palestinian question in a rather objective manner far away from personal emotions.[89]

REPRESENTATIONAL ART

Representational art in Palestine took a different direction than in other Arab countries or in Israel. It was used to depict the suffering of the Palestinian people. Kamal Al-Mughanni, Isma'il Shammout, Sulaiman Mansour, and Fathi Al-Ghubain are among the well-known Palestinian representational artists.[90]

Following the Israeli occupation of the West Bank and Gaza Strip, representational art formed a new means of resistance. A lot of art works appeared and art exhibitions became popular. Consequently, art works and artists became the focus of the oppressive measures of the Israeli military occupation. Art works were confiscated, exhibitions were closed, artists were arrested, and they were not allowed to transport their art works from place to place. In fact, the occupation did not spare any means to stop art from playing its role as a form of resistance.

As all Palestinians, artists were subject to the same oppressive measures of the occupation. Kamal Al-Mughanni, a graduate of the Art Academy in Alexandria, Egypt, and an instructor at An-Najah National University in Nablus, was charged with affiliation with a Palestinian resistance movement,

لوحة إلى أبن لإسماعيل شموت

Scenes from Palestinian memories and challenges

was sentenced to two years in prison, and his house was blown up. Sulaiman Mansour, a graduate of Bezalel Academy of Arts and Design in Jerusalem, was summoned by the Israeli intelligence for investigation and was put under surveillance while his art works were confiscated. Fathi Al-Ghubain from Gaza, who was known for his creative use of the colors of the Palestinian flag (white, black, red, and green) in his works, was imprisoned for seven months, his 1979 exhibition in Ramallah was closed, and his works were confiscated.

8

INTIFADA

~❦~

In May 1983, a formal peace treaty was signed between Israel and Lebanon, but it was never actualized. Pursuant to the treaty, Israel pulled out of Beirut and the Shouf Mountains and withdrew its forces south of the Awali River, to a distance of 45 kilometers from the northern border of Israel. Two divisions of the South Lebanese Army, under the command of Major Sa'ad Haddad, were stationed in the area between that line and Israel, known as the "security zone." Israel was deeply mired in "the Lebanese swamp" for many years. Acts of terror against IDF soldiers continued, and new casualties were added to the 670 Israeli victims of the Lebanon war of 1982 on a daily basis. There was mounting protest from Israelis, even IDF soldiers, who were increasingly critical of the government and of what was happening in Lebanon. On August 28, 1983, Prime Minister Menachem Begin announced his intention to resign his post and to quit politics altogether. He did not enumerate his reasons, but declared, "I can go on no longer." His successor as prime minister was Yitzhak Shamir.

In the elections for the 11th Knesset (1984), the left-wing bloc and the right-wing bloc were tied, which led to the formation of a national unity

8

THE INTIFADA OF 1987

The following folk poem portrays the circumstances prevailing prior to the outbreak of the intifada and also expresses the objectives of the intifada:

> *The 1967 War was over*
> *All the land of Palestine was occupied*
> *In every patch of land there was a tragedy*
> *In every house a sad old man*
> *In every village there was poverty*
> *And in every camp an orphaned child!*
> *They reckoned the case was over*
> *And thought they had gotten rid of us*
> *Once and for all!*
> *They thought that after all the suffering*
> *We had lost our patience*
> *Or given up our steadfastness.*
> *A million times did we tell them:*
> *No to Camp David*

government. In 1985 this government, headed alternately by Shimon Peres and Yitzhak Shamir, decided to complete the withdrawal of the IDF from Lebanon, meaning Israeli forces would return to the international border, while establishing a buffer zone in cooperation with the South Lebanese Army (SLA) and the stationing of a UN observer force north of the buffer zone. Palestinian terrorists were thus distanced from South Lebanon, but a new and far more radical element appeared in their stead—Hezbollah, a terrorist organization under Syrian control with funding from Iran.

In April 1984, the Israeli public learned for the first time about Operation Moses—a complex, secret operation that lasted several months, in the course of which more than 6,000 Jewish immigrants fleeing Ethiopia were brought to Israel. Israeli society once more experienced moments of solidarity and feelings of pride in the success of the operation. During this period, defense issues cast a shadow on everything else. Violence and terror toward Jews and Israelis increased outside Lebanon too: a shipload of terrorists on their way to perpetrate a mass terrorist attack in Tel Aviv was torpedoed and sunk by an Israeli navy gunboat; eighteen Israelis were murdered in airports in Vienna and Rome; terrorists took over a private Israeli yacht moored at Larnaca in Cyprus and murdered the three Israelis on board; about two weeks later, a terrorist group took over the *Achille Lauro* cruise ship and murdered a disabled American Jewish man in cold blood.

Terrorism was also on the rise in the heart of Israel itself: dozens of Israelis were murdered by bombs on buses, knife attacks, kidnappers, Molotov cocktails, and drive-by shootings of cars with children inside. Responding to the rampaging terror, the Israeli air force bombed the PLO headquarters in Tunis (2,460 kilometers from Israel), wounding many PLO members. The Tunis attack was the most distant one the IAF had ever carried out, and signified Israel's resoluteness of purpose to defend the lives of its citizens, even if that meant taking action outside the state's borders.

In April 1984, the Israeli security services uncovered a well-trained, well-organized Jewish underground, comprising several dozen young residents of settlements, among whom were a few senior IDF officers (in the reserves) and several leading settler activists. These people murdered Arab political leaders and carried out other terror attacks during 1980–1984. The discovery and imprisonment of the Jewish underground shocked Israeli society, as people had a hard time believing that young Jewish people, the cream of the crop of Israeli youth, had planned, organized, and carried out the murders

A million NOs to it and to all those behind it
No to autonomy:
It is futile and deformed!
No to elections
They take our rights away
They replace our rulers
And divide us more and more.
Our demand is one:
An independent state
That only—will last forever.

FORMATIVE STAGES OF THE INTIFADA

The formative stages of the popular uprising (intifada), which erupted on 9 December 1987, emanate from the forty years of national deprivation and from the twenty years of Israeli occupation and the Israeli policies that aimed to terminate the existence of Palestinian people on their land. The roots of the intifada go far back to the establishment of the all-Jewish state of Israel on the land of Palestine, which completely excluded all others. The Zionist founders of the State of Israel simply denied the rights of any other people in Palestine in order to justify the existence of their own state and to be able to maintain its security. Israel's refusal of UN Security Council Resolution 194, which called for the repatriation of Palestinian refugees, as well as other resolutions, was a reflection of the Israeli policy of rejecting and denying Palestinian national rights. The multitude of laws of the Israeli occupation (totaling over a thousand) were not only aimed at keeping the Palestinians under Israeli rule and deprived of their rights and enslaved to Israel but were also aimed to humiliate them and strip off their identity and keep them under inhumane circumstances.

For Palestinians, Palestine embodies their humanity. The intifada was merely a means for them to reclaim their humanity, and for years since the occupation it was an eruption just awaiting the suitable historical moment to go off.

Palestine disappeared from the political map after 1948 when Israel was established on around 80 percent of the land area of Palestine and after the annexation of the West Bank to Jordan and the Gaza Strip to Egypt. Following

The photos shown here illustrate the characteristics of the early days of the intifada[1]

of Palestinian political leaders and civilians. The underground leaders were tried, convicted, and sentenced to prison terms of varying lengths. Some were pardoned by President Chaim Herzog a few years later. Despite serious criticism of the settlers, and despite the growing trend to question the entire settlement enterprise, the settlement movement dug in its heels and refused to back down.

THE INTIFADA BEGINS

On December 8, 1987, an Israeli truck crashed into a Palestinian car in Gaza and four Palestinian passengers were killed. The Palestinians claimed that the collision was intentional—that it was malicious murder. At the funeral of those killed, the crowd attacked an IDF post in Gaza and threw stones; the rioting resumed the next day and continued over subsequent days. This incident is said to have marked the start of the Palestinian war against Israel: the intifada (uprising).

The intifada initially featured throwing stones and Molotov cocktails at IDF soldiers and vehicles, crowds gathering to confront the IDF in Gaza, blocked streets, snatched weapons, and so forth, on a daily basis. The intifada was initially driven by Palestinian women and children. Meanwhile, a local,

that, the Palestinians lived in a sort of sociopolitical maze—being deprived of a citizenship, a national identity, and the protection of a state within the wide international community. It is quite baffling that the Palestinians were left without a state of their own in an era in human history when nationalism reached its peak and political entities were being established in the formerly colonized parts of Africa, Asia, and Latin America.

On 6 June 1967, Israel occupied the West Bank and Gaza Strip, Egyptian Sinai and the Syrian Golan Heights. This event heralded the end of Arab unity and was a clear sign of the inability of the Arab countries to liberate Palestine. More important, it was an obvious indicator to the Palestinians that the liberation of their country had become incumbent upon them.

As a result of the 1967 war, all Palestine was now under Israeli rule. Ironically, Palestinians were now able to get in contact with their families and relatives in the West Bank, Gaza Strip, and in the Palestinian territories occupied in 1948. Following the war, Israel did not have a clear policy concerning the newly occupied territories. So the first five years of occupation were characterized by open Israeli job markets, which in fact had a rather positive effect on the life of the Palestinians.

Following that honeymoon period, the Israeli occupation began confiscating lands and building settlements. Israel governed the occupied territories by direct military rule, whose main interest was focused on security for the Israeli army and settlers, with total disregard to the needs of the Palestinian inhabitants. Services in the occupied territories were administered by military officers: so there was an officer for health, another for education, a third for agriculture, a fourth for labor, and so on. As a result, services worsened and the infrastructure deteriorated desperately, even though the inhabitants were paying full taxes.

In 1976 Israel conducted municipal elections, hoping to bring about a local Palestinian leadership that would accept the policies and practices of the occupation authorities. Contrary to the expectations of Yitzhak Rabin, then Israeli prime minister, the National Front won eighteen out of twenty-four municipal councils; the other councils went to the traditional conservative leaders. In fact, Rabin had expected the National Front would boycott the elections, as it had done in the elections for the mayoralty of Jerusalem. The aim of the Jerusalem elections at that time was to give legitimacy to the annexation of the city by Israel, and it was hoped that the candidates who were collaborating with Israel would win.

independent young leadership was emerging, trying to take care of the essential needs of the population as part of the struggle against IDF forces and collaborators with Israel. The uprising in Gaza spread to include the Palestinians in Judea and Samaria, who were also at boiling point (in the Balata refugee camp next to Nablus, for example, a rebellion was under way even before the intifada began).

The intifada came as a surprise to Israel, Jordan, and even the PLO. Each side, in its own manner, crafted a response to this new phenomenon. The IDF was forced to overhaul its policies and the conduct of its soldiers in the occupied territories. The army was not suitably equipped to deal with serious mass protests involving stones and Molotov cocktails thrown at soldiers. The Palestinians (including teenagers and children) showed great courage and attacked soldiers on the street, in their armored vehicles and at their military outposts. The surprise was so great that an appropriate response to the Palestinians' irregular methods of warfare was not found. Because they were reluctant to use force against men, women, and children who fought only with stones, the soldiers found themselves in dangerous situations: surrounded, under attack, and wounded, sometimes totally helpless.

Initially, the IDF adopted a military policy that directed its soldiers to batter the demonstrators with all possible force. The army issued clubs to the troops, which they used as weapons of deterrence and punishment. This policy led to terribly violent scenarios fueled by anger and frustration, and there were many instances of severe injury to Palestinians, including broken bones: "In many cases, junior officers joined their soldiers in beating people unnecessarily. It was unclear whom it was permissible to hit, and when, and where, and for what reasons. [. . .] Many reports from the field stated that people— sometimes entire families—were being beaten in their own homes, without cause."[2] Later, the IDF issued restrictions on the use of violence, although around the world and even in Israel there was trenchant criticism of the policy of violent force used by IDF soldiers toward the Palestinians.

A few days after the outbreak of the intifada, the National Committee

Palestinians throwing stones at Israeli forces

The results of the 1976 municipal elections compelled Israel to avoid a repetition of this experiment, and so started aggressions against the elected leaders including expulsion and even assassination. Soon after, the Israeli occupation formed a civil administration and attempted to create a substitute Palestinian leadership—the pro-Israeli Village League Plan, which failed because of little base support. In the meantime, settlement construction and expansion took a different pace, and oppression of the Palestinians never stopped or eased up. The economic situation deteriorated and there was great unemployment among graduates of local Palestinian universities, all of which had been established under Israeli rule.

When the occupation's calculations failed, it invaded Lebanon in the summer of 1982 to strike the Palestinian Liberation Organization. Israeli forces entered Beirut, destroyed the power of the PLO, and dispersed its leadership. Arabic and international neglect of the Palestinian question reached its peak. In the occupied territories, conditions deteriorated to unprecedented levels. Suppression and negligence of the needs of the Palestinian people by the occupation also reached its highest levels. The Palestinians started the intifada in 1987, a peaceful, grassroots uprising, which came about as the only appropriate reaction to twenty years of oppressive Israeli occupation.

THE LAST MONTHS OF 1987

Following the deterioration of conditions in the West Bank and Gaza Strip, there was an increase in acts of violence during the last months of 1987, such as hurling Molotov cocktails, knife stabbings, setting tires on fire, and strikes by school and university students. Gaza had become a heavy burden for Israeli security merely because of the killing of several Israelis by Palestinian resistance men and the success of individual acts of heroism in hunting down important Israeli symbols, such as the killing of the leader of the military police in August 1987.

In early October and under mysterious circumstances, Israeli forces fired at a car, killing all three Palestinian passengers. In the same month, a bloody fight took place in the Gaza Strip between Israeli forces and a group of the Islamic Jihad Movement, which led to the deaths of all members of the IJM and Victor Rajwan, member of the Shin Beth (Israeli intelligence). Popular resentment continued to mount and demonstrations broke out in the Gaza Strip. Increasingly, new and creative resistance operations were seen

of the Heads of Arab Local Councils in Israel decided to declare a one-day general strike by Arab Israelis in solidarity with the Palestinian residents of the territories and the uprising. The strike degenerated in some places into actual violence (in Jaffa, Lod, Nazareth, and Wadi Ara). Stones and Molotov cocktails were thrown and roads were blockaded. This was the first time that Arabs living within Israel identified a common cause with Palestinians in the territories and joined them in demonstrating against Israel. It was the beginning of a joint struggle by both Palestinian populations against Israeli rule in the territories, and in favor of the establishment of a Palestinian state. From the outset, the intifada took the form of a civil rebellion against a regime of occupation: "The rebellion rose from below: in the alleys of the refugee camps, among Palestinian youth, in university and high school classrooms, among the laborers going out to work in Israel, among those released from Israeli jails, among the masses of the people. [. . .] This rebellion had an utterly revolutionary character. The rebellion was unplanned, and it erupted suddenly, like a volcano."[3]

REASONS FOR THE INTIFADA

Initially, the occupation beginning in 1967 improved things for Palestinians from several standpoints: new work options opened up, the standard of living rose, and there was a sense of economic progress. As time went by, however, ill feeling increased among Palestinians in the territories. This was evident in three spheres:

The Personal Aspect: Palestinians experienced humiliation at every point of meeting with Israelis: at checkpoints, in the attitudes toward Palestinian workers in their workplaces, in seeking permits for everything imaginable, when their cars were searched, when their homes were searched. Encounters with soldiers only emphasized their status as a conquered people, perceived as inferior, subject to arbitrary decisions and policies on the part of Israelis, and thwarted in their attempts to progress economically, professionally, and personally.

The Palestinian Leadership: The Palestinians in Judea and Samaria (the West Bank) and Gaza learned that their leaders living outside those territories were promulgating policies that decided their fate, while lacking awareness of their suffering, inadequately considering their needs, and perhaps achieving nothing whatever. The Lebanon war of 1982, which severely

everywhere. The glider operation, for instance, which was carried out by Khaled Aker at the end of November against an Israeli base in the north of Israel, led to the death of a number of Israeli soldiers, and generated a feeling of pride and confidence among Palestinians everywhere.

On 8 December 1987, just one day before the eruption of the intifada, an Israeli truck driver in Gaza deliberately hit an Arab car, killing several of its passengers and seriously wounding the others. The next day, over 6,000 people from Jabalia refugee camp, from which three of the people killed in the truck accident had come, participated in the funeral procession. The procession turned into a huge demonstration. As usual, the Israeli military forces met the demonstrators with live ammunition, tear-gas bombs, beating, and arrest. Scores of demonstrators were injured and one was killed; Hatem Al-Seesi was the first martyr of the intifada. When news of this incident leaked out, sweeping demonstrations erupted all over the West Bank and Gaza Strip.

SPONTANEITY OF THE INTIFADA

The intifada erupted spontaneously and without any central organization or interference from the Palestinian Liberation Organization. It had no preset plans, though there was a widespread desire among all the Palestinians to overthrow Israeli rule in the territories occupied in 1967. Very soon, however, the intifada had a national command representing the popular and revolutionary committees in all cities, villages, and camps. This leadership comprised the four major factions of the PLO: Fatah, the Popular Front, the Democratic Front, and the Communist Party. National popular committees were also set up in villages, cities, and camps to organize resistance actions. These committees were accountable to the Unified National Command of the Intifada.

The Palestinians were totally convinced that the road of continued struggle was the only means available to them

Palestinians demonstrating against Israeli occupation in the 1987 intifada

weakened Arafat's power within the PLO, provided an opportunity to those who had opposed his policies to propose a different path. Young Palestinians who emerged at that time offered a new agenda for the region via paths that had not been pursued: through negotiation and compromise with Israel.

The National Perspective: Palestinians felt the ground giving way underfoot. Israel took control of the water resources in Judea and Samaria and channeled most of the water to the settlements. Looking to establish new settlements, Israel also seized a great deal of Palestinian land, including privately owned land. Aiming to ensure that Jerusalem would remain its capital and a united city, Israel annexed most parts of East Jerusalem and the Old City and constructed a ring of new Jewish neighborhoods around the edges of the city. Governance of Judea, Samaria, and Gaza was given to a civil administration that controlled appointments of government-paid jobs (such as teachers), the school curriculum, the newspapers, the economy, taxation, and the bureaucracy in general. The threatening presence of the Israeli security services greatly contributed to the feelings of fear, defeat, and outrage that accumulated under the surface, until the spontaneous uprising gave vent to them.

THE DEVELOPMENT OF THE INTIFADA

When the intifada began to spread and make an impact, various interested parties in Palestinian society promptly began trying to take control of its momentum and direct it to serve their own ends. The youthful local leadership won out initially, captaining a "civil rebellion" that sought to arrive at a dialogue with Israel over a solution based on compromise between the two peoples. The point of departure for such a struggle is that guns are not used and its principles are: civil disobedience (as in the nonpayment of taxes), circumventing the imposed institutions of governance via the establishment of autonomous institutions instead (e.g., educational institutions), fostering economic independence (such as discouraging the purchase of imported goods), and taking control of the street (closing shops, holding demonstrations). This was the strategy initially adopted by Palestinians in the territories.

They set up hundreds of "people's committees," encompassing thousands of activists, who worked to help those in need and brought basic supplies to the sealed refugee camps, set up committees to care for the wounded, provided training in first aid, and conducted both formal and informal

to end Israeli occupation, to establish their independent state, and to achieve their right to self-determination. The Palestinians were looking forward to the time when their "right to return" would become a reality; i.e., when all Palestinian refugees living in the Arab world would return to their lands and homes and property in Palestine.

The continuous struggle of the intifada yielded a strong political position for the Palestinians and the Palestine Liberation Organization. The intifada was considered an attrition war against the occupation. As such the intifada resulted in the loss of Israeli lives and damage to the Israeli economy, in addition to the negative effect on the morale of the Israelis. More significant, the intifada put the Palestinian question on the agenda of the United Nations as an

Scenes from the Palestinian 1987 intifada: (top) a small boy throwing stones at an Israeli tank in the Gaza Strip; (botton) Palestinians youths throwing stones at Israeli occupation military jeeps

issue to be resolved urgently. Equally important, the intifada reinforced the position of the Palestine Liberation Organization as a symbol of struggle and as the representative of the Palestinian people after it had been displaced and weakened by the Israeli invasion of Lebanon in 1982.

education, and created an alternative judicial system. Committee activists
encouraged farmers to recommence farming, and thousands of students
and other young adults were sent to help them. Merchants organized collective strikes and were able to prevent the Israeli army from forcibly opening
Palestinian shops. Israeli products were boycotted, workers employed in Israel
and in the settlements periodically went out on strike, and clerks at the civil
administration quit their jobs. To cope with the harsh living conditions that
resulted from the civil revolt, the people were taught to grow their own food
(by planting vegetables, raising pigeons and rabbits, etc.).

Over time, the people's committees were taken over by PLO representatives led by Fatah. This changed the way the committees functioned,
transforming them into a violent, authoritarian force, employed not only
against the Israeli occupation but also against collaborators and others on the
Palestinian street. Activists began using firearms in battling with soldiers and
settlers, and were mercilessly suppressed by Israel. Both sides suffered many
casualties and were engrossed in a war of attrition with no winners.

RESULTS OF THE INTIFADA

The intifada had different consequences for the Palestinians than it did for
the Israelis, but there was also a joint result.

THE PALESTINIANS IN JUDEA, SAMARIA, AND GAZA

- The intifada caused all strata of society to come together in joint
  action, which left a changed social fabric in its wake. Rural people,
  women and children, workers, youth, educated people, merchants,
  and elite families all lent their efforts to the common struggle,
  which contributed to solidarity and to Palestinian national
  cohesion.

- The trend toward a political resolution of the conflict "went
  public."

- Jordan decided to cut itself off from the Palestinians and from
  Judea and Samaria, and for the first time the Palestinians became a
  people responsible for their own destiny. This was an acknowledgment on King Hussein's part that the Palestinians were a people

During the years of the intifada (1987–1992), the Israeli army killed around 2,000 Palestinians, imprisoned about 110,000, and demolished around 500 Palestinian houses. On the other hand, the Palestinians killed around 900 collaborators, 80 Israeli soldiers, and 180 Israeli civilians. The statistics below show the severity of the Israeli reaction to the intifada in its first two years.

STATISTICS OF THE FIRST TWO YEARS OF THE INTIFADA (9 DEC. 1987–9 DEC. 1989) DUE TO ISRAELI MILITARY PRACTICES AGAINST PALESTINIANS

1. Killed

Men	890
Children	143
Women	116
Prisoners	16
TOTAL	1,165

4. Deported

Already deported	58
Mothers and children	88
TOTAL	146

2. Disabled

Full or partial paralysis	131
Injury-related	1,800
Total or partial loss of sight	150
TOTAL	2,081

5. Arrested & Detained

Arrested	49,093
Administrative detention	4,908
Detained	6,313
TOTAL	60,314

3. Wounded & Hospitalized

Live metal bullets	12,000
Rubber bullets	40,564
TOTAL	62,564

6. Property

Demolished houses	829
Closed houses	149
Destroyed garages, farms, etc.	77
Supporting walls	236
TOTAL	1,291

in their own right, responsible for their own fate, and capable of sovereignty.

- The local leadership, which attained power and influence vis-à-vis the PLO, whose leadership mostly lived outside the region, demanded Arafat come up with a practical political plan to resolve the conflict.

- The intifada hastened the Palestinian National Council's Declaration of Independence for Palestine (in November 1988, in Algiers), which included recognition of UN Resolution 242 and the existence of two states for two peoples.

THE ISRAELIS

- The intifada, which had come as a complete surprise, created bewilderment in Israeli society and damaged the sense of superiority many Israelis had harbored toward the Palestinians.

- The violent outbursts among Arab citizens of Israel shocked and frightened the Jewish public. The suspicion and the rift introduced by the intifada became more severe as time passed.

- The intifada stimulated a trenchant debate in Israeli society about what kind of combat is right and ethical. For many Israeli soldiers, fighting a civilian population was difficult from a moral standpoint and doubts about the justice of what Israel was doing, doubts that had already surfaced during the Lebanon war, were reinforced and began having an impact within the ranks of the military.

- As debate continued concerning what might be a proper solution, the rift widened between proponents of territorial compromise on the one hand, and those of Greater Israel on the other, who were not prepared to concede even "a single inch" of land:

The Intifada thoroughly shook up Israeli society. [. . .] What the Arab armies had not succeeded in doing during years of warfare with their airplanes and missiles, the Palestinians in the territories did with rocks, knives and Molotov cocktail. [. . .] Israeli society was frustrated and disturbed, because people felt that Israel was confronting a situation that had no solution using methods tried thus far.[4]

THE INTIFADA IN PALESTINIAN FOLK SONGS

The demands of the intifada were reflected in Palestinian folk songs:

The demand for self-determination
The right of return and the state
Through the Intifada we go
To the International conference

The intifada did not resort to military power. In fact, the militarization of the intifada was rejected by the entire popular forces. This is portrayed by the following folk song:

Demonstrations and confrontation
Graffiti writing and hanging flags
The Intifada is moving forward
It is continuing and getting stronger

The intifada clearly condemned the position of the United States and its bias to Israel. According to one folk song:

To the American veto, the Zionist says:
"You are my partner!"
O my comrade sing with me
No for imperialism.

Although the intifada was totally nonviolent, Israel responded with very cruel oppressive measures, including bone breaking, expulsion, and imprisonment without charge or trial.

The intifada encompassed all sectors and classes of Palestinian society: old and young, men and women, boys and girls, rich and poor. Each and every one of them attempted to express his/her rejection of the occupation and its oppressive and brutal practices. All Palestinians took part in demonstrations, strikes, and sit-ins, and they only used stones in their confrontation with one of the most powerful military institutions in the region, which wanted to crush these unarmed people.

Israel was uncertain about how to deal with the intifada yet insisted

Demonstration of "Women in Black"—one of the protest movements founded following the intifada

CONCLUSION: ISRAEL AND THE PALESTINIANS

The argument over what Israel's policy should be vis-à-vis the occupied territories thenceforth became much more strident. Israeli society understood—though late—that despite its best intentions and its resolve to maintain humanistic standards of conduct in the occupied territories, Israel had become a people of conquest, with all that implied. Ruling over the Palestinians engendered arrogance and promoted indifference to the suffering of the other and to the belligerent, violent attitude that had penetrated the heart of Israeli society. Despite protest movements that organized demonstrations against the occupation and demanded a peaceful compromise, the settlements grew and multiplied throughout the occupied territories. The violence and terror continued to cause many casualties on both sides, while many people seemed to forget that there could be no resolution of this conflict using force, but rather what was needed was negotiation.

on crushing it instead of giving it due thoughtful consideration. The Israelis chose to overlook the persistence of the Palestinians to fight against the occupation, and their displacement, dispersion, and dispossession.

DECLARATION OF INDEPENDENCE (15 NOVEMBER 1988)

The intifada encouraged the PLO to declare the independence of Palestine on 15 November. The declaration came to emphasize the right of the Palestinians to establish their own independent state with Jerusalem as their capital. The following are excerpts from the document of independence:

> The State of Palestine is the state of Palestinians wherever they may be. The state is for them to enjoy in it their collective national and cultural identity, theirs to pursue in it a complete equality of rights. In it will be safeguarded their political and religious convictions and their human dignity by means of a parliamentary democratic system of governance, itself based on freedom of expression and the freedom to form parties.
>
> The rights of minorities will duly be respected by the majority, as minorities must abide by decisions of the majority. Governance will be based on principles of social justice, equality and non-discrimination in public rights of men or women, on grounds of race, religion, color or sex, under the aegis of a constitution which ensures the rule of law and an independent judiciary. Thus shall these principles allow no departure from Palestine's age-old spiritual and civilizational heritage of tolerance and religious co-existence.
>
> The State of Palestine is an Arab state, an integral and indivisible part of the Arab nation, at one with that nation in heritage and civilization, with it also in its aspiration for liberation, progress, democracy and unity. The State of Palestine affirms its obligation to abide by the Charter of the League of Arab States, whereby the coordination of the Arab states with each other shall be strengthened. It calls upon Arab compatriots to consolidate and enhance the emergence in reality of our state, to mobilize potential, and to intensify efforts whose goal is to end Israeli occupation.

PALESTINIAN TEXT / النص الفلسطيني

The intifada was a turning point in the relations between Israel and the Palestinian people. For the first time, the two peoples stood face-to-face as partners in the necessity to resolve the conflict between them. This accelerated the opening of channels of dialogue between the two peoples, which eventually led to the signing of the Oslo Accords.

POETRY OF THE INTIFADA

The following poem is among many written to celebrate and commemorate the intifada. The poem was written by Muhammad Al-Shahhat and is entitled "Rise Up: The Stone Has Risen Up":

Here are the children coming out of the depths of the earth
Carrying in their hands
The song of blood and stones
O! Our blood, our blood
Repeat the sound of our song
And write in the chronicles of history
About the generation of stone-throwers
It is the generation which brought good tidings
It is the generation which brought good tidings.

Abdo Muhammad Sultan wrote a poem titled "The Return of Hope":

O Arabs! Hope has come into view
Get over your slackness and laziness
And give up your tardiness and disagreement
Arguments have tired us out!
O Arabs! Get up from heedlessness—
In Palestine a momentous event is stirring up
The revolution of free men has been kindled
Who will lend a hand to see it through?
O Martyr of righteousness! Your death was not in vain
The struggle lives on and will forever continue.
You have warded off injustice until it cleared away
You never let despair or weariness get to you.
The stones have made a clatter
And to Palestine they have brought back hope
They wrote down the glories of a valiant people
O, How many disasters this people has met and bore!

CONCLUSION

The intifada passed through three different phases, which coincided with some very critical regional events. The first phase, which started in December 1987 and continued through the first Gulf War in 1991, was characterized by an effective unity and recognition of the right of Palestinians to self-determination. During this phase the Palestinians were able to emphasize their right of existence and their right to fight against Israeli military occupation. In this phase the Palestinians also gained much international support.

The second phase started with the end of the first Gulf War until the Oslo Accords. At this time the intifada had started to wither away because of the Israeli suppression, and because of the seclusion policy imposed on the Palestinians and the damage inflicted on the Palestinian economy. This phase was marked by a change in the center of power from ordinary people who had started the intifada to the higher Palestinian leadership, who were involved in the Arab-Israeli peace process initiated by the United States, first in the Madrid conference and later in the bilateral agreements in Washington. All Palestinians were on the lookout for what the peace process might bring about.

The third phase started with the signing of the Oslo Accords on 13 September 1993. This agreement marked the end of the intifada, even though it was always likely to erupt again.

9

THE 1990S

⟿

**BROKEN DREAMS—ATTEMPTS AT PEACE AND
THE REALITY OF WAR AT THE TURN OF THE MILLENNIUM**

After many years of terror, struggle, and bloodshed between Israel and the Palestinian people, Yasser Arafat, chairman of the Palestinian Authority, and Israeli prime minister Yitzhak Rabin signed the Oslo Accords in a ceremony on the White House lawn on September 13, 1993. The ceremony, both impressive and moving, was sponsored and supported by U.S. President Bill Clinton. The signing was accompanied by an historic handshake, imbued with hope and not a little trepidation, between the two former enemies. The event was a surprising breakthrough in the complex, bloodstained relationship between these two people fighting over the same homeland. The agreement, based on mutual recognition and collaboration for the sake of peace, signaled the decision to embark on the path of peace, dialogue, and compromise, as opposed to war and extremism. It understandably aroused expectations for a future of peace and normalization in the Middle East. During the signing ceremony, the Israeli prime minister said:

▼

9

REACHING FOR A SETTLEMENT:
AGREEMENTS TOWARD THE UNKNOWN

During the last decade of the last century, the idea of establishing a Palestinian state became more acceptable at the Palestinian and international level. The clearest manifestation of this was represented by the Palestinian National Council meeting held in Algiers on 15 November 1988. At that meeting, the PLO accepted the idea of establishing a Palestinian state alongside Israel on the basis of UN Resolutions 242 and 338.[1] According to observers, "The emergence of a Palestinian state in the occupied areas is inevitable, regardless of how long the process will take or how painful and complicated it will be." The beginning of the negotiations between the Palestinians and the Israelis in Madrid in November 1991, followed by the Oslo Accords in September 1993, and Oslo Accords II in September 1995, showed that the Palestinians were ready to go so far toward the establishment of their state through temporary measures. This is evidenced by their acceptance of the Gaza-Jericho project as phase one, on the condition that this would result in the complete withdrawal of the Israeli army from the occupied territories, guarantee their right to self-determination, and the building of their state led by a national

We have come from Jerusalem, the Israeli people's eternal capital, from an anguished and grieving land [. . .] We have come to try and put an end to the hostilities, so that our children, our children's children, will no longer experience the painful cost of war, violence and terror [. . .] We are destined to live together on the same soil, in the same land. We, the soldiers who have returned from battle stained with blood, we who have seen our relatives and friends killed before our eyes [. . .] we who have fought against you, the Palestinians, say to you today in a loud and a clear voice: Enough of blood and tears. Enough. We have no desire for revenge. We harbor no hatred towards you. We, like you, are people who want to build a home, to plant a tree, to love, to live side by side with you in dignity, in empathy, as human beings, as free men. We are today giving peace a chance, and saying again to you: Enough. No more. Let us pray that a day will come when we all will say: Farewell to the arms.

What occurrences, processes, and events paved the way for the Oslo Accords, and what enabled the surprising turnabout in the relations between the two peoples? These issues are the focus of the first part of this chapter.

EVENTS THAT PRECEDED THE SIGNING OF THE OSLO ACCORDS

During the last decade of the twentieth century, many powerful political processes took place that led to the formulation of a new "world order" that was different from the model that had existed for the past fifty years. In the summer of 1991, the Soviet Union, once a world superpower, collapsed. This dramatic turn of events, occurring as an astounded world looked on, expedited the disintegration of the Eastern European communist bloc and marked the end of the Cold War. The collapse of the Soviet Union left the United States as the lone superpower and ultimately presented capitalism and the free-market states as the prevalent way of life. The

The signing of the "Oslo Accords" in Washington

authority in the West Bank and Gaza Strip, and also to the recognition that the Palestinian people form a political entity whose collective existence ensures its right to express itself politically as a state."[2]

The document that President Arafat sent to Israel's prime minister Yitzhak Rabin on 9 September 1993 included the PLO's recognition of Israel's right to live in security and peace. Furthermore, "The PLO commits itself to the peace process in the Middle East and to a peaceful solution to the conflict between the two sides. The PLO affirms that items in the Palestinian Charter that are not in line with the commitments mentioned in this letter are invalid." This was an official Palestinian recognition that their issue would be solved through negotiations, and if these negotiations failed, new negotiations would start.[3]

The Oslo Accords signed in 1993 between the PLO and Israel was a declaration of principles, phased interim agreement that was supposed to expire in no more than five years and lead to the final settlement for the conflict on the basis of Resolutions 242 and 338 as stipulated in the agreement. Israel exploited the accords to create new frightening realities on the ground. It confiscated large areas of Palestinian land to expand existing settlements and to build new ones at the expense of the Palestinians' rights to the land, water, and air. Israel also managed to divide the land into isolated enclaves, surrounded by detour routes separating Palestinians from one another, from their land, and from their source of living.[4]

POSITIONS IN THE PALESTINIAN POLITICAL ARENA

In response to the new political developments, two positions appeared in the Palestinian arena: the position of the PLO leadership and that of the opposition.

POSITION OF PLO LEADERSHIP

Since the leadership of the PLO agreed to participate in the peace process, discussion among the Palestinians has centered on the role of armed struggle in achieving the Palestinian national goals. The discussion intensified further after the Likud under the leadership of Binyamin Netanyahu assumed office in 1996, the faltering negotiations, and the violent clashes between the Palestinian security forces and the Palestinian masses. Some Palestinians called for repeating the uprising of September 1996 (Al-Nafaq uprising).

status and the power that now fell to the United States both encouraged and challenged it to assume an active role in international leadership. The dissolution of the communist bloc and the collapse of the Soviet Union also had an effect on events in the Middle East. Its Arab protectorates lost their main source of political support and their subsidized arms supply. Their rulers began seeking alternatives, and thus sought a closer relationship with the United States, whose international status and prestige continued to grow. This power was validated by the Gulf War.

GULF WAR (JANUARY 17, 1991–FEBRUARY 28, 1991)

The invasion of Kuwait by Saddam Hussein, ruler of Iraq, enraged much of the world. The UN secretary general's demand that Saddam Hussein immediately withdraw from Kuwait received no response. The countdown to war began with United Nations backing and United States approval, and with an American commitment of half a million soldiers. President George H. W. Bush put together an international coalition, joined by British, French, and Arab forces (Egypt, Syria, Saudi Arabia, and the Gulf states). This was a rare political accomplishment to assemble, on one united front, Western superpowers that would fight against Iraq together with Arab countries that opposed Saddam's move. The Gulf War (Operation Desert Storm) was a technological and telecommunications war. The television networks aired worldwide broadcasts of amazing maneuvers by advanced aircraft and "smart" long-range missiles that hit their targets with the utmost precision. They did not broadcast the killing, bloodshed, and human horror that took place in Iraq; these scenes were aired almost exclusively on Iraqi television.

During the war, Saddam Hussein fired "Scud" missiles (suspected to be carrying chemical or biological warheads) at Israel in an attempt to drag it into the war and break up the coalition. In keeping with the United States' request, and despite public pressure on Prime Minister Yitzak Shamir, Israel exercised restraint. With the liberation of Kuwait, the UN imposed severe restrictions against Iraq and demanded that it destroy the chemical and biological weapons of mass destruction in its possession.

The United States ended the war determined to take advantage of its influence and prestige to find an overall solution to the Israeli-Arab conflict and to halt the nuclear build-up in Iran and Iraq. These radical international processes also had a significant effect on the situation in Israel. The collapse of the Soviet Union and the downfall of the bloc system robbed Israel of its

They based their argument on what appeared to be a Palestinian consensus that the events of 1996 played a direct role in activating the negotiations and the role of the American sponsor, forcing Netanyahu to meet with Arafat, and obliging the Likud to stop stalling and evading the implementation of the agreements signed between the two sides.

There were doubts whether the PLO and the Palestinian Authority could successfully combine the political and diplomatic work it was undertaking in the framework of the peace process with military work in the same way as the Algerians did under the leadership of the Liberation Front during their peace negotiations with the French in Evian or the Vietnamese with the Americans. Would it be possible for the Palestinian Authority to reconcile its orientation toward a peaceful settlement with its commitment to renounce violence and fight terrorism?

> The five-year experience of negotiations between Palestine and Jordan and Israel has indicated that the political and diplomatic path was fruitful and productive. Results of the negotiations have affirmed that, under the current regional and international circumstances, the Palestinians can extract many of their rights in peaceful ways, including liberating large sectors of the Palestinian people from occupation, and freeing large areas of the land, in addition to taking several steps forward towards the formulation of a Palestinian entity and building the future state.[5]

The PLO went to Madrid and Oslo with the aim to reach, through negotiations, acceptable solutions to the Israeli-Palestinian conflict with its full recognition that participation in this process is based on conditions that contravene its insistence to resume armed struggle. The PLO agreed to these conditions and offered written assurances to that effect. The letters exchanged between Arafat and Rabin after Oslo and all the agreements signed by them included clear commitments to abandon violence and fight terrorism. Later, the PLO annuled all items in the Palestinian National Charter that referred to armed force as the main form of struggle for the Palestinian people to achieve its national goals.[6]

POSITION OF THE PALESTINIAN OPPOSITION

The Palestinian opposition viewed the signing of the Oslo Accords as a violation of the decisions of the twentieth session of the Palestinian National

special status as an essential strategic U.S. ally. At the same time, Israel established formal, and in some cases friendly, ties with the governments of former communist bloc countries and the Commonwealth of Independent States (CIS) Some one million new immigrants arrived in Israel during this period (mainly from the Soviet Union, but also from Ethiopia), and had a positive influence on life in Israel on many levels, including the Israeli-Arab power balance. In the Arab world, some people understood that time was not necessarily on their side. Israeli public opinion also vacillated over the years, particularly since the unexpected outbreak of the intifada in 1987, which took a heavy toll in human lives. Many Israelis were unable to ignore what was happening in the occupied territories; they understood that there was a price to retaining control of the territories, because Israeli soldiers, albeit well-nigh invincible in battle, were rendered helpless when confronted by women and children; and because the intifada had no military solution, it was necessary to find a way to end the conflict at the negotiating table. The changes in the international and Middle Eastern arena (acceptance of the principle of dividing the land and adoption of UN resolutions 242 and 338 by the PLO) had a strong influence on a large sector of the war-weary Israeli public, which refused to pay the price of occupation and strove to conduct "normal" lives.

The United States government, which embarked on the Gulf War fully conscious that world peace involved maintaining stability in the Middle East and on preventing the use of weapons of mass destruction, understood that its first priority was to achieve a political order acceptable to all sides. Adding to the pressure exerted by the United States government on Prime Minister Shamir was mounting public pressure at home, without which it is difficult to understand Shamir's agreement to attend the Madrid Peace Conference.

MADRID PEACE CONFERENCE—THE MIDDLE EAST ISSUE ON THE INTERNATIONAL AGENDA

The Madrid Conference, which convened in October 1991, saw for the first time the international community rallying around the United States in a concerted effort to resolve the Arab-Israeli conflict. With great determination and persistence, U.S. secretary of state James Baker managed to formulate a framework and system of rules that were accepted by all the parties. The conference was conducted along two tracks: (1) the bilateral track between Israel, Syria, Lebanon, and the joint Jordanian-Palestinian delegation focused on

Council held on 28 September 1991, which set the bases and premises for any peace efforts.[7] These included:

a. assuring the right to self-determination;

b. the complete withdrawal of the Israeli army from the Arab and Palestinian territories occupied in 1967;

c. solving the refugee problem in accordance with UN resolution 194;

d. the necessity for any temporary arrangements to include the right of the Palestinian people to maintain its sovereignty of its land, water, natural resources, and all political and economic affairs;

e. providing international protection to the Palestinian people prior to exercising its right to self-determination; and

f. securing guarantees for the removal of the present illegal settlements.

The position also believes that all the agreements signed between Israel and the Palestinians, including the Oslo Accords (1993)[8] and the Cairo Agreement (1994),[9] have led to more partitioning of the Palestinian issue and to the dissipation of the refugee problem. Contrary to UN Resolutions 194 and 237, the peace agreements turned the refugee problem into an Arab-Israeli issue that could be handled within the multilateral negotiations. For instance, the issue of the Palestinians displaced in 1967 would be relegated to a quartet committee (Israeli, Egyptian, Jordanian, and Palestinian). Unlike UN Resolutions 194 and 237, which made the return of the refugees immediate and unconditional, the new peace agreements gave Israel the right to look into each individual problem separately.

The opposition also believes that Israel signed the peace agreements for the specific purpose of breaking the first intifada, especially as the Israeli leadership had come to the conclusion that the intifada could not be stopped by military measures. Israel had in fact tried all methods of suppression against the Palestinians, including killing, breaking bones, arrest, and demolishing homes. Despite Israel's use of its huge military machine—warplanes, tanks, artillery, and live and rubber bullets—the intifada still persisted.[10]

arrangements for peace; (2) the multilateral track, attended by Saudi Arabia and Morocco, where questions affecting the entire Middle East were considered, such as water shortages, environmental quality, economics, and so forth.

The conference, which opened with an impressive ceremony at the Royal Palace in Madrid, ultimately accomplished nothing of import. There was no progress on any of the peace objectives concerning Syria, Lebanon, and Jordan. No agreements were signed. Its significance lay in creating an expectation for peace and granting the Palestinians the status of necessary partners in the peace process. The nine months and five rounds of joint talks in Washington that followed the conference also failed to achieve any real progress. The United States government, as well as broad segments of Israeli society, expressed outright criticism of Prime Minister Shamir, who confessed at the end of his term that if it had depended on him, he would have dragged out the talks for an additional ten years.

The Madrid Conference was the first attempt to implement an international and regional policy that had been formulated following the processes of change described above. This was an opportune moment in which the goals and interests of many forces converged in order to solve the intractable problems of the Middle East. As it turned out, however, the groundwork had not yet been laid, and time was still needed for a breakthrough.

The victory of Yitzhak Rabin, chairman of the Labor Party, in the June 1992 elections aroused great expectations among the Israeli population, both in the economic-social realm and the diplomatic-security arena, and sparked hope for a renewal of the peace process and progress toward a solution. The Rabin government set itself the goal of "changing national priorities." Large budgets were channeled to the educational system, closing gaps between the Jewish and Arab-Israeli sectors, and to absorbing the large wave of immigration from the Soviet Union. Rabin attributed utmost importance to obtaining 10 billion dollars worth of U.S. guarantees for infrastructure and economic development. However, his top priority was to renew the peace process and revitalize relations with the United States, which had deteriorated. Rabin did not like the "framework" created in Madrid, preferring a gradual approach during which it would be possible to improve Israel's domestic situation together with its regional and international status.

The United States government, on the other hand, believed that Iran and Iraq, which were believed to be arming themselves with weapons of mass

REGIONAL AND INTERNATIONAL CIRCUMSTANCES AND ELEMENTS

THE INTERNATIONAL LEVEL

Despite the substantial achievements of the intifada on the ground, the proper circumstances for adopting peace as a practical political option by all parties concerned were not yet obtainable. The socialist system and the Warsaw Pact collapsed, and the Soviet Union disintegrated in 1989 marking the end of the Cold War. And it was necessary for the first Bush administration to take a breather before it could absorb the international developments and establish new strategies and rules for what was later known as the new world order, led by the United States, now being the unipower in the world.

Palestinian-American relations were activated. George Shultz, then U.S. secretary of state, tested the possibility of setting the political process in motion. Yet nothing emerged except the declaration by the PLO of its preparedness, at the formal, practical, and theoretical levels, to accept a settlement of the conflict on the basis of UN Resolution 242. It was only the pressure exerted by the intifada that made Israel eventually recognize the existence of the Palestinian people and, later, the PLO, after a long history of denial and dismissal of the role of the PLO.[11]

THE ARAB LEVEL

On 2 August 1990, the second Gulf crisis started, and on 17 January 1991, the international war against Iraq broke out. This period witnessed the worst Arab disintegration to date; this became clearly evident in the participation of some Arab countries in the international coalition, both militarily and politically, against a fellow Arab country. This acted as a further catalyst for the disintegration of the Arab official system and resulted in the even wider expansion of the U.S. hegemony in the region. The war also resulted in a change in the U.S. strategy. Prior to the war, the United States utilized Israel to control the area. Now with its military bases and forces spread in the whole region, the United States could secure its own interests directly.

The Gulf War made the absence of any international power that could stand in the face of the United States quite evident. It was also clear now that the U.S. policy was able to force its allies to adopt the participatory approach only as much as its interests in the area allowed. The United States used its achievements in the war to enhance its hegemony even on its European allies.[12]

destruction, constituted the focal point of danger to regional and world stability, and therefore tried at (almost) all costs to distance Syria from the influence of both. This is the context for understanding why the United States
opted to focus on the Syrian track in the peace process. Rabin went along
with this trend, but beyond improving the atmosphere, no particular progress
was achieved in the talks with Syria. Syrian President Assad's insistence that
the principle of withdrawal from the Golan Heights be accepted as a precondition for negotiations stood in the way of any possible progress.

In parallel, Rabin continued operating along the Palestinian channel.
As a preliminary step, the government decided to stop establishing settlements in the West Bank, and indicated that it would agree to include the
component of withdrawal in a future agreement. In July 1992, the Arab foreign ministers convened in Damascus with the objective of coordinating their
position for the upcoming sixth round of talks in Washington. In the declaration released on 25 July, the term "peace agreement" was mentioned for
the first time. But aside from this, it negated most of Israel's peace policy and
demanded that Security Council agreements 242 and 338 be carried out in
full—according to the Arab interpretation, calling for the Palestinian right to
self-determination, the establishment of an independent state on their land,
and official inclusion of the PLO in the peace process. It also condemned the
illegal Israeli settlements and insisted on creating a process that would devise
a "general solution on all fronts and channels . . . while rejecting any attempt
to split up and to hold discussions with each side separately." This approach
set the tone for the unfruitful Washington talks, with the PLO blocking every
attempt to make progress that deviated from the declaration it had released,
and with Assad insisting on the principle of withdrawal as a condition for
negotiation.

Although the flames of the peace process began to flicker, Islamic extremist groups such as Hamas and the Islamic Jihad still perceived it as a
threat. They opposed peace with Israel on principle, and the Madrid process
in particular. They voiced criticism of and opposition to Yasser Arafat and believed that violence and terror against Israeli targets would undermine popular Israeli support for peace and lead to Israeli retaliation that would collapse
the process.

At the time, Hamas increased its terror activities. Rabin decided to
adopt extreme measures in an effort to stop its assault on the peace process.
In response to the kidnapping and murder of Israeli soldiers, and in order to

As soon as the war was about to come to an end, the United States started to reformulate its policies in the region in view of the new realities. As regards the peace process, there was a return to the UN resolutions relevant to the conflict. On 6 March 1991, George H. W. Bush, then U.S. president, announced his four-point policy:

1. The principle of land for peace;
2. Implementation of international legality on the basis of UN Resolutions 242 and 338;
3. The legitimate rights of the Palestinian people;
4. Security and peace for Israel.[13]

In September 1991, all the parties involved in the conflict were invited to Madrid after the shuttle diplomacy conducted by U.S. Secretary of State James Baker. The Palestinian side had to accept participation within a joint Jordanian-Palestinian delegation that represented the Palestinians of the West Bank and Gaza but not the PLO. The talks were sponsored by the United States and the Russian Federation. The role of sponsors was relative to their role and presence in the area and at the international level. In other words, the United States was the main sponsor while the Russian Federation enjoyed only a nominal role. In fact, the latter did not attempt to prove its presence at all during the peace process.

The form of the Palestinian participation indicated a retreat in the role of the PLO, which was punished for supporting Iraq during the second Gulf War. This was also indicative of the weak role of the intifada, which had lost momentum after four years, and following Israeli-American attempts to create an alternative leadership for the intifada. Under these unfavorable circumstances and for fear of being dismissed totally, the PLO had to accept the arrangements made prior to the peace conference.

However, the PLO worked diligently to alter the situation through supervising the Palestinian delegation and soon it was able to overcome all obstacles by signing the "Declaration of Principles" in Oslo on 20 August 1993. The United States accepted the agreement, and later sponsored its signing in Washington on 13 September 1993. The declaration was in line with an article that was included in the U.S. Letters of Assurances which stated that "All tracks are invited to achieve one final accord, but the Palestinian track

weaken the organization's infrastructure in the West Bank and Gaza Strip, he deported some 400 Hamas activists to Lebanon in a single night, an action that was fiercely criticized even among the Israeli public. The political attenuation of President Bush, who in the summer of 1992 was at the height of a failed election campaign, contributed to the deterioration of the peace process that had begun in Madrid.

United States president-elect Bill Clinton, who took office in the beginning of 1993, adopted the approach of his predecessor regarding Middle East policy: blocking Iran and Iraq in the east, and investing in Israeli-Arab peace in the west. He also hoped that his support for Israeli-Syrian and Israeli-Palestinian reconciliation would diminish the capability of Iran and other fundamentalist states to interfere with and undermine the peace process, and therefore favored focusing on the Syrian channel. This approach was based on the understanding that Rabin was prepared to offer significant concessions, and on the assumption that Assad wanted peace. Rabin again accepted the U.S. preference, without neglecting the Palestinian track. In effect, all of the attempts to reignite the peace process came to naught. American diplomacy failed on both the Syrian and Palestinian tracks. It seemed that relations were once again at a standstill—and then the Oslo option emerged.

THE OSLO ACCORDS

The Oslo talks formally began in May 1993, the day after the Knesset repealed the law prohibiting contact with the PLO. In practice, informal contacts with PLO representatives had begun much earlier; Deputy Foreign Minister Yossi Beilin had created a secret and informal channel of communications with the PLO through the upper echelons of the Norwegian government. An emissary from among Beilin's close associates had met with Ahmad Qureia (Abu Alaa), the PLO financial officer and close associate of Abu Mazen, on Beilin's behalf. The talks were conducted in complete secrecy; Beilin was in no hurry to report to Foreign Minister Shimon Peres, and Peres took his time reporting to Prime Minister Rabin. During that period, Rabin lost faith in the formal talks in Washington, and was seeking an indirect way to communicate with the PLO. When it came to his knowledge that talks were being conducted in Oslo, he gave them the "green light," and in May 1993 he appointed Uri Savir, director of the Foreign Ministry, to head the Israeli team, granting the talks a formal status. In early August, the parties reached a theoretical framework

will be divided into a transitional track and a final track, each lasting for five years."[14] The interim phase ended even before Israel could meet any of the obligations stated in the agreements, and without reaching a final solution to the conflict.

Despite all the obstacles, expectations, and tension involved in the process, we believe that the entire area entered into a stage of adjustment to peace as a viable option so that there was no turning back. Some people believed that all the obstacles, expectations, and tension were part and parcel of the pursuit of peace.

The escalation of Israeli violence against the Palestinian people contributed to the deterioration and stagnation of the peace process initiated in Madrid. For example, without any prior warning, Israel deported 413 Palestinians to Lebanon. While Israel tried to make progress on the Syrian track, the negotiations stumbled because the Syrian president Hafez Al-Assad insisted on the withdrawal of Israel from the Golan Heights, which were occupied in 1967, as a precondition for initiating any peace negotiations. Moreover, the attempts of Clinton, the newly elected American president who hoped to follow in the footsteps of his predecessor, George H. W. Bush, to make progress on both the Syrian and Palestinian tracks, failed miserably.

Consequently, Israeli diplomacy moved and opened secret channels with the leaders of the PLO.[15] In early August 1993, both sides laid a framework for the peace process by drafting an agreement which was officially signed on 13 September 1993. The draft agreement included the following points.

1. The two sides confirm the establishment of a Palestinian Self-Government Authority in the West Bank and the Gaza Strip, for a interim period not exceeding five years;

2. Permanent status negotiations will commence no later than the beginning of the third year of the interim period;

3. Israel will redeploy its forces in phases beginning from Gaza and then from cities and their surroundings in the West Bank; and

4. The issues of the Israeli settlements in the West Bank, Jerusalem, refugees, water, and sovereignty will be discussed in the final status negotiations.[16]

for an agreement (the Declaration of Principles), which detailed the stages of formulating a peace agreement between Israel and the Palestinians. The draft of the agreement emphasized the following points:

1. An independent Palestinian authority would be established in the West Bank and Gaza Strip for a five-year interim period.

2. At the end of the second year, negotiations would be held regarding a permanent agreement. Israeli armed forces would redeploy in a number of stages—first, a withdrawal from Gaza, followed by a withdrawal from the Palestinian cities in the West Bank, and ultimately, a series of additional redeployments.

3. No reference would be made during these talks to difficult questions such as: the future of the Israeli settlements in the West Bank, the question of Jerusalem, water rights, and the refugee problem. All these would be discussed in the final agreement negotiations.

On September 10, Israel and the PLO exchanged letters declaring mutual recognition: the State of Israel recognized the PLO as the representative of the Palestinian people, while the PLO recognized Israel's right to exist in peace and security, undertook to desist from terror and to change the articles in the Palestinian National Covenant calling for the destruction of the State of Israel.

Since Rabin had maintained secrecy and concealed the Oslo proceedings from even his closest assistants and the security establishment, the Israelis, the Palestinians, and the rest of the world learned of the Oslo talks only at the beginning of September—just a few days before the signing of the agreement. Even the American government was surprised by the breakthrough in Oslo and displayed neither disappointment nor anger at their lack of involvement. On the contrary, President Clinton endorsed the signing ceremony—held on September 13, 1993—and imbued it with a universalistic-optimistic spirit and a dimension of international obligation. The Oslo Accords were the product of changing international circumstances, intersecting processes and interests, and also of leaders who knew how to identify the window of opportunity that had arrived. But it was just a starting point, and from then on, it became necessary to guide the process along a rocky path strewn with obstacles toward the longed-for goal of peace.

ISRAELI TEXT / טקסט ישראלי

THE OSLO ACCORD: ONE STEP FORWARD, TWO STEPS BACKWARD

Not only was the Oslo Accords an important event in the process of the political peace settlement, but it was also a historical turn in the course of the
Palestinian issue and the Arab-Israeli conflict. It was the first agreement to be
signed by the Israelis and Palestinians according to which the implementation of the political settlement on the Palestinian-Israeli track was initiated
and according to which the Palestinians were given a limited self-rule in the
West Bank and the Gaza Strip. The agreement was also the bridge that gave
Israelis access deep into the Arab and Muslim world. Finally, it led to a full
separation between the Palestinian track and the other tracks, bilateral as well
as multilateral.

The signing of the accords (the Declaration of Principles) expressed the
desire of the two sides to reach a peaceful settlement between them by adopting the phased-solution format, from a transitional to a permanent solution.
By so doing, the accords met two Israeli demands: bilateralism and the post-
ponement of highly sensitive issues, thus providing Israel with extra time. The
accords made reference to the UN Resolutions 242 and 338, stipulating that
the settlement should reflect the content of the two resolutions: "Therefore,
the two resolutions are not subject to the implementation of the Palestinian
and Israeli sides, but to the outcome of the negotiations."[17]

The Declaration of Principles provided details of the two phases of the
interim solution. The first phase granted the Palestinians a self-rule in Jericho
and the Gaza Strip; the self-rule would then expand gradually to other cities
in the West Bank. The declaration left the specification of the areas and powers of the self-rule to detailed negotiations about the implementation of each
individual phase. The agreement also imposed on the Palestinians a number
of obligations toward the security of Israel. The agreement specified a period
of five years for the implementation of the interim stage, whereas the second
phase of the negotiations would start two years after the implementation of
the first phase.

The ambiguity that characterized the text of the Declaration of Principles
played a significant role in prolonging the negotiations and in creating differences over the implementation of the articles of the interim phase and coming
to an agreement about it. The Oslo Accords stipulated the immediate implementation of the transitional phase and a period of no more than three years
before proceeding to the next stage. However, the Israelis were deliberately

Most of the Israeli public responded to the signing of the Oslo Accords with enthusiasm and excitement. Others, however, expressed doubt, skepticism, and even outright opposition. With the initial implementation of the agreement, a heated debate arose between its supporters—who saw it as a ray of hope for ending the conflict for the sake of a better future—and its opponents—who claimed that Israel was conducting negotiations with murderers and handing half of the homeland over to them. Within the opposition camp, two groups with different approaches joined forces: the national-security approach and the religious-messianic approach, to form a unified front in order to foil the agreement.

A similar debate arose on the Palestinian side. Opponents of the agreement—mainly the extremist religious organization Hamas—embarked on a fierce terror campaign, including suicide attacks, also with the aim of undermining the peace process. Given the initial implementation's rocky start, both leaders were called upon to generate mutual trust, and at the same time maintain public support.

1994—A FATEFUL YEAR

The transition from the heights of the Declaration of Principles to the definition of objectives and hopes of implementation was complex and difficult, but necessary. Israel and the PLO devoted 1994 to talks on implementing the first stage of the declaration, as in the "Gaza and Jericho First" agreement signed in Cairo in May 1994. The talks immediately led to the formal establishment of an independent Palestinian Authority, which already began functioning in Gaza that summer, as well as to the Paris Agreement, which arranged economic ties between Israel and the Palestinian Authority.

The agreements sparked a wave of hope on both sides, articulated by Yitzhak Rabin in his speech at the signing ceremony of the Gaza and Jericho agreement: "In the alleyways of Khan Yunis and the streets of Ramat-Gan, in the houses of Gaza and the plazas of Hadera, in Rafah and Afula . . . a new reality is being born today. One hundred years of Palestinian-Israeli conflict and millions of people who want to live are watching us. May God be with us."

However, the realization that the process was indeed being fleshed out sparked a wave of terror aimed at sabotaging the peace process and bringing about its collapse. On February 25, an extreme right-winger and resident

very slow and continually stalled the implementation process beginning just one month after signing the declaration.[18]

THE CAIRO AGREEMENT:
PALESTINIAN AMBITIONS VS. ISRAELI CONDITIONS

On 4 May 1994, an agreement for the implementation of Palestinian self-rule in Jericho and the Gaza Strip was signed in Cairo. It took negotiators eight months to reach the agreement due to Israeli stalling. According to this agreement, the Palestinian Authority was set up and was granted only civil powers in 80 percent of the area of the Gaza Strip in addition to the center of the city of Jericho. Following the signing of this agreement, a great deal of financial assistance flowed into the Palestinian territories. A police force was formed and it later developed into nine different security apparatuses. Some ministries and departments were also set up.

In June 1994, Yasser Arafat, as head of the Palestinian Authority, established the first transitional government, which continued to fulfill its responsibilities until the Legislative Council was elected on 2 January 1996. However, many vital agreements were left unimplemented because the Israeli side simply stalled on them, including the Gaza airport and seaport, the release of Palestinian prisoners from Israeli prisons, and the safe passage between Jericho and the Gaza Strip.[19]

Months after signing the Cairo Agreement and starting its implementation particularly by the entry of the Palestinian Authority and the Palestinian police force to the West Bank, the agreement appeared to be exploding with clashing views on a large number of issues. Israel started to extort lots of demands and conditions from the PA for its security, particularly in light of the increasing number of resistance activities. The PA's "good conduct" was appraised by Israel and the United States for its efforts at coordinating security arrangements with the Israelis, including the destruction of the infrastructure of Hamas and the Islamic Jihad.

Security coordination led to an even wider gap among Palestinians who opposed and others who supported the signed peace agreements. Political affairs were thus polarized in two major positions: those who supported the peace approach and the signed agreements, on the one hand, and those who supported the continuation of the intifada, on the other. This became quite evident after Baruch Goldstein, an extremist Jew, on 25 February 1994, shot

Signing the peace agreement with Jordan at the Arava border crossing near Eilat

of Kiryat Arba, named Baruch Goldstein, murdered twenty-nine Muslims praying in the Cave of the Patriarchs. A few weeks later, as an act of revenge, suicide bombers blew themselves up in the cities of Afula and Hadera, killing twelve Jews. This escalation of the violence, in which extremist opponents from both sides were involved, has in essence not abated to this day.

There were also glimmers of light: the Oslo Accords paved the way to a peace treaty with Jordan. There was no debate regarding this agreement, and it presented a chance for good relations and true cooperation with King Hussein's friendly government. With the Palestinians conducting independent negotiations with Israel, King Hussein now saw himself as freed from obligations regarding the Palestinian issue. On October 26, 1994, after Israel agreed to minor border amendments and arrangements for the water problem, a peace agreement was signed between the two countries. The signing ceremony was conducted at the Arava border crossing near Eilat, in the presence of President Clinton. In his speech at the ceremony, King Hussein declared that "All children of Abraham . . . [will] remember it as a dawning of the new era of peace."

On October 31, 1994, just a few days after the signing of the treaty with Jordan, the First Middle East Economic Summit opened in Casablanca. The central topics discussed were: Arab-Israeli normalization, potential areas of collaboration between Israel and the Arab world, and consideration of economic solutions for raising the standard of living of the region's population.

indiscriminately at Palestinian worshipers inside Al-Ibrahimi Mosque in Hebron, killing thirty and injuring over a hundred.

From this point on, the Oslo Accords and its subsequent phases entered into an endless series of Israeli stalling and deferment. Meanwhile, Israel and Jordan signed a joint agreement on October 26, 1994, following Jordan's decision of disengagement with the Palestinians.[20]

TABA/WASHINGTON AGREEMENT (OSLO II):
DID IT OFFER A SOLUTION?

According to the Oslo Accords, the implementation of the second phase of the transitional stage was supposed to begin six months after signing the accords. This phase included expanding the powers of the Palestinian Authority and the areas under its control in the West Bank cities and rural areas. However, negotiations took almost eighteen months before the two sides signed the Taba Agreement, which called for the expansion of Palestinian self-rule in the West Bank. Unfortunately, the Palestinians were forced to make numerous concessions due to the ambiguous phrasing of the Declaration of Principles. The Palestinians also had to give in to Israeli demands in order to make some progress in the settlement process.

The Taba Agreement was signed in Washington on 28 September 1995, but it proved to be worse than its predecessor. The agreement included a formula that was devised by Shimon Peres whereby the West Bank, excluding East Jerusalem, would be divided into three categories: Areas A, B, and C. The first, Area A, included the center of six major cities: Ramallah, Qalqilieh, Bethlehem, Tulkarem, Nablus, and Jenin, with the exclusion of Hebron. This area comprised only 3 percent of the total area of the West Bank. According to the agreement, the civil and security control in Area A would be transferred to the Palestinian Authority just like Gaza.

The second category, Area B, included the majority of the Palestinian rural areas. These areas were classified as a buffer zone. Civil administration of Area B would be transferred to the PA, but would remain under the military control of Israel. Area B covered 20 to 25 percent of the total area of the West Bank. The third category was labeled Area C and it included border areas, settlements, and Israeli military security areas. These areas would remain under full Israeli control.

According to the agreement, Israel was supposed to redeploy its forces

The Casablanca Summit was considered a success and heralded as a break-through in the peace process. And yet, some are of the opinion that Shimon Peres's talk of a "new Middle East" caused Egyptian President Mubarak to fear that Israel was plotting regional hegemony at his expense, which may explain Mubarak's reserved attitude toward the peace process overall. Despite this, the Israeli-Jordanian peace treaty and the Casablanca Summit are viewed by some as the high point of the years 1992–1996.

Yitzhak Rabin, who as chief of staff led the great victory of the Six-Day War and as defense minister was forced to deal with the intifada and its dif-ficulties, understood that the path of violence led nowhere. Together with Shimon Peres and others, he made an historic turnabout and attempted to walk the path of peace. In a speech he gave to the United States Congress on July 26, 1994, he said:

> I, Military I.D. No. 30743, Retired General in the Israeli Defense Forces, consider myself to be a soldier in the army of peace today.
>
> I, who served my country for 27 years as a soldier, I say to you, Your Majesty, the King of Jordan, and I say to you, our American friends:
>
> Today we are embarking on a battle which has no dead and no wounded, no blood and no anguish. This is the only battle which is a pleasure to wage: the battle of peace.

The event that concluded 1994 was the awarding of the Nobel Peace Prize to Yitzhak Rabin, Shimon Peres, and Yasser Arafat. This decision re-flected the extreme importance that the international community attributed to the peace process between Israel and the Palestinians.

Indeed, in an atmosphere of increasing antagonism and terror, Rabin and Peres continued promoting the interim agreement, Oslo II, signed on September 25, 1995. This agreement, which increased Palestinian self-government in the West Bank, was preceded by negotiations that were more difficult and protracted than anticipated. The situation in the West Bank was more complex and entangled than that of the Gaza Strip. The West Bank has many more settlements and settlers (who felt as if they were fighting for their homes), borders Jerusalem, and is close to major cities in Israel. An ad-ditional reason for the difficulty of the negotiations was that the discussions were getting closer to the question of the Palestinian Authority's permanent status, and the upcoming (1996) Israeli elections. Given the circumstances,

from Area A within three months of signing the agreement. This is what actually happened on the ground. Yet, redeployment from Areas B and C was divided into three stages, the last of which was to be completed by September 1997, and whereby the PA would be in control of 30 percent of the area of the West Bank. But this did not materialize as Israel kept stalling. So as soon as the PA police force entered the Palestinian cities (excluding Hebron), having fulfilled all Israeli conditions concerning the size of the police force, the type and number of arms, and the distribution of police centers, Israel started to confiscate more lands in Area B in order to expand its settlements and to construct bypass roads to provide safe passage to Israeli settlements in the West Bank. Meanwhile, negotiations continued in order to implement the agreement and to finalize the redeployment, but nothing was achieved.[21]

The redeployment of the Israeli forces outside the cities showed how bad the agreement was. The cities of the West Bank were split up in an unprecedented manner, making it impossible for the Palestinians to move in or out of the West Bank and Gaza cities, even though they were under PA control. In fact, the Israeli Labor government imposed frequent closures over the major Palestinian cities for varying lengths of time. During these closures, and with total disregard for all the agreements, Israel gave itself the right to enter the PA areas to carry out arrests, shootings, and hot pursuit of "wanted" Palestinians.

The Taba Agreement disclosed the real intentions of the Israelis regarding the maximum extent to which they were willing to go in granting the Palestinians their rights in the framework of a permanent settlement. It was quite evident that Israel was willing to allow the expansion of the PA areas to a maximum not exceeding 50 percent of the total area of the West Bank besides the areas in Jericho and Gaza Strip already under PA control. It was also obvious that Israel wanted the Palestinian entity to be demilitarized and surrounded by security belts of buffer zones, military installations, and settlements. Furthermore, Israel continued to delay the discussion of final-status issues, in the meantime, continuing to create new realities on the ground such as the case with Jerusalem and the construction of settlements, which intensified significantly under the rule of the Israeli left government.

In this regard, Dan Meridor, a Likud leader, said:

> The late Rabin and Peres deserve our appreciation because they increased the number of Jews in Judea and Samaria by 40% during the

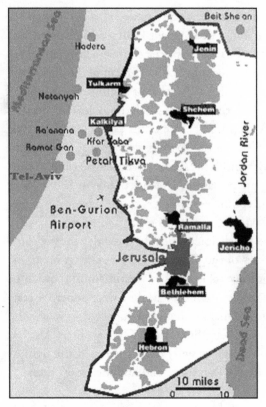

Map of division into areas according to Oslo

the Palestinians aspired to gain control of as large an area as possible, while Rabin and Peres' wanted to hold on to as many bargaining chips as possible for the final negotiations.

In the main, the agreement reached at the end of this period divided the West Bank into three areas: Area A, which included the large Palestinian cities from which Israel would withdraw entirely; Area B, which included some 450 villages under Palestinian civil authority but where Israel would maintain overall military control until 1997; Area C, which included state lands, sparsely populated areas, and Jewish settlements that were to remain solely under Israeli sovereignty. All in all, less than 30 percent of the West Bank would be transferred to Palestinian control at this stage.

The increasing opposition to the Oslo process among the Israeli public was expressed at the parliamentary level. When the Oslo II agreement was brought before the Knesset, it passed by a tiny margin: sixty-one voted in favor, fifty-nine against. The tremendous importance of the agreement lay in its success in facilitating a transition from the first to the second stage, promoting Oslo from the realm of the potential to the actual, and in effect bringing the Palestinians to imminent statehood.

Between November 1994 and June 1995, considerable efforts were made to revive the Syrian-Israeli channels of communication. Rabin, under unrelenting American pressure and despite the frustration engendered by broad,

last four years. While they were in office, thousands of houses were built and the number of Jews there increased from 100,000 to 140,000. The Israeli Left also deserves our gratitude because they did not voice any objections during the last four years. We will not do less than the Labor government. The establishment of settlements is one of the factors that determine the map of the state.[22]

After signing the Taba Agreement, the final settlement of the conflict was governed by a stage whose characteristics were totally unknown due to several variables, which can be summarized as follows:

- The start of the intense election race between the Likud and the Labor parties in preparation for the fourteenth Knesset elections of 1996 was preceded by dramatic developments, the most important of which was the assassination of Rabin and the political chasm that occurred in the Israeli society as a result; the transition of the Israeli society to a stage of internal violence against anybody who calls for peace with the PNA and against Israel's withdrawal from the West Bank, which reinforced the Likud opportunity for winning the elections and led to the failure of the Labor election program;

- The stumbling of the other peace tracks and the failure of Israel to propose any bold initiatives to the Arab countries; and at the same time, the lack of progress in the Palestinian Israeli negotiations, and the escalation of resistance operations against Israeli targets and the political confusion that came about as a result;

- The intensification of the internal Israeli conflicts between the secular coalition and religious conservative groups causing multiple differences relating to religion and state to appear, in addition to the ethnic, ideological, national, and religious divisions;

- Finally, the widespread frustration and discontent of the Palestinians regarding the results of the faltering peace process and the disappointment concerning the promises of economic prosperity resulting from the peace process.[23]

It can be said that the Israeli achievements of the peace agreements came

seemingly unbridgeable, differences, recognized that there would be no resolution of the Arab-Israeli conflict without Syrian participation. This round
of talks, conducted on various levels, was characterized by a lack of clarity,
a disregard for the basic rules of diplomacy, mutual suspicion, and a lack of
determination. Ultimately, Prime Minister Rabin refused to continue negotiations in such a fashion and the talks again reached a dead end.

1995—A TOUGH YEAR FOR PEACE

Despite the undeniable achievements gained on both sides as a result of the
Oslo process—indeed, perhaps because of them—opposition to the peace
process spread and it became increasingly unpopular. During the years
1993–1996, nearly 300 Israelis were killed in terror attacks (most of them
by Hamas). As a result, many Israelis began to have reservations about the
Oslo process and associate it with a genuine loss of personal security. Yasser
Arafat's personal conduct also contributed to this trend. Without a doubt, his
situation was very complicated. He had to walk a tightrope, simultaneously
appeasing two conflicting publics: he had to convince Israel that he was a devoted ally in the peace process; and at the same time, he had to win the faith
of the Palestinians and convince them that he was an able and brave leader,
coax his opposition into accepting him as such, and garner their support for
the difficult negotiations that lay ahead. Arafat did not succeed in navigating
between his two obligations. Moreover, his rhetoric toward the Palestinian
population was peppered with phrases such as "this is a jihad (a holy war),"
"Jerusalem will be liberated," and "agreements with heretics are not always
binding." Statements of this nature clearly did not help Arafat convince the
Jewish Israeli public of his efforts to eradicate terror. Even the Labor Party
claimed that "the PLO is trying to divest Israel of its security by means of
diplomacy, while the extremist organizations are finishing the job by using
force; there is complete cooperation between them." The increasing terror attacks, the large number of wounded, and Arafat's anemic responses generated
a widespread lack of faith, disappointment, and reservations among the Israeli
public regarding the entire process.

   After signing the Oslo II agreement, the Israeli right wing's opposition to
government policy became increasingly aggressive. This opposition included
disturbances of the peace, violent demonstrations, calls for a civil uprising, and
unprecedented vehement expressions against the government and against Rabin,

to a halt at this stage, especially in regard to the normalization of Arab-Israeli relations.

Operation Grapes of Wrath against Lebanon in April 1996 was yet another turning point in the deterioration of the situation. During the operation, the Israelis committed the Qana massacre. They bombed a UN compound where 800 people from the nearby village of Qana had taken refuge, killing 106 and injuring 116, in addition to 4 Fijian members of the UN peacekeeping force. These incidents revived the popular Arab feelings of enmity and hatred against Israel and constrained formal Arab relations with Israel much further.

Palestinians, Israelis, and Americans negotiating at Wye River Plantation

THE HEBRON AND WYE RIVER AGREEMENTS: ANOTHER STEP BACKWARD

Amid very unfavorable conditions, the Israeli elections brought the Israeli Right to government. The Likud, led by Binyamin Netanyahu, came out victorious, and in May 1996 Netanyahu took office. Netanyahu's election campaign was in fact based on a total opposition of the Oslo Accords, claiming that the Palestinians had taken more than they should have taken or deserved. Soon, the peace process encountered a very serious crisis. The agreement concerning the redeployment of Israeli forces from Hebron, the heavy legacy that Peres left for Netanyahu, came to a complete impasse. It would have been totally impossible had the Americans not put their full weight behind it and had the Palestinian Authority not made additional concessions, including the modification of the Oslo Accords in return for illusive American promises to speed up the redeployment and the start of the final status negotiations.[24]

On 24 September 1996, only four months after Netanyahu took office, and in order to create more insurmountable impediments for the peace negotiations and to step up the Judaization process of Jerusalem, Netanyahu

Incitement against Rabin: "Trial to the criminals of Oslo"

such as that of Elyakim Haetzni: "Yitzhak Rabin is not my prime minister, his government is illegal and illegitimate, and I will not comply with his orders." The radicalization and escalation of incitement were expressed in demonstrations during which signs and banners were waved proclaiming "Death to Arafat," "Death to Rabin," "Rabin the Traitor," and "In Fire and Blood, We Will Deport Rabin." Placards were also brandished depicting Rabin as an S.S. officer or wearing Arafat's traditional headdress (keffiyeh). As a result, there were more than a few acts of physical violence against public leaders from the left.

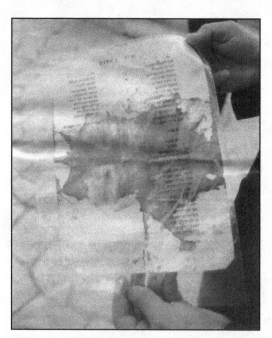

Paper with the words of "Song of Peace" found in Rabin's pocket at the time of his assassination

The leadership of the extremist camp, which included public figures, rabbis, and politicians, approved every action aimed at interrupting the peace process and fueling the flames of the opposition. They did not protest when Rabin's life was declared fair game, or when Jewish (halakhic) rulings were issued that permitted his persecution, they ignored, and even secretly reveled in, the "wonderful" young people who disseminated their teachings among the public. It subsequently became apparent that in this

decided to officially open a tunnel beneath Al-Aqsa Mosque in the holy city.
The reaction of the Palestinian people was strong and firm. Demonstrations,
sit-ins, and confrontations with the Israeli army broke out in all Palestinian
cities, villages, and camps.

Being part of the negotiations process, the Hebron Agreement (January
1997) was purely a security agreement. Dan Rubenstein described it as a
"project for partitioning Hebron."[25] According to the agreement, the city was
divided into two parts, one Arab and one Jewish, while the center of the city,
including Al-Ibrahimi Mosque (Hebron Mosque), remained under Israeli
control. The Israeli army established roadblocks and safe passages for the settlers inside the city and on the outskirts. The agreement rescheduled the redeployment of Israeli forces to the end of June 1998, instead of September 1997
as had been agreed on in the Taba Agreement. Yet even this new agreement
has not been implemented to date. The five-year transitional period ended
a long time ago, and so far there have been no attempts to initiate the final-
status negotiations, which, according to the Oslo Accords, should have begun
in the second year of the transitional period.[26]

Before leaving office, Netanyahu signed the Wye River Memorandum
with the PA on 23 October 1998, extorting yet a new and critical concession
from the Palestinians. The two sides agreed to take all the necessary measures
to prevent "terror and crime" and resistance operations. The Palestinian side
further agreed to devise a security plan to be reviewed by the United States
and had to resume security cooperation with the Israeli side. A Palestinian-
American committee was set up to review the steps taken by the Palestinians
against radical groups.

According to the security plan, the Palestinians would apprehend individuals suspected of participating in acts of violence and interrogate and
prosecute them. The PA would criminalize the possession of firearms and
work on the confiscation of unlicensed weapons in areas under its control. A
high-ranking American-Palestinian committee would oversee the security coordination to combat extremists. In return, Israel would transfer 14.2 percent
of the West Bank area to the PA. Also, a joint committee would be set up to
discuss the postponed third phase of redeployment.

The Palestinian side fulfilled all of its obligations according to the Wye
River Memorandum. Netanyahu's government, however, did not meet any of
its obligations. This increased tension in the entire Arab region, and hopes for
building a new Middle East vanished.

context of delegitimization and demonization of advocates of the policy, an extremist, unbridled group—who believed that the only way of stopping the peace process was to murder the prime minister—was at work. On November 4, 1995, Yigal Amir, a religious student at Bar Ilan University and an extremist right-wing activist, shot and killed Yitzhak Rabin. Three bullets put an end to the life of the Israeli prime minister at the conclusion of an inspiring mass rally for peace. The State of Israel went into shock, and the entire peace process plunged into crisis.

ISRAEL UNDER THE LEADERSHIP OF SHIMON PERES (NOVEMBER 1995–MAY 1996)

After Arafat and Rabin signed the Oslo Accords, many people in Israel and in the Palestinian Authority were hopeful that peace was in sight. However, in the days that followed, the dream turned into a nightmare. Was it the Rabin assassination that placed peace beyond reach? Was it the leaders who were responsible for the rift? Or were there other forces at work that prevented the continuation of the process? The rest of this chapter will explore these questions.

Shimon Peres was appointed prime minister in November 1995. He decided to schedule the Knesset elections for May 1996, in the hope that he would win and be able to move the peace process forward; however, things went awry and Shimon Peres's tenure was very brief. On the Syrian front, Peres did not manage to formulate a peace agreement with President Assad, so the Syrians set about destabilizing the northern border in order to push Israel into continuing negotiations. They encouraged terror attacks and the shelling of settlements from the Lebanese border by Hezbollah, which also intensified its activities against the IDF in the "security strip" in South Lebanon. The loss of lives and property mounted, and residents along the northern border lived in constant fear. Israel was forced to respond militarily and tensions along the northern border increased.

In an operation known as "The Grapes of Wrath" (April 1996), Israel shelled South Lebanon for several days, aiming to destroy Hezbollah's infrastructure, and around half a million civilians fled for Beirut. The IDF accidentally shelled a UN building in the village of Qana with hundreds of Lebanese civilians inside; some one hundred people were killed. (Peres paid the price for this disaster in the elections, as many Israeli Arabs refrained from voting for him, thus contributing to his defeat.)

This period witnessed a series of Israeli security measures against the Palestinians including arrests, house demolitions, and the destruction of the infrastructure of Palestinian institutions. A 1997 report prepared by the U.S. State Department about the human rights of Palestinians in the areas under the PA confirmed "an increase in the violations, arrests and torture of Palestinians by the Israeli Shabak security agents and in institutional racial discrimination against Arabs in Israel."[27]

Netanyahu and his government's position in regard to the peace process with the Palestinians and the Arabs was clearly expressed by Dan Meridor, the Liberal minister, who wrote:

Arafat and Barak entering a builidng at Wye River Plantation

> In 1923 when Jabotinsky wrote his famous article "The Iron Wall," an article that is still considered to be the intellectual basis for the political camp I belong to, his basic claim was "we have to give up any aspirations for peace now, because it is impossible to reach an agreement with the Arabs now as long as they believe that they could get rid of us." Jabotinsky believed that we first had to build our power, and only after that, when Arabs would be completely unable to expel us, they would be forced to accept our existence. Some moderates among them would take the initiative to negotiate with us to find some settlement. There would be no peace until we possessed the power, and after they would lose hope. And this is exactly what has happened.[28]

On 4 April 1999, the Israeli Knesset passed a no-confidence vote against Netanyahu's government. The government dissolved itself and agreed to hold early elections on 17 May 1999. Ehud Barak was elected Israel's prime minister and wanted to resume what Rabin, Peres, and Netanyahu had achieved in the peace process.

On 4 September 1999, Barak and Arafat signed the Sharm El-Sheikh

On the Palestinian front, many difficulties arose following the increase in terror, and among Israelis there was a sense that Arafat had not given up his policy of using force despite the fact that he had signed the Oslo Accords. During February and March 1996, sixty Israelis were murdered in terror attacks in Israel, and dozens were wounded. The attacks cast a heavy shadow on the efforts for peace, and led to a change of heart of many Israelis who in the past had supported the Oslo Accords and had truly believed in the steps that Arafat had taken.

ISRAEL UNDER THE LEADERSHIP OF BINYAMIN NETANYAHU (MAY 1996–MAY 1999)

In May 1996, Binyamin Netanyahu, a Likud candidate, won the elections, and became the first prime minister of Israel elected by "direct election," a system voted in by the Knesset in 1992. According to this system, every citizen had two votes through two separate ballots: one for prime minister, and one for the party they supported in the Knesset. Netanyahu's stance against the Oslo Accords was well known, and his success in the elections reflected a change in the sentiments of the Israeli public regarding peace with the Palestinians. Upon taking office, Netanyahu announced that he was committed to the Oslo Accords, but there is a question as to whether his opposition to the peace process affected its implementation, and by what means.

In August 1996, Netanyahu overturned Rabin's decision to freeze construction in the settlements, in contravention of the Oslo Accords. On September 24, 1996, at the conclusion of the Yom Kippur fast, Netanyahu ordered that a new opening be made at one end of the "Western Wall Tunnel," which triggered three days of violent confrontations. The Western Wall Tunnel leads from the Western Wall plaza along the base of the Temple Mount, and the new exit into the Muslim Quarter had been completed a year earlier. Rabin and Peres preferred not to open the tunnel to visitors so as to prevent tension, but Netanyahu decided to open it, based on the view that one must not bow to directives from the Palestinians.

Regarding the tunnel, Netanyahu said, "We are touching the bedrock of our existence." Arafat, chairman of the Palestinian Authority, called on his people to take to the streets and demonstrate, and the three days of violence, which spread to all of the cities in the West Bank and Gaza Strip, claimed

Memorandum, which concentrated on the resumption of final-status negotiations, resolving outstanding issues such as the release of Palestinian prisoners, the safe passage between Gaza and the West Bank, and beginning construction work on Gaza seaport. It also dealt with other detailed issues concerning the city of Hebron, such as reopening Al-Shuhada' Street and convening the Joint Liaison Committee to review the status of Al-Ibrahimi Mosque.

In Israel, the political situation was becoming tense in light of the diminishing popularity of Barak and his party due to the apprehension of the Israeli public that Barak might make fundamental concessions at Camp David concerning Jerusalem and the Palestinians' right to return to their homeland. Similarly, on the Palestinian side, the political and popular situation was uptight. The Palestinians were afraid that the PA might make concessions that could harm their right to establish their independent state on the land occupied in 1967 in accordance with UN Resolution 242. They were also afraid of concessions that might affect their right to return in accordance with UN Resolution 194.[29]

On 5 July 2000, both Arafat and Barak were invited by U.S. President Bill Clinton to come to an agreement about final-status issues. The meeting was known as Camp David II. However, it was immediately evident that Barak had come to the meeting with the intention of failing it and blaming its failure on the Palestinian side. The Israeli media, in its turn, intentionally depicted what it termed Israeli concessions in a much exaggerated manner. For example, it was claimed that Israel agreed to establish a Palestinian state on 95 percent of the West Bank and Gaza. It also intensively promoted Israel's intentions to dismantle settlements which lie outside settlement concentration areas, or to allow these settlements to remain inside the Palestinian state where settlers would be treated as foreign residents. Also, Israeli media claimed that Israel accepted the return of a large number of Palestinian refugees over a number of years. Clearly, such staged allegations were meant to blame failure of the meeting on the Palestinian side.

The failure of Camp David II was no more than a direct expression of the continued Israeli policy of imposing substantial realities on the ground. Nevertheless, the Israelis persisted that it was the Palestinians who undermined the meeting by their inflexibility. They complained that the Palestinians wanted all the hand that Israel had extended to them instead of the palm and some fingers.[30] In a similar fashion, the Israelis believed that Sharon's visit to

The Western Wall tunnel

many victims: fourteen IDF soldiers and over sixty Palestinians were killed, and dozens were wounded on both sides. Following intervention and pressure from the Clinton administration, the riots subsided and negotiations with the Palestinians resumed.

In keeping with the Oslo Accords, Israel was supposed to withdraw from most of the areas of Hebron and to redeploy, and Netanyahu announced that he would fulfill his obligations. In January 1997, Arafat and Netanyahu signed the Hebron Agreement, which included, among other things, the following steps: Israel would pull the IDF out of Arab Hebron, and would carry out three additional withdrawals during the year; the Palestinians would desist from terror activities and propaganda and would ceremoniously rescind the articles in the Palestinian Convention that contradicted the Oslo Accords. In addition, it was agreed that discussions on a permanent settlement would be renewed within two months.

On January 16, 1997, the Israeli flag was removed from the government building in Hebron, and the next day, the building was transferred to the Palestinian Authority, along with most of the city. The Jewish settlement in Hebron was not evacuated, and the IDF remained to protect it and the Cave of the Patriarchs. In the difficult atmosphere prevailing during that time, Israeli society experienced a terrible calamity. In February 1997, seventy-three soldiers were killed in a crash between two helicopters on the Lebanese border; the public sank into deep mourning. Following the accident, the debate regarding the IDF's continued presence in the security strip in South Lebanon intensified. The security strip was annexed during Operation Peace for the Galilee in June 1982, claiming the lives of hundreds of civilians and soldiers; many thought that the price was too high. Hezbollah continued shelling the civilian population in the north, despite the IDF's presence in the strip, and it seemed as if there was no advantage to maintaining a military presence in Lebanon. On the other hand, there were those who feared that a withdrawal would be considered a victory for terror, and warned that the Hezbollah would

Al-Aqsa Mosque was simply a visit and not the spark that ignited the intifada of Al-Aqsa.

OSLO AND AL-AQSA INTIFADA

Since the signing of the Declaration of Principles in September 1993 and until the outbreak of the Al-Aqsa Intifada in September 2000, political, economic, and social conditions in the West Bank and Gaza had deteriorated much further despite the presence of a national authority, which came as a result of the implementation of the first phase of the Oslo Accords, specifically the Gaza-Jericho First Agreement. Moreover, Barak's government, during which the second intifada broke out, continued to impose its fait accompli policies on the entire West Bank and Gaza, or what some political analysts termed a "preemptive strategy."[31] This strategy manifested itself in the following ways:

1. Settlements were not dismantled nor was the construction of new settlements discontinued. To the contrary, more settlements were built during Barak's government than any of his predecessors, Rabin, Peres, and Netanyahu. More astounding was the fact that

A view of Arab-occupied Jerusalem through barbed wire

Arafat, King Hussein, Clinton, and Netanyahu at Wye
Plantation

draw closer to the fence near the northern settlements and endanger their security. Following the helicopter disaster, the "Four Mothers" movement was established, which led the struggle for the withdrawal from Lebanon through roadside demonstrations, advertising, and collaboration with artists and politicians.

Negotiations with the Palestinians resumed in May 1997, because both parties to the conflict, and President Clinton, sensed the urgency: Israelis had suffered serious attacks on buses, in restaurants, nightclubs, and bustling city streets, and the Palestinians felt that Israel's construction of settlements in Judea and Samaria was pushing them off their land. The multilateral negotiations continued during 1998, but only toward the end of the year did the leaders and their advisors meet in the United States at the Wye Plantation (near Washington D.C.) with the objective of signing a new agreement. The main points of disagreement were the settlements and the occupied territories, the status of Jerusalem, and the "right of return."

The Wye Plantation Agreement was signed on October 23, 1998, and heralded the continuation of the Oslo process. The following matters were determined: 13 percent of the area of Judea and Samaria would be transferred to the Palestinian Authority, and in exchange, the authority would fight against terror and its infrastructure, and the Palestinian National Assembly (PNA) would disassociate from the Palestinian National Charter. It was also decided that President Clinton would visit Gaza and Jerusalem. Indeed, in the framework of his visit, the PNA did rescind the articles that contradicted the Oslo Accords.

In November, Israel transferred 9 percent of Area B to Area A (to the Palestinian Authority), the Palestinian airport in Dahariya began operating, and 250 Palestinian prisoners (without blood on their hands) were released.

However, on December 21, 1998, new Israeli elections were scheduled in light of the lack of faith expressed by the Knesset vis-à-vis the prime minister.

the land that the PA "gained" as a result of the Oslo Accorda was much smaller than the land that the Israelis took possession of in the last years for the purpose of building settlements and constructing bypass roads;

2. All crossing points, including Gaza airport, were totally controlled by Israel according to the agreement;

3. Water resources in the West Bank and Gaza Strip, which had been believed to be sufficient to cover the needs of four million Palestinians, were stolen in broad daylight and in sight of the Palestinians and were diverted to Israeli settlements.

The level of living standards in the PA areas dropped by 30 percent, thereby disappointing economic observers who dreamed of transforming Palestine into the "Singapore of the Middle East." The fate of Jerusalem, the final borders, water resources, and sovereignty remain unknown until now.[32]

AL-AQSA INTIFADA: A RESULT OF THE OSLO ERA

The first intifada (1987) introduced an important stage in the history of the national and political struggle of the Palestinians since it "moved the conflict to the land of conflict." It enabled the Palestinians to take the initiative by adopting new methods not previously familiar to the Israelis, and by making "the cost of the occupation of Palestinian territories extremely high to the Israelis. This prompted Rabin to say, 'Only a miracle can save us from the Intifada.'"[33]

The new developments the world witnessed in the late 1980s upset the balance of power in favor of the United States and its ally Israel. In the Madrid Conference, the United States imposed its own vision of the solution to the Arab-Israeli conflict first by redefining the conflict. The United States characterized the Palestinian territories as "territories in conflict" rather than "occupied territories." This solution was based on Washington's vision of the world, in which Israel constitutes an integral part.

It was the intifada of 1987 that led to the Oslo Accords, or the much-awaited "miracle" in Rabin's words; ironically, it was the Oslo Accords itself that led to of the outbreak of Al-Aqsa Intifada.

Binyamin Netanyahu opposed the Oslo process, but also acted to fulfill its obligations, and in so doing aroused the opposition of both the left and the right in Israel, each for its own reasons.

ISRAEL UNDER THE LEADERSHIP OF EHUD BARAK (MAY 1999–FEBRUARY 2001)

Ehud Barak won the elections, also through the direct election system. Barak was elected by a very large margin (he received over 50 percent of the vote), but his party, the Labor Party, was not sufficiently strong to back him up. The coalition that Barak established lacked the broad common denominator necessary to support him in the areas of security, economy, and social concerns. During this period, there was a world crisis in the hi-tech industry, and in Israel, unemployment was on the rise and with it, frustration. The people expected the Barak government to provide solutions to the security situation and the economic crisis, including unemployment, but the situation continued to deteriorate in both areas.

In the diplomatic arena, Barak preferred first to deal with peace with Syria, and only afterward to continue implementing the Oslo process. He drew up tight schedules for signing peace agreements with Syria (including withdrawal from Lebanon) and the Palestinians, and set about working on them with great determination. After the negotiations with Syria failed, Barak decided to take the IDF out of Lebanon without an agreement. The IDF secretly withdrew from southern Lebanon on the night between May 22–23, 2000, with no fighting or casualties. Most Israelis were very happy about the withdrawal from Lebanon, but some were critical, claiming that it constituted a dangerous precedent, which could be interpreted as flight, and would encourage the Palestinians to continue using terror as a weapon. There was also a strong concern that Hezbollah was drawing nearer to the security fence and to Israeli residential communities at the border.

From this stage onward, Barak made a concerted effort to continue the Oslo process, and the question arises as to why he and Arafat failed to implement it, even though both claimed that they were acting in full force.

In July 1999, accelerated negotiations were held between the Israeli and Palestinian delegations. The Israeli team insisted on the following principles at the outset: Jerusalem would remain under Jewish sovereignty; most of the settlers would be allowed to remain in their homes by annexation of continuous

The Oslo Accords led to the establishment of the Palestinian Authority in some Palestinian cities, camps, and villages. Yet the Israelis viewed the PA as a tool for their own security, just as Rabin himself had regarded Oslo as no more than a security agreement. Indeed, Israeli politics has confined the Palestinian Authority to this role.

Ariel Sharon's visit to Al-Aqsa Mosque in East Jerusalem, September 2000

Al-Aqsa Intifada, which broke out in the presence of the Palestinian Authority, posed a number of critical questions to the Palestinian society at large, including the PA and the opposition. The most important questions concerned the existence of a Palestinian political program or a national reference, the relationship between the PA and the opposition, and the assurance of personal and collective security for all the Palestinian people.

The continuation of the intifada became an urgent issue despite the approximation in position over the intifada between the PA and the other national and Islamic forces. While the PA saw the intifada as a means for improving its negotiation position, the other national forces viewed it as a strategic option.

Despite several American and Israeli peace proposals and plans, they never came close to acceptance of the establishment of a just and final peace, or at best establishing a secure Palestinian entity on an area not exceeding 45 percent of the West Bank.[34]

Al-Aqsa Intifada broke out on 28 September 2000, following the frustration the Palestinian people felt as a result of the failure of the peace process, which had lasted for seven full years. It became clear that the dream of establishing a Palestinian state with East Jerusalem as its capital had become impossible. Israel had failed to meet its obligations under the Oslo Accords, which were signed by the successive governments, and continued to expand its oppressive measurements and settlement activities in addition to the disrespect it had shown for the Palestinian negotiators. Moreover, Israel's real

blocks of settlement by Israel; establishment of a demilitarized Palestinian state while meeting Israel's security needs; no "right of return" for the Palestinians.

Barak also demanded that any interim agreement be part of the permanent arrangement. He claimed that without a permanent status arrangement the Palestinians would enjoy additional concessions with each stage of the negotiations, while Israel would be losing its bargaining tool for determining the permanent status. Barak claimed that the Palestinians would keep using terror to force Israel into agreeing to additional demands and that therefore the borders must be determined in advance.

The Palestinians insisted on their right to all of the occupied territories and control over East Jerusalem and the Temple Mount, and were not prepared to relinquish the principle of the "right of return."

SHARM DOCUMENT (SEPTEMBER 1999)

After much discussion, Barak and Arafat met at Sharm a-Sheikh in September 1999. There they signed the Sharm document, which included postponing implementation of the Wye Plantation Agreement to February 2000, a schedule for discussions about the permanent status, the release of 350 prisoners, and Palestinian commitment to collaboration on security and the prevention of terror.

Politically speaking, Barak was very much constrained. With every new agreement, his coalition deteriorated further, added to which was a religious crisis between the *Shas* and *Meretz* parties, both of which were coalition members. The Knesset was split between those who supported a broad compromise with the Palestinians and those who opposed it. Despite his shaky political position, Barak gave an order to continue with the negotiations, and he was determined to adhere to the schedule that he had set for himself. The teams worked long days and nights on the (secret) Swedish channel and on the (open) American channel, but it seemed that the differences were insurmountable.

CAMP DAVID (JULY 2000)

On May 15, 2000 (Israeli Independence Day), Barak announced in the Knesset that the villages linked to Jerusalem would be transferred to the Palestinian Authority (Abu Dis, al-Eizariya, and Sawahra), according to the Sharm Agreement. However, just then the Palestinians announced *Nakbah* (Palestinian Catastrophe of '48) Day, which led to mass riots similar

intentions had become quite apparent after the Camp David II summit with its absolute refusal of the establishment of a sovereign Palestinian state. Israel never ceased to demolish Palestinian houses and take possession of others, deny access into and out of the West Bank and Gaza Strip, and impose its total control on the movement of the Palestinians.

Palestinians defending Al-Aqsa Mosque as Israeli police throw tear gas at them

On top of all that came Sharon's visit to Al-Aqsa on 27 September 2000, which sparked off Al-Aqsa Intifada and was accompanied by severe Israeli oppressive measures, followed by an incursion into all Palestinian territories. Israel used its air, naval, and land forces against unarmed Palestinian civilians, resulting in hundreds of deaths and thousands of injured people, including children, and old men and women. The number of casualties in the first month of Al-Aqsa Intifada was equal to those in the first year of the first intifada.[35]

The second intifada highlighted the following facts:

1. Israel's strategy to use military force in any confrontation;

2. Israel's disrespect of signed agreements, international treaties, and conventions;

3. Israel's lack of desire to reach a just and comprehensive peace;

4. The absolute siding of the United States with Israel in every step and in any forum, making it impossible for the Palestinians to trust the United States as an honest broker in the peace process;

5. The reawakening of the Palestinians' sense that struggle was indispensable for regaining their land, and the resurgence of their sense of nationalism and their realization of the risk inherent in betting on the credibility of Israel or the United States;

6. The crucial role of the intifada in unifying the Palestinians: Palestinians living behind the Green Line (1948 territories) organized nonviolent solidarity demonstrations in protest of what

Barak and Arafat with Clinton at Camp David

to those of the Western Wall Tunnel incident. Two "Days of Rage" declared by the Palestinians led to injuries on both sides, an increase in tension, and an additional decline in mutual trust.

During the summer, the negotiations between the Israeli and Palestinian teams were again cut off. Given this situation, U.S. President Clinton pressed for a summit meeting at Camp David to try to salvage what was left of the peace process. Clinton said, "Movement now depends on historic decisions that only the two leaders can make . . . to remain stalled, is simply no longer an option, for the Israeli-Palestinian conflict . . . knows no status quo . . . the longer we wait, the more difficult the decisions are likely to become."

Just before Barak's trip to the summit meeting, on July 10, 2000, his government lost a vote of confidence in the Knesset; Israel was headed toward new elections. A week later, a demonstration of some 150,000 right-wingers was held at Rabin Square protesting Barak's departure to Camp David, and it was clear that his trip sorely lacked political backing.

The teams at the summit meeting worked furiously, but failed to advance the negotiations. According to descriptions by various sources, Clinton

was happening to their fellow Palestinians. The Israeli police moved to violently crush "the citizens of the state." Thirteen young people were killed due to "unjustified" excessive force by the Israeli police against "the Arabs," according to the Or Committee that was set up by Barak's government, though none of the members of the police force were prosecuted. These events showed the depth of the crisis the "Jewish democratic state" was living; a state where one finds suffering and social discrimination and oppression against the Arab minority; and a state which ranks Arabs at the bottom of the social ladder below oriental and Falasha Jews;[36]

7. The ability of the intifada to stir up the feelings of Arabs in all Arab countries, and to move the ethnic and religious zeal of the Arabs. It showed the readiness of the Arabs to sacrifice for the sake of the Palestinian cause and Al-Aqsa. The Arab street exerted pressure on the Arab governments to adopt clearer positions on dealing with Israel and all its allies. Egypt withdrew its ambassador to Israel, while Tunisia and Morocco severed their diplomatic relations with Israel.

SHARM EL-SHEIKH DOCUMENT AND TABA NEGOTIATIONS: AN ATTEMPT TO BUY TIME

The second intifada pushed U.S. President Bill Clinton to hold a summit conference in Sharm El-Sheikh on 17 October 2001, with the participation of the representative of the European Union and the UN secretary general. The conference aimed at ending violence and bringing the parties back to the negotiating table. The negotiations failed after Israel refused to discuss its obligations unless Arafat stopped the intifada, presuming that the decision to end the intifada was in Arafat's hands, and overlooking the real reasons behind the intifada.[37]

The negotiations between the Palestinian and Israeli sides resumed in Taba on 20 January 2000, on the basis of a plan presented by Clinton on 23 November 2000. It was the last round of negotiations conducted by Barak's government. Consequently, in an attempt to reach a framework agreement

was very angry at Arafat and blamed him for the summit's failure. Arafat on his part was very worried about relinquishing Jerusalem, and told Clinton that he spoke for "a billion Muslims who would never forgive me if I do not receive complete sovereignty over Jerusalem. I do not have a mandate to give it up. It isn't me, but the entire Muslim world."

Israel was worried mainly by the demand for the "right of return" and the potential confiscation of the Temple Mount. Prime Minister Barak charged that during the Camp David conference he had agreed to far-reaching concessions, while Arafat hadn't budged an inch from his original position. Barak, who was putting his political career and his life on the line for the peace agreement, expected Arafat to do the same.

AL-AQSA INTIFADA (OCTOBER 2000)

On September 28, 2000, on Rosh Hashanah—the Jewish New Year—a new and problematic wave of violence erupted that came to be known as the Al-Aqsa Intifada. The outbreak of the riots was timed with the highly publicized visit of MK Ariel Sharon and his right-wing cronies to the Temple Mount on September 28, 2000, with the approval of Prime Minister Barak. The Palestinians had prohibited Jews from ascending the Temple Mount, and Sharon's visit was a statement of protest against Israel's capitulation. But was this the real reason for the eruption of the riots? Sharon's motives were unclear, but it is also not known to what extent the visit served as Arafat's excuse for an action that had already been planned, or was a genuine trigger for the spontaneous eruption of violence.

Sharon's visit on the Temple Mount was protested in demonstrations by Palestinians from the West Bank and Israel. The police shot rubber bullets at the demonstrators and dozens of policemen and Palestinians were injured. The following day, violence again erupted on the Temple Mount. Five Palestinians were killed and dozens were injured on both sides. Within ten days, Judea, Samaria, and the Gaza Strip were ablaze. The Palestinians launched an armed struggle that included explosive devices, car bombs, and suicide attacks. Judea and Samaria burned, and the IDF responded with force.

The grave events of this period include the kidnapping and murder of three soldiers on Mt. Dov (near Mt. Hermon) by Hezbollah, shooting at the Jewish community in Hebron, shooting at the Gilo neighborhood in Jerusalem, terror attacks in the cities, and a savage lynching carried out in Ramallah in which two reserve soldiers were killed. Despite this, world opinion grew for a permanent settlement after the failure of the Camp David II summit and before the Israeli elections, Israel, immediately before the negotiations, announced three principles as a basis for negotiations.

1. Israel rejects the right of return to Palestinian refugees;

2. Israel will not sign any document that transfers sovereignty over Al-Haram Al-Sharif to the Palestinians;

3. Israel will keep 80 percent of the settlers in settlement enclaves under its control.[38]

The Taba negotiations started at the time when both sides had announced that there was no opportunity for reaching an agreement. Israel demanded that negotiations be conducted with four different committees, each dealing intensively with one specific issue: Jerusalem, the refugees, the land, and security.[39]

The issue of the Palestinian refugees was the most complicated. The Israeli side showed two maps, one for the West Bank and another for Jerusalem, which indicated the Israeli position on Jerusalem and the settlements. The maps showed that Israel wanted to annex sixty of the big settlements, totaling 6 percent of the area of the West Bank. On 23 January 2001, Israel stopped the Taba negotiations and Barak asked senior negotiators to return to Israel for consultations. On 28 January 2001, negotiations were brought to an end after the two sides failed to reach any solutions. The Palestinian side said, "The Israeli side offered nothing new at Taba, and it was not possible to reach an agreement there due to the existence of a gap regarding all four issues and also because it was not possible to bridge this gap under the sword of the Israeli elections and the pressure of time."[40]

In a speech delivered at the First Conference of the European Gathering in support of the right of return of Palestinian

A Palestinian man watches helplessly as an Israeli Caterpillar, guarded by an Israeli solider, uproots a Palestinian olive tree

increasingly anti-Israel, and Israel was perceived as a cruel occupying force. Israeli soldiers were shown on television screens around the world shooting at women and children, beating Palestinians and destroying homes, and Israeli tanks were shown plowing through the streets of Palestinian cities.

Joining the protest against Sharon's visit to the Temple Mount were Palestinian citizens of Israel who held stormy demonstrations across the country, closed main arteries, threw stones at cars, and injured civilians. The behavior of Israel's Arabs was perceived by most of the Jewish population as a real threat. The police force responded disproportionately, with disastrous results. Israeli policemen killed thirteen Israeli-Palestinian adults and adolescents, and testimonies show that officers often fired even when there was no risk to them. These violent incidents between policemen and Arab civilians exposed the fragile, precarious condition characteristic of Jewish-Arab relations in Israel.

The use of live ammunition against demonstrators was unreasonable in the eyes of many, and the Barak government established the Or Commission, a national commission of inquiry headed by Justice Theodore Or, to look into the matter. The commission published its findings in September 2003, after questioning policemen and officers, Arab MKs, and Israeli Arab demonstrators. The report criticized the violence exercised against the Arabs, but also the functioning of Prime Minister Barak, Domestic Security Minister Shlomo Ben Ami, and the upper echelons of the police. In addition, the report pointed to the harsh discrimination against the Arab sector in Israel and saw it as an inciting factor:

> The events, their irregular nature and grave consequences, were the outcome of factors that ran deep [. . .] The state and its government had for generations failed in dealing thoroughly and comprehensively with the difficult problems posed by a large Arab minority within the Jewish state [. . .] The government handling of the Arab sector has been characterized mainly by disregard and neglect.

Attempts at dialogue between the leaders regarding the intifada led nowhere. Barak demanded that Arafat put an end to the violence and terror, and claimed that if he was unable to control his people, then "he was the head of a gang and not a leader." On October 17, 2000, Barak and Arafat signed the Second Sharm Memorandum to calm things down, but it was

refugees, organized by French cities twinning with Palestinian camps and the French town Montataire held on 27 January 2001, Arafat said:

> We have dealt positively with all international efforts, and we have showed a lot of flexibility. We have agreed to less than 25% of the area of historic Palestine, and we have also accepted UN Resolutions 242 and 338 which call for Israel's withdrawal from all Arab and Palestinian occupied territories, including Jerusalem, to pre-1967 borders. We also want to see the implementation of UN Resolution 194 implemented and we want to see an end to the war waged by Israel against the un-armed Palestinian people. We appeal to all international conventions, especially the World Declaration for Human Rights.[41]

ECONOMIC AND SOCIAL VARIABLES IN THE 1990S

As mentioned earlier, the early 1990s witnessed a number of international and national changes, which greatly impacted the Palestinian struggle. Internationally, there were the collapse of the Soviet Union and the outbreak of the Gulf War. Nationally, there were the first intifada and Israel's intensive attempts to crush it, followed by initiatives for peace represented by the Oslo Accords in 1993. All these important political events had a serious affect on the Palestinian economy, which had not had the chance to recover after the first intifada, or to develop because of the Israeli occupation.

The 1991 Gulf War affected not only the Gulf countries but also Palestine, whose economy depended to a large extent on the transfer of funds from Palestinians working there to their families. Remittances to the PLO declined critically. In addition, Israel issued a new order requiring Palestinian workers to obtain special permits for work in Israel behind the Green Line.[42] As a result, a considerable number of workers became unemployed. This was accompanied by frequent military closures that prevented workers from reaching their workplaces. Consequently, the individual income and Palestinian gross national product fell greatly, especially since income from work behind the Green Line comprised 22 percent of the gross national income.[43]

Under such dire circumstances, workers started to look for an alternative—seeking jobs in the West Bank and Gaza. Unfortunately, the West Bank and Gaza could not absorb the large workforce. Consequently, there was a decrease in the daily wages from an average of $16.60 to $12.70.[44]

not implemented. Arafat claimed that he did not have the power to stop the terror, but Barak told the Americans, "He's lying to all of us. I don't have the option of not responding . . . one day we'll really need to strike at him, efficiently; at this stage, we're still holding back, but it's not beyond our capability."

During November 2000, the Palestinians perpetrated serious terror attacks in Gush Katif in the Gaza Strip by day, and the IDF responded with unprecedented force by night, wounding dozens of people and causing power outages in large areas of the city. Tunisia and Morocco had already cut diplomatic ties with Israel, and Egypt subsequently recalled its ambassador. At the end of November, Barak suggested disbanding the Knesset for new elections, and his suggestion was accepted by a sweeping majority. In December, Barak resigned and asked for elections in February 2001, in the hope that if he succeeded in achieving a peace agreement the people would stand behind him.

But the window of opportunity for signing a peace agreement was fast closing, because Clinton was about to end his period of office in January 2001, and Barak had lost his legitimacy vis-à-vis the public. Barak instructed his staff to maintain daily ties with Arafat's office with the aim of accelerating the negotiations, but neither side was willing to compromise. The Clinton government appointed a committee that would come to the area and put an end to the violence, but the Palestinians did not stop their brutal terror attacks, in which dozens of Israelis were killed. In order to protect its civilians and prevent the entry of suicide bombers, Israel adopted a policy of "closure" (placing checkpoints between Palestinian communities and stringently monitoring all travelers entering and leaving Israel), which caused the local Palestinian population great suffering. Israel also adopted a policy of targeted killings (direct attacks against specific masterminds and perpetrators of terror), which resulted in the inadvertent harming of innocent Palestinians. In spite of, and perhaps because of, this situation, both the Israeli and Palestinian teams felt that an agreement could be reached only if U.S. President Bill Clinton devoted himself to the cause.

CLINTON PARAMETERS (DECEMBER 23, 2000)

Clinton answered the call. Although he was at the end of his tenure, he decided to undertake the challenge notwithstanding the risk of failure. Clinton

The peace process and the Oslo Accords (1993) brought great expectations of economic improvement. People were hoping for more job opportunities and huge investments, which would lead to an instant economic boom. The PA tried its best to create suitable conditions for mul-

Palestinians waiting to cross through an Israeli military checkpoint near Beir Furik

tiple development, developing the economy, concluding commercial deals, and planning the construction of the Gaza airport and seaport.[45] This led to some positive results that lasted for less than a year. In the field of tourism, for example, the number of tourists to Bethlehem went up from 600,000 visitors in 1990 to a million in 1995. However, in 1996, the number of visitors to the city dropped by 8.5 percent due to the repeated military closures and to political instability.[46]

The period between 1995 and 1998 represents the second time that Palestinian workers sought jobs in the West Bank and Gaza due to Israeli closures and to the difficulty of obtaining permits to work in Israel. Most job seekers turned to the job opportunities made available by the PA, e.g., in the security and police forces, or in the various ministries. This explains the increase in government employees from 61,000 in 1995 to 79,000 in 1996.[47] Yet the majority could not find jobs, became unemployed and, as a consequence, caused a rise in the inflation.

Under these circumstances, there was record recession in all aspects of the Palestinian economy, taking into consideration that the Palestinian society is a young one in which young people constitute more than half the population. So finding job opportunities for both old unemployed workers and for young workers became a crisis.

With the outbreak of the second intifada at the end of December 2000 the economic conditions in the Palestinian territories became more unbearable. The transportation industry considerably declined due to the repeated closures, the difficulty of reaching the market, restrictions on movement, the difficulty of getting raw materials, and the destruction of industrial

worded the parameters for an agreement taking into account the demands of both sides but also stipulating mutual concessions, and hoped that both parties had reached the stage of being ready to sign. Following are the main points of the Clinton Parameters, which the president believed could lead to a resolution of the conflict:

- Borders and territory: The territories to be annexed by Israel in the West Bank would be 4–6 percent, and Israel would transfer to the Palestinians between 1 and 3 percent (exchange of territories, but not one to one). Guidelines were given for the permanent map: maximum Palestinian contiguity and minimum impingement on Palestinians by border corrections.

- Jerusalem: The Arab areas would be under Palestinian sovereignty, and the Jewish areas under Israeli sovereignty; the same would apply to the holy places. The site of the mosques—to Palestine; the Western Wall—to Israel.

- Security: Palestine would have no army, but would have security and police forces; an international force would supervise and control the implementation of the agreement (the force would be withdrawn only with Israel's agreement). Jordan Valley: Israel would be able to maintain three early warning stations, whose status would be reviewed after ten years.

- Period of preparation and arrangement: Israel would have three years to transfer army bases and settlements in an orderly manner.

- Refugees: A three-part solution for the refugees: in Palestine, in third-party host countries, and in Israel itself. "The solution will have to be consistent with the two-state approach: . . . the state of Palestine as the homeland of the Palestinian people and the state of Israel as the homeland of the Jewish people. . . . The Israeli side could simply not accept any reference to right of return that would imply a right to immigrate to Israel in defiance of Israel's sovereign policies on admission or that would threaten the Jewish character of the state."

- End of the conflict and all claims: Signing of a contract that

installations.[48] Such Israeli measures destroyed the industrial sector, hampered its development, and, consequently, increased unemployment. (According to official statistics the industrial sector comprises 18 percent of gross national income and employs 18 percent of Palestinian workers.[49]

The agricultural sector did not fare any better than the industry sector. Israel confiscated the agricultural lands, destroyed the infrastructure, prevented farmers from using agricultural areas adjacent to settlements, and controlled water resources.[50] In 2001 alone, the construction of bypass roads swallowed 31,730 dunams of land planted with fruitful trees, mostly olive trees.[51]

As regards settlements in the West Bank and Gaza, by the early 1990s, Israel had built 194 settlements: agricultural, military, or industrial. After Oslo, the successive Israeli governments intensified the construction of settlements in the West Bank, Gaza, and around Jerusalem. Israel adopted a policy based on a combination of two types of measures:

1. discontinue the building of settlements, but increase the number of housing units in settlements (Rabin's government—Labor Party);

2. expand existing settlements and build new ones (the Likud government [1996–1999], under Netanyahu, Barak, and Sharon).[52]

In summary, Israel managed to destroy the Palestinian economy by adopting a large number of practices, including the following:

1. confiscation of land

2. frequent closures

3. restrictions on transportation and movement

4. obstacles for Palestinian imports and exports

5. restrictions on transport of raw materials

6. preventing Palestinians from reaching their work places.

constitutes an end to the conflict. Its implementation, including release of the Palestinian prisoners, constitutes an end to all claims.

Clinton said that if the teams and their points of view could be reconciled, Barak would meet with Arafat to sign an agreement. The Israeli government approved the proposal in theory, on condition that Arafat also responded positively, which he did. In actuality, however, both sides went on to act in direct contravention of the proposed compromise. The Barak government continued developing settlements in Judea, Samaria, and the Gaza Strip, and Arafat on his part continued to endorse violence and terror.

Barak told Clinton that without an end to terror, he would be unable to sign any agreement because the Israeli public would not stand for it. Indeed, incitement in Israel against Barak increased, and the verbal extremism echoed that of the days of the Rabin government.

TABA TALKS (JANUARY 21, 2001)

With the end of Clinton's term of office as president of the United States (January 20), and with the upcoming elections in Israel in February 2001, the negotiation teams met in January in Taba to discuss the Clinton Parameters. The talks failed, and the negotiations remained stuck for many years. The failure of the Taba Talks closed a circle of ongoing attempts during the Barak/Arafat period to achieve a peace agreement between the Palestinians and Israel.

Many interpretations have been offered of the Taba Talks, but the general impression was that they didn't stand a chance. Toward the end, Barak considered meeting with Arafat, but then the chairman of the Palestinian Authority made an offensive speech against Israel at the Economic Conference at Davos. Arafat attacked Israel as a "fascist state" conducting a "barbaric" and cruel war against the Palestinians, and accused Israel of attacking the Palestinians with "uranium bombs." An unbridgeable gap developed between Arafat and Barak, but the Israeli and Palestinian negotiation teams claimed that "the Taba talks were unprecedented in their positive atmosphere [. . .] the sides declare that they have never been closer to reaching an agreement."

The negotiations that took place between Barak and Arafat have been widely interpreted, and the interpretations will probably multiply over time. One school of thought views Arafat as responsible for the failure; another

THE SOCIAL SITUATION

The economic deterioration in the 1990s had a negative impact on the social situation, especially education. From 1990 to 1993, the intifada was going through its second stage; during this time the educational process witnessed numerous interruptions that often lasted for several days at a time. This reflected negatively on the students in the primary stage. When the PA assumed its responsibilities in 1994, it did its utmost to improve the educational process, such as holding training workshops for teachers. The PA continued to use school curricula from neighboring Arab countries such as Jordan until new Palestinian curricula were prepared. The PA also had to confront the challenges of a young society, which required opening a hundred new schools every year. There was emphasis on offering equal educational opportunities to males and females.[53]

With the beginning of the third millennium, the total number of Palestinian school students was 914,269 distributed as follows:

1. 68 percent in government schools

2. 25.6 percent in UNRWA schools

3. 6.4 percent in private schools.[54]

These large numbers of students required the PA to allocate huge sums of money to provide new schools, additional classrooms, and school furniture, print school textbooks, and pay salaries to more than forty thousand teachers. The ministry of education relied on direct and indirect donations to cover these expenses.

As soon as the second intifada (Al-Aqsa Intifada) started, the educational process was hampered by interruptions caused by the inability of teachers and students to get to their schools due to closures and roadblocks, or due to the arrest of teachers and students. In the first year of the intifada, eighty-seven students were killed, which is equal to 2 percent of the total number of martyrs.[55] Students also suffered from psychological trauma because their homes and schools were shelled.

In the 1990s, the Palestinian territories witnessed a greater participation of women in the economic, political, and social fields. This is evidenced by the participation of women in the 1996 legislative elections, and by the appointment of women to several ministerial positions.

blames Barak. Some believe that U.S. policy hampered the process, while others claim that the power of the extremists on both sides obviated any compromise.

The dream of peace, which many on both sides hoped to achieve, lay shattered and broken, postponed for another time.

New and important laws relating to women—whether in the Egyptian laws in effect in Gaza or the Jordanian laws in the West Bank—were issued, dropped, or modified. For example:

1. Personal Law: prepared in 1998 but not endorsed until much later;

2. Civil Service Law: issued in 1998 and reflected parity between men and women civil servants in pay and appointment;

3. Higher Education Law: aimed to improve education and to make primary education (grades 1–10) compulsory and free;

4. Labor Law: issued in 2000 and emphasized parity between men and women in pay; it also fought discrimination.[56]

Yet, the outbreak of the second intifada did not allow the Palestinians to put these laws in effect.

NOTES

THE DUAL-NARRATIVE APPROACH

1 We thank the U.S. Department of State, the U.S. Embassy in Tel Aviv, the U.S. Consulate in Jerusalem, and the EU for financially supporting this project. We thank the Ford Foundation and Dr. Dieter Hartmann from Germany for their contributions; and Dr. Falk Pingel, Jonathan Kreiner, and Achim Rohde of the Georg Eckert Institute for their support and assistance. Many thanks to the Talitha Kumi School in Beit-Jala and Berlin. We are grateful to all the Palestinian and Israeli teachers who worked on this project and to Dr. Shoshana Steinberg and Summer Jaber-Massarwa for documenting the process. We thank Shimon Ben Naim for his faithful hard work and perseverance in translating successive versions of the texts over several years. We thank Dr. Saliba Sarsar for his hospitality at Monmouth University and the Fulbright Scholarship Program that enabled us to spend the spring semester of 2007 at Monmouth University.

2 For book copies, please write to Prof. Sami Adwan, sadwan@bethlehem.edu.

3 "Double wall" is a metaphoric and psychological term describing the wall surrounding our ethnocentric narratives. You need to open or penetrate through the wall surrounding your narrative, as well as the wall surrounding the other's, hence the term "double wall."

4 In the summer of 2006, two teachers from Barcelona who participated in the teachers' seminar at the Eckert Institute described a very interesting process they

designed with their pupils in order to teach our booklet, translated into Catalan (Adwan and Bar-On, 2006): they asked their two classes to prepare themselves for a seminar on three dates in our conflict (1917; 1948; the First Intifada) as part of their history classes and did not tell the pupils that they provided each class with only one of the two opposing narratives, as those appeared in the PRIME booklet. When the pupils presented their work at the seminar two weeks later, they were surprised to hear the narrative presented by the other group, so different from their own. Only then did the teachers tell them about our booklet. One can see how the innovative presentation in our text stimulated further innovation by these Catalan teachers.

5 See http://prime-peace.org/tmp/teacherguide.php?sid=all.

1[A]. FROM THE BALFOUR DECLARATION
TO THE BRITISH MANDATE IN PALESTINE / *ERETZ YISRAEL*

1 Before the founding of the State of Israel, the Jews called the land *Eretz Yisrael* [Hebrew for "The Land of Israel"—its traditional Jewish designation], while in English it was generally called "Palestine," often also by Zionist Jews; hence this text will use both terms, "Palestine" and "The Land of Israel," depending on the context.

2 The Enlightenment is the generally accepted term; Jews also refer to it as the *Haskalah*.

3 Kolet, S., *Hara'ayon hatzioni vehakamat medinat yisrael*, Maalot, 1985.

4 Sykes, C., *Mibalfour ve'ad Bevin*, Ma'archot, 1966.

5 Weizmann, C., *Masa uma'as*, Schocken, 1963.

6 The Avalon Project, Yale Law School: http://avalon.law.yale.edu/20th_century/palmanda.asp.

7 Lifshitz, M., *Zionut*, Or Am, 1993, 127.

8 Yana'it, R., Y. Avrahami, Y. Etzion (eds.), *Hahaganah beyerushalayim*, 1973.

9 Naor, M. (ed.), *Lexicon ko'ach hamagen—hahaganah*, 1994.

1[B]. THE BALFOUR DECLARATION

1 Al-Hout, Bayan N., *Palestine: The Cause, the People, the Culture*, 357.

2 Ibid., 476–77.

3 Zu'aiter, Akram, *The Palestinian Question*, 50–51.

4 Al-Kayyali, Abd Al-Wahab, *The History of Modern Palestine*.

5 Ibid., 50–51.

6 Jbara, Taysir, *The History of Palestine*, 1,998.

7 Al-Kayyali, ibid., 108.

8 Masalhah, 19.

9 Al-'Uwaissi, Abd Al-Fattah, *The Roots of the Palestinian Cause (1799–1922)*, 29.

10 Ibid., 209.

11 Al-Sifri, 'Isa, *Arab Palestine Between the Mandate and Zionism*, 29.

12 Ibid., 37.

13 Ibid., 38.

14 Jbara, ibid., 123.

15 Al-Kayyali, ibid., 123.

16 Zu'aiter, 66.

2[A]. THE LAND OF ISRAEL AND THE *YISHUV* IN THE 1920S

1 Bar-Navi, E. (ed.), *Ha'atlas hahistori letoldot am yisrael*, Yediot Aharonot, Sifrei Hemed, Tel Aviv, 1994, 209.

2 Kimmerling, B., and S. Migdal, *Palastinim: am behivatzrut*, Keter, 2000, 36.

3 Porat, Y., and Y. Shbeti (eds.), *Hahistoria shel eretz-yisrael*, vol. 9, *Hamandat vehabayit heleumi*, Keter and Yad Ben Zvi, 1982, 310–11.

4 Golani, M., *Milchamot lo korot me'atzman: al zikharon vekoach bechira*, Modan, 2002.

5 Avalon Project, Yale Law School, British White Paper of 1922, at: http://avalon.law.yale.edu/20th_century/brwh1922.asp.

6 Kolat, S., *Hara'ayon hatzioni vehakamat medinat yisrael*, vol. 2, 1985, 13.

7 Ibid., 16.

8 Ibid., 28.

9 Naor and Giladi, *Eretz yisrael bemea haesrim—meyishuv lemedina*, Ministry of Defense, 1990.

10 Domka, A., *Ha'olam vehayehudim bedorot ha'acharonim*, helek bet 1, Zalman Shazar Center, 1999, 108.

11 Ibid., 106.

12 "Meyomano shel colonel Kisch," in Domka, 107.

13 Segev, T., *Yamei hacalaniyot—eretz yisrael betekufat hamandat* [published in English as: *One Palestine, Complete: Jews and Arabs under the British Mandate*], Keter, 1999, 267.

2 [B]. PALESTINE IN THE 1920S

1 Abd Al-Mun'im, Mohammad Faisal, *We and Israel in a Crucial Battle.*

2 Jbara, 127.

3 Shufani, Elias, *A Digest of Palestine's Political History*, 385.

4 Khillah, 127.

5 Al-'Uwaisi, Abd Al-Fattah, *The Roots of the Palestinian Problem*, 242.

6 Ibid., 209

7 Al-Sifri, 'Isa, *Arab Palestine Between the Mandate and Zionism (1799–1922)*, 73.

8 *Palestine: The History and the Cause*, 67.

9 Jbara, 130.

10 Al-Sifri, 79.

11 Jbara, 131.

12 *Palestine: The History and the Cause*, 68.

13 Ejbara, 131.

14 Ibid., 133–134

15 *Palestine: The History and the Cause*, 70.

16 Ibid., 69–70.

17 Jbara, 137.

18 Al-Kayyali, Abd Al-Wahab, 202.

19 Ibid., 223.

20 Shufani, 387.

21 Jbara, 140.

22 Ibid., 141–42.

23 Ibid., 145–49.

24 Tahbub, 44.

25 Al-Hizmawi, 207.

26 *Palestine: The History and the Cause*, 64–65.

27 Al-Hizmawi, 151.

28 Hadawi, Sami, *The Harsh Siege on Palestine, 1914–1979*, 76.

29 Al-Hizmawi, 206.

30 Ibid., 5.

31 Al-Sifri, 107–110.

32 Al-Kayyali, 193.

33 *Summary of the History of the Palestinian Educational System in the Twentieth Century*, 6.

34 *Al-Karmil*, July 1, 1928.

35 *Palestine*, July 22, 1930.

36 Second International Conference for Palestinian Studies, 185.

37 *Palestine*, November 2, 1922.

38 Al-Rajabi, S. M., *The Jewish Community in Hebron*, 104.

39 Jbara, 164.

40 Al-Rajabi, *Jewish Community*, 135.

41 Ibid., 148.

42 Tuqan, 281.

43 Ibid., 169.

44 Ibid., 220–22.

45 Ibid., 222.

46 Ibid.

47 Ibid., 172.

3 [A]. THE LAND OF ISRAEL BETWEEN 1931 AND 1947

1 Ayin Hillel (pseudonym of Hillel Omer), *Tchelet vekotzim*, Sifriat Poalim, 1987, 94.

2 *Toldot hayishuv "choma umigdal,"* Information Center, 1978.

3 There is no exact census figure for the Jewish population in that period; this text relies on the Yad Vashem website at: www.yadvashem.org.

3 [B]. THE PALESTINIAN-ISRAELI CONFLICT: THE 1930s AND 1940s

1 Al-Hout, Bayan, *Leadership and Political Institutions in Palestine*, 238.

2 Al-Kayyali, Abd Al-Wahab, *Palestine: A Modern History*, 219.

3 Shufani, Elias, *A Digest of Palestine's Political History*, 409.

4 Al-Kayyali, ibid., 223–25.

5 Institute for Palestine Studies, *Palestine: Its History and Cause*, 59–60.

6 Jbara, Taysir, *The History of Palestine*, 176–77.

7 Al-Hout, ibid., 477.

8 Shufani, ibid., 447.

9 Ibid., 232–37.

10 Jbara, ibid., 192–94.

11 Ibid.

12 Ibid., 192–94.

13 Al-Kayyali, ibid., 251–52.

14 Institute for Palestine Studies, ibid., 67.

15 Ibid.

16 Al-Hout, 317–28.

17 Al-Khalidi, Walid, *Before Diaspora*, 189–91.

18 Ministry of National Defense, Lebanese Army, *The Palestinian Question and the Danger of Zionism*, 223–26.

19 Zu'aiter, Akram, *The Palestinian Question*, 99.

20 Sharif, Hussein, *The Political Perception of Jews in History*, 353.

21 Ibid., 282.

22 Abd Al-Mun'im, Mohammad Faisal, *We and Israel in the Battle for Destination*, 121.

23 Ibid., 122.

24 Ibid., 185.

25 Jbara, Taysir, *The 1936 Strike in Palestine*, 20.

26 Ibid., 23–27

27 Ibid., 27–28.

28 Al-Kayyali, ibid., 262.

29 Institute for Palestine Studies, ibid., 68.

30 Al-Hout, ibid., 332.

31 Al-Kayyali, ibid., 263.

32 Ibid., 263.

33 Zu'aiter, ibid., 103.

34 Ibid., 105.

35 *The Palestinian Question and the Danger of Zionism*, 233.

36 Al-Hout, ibid., 354–58.

37 Al-Kayyali, ibid., 234, 244–45.

38 Institute for Palestine Studies, ibid., 73.

39 Al-Kayyali, ibid., 284–96.

40 Al-Khalidi, ibid., 190.

41 *The Palestinian Question and the Danger of Zionism*, 239–40.

42 Al-Hout, ibid., 383.

43 Ibid., 384, and Institute for Palestine Studies, ibid., 75.

44 Al-Hout, ibid., 386.

45 Ibid., 386–99.

46 Zu'aiter, ibid., 142.

47 Al-Hout, ibid., 386–99.

48 *The Palestinian Question and the Danger of Zionism*, 241.

49 Institute for Palestine Studies, ibid., 86.

50 Ibid., 85.

51 Al-Hout, ibid., 383.

52 Zu'aiter, ibid., 191–97.

53 Al-Tarazi, Nasri, and Hajjaj, Osama, *The Palestinian Question in Drawing and Words*, 54–56.

54 Al-Khalidi, ibid., 306.

55 Al-Tarazi and Hajjaj, ibid., 57.

4[A]. THE WAR OF INDEPENDENCE AND THE FOUNDING OF THE STATE OF ISRAEL

1 Naveh, E., and Yogev, E., *Historiot*, Tel Aviv: Babel, 2002, 163–64.

2 For a discussion of the refugee problem, see B. Morris, *Leydata shel beayat haplitim hapalastinim, 1947–1948*, Am Oved, 1991.

3 Naveh and Yogev, *Historiot*, 161–62.

4[B]. *AL-NAKBAH*, 1948

1 Al-Sifri, 'Isa, *Arab Palestine Between the Mandate and Zionism*, 100.

2 Sayigh, Rosemary, *Palestinian Peasants from Uprooting to Revolution*, 88.

3 Ibid., 84.

4 Morris, Benny, *The Birth of the Palestinian Refugee Problem*, 159.

5 Ministry of National Defense, Lebanese Army, *The Palestinian Question and the Danger of Zionism*, 263.

6 Ibid., 266.

7 Ibid.

8 Zu'aiter, Akram, *The Palestinian Question*, 226.

9 Institute for Palestine Studies, *Palestine: Its History and Cause*, 122.

10 Ibid., 122.

11 Ibid., 124.

12 Ben-Gurion, David, *Memories of the War, 1947–1948*, 316.

13 Zeitawi, Nihad, in *Destroyed Palestinian Villages*, no. 4 (ed. Kana'neh), 57.

14 Mir'i, Ibrahim, in *Destroyed Palestinian Villages*, no. 16 (ed. Kana'neh), [tk]

15 Sayigh, ibid., 105.

16 Ibid., 132.

17 *Majallat Al-'Ummah*, August 1982.

5[A]. THE STATE OF ISRAEL: THE FIRST DECADES, 1950S AND 1960S

1 Bar-On, M., *Hamaavak al hesegei tashach—mediniut Habitachon shel yisrael*, in *Haasor harishon*, T. Tzameret and H. Yablonka (eds.), Jerusalem, 1997, 14.

2 Morris, B., *Tikkun taut: yehudim ve aravim beeretz yisrael, 1936–1956*, Tel Aviv: Am Oved, 2000, 193.

3 See www.nfc.co.il/archive/003-d.

4 Amir, E., *Mafriach hayonim*, Tel Aviv: Am Oved, 1994.

5[B]. YEARS OF HOMELESSNESS AND DESPAIR

1 Institute for Palestine Studies, *Palestine: Its History and Cause*, 133.

2 Ibid., 135.

3 Abu Zahra, Ibrahim, *The Zionist Movement, Colonialism and Transfer of Palestinians*, 75.

4 Ibid., 77.

5 Ibid., 64–65.

6 Ibid., 65–66.

7 Jbara, Taysir, *The History of Palestine*, 336–37.

8 Ministry of National Defense, Lebanese Army, *The Palestinian Issue and the Danger of Zionism*, 274.

9 Jbara, 319–21.

10 Ibid., 319–21.

11 *Palestine: Its History and Issue*, 142.

12 Khalaf, Salah, *A Palestinian Without an Identity*, 22.

13 Abu Zahra, 55.

14 The Campaign for Defending the Rights of Palestinian Refugees, *Palestinian Refugees in Diaspora*, 4.

15 Kanafani, Ghassan, *Men in the Sun*, 85–86.

16 Ibid., 106.

17 Zu'aiter, Akram, *The Palestinian Problem*, 262, 267.

18 Abu Zahra, ibid., 81.

19 Zu'aiter, ibid., 257–58.

20 Abu Zahra, ibid., 68.

21 Al-Deek, Mufeed, "Unpublished Pages from Moshe Sharett's Memoirs," 47.

22 Zu'aiter, ibid., 260.

23 Al-Tarazi, Nasri, and Hajja, Osama, *The Palestine Problem in Drawing and Words*, 77.

24 Al-Hourani, 177–82.

25 Ibid., 177–82.

26 Abu Zahra, ibid., 45.

27 Al-Hourani, ibid., 180–82.

28 Abu 'Eleiwi, Hasan, *The Palestinian Encyclopedia*, vol. 2, 70–78.

29 Abbas, Ihsan, *The Palestinian Encyclopedia*, vol. 4, 25–26.

30 *Palestine: Its History and Issue*, 147–48.

31 Al Deek, ibid., 43.

32 *Palestine: Its History and Issue*, 149.

33 Ibid., 152.

34 *The Palestinian Issue and the Danger of Zionism*, 291.

35 Ibid., 294.

36 Al-'Aqqad, Salah, *The Contemporary Arab East*, 469.

37 Al-Duri, Abd Al-Aziz, ed., *The Palestinian Issue and the Arab Israeli Conflict*, 296–29.

38 Ibid., 296–98.

39 *Palestine: Its History and Issue*, 165.

6[A]. THE SIX-DAY WAR OF JUNE 5–10, 1967

1 Wallach, in Mikelson, Z., and Meltzer (eds.), *Hama'avak lebitachon yisrael*, 1999, 130.

2 Gluska, A., *Eshkol ten pekuda*, 2004, 313.

3 Wallach, ibid.

4 Shapira, A., *Siakh lochamim, pirkey hakshava vehitmodedut*, Siach Lochamim [published in English as: *The Seventh Day: Soldiers Talk About the Six-Day War*].

5 Rabin, Y., *Pinkas sherut*, 1979, 157.

6 Rubinstein, D., *Gush Emunim*, 1982, 30.

7 Amikam, A., "Yediot Aharonot 23.6.67," in A. Ben-Ami (ed.), *Hacol: Gevulot hashalom shel eretz yisrael*, 1967.

8 Shapira, in *Siach lochamim*, 271–72.

9 Pedatsur, R., *Nitzahon hamevukha—Mediniyut memshelet Eshkol bashtahim hakvushim leahar milhemet sheshet hayamim*, Bitan, 1996, 55–56.

10 Alon, Y., *Kelim sheluvim*, Hakibbutz Hameuhad, 1980, 165.

11 Pedatsur, *Nitzahon hamevukha*, 152–53.

12 Braverman, N. G., (ed.), *Kovetz mismakhim betoldot hamedina*, Ministry of Defense, 1981.

13 Harkaby, Y., *Ha'amana hafalastinit umashma'uta*, Publications Service of the Information Center, 1974.

14 Bekhor, G., *Leksikon ashaf*, Ministry of Defense, 1991.

6[B]. ISRAELI AGGRESSION AGAINST ARAB AND PALESTINIAN LANDS: JUNE 1967 WAR

1 Zu'aiter, Akram, *Palestinian Problem*, 291–93.

2 Al-Shar', Sadiq, *Our Wars with Israel, 1947–1973*.

3 Ibid.,

4 Ibid., 449.

5 Institute for Palestine Studies, *Palestine: Its History and Problem*, 238–39.

6 Green, Stephen, *American Secret Relations with a Militant Israel, 1948–1967*.

7 Jabara, Taysir, *The History of Palestine*,

8 Herzog, Chaim, *The Arab-Israeli Wars*.

9 Al-Shar', *Our Wars*, 471.

10 Yousef Ka'wash, *The June 1967 War*, 78.

11 Al-Shar', *Our Wars*, 384–485.

12 Al-Budairy, Musa, *Palestinian Society on the West Bank and in the Gaza Strip*, 54–55.

13 Shaker, Mahmoud, *Encyclopedia of Jewish History*, 384–485.

14 *A Summary of the History of Palestine*, 88.

15 Al-Ghul, Omar Hilmi, *Palestinian Developments*, 25.

16 Al-Tarazi, Nasri, and Osama, Hajjaj, *The Palestine Problem in Drawing and Words*, 77; and *Palestine: Its History and Problem*, 187–88.

17 Al-Tarazi and Hajjaj, ibid., 82.

18 Al-Tarazi and Hajjaj, ibid., 83.

19 Al-Shar', *Our Wars*, 514.

20 Al Budairy, 45–55.

21 *Palestine: Its History and Problem*, 187.

7[A]. FROM THE SIX-DAY WAR TO THE FIRST INTIFADA: ISRAEL IN THE 1970s AND 1980s

1 Avineri, A., *Hamapolet*, Revivim, 1977.

2 Oz, A., *Po vesham beeretz yisrael, bestav 1982*, Tel Aviv: Sifriyat Ufikim, Am Oved, 1983, 32.

3 Ibid., 41.

4 Kimmerling, B., and Migdal, S., *Palastinim—am behivatzrut*, Keter, 2000, 221.

5 Rubinstein, D., *Mi leadoni elaay, gush emunim*, Hkibbutz Hmeuhad, 1982, 30.

7[B]. PALESTINE AND PALESTINIANS, 1967–1987

1 See http://www.palestinehistory.com/arabic/argalamp.htm.

2 Institute for Palestine Studies, *Palestine: Its History and [?]*, 178; *Palestinian Encyclopedia*, vol. 5, 589.

3 Al-Tarazi, Nasri, and Hajjaj, Osama, *Palestine Problem in Drawing and Words*, 84

4 In the British daily *The Times*, Lord C. Maghew in 1986 challenged any Zionist to offer any evidence that proves the charge. He offered 5000 pounds to the one who provides the evidence. See *Palestinian Encyclopedia*, part 2, vol. 5, 19.

5 Kattan, Henry, *The Palestinian Problem*, 130

6 Ibid., 131.

7 Ibid., 133–36.

8 *The Political Encyclopedia*, vol. 1, 156.

9 Kattan, ibid., 138.

10 *Palestinian Encyclopedia*, part 2, vol. 5, 33.

11 Ibid., 986–87.

12 Ibid., 208.

13 Ibid., 216.

14 Abd Al-Hadi, Mahdi, *The Palestinian Problem and Political Solutions*, 507 in Kattan, 127.

15 *Palestinian Encyclopedia*, part 2, vol. 5, 229 in Abd Al-Hadi, Mahdi, 576–77.

16 *Palestinian Encyclopedia*, part 2, vol. 5, 32.

17 Institute for Palestine Studies, 178.

18 Ibid., 181; *Palestinian Encyclopedia*, part 2, vol. 5, 585. Special Studies

19 Al-Tarazi and Hajjaj, ibid., 86.

20 *Palestinian Encyclopedia*, part 2, vol. 5, 202.

21 Ibid., 204. Special Studies

22 Ibid., 206–208.

23 Abd Al-Hadi, Mahdi, 414, *Palestinian Encyclopedia*, part 2, vol. 5, 208.

24 Abd Al-Hadi, 413.

25 Ibid., 414.

26 *Palestinian Encyclopedia*, part 2, vol. 5, 208.

27 Ibid., 209.

28 Ibid., vol. 4, 773.

29 Ibid., part 2, vol 5, 212.

30 Ibid., part 2, vol. 5, 598; vol. 6, 191; vol. 2, 209.

31 Ibid., part 2, vol. 5, 611; *Political Encyclopedia*, vol. 2, 209.

32 Abd Al-Hadi, 545.

33 Ibid., 547; *Palestinian Encyclopedia*, part 2, vol. 5, 621; *Political Encyclopedia*, vol. 2, 209.

34 *Political Encyclopedia*, vol. 2, 210.

35 Institute for Palestine Studies, 208.

36 Islamweb, Land Day, and Resisting the Judaization, from www.islamweb.net.

37 The National Committee for Defending Arab Land in Palestine, "The Black Paper on Land Day," 172–73.

38 Islamweb, Land Day, and Resisting the Judaization, from www.islamweb.net.

39 National Committee for Defending Arab Land, "Black Paper," 76.

40 Al-Tarazi and Hajjaj, ibid., 97.

41 *Palestinian Encyclopedia*, part 2, vol. 6, 193.

42 *Palestinian Encyclopedia*, part 2, vol. 6, 194.

43 Ibid., part 2, vol. 6, 192.

44 Kattan, ibid., 138.

45 *Palestinian Encyclopedia*, part 2, vol. 5, 193, 233.

46 Ibid., part 2, vol. 2, 211.

47 Ibid., part 2, vol. 5, 233.

48 Ibid., part 2, vol. 5, 332.

49 Al-Tarazi and Hajjaj, 103.

50 Al-Husseini, Yousef, *Palestine and Israeli Aggression on Islamic Italy Sites*, 26–27.

51 Ibid., 30.

52 Ibid., 29, 31.

53 Ibid., 33–36.

54 Ibid., 47; Sa'd al Din al Alami, 70.

55 Al-Husseini, 47–48; Sa'd al Din al Alami, 70.

56 Al-Husseini, 48–49, 50; Al-Alami, 337.

57 Ibid., 49–50, 50; Al-Alami, 376–82.

58 Ibid., 110–22. See Al-Alami, 160–62, 299–302, 314.

59 Al-Husseini, 51.

60 Al-Alami, 104.

61 *Palestinian Encyclopedia*, part 2, vol. 6, 570.

62 Ibid., 571.

63 Ibid., 572.

64 Ibid., 574.

65 Ibid, 574-575

66 Abdallah, Samir, *The Impact of the Occupation on the Productive Base of the Palestinian Economy*, 10.

67 Ibid., 12.

68 Ibid., 12, 15.

69 Ibid., 67.

70 Gohatsky, 304 in Samir Abdullah, 22.

71 Ibid.

72 Ibid.

73 *Palestinian Encyclopedia*, part 2, vol. 3, 123.

74 *Palestinian Encyclopedia*, part 2, vol. 3, 161.

75 Ibid., 159.

76 Ibid., 134, 161.

77 Ibid., 134.

78 Ibid.

79 Ibid., 165.

80 Ibid., part 2, vol. 4, 33, 36.

81 Ibid., 41.

82 Ibid., 33.

83 Ibid., 46.

84 Ibid., 172–73.

8[A]. INTIFADA

1 Schiff, Z., and Yaari, E., *Intifada*, Schocken, 1990, 160.

2 Ibid., 146.

3 Ibid., 43

4 Ibid., 325–26.

9[B]. REACHING FOR A SETTLEMENT: AGREEMENTS TOWARD THE UNKNOWN

1 *Ha'aretz*, November 20, 1988.

2 Horovitz, Dan, and Lisak, Moshe, *Democracy and Security in an Endless Conflict*, 28.

3 Hawatmeh, Nayef, *Oslo and the Other Balanced Peace*, 311.

4 *The Uprising and the Palestinian Nakba*, 178.

5 "Studies in the Israeli Society," 88.

6 *Oslo Peace Between Illusion and Reality*, 236.

7 *The Rough Road*, 28.

8 Ibid., 204.

9 *Oslo Peace*, 49.

10 *The Rough Road*, 38.

11 Ghalyoun, Burhan, *Arabs and the Battle for Peace*, 171.

12 Abu Hadba, Ahmed, *The Palestinian Economy and the Limits of Israeli Control*, 75.

13 See www.sis.gov.ps.

14 *Oslo Peace*, 162.

15 Aronson, Geoffrey, *The Politicians of Fait Accompli in the West Bank and Gaza Strip*, 118.

16 *Oslo Peace*, 214.

17 Ibid., 94.

18 *The Uprising and the Palestinian Nakba*, 236.

19 Ibid., 209.

20 Ghalyoun, *Arabs and the Battle for Peace*, 184.

21 Ibid., 176.

22 *Ha'aretz*, July 19, 1996.

23 Darwish, Marwan, *The Fourteenth Knesset Elections*, 36.

24 Shavit, Arieh, *Ideology and Economy in Israel*, 72.

25 *Ha'aretz*, January 16, 1998.

26 *The Uprising and the Palestinian Nakba*, 201.

27 *Ha'aretz*, February 1, 1998.

28 Arieh Shavit in *Ha'aretz*, July 19, 1996.

29 Hawatmeh, *Oslo and the Other Balanced Peace*, 198.

30 Aronson, *The Politicians of Fait Accompli*, 78.

31 Benvenisti, Meron, *The Uprising Economy*, 230.

32 Aronson, *The Politicians of Fait Accompli*, 217.

33 Haydar, Aziz, *Palestinians in Israel Under the Oslo Agreement*, 92.

34 Ibid., 173.

35 See www.bma.alquds.com.

36 See www.regaz.com.

37 Al-Atrash, Azmi, *Palestinian Economy and Israeli Occupation*, 197.

38 See www.oppc.pna.net.

39 See ibid.

40 See ibid.

41 *The Uprising and the Palestinian Nakba*, 231.

42 Hilal, Jamil, *Poverty in the West Bank and Gaza*, 11.

43 See www.miftah.org.

44 Hilal, *Poverty in the West Bank and Gaza*, 11.

45 "Private Sector Economy in the West Bank and Gaza," 3.

46 Ibid.

47 Hilal, *Poverty in the West Bank and Gaza*, 21.

48 "Private Sector Economy in the West Bank and Gaza," 23.

49 See www.palestine-info.com.

50 See www.miftah.org.

51 See www.minfo.org.

52 See ibid.

53 See www.nic.gov.ps.

54 See www.isesco.org.

55 See ibid.

56 See www.minfo.org.

ISRAELI GLOSSARY

ARMISTICE AGREEMENT

Treaties signed by the Arab states with the state of Israel that followed its military achievement at the end of the 1948 war. Egypt was the first country to sign (in February, 1949) followed by Lebanon (in March), Jordan (in April), and Syria (in July). These were not peace treaties but arrangements that ended the war, by which the Arab countries acknowledged their inability to defeat the state of Israel militarily.

School for the children of the first Aliyah

ALIYAH (ASCENT)

The term used to characterize the immigration of Jews to the Land of Israel. It originated in ancient times when Jews were commanded to ascend to Jerusalem during certain

PALESTINIAN GLOSSARY

AL-AQSA INTIFADA

The provocative visit by Ariel Sharon and other Zionists to the compound of Al-Aqsa Mosque on 28 September 2000 infuriated the Palestinians and sparked off the second intifada, or uprising, against the Israeli occupation.

AL-BURAQ WALL

The name given to the western wall of the Al-Aqsa Mosque. For Muslims, it is sacred because on the night of the Isra' (nocturnal journey form Mecca to Jerusalem) Prophet Mohammed (peace be upon him) tied his horse, Al-Buraq, to that wall before the Mi'raj (the Prophet's ascension to the heavens). Jews believe that it is constructed on the remains of Solomon's Temple and call it the "Western Wall" or the "Wailing Wall." The court next to this wall is part of the *Waqf* (endowments) belonging to the Abu Madyan family. During the British mandate of Palestine, the Jews attempted to purchase the court from the Muslims several times but were not successful.

holidays. It connotes that immigration to the Land of Israel represents an elevated status. There were five waves of Aliyah prior to the establishment of the State of Israel, starting in 1882. Each wave was characterized by the origin, economic and social status, and ideology of the immigrants. The immigration of Jews to the Land of Israel continued after the creation of the state of Israel.

THE DISTURBANCES (THE RIOTS)

The term that the Jews used in order to characterize the violent Arab attacks against the Jewish population during the Mandate period. It refers to the Disturbances of 1920–1921, 1929, and 1936–1939.

Haim Weizman became the first president of the state of Israel

EMANCIPATION

A legal process that ended the discrimination of certain individuals and groups and provided them with equal rights and equal opportunities. The Emancipation enabled the Jews to assimilate into the rest of society, and opened new fields that were previously forbidden to them.

ENLIGHTENMENT

A cultural and scientific movement in Europe in the eighteenth century claiming that human reason, rather than external authority, is the only way to comprehend the world. The movement resisted religious authority and worked to secure individual liberty. It shaped the ideas of the French Revolution and had great influence on Jewish society in Western and Central Europe.

ERETZ YISRAEL (THE LAND OF ISRAEL)

The name that the Jews used for the territory that the Arabs called "Palestine." The name refers to the land (not necessarily to a specific state) where Jews

AL-HUSSEINI, HAJ AMIN (AL-MUFTI) (1897–1970)

Born in 1897, he went to school in Palestine. He studied Islamic Shari'a (jurisprudence) as well as French and Arabic philology. In 1912, he moved to Cairo for further study. He joined a military academy in Istanbul, and graduated as an officer. He was appointed mufti of Jerusalem in 1921 by the high commissioner and subsequently became chairman of the Supreme Muslim Council in Palestine. Soon he became an important figure in the national movement and was known for his political wisdom and diplomatic skills. He was known for his political sense and diplomatic talent, by virtue of which he acquired a name and extensive publicity for himself.

AL-HUSSEINI, MUSA KATHEM (1853–1934)

Born in Jerusalem in 1853. He attended the best Turkish educational institutions. He held many posts, most importantly, district governor in many states under the Ottoman Empire. He succeeded his brother Hussein Salim Al-Husseini as mayor of Jerusalem but he was pulled out of this position by the British mandate in 1920 because of his nationalist views. From then until his death in 1934, he was the unrivaled head of the Palestinian Nationalist Movement.

AL-NAFAQ UPRISING 1996

Another episode in the struggle of the Palestinians in which they showed their tenacity in holding to their land and holy sites. On the morning of 25 September 1996, the Palestinian people surprised the whole world and Israel with their uprising against Israeli occupation after Israel opened a tunnel underneath the Al-Aqsa Mosque. For three days, all sectors of the Palestinian people stood together against the Israeli military forces in defense of their holy places.

AL-QASSAM, IZZ AL-DIN (1871–1935)

Born in 1871 in the township of Habla near the city of Latakia, Syria. Studied at Al-'Azhar and worked as a teacher in Sultan Ibrahim Mosque. Al-Qassam was known for his sincere nationalism and religious fervor. He took part in

lived and enjoyed religious and political independence during the period of the first and second temples. Even during the years in exile the Jews continued to keep some settlements on the land. According to Jewish religious belief, the land was promised by God to the Jewish people, and in the Bible it is called "the Promised Land." Therefore the Zionist movement chose Eretz Yisrael ("Land of Israel") as the destination for establishing the Jewish state. The geographical borders of the Land of Israel are not defined. They were changed throughout history according to political circumstances, and are defined today according to one's political view. The official name of the Land of Israel during the Mandate period was "Palestine—Eretz Yisrael," as it appears on coins and stamps of the period. The Roman Emperor Adrian labeled the land "Palestina" at the end of the Bar-Kochba rebellion (135 AC), aiming to eradicate any reference to Jewish existence in the land. The area around Jerusalem became a Roman province named Judea.

ETZEL (IRGUN, OR THE NATIONAL MILITARY ORGANIZATION)

An underground military group, founded as a reaction to the riots of 1936,

The weapon ship of the Irgun, *Altalena*, is burning in front of the beach at Tel Aviv

which did not submit to the authority of the elected institutions of the Jewish community in Palestine (the *Yeshuv*). The Etzel refused to operate under the restraint policy imposed on the Haganah, the underground military organization of the *Yeshuv*. The Etzel was under the authority of Zeev Jabotinsky; the leader of the Revisionist Party. It numbered a few hundred members and operated against officials of the British administration and against the Arab public.

David Ben Gurion

DAVID BEN GURION (1886–1973)

The most prominent leader of the Zionist movement. He was born as David Green in 1886. As a young person he was active in the Zionist movement and held various positions in its institutions. He viewed the creation of

the revolt of Sheikh Salah El-Ali in 1920 against the French in Syria and had to flee to Haifa in 1922. He taught at the Islamic School in Haifa and then was the chairman of the Muslim Youth Association, 'imam and preacher at the Al-Istiqlal Mosque in Haifa. After witnessing the injustice and oppression of the British in Palestine, he called for resistance and struggle against the British and the Jews. He died in battle with the British near Jenin in 1935.

AL-RASHIDIYYA SCHOOL

A school in Jerusalem built in 1903 and named after Ahmad Rasheed Bey, district governor of Jerusalem during the reign of the Ottoman Sultan Abdul Hameed II. Teaching at the school started in 1906. Graduates of the school include some well-known figures, such as Raghib Al-Nashashibi (Jerusalem mayor, 1920–1934) and Abd Al-Kareem Al-Karmi (Abu Salma), famous Palestinian poet.

AL-SHUKAYRI, AHMED (1908–1980)

An outstanding Palestinian lawyer, and the first head of the PLO. He was born in 1908 in Tibnin, south of Lebanon. He completed primary school education in Acre. He finished secondary school in Jerusalem in 1926. He joined the American University in Beirut. A year later he was expelled by the French Mandatory Power in Lebanon for leading a huge demonstration organized by Arab students on the occasion of May 6th. He returned to Palestine where he studied at the Institute of Law in Jerusalem. After graduating from the institute, he trained and worked in the law office of Awni Abdul Hadi, one of the founders of Hizb Al-Istiqlal (the Independence Party) in Palestine. During this period, he met some of the leaders of the Great Syrian Revolution, who had taken refuge in Palestine, such as Shukri Al-Quwatly, Riyadh Al-Sulh, Nabih Al-Athma, Adel Al-Athma, and Adel Arslan. In 1945, he was chosen by Musa Al-Alami to open an Arab media office in Washington, D.C., to promote the

Ahmad Shukairi (1908–1980), the first PLO chairman

an independent and sovereign state for the Jews as the major Zionist goal, and demanded that all Zionist organizations relate to the institutions of the Yeshuv. He led the struggle for independence and the war that followed. Ben Gurion was the first prime minister and defense minister of Israel, holding these positions during most of the first decade of the state. He passed away in 1973.

HAGANAH (DEFENSE ORGANIZATION)

An underground Jewish military organization established to defend the Jewish community in the Land of Israel. The organization was founded in 1920 and

"Haganah" fighters, Tel Aviv, 1948

was under the official authority of the Yeshuv, with unofficial acceptance by the British administration. The organization increased its military capacity and scope after each wave of violence. It was able to produce some weapons, to buy arms abroad, and to deliver them illegally to the Jews in the Land of Israel. At its height the organization numbered about fifty thousand members.

BENJAMIN ZE'EV HERZL (1860–1904)

Theodor Herzl

Considered the father of the Zionist movement. Having experienced anti-Semitism as a student and journalist, Herzl became a Zionist activist. His book *The Jewish State* presented his Zionist ideas and contributed to the spreading of Zionism worldwide. He founded the first Zionist Congress and created the first Zionist institutions, thereby turning the various Zionist groups into one national movement. He worked without success to convince the great powers to grant an official "Charter" for the creation of a Jewish state, but he did succeed in popularizing the Zionist movement and having it recognized

Palestinian cause. Then he represented Palestine at the Arab League (1962–1969). At the First Arab Summit (January 1964), he was appointed president of the Palestine Liberation Organization, which was then under the supervision of the Arab League. He continued to guide the policy of the PLO until 1969, when he resigned his position as head of the PLO and as the representative of Palestine and devoted his time to writing.

ARAB NATIONALISM

The belief that all speakers of Arabic constitute a nation tied together by bonds of common feelings, aspirations, history, beliefs, traditions and customs, and norms.

ARAFAT, YASSER (1929–2004)

Symbol of the Palestinian national movement. He devoted most of his life to the Palestinian cause. He was leader of the student movement in Cairo, leader of Fatah, a political leader who signed a peace agreement with Israel. He lived in Egypt, Jordan, Lebanon, and Tunis. Yasser Arafat (Abu 'Ammar) was born in Gaza on 24 August 1929. His original full name was Mohammad Abdel Rahman Abdel Raouf Arafat Al-Qudwa Al-Husseini. He studied civil engineering at the University of Cairo. During his undergraduate studies he joined the Muslim Brotherhood and the General Union of Palestinian Students, becoming president from 1952–1956. He worked in Kuwait and set up a private company. He founded the Fatah movement in Kuwait in 1964. Fatah later became the main movement in the Palestine Liberation Organization. He succeeded Ahmed Al-Shukayri as chairman of the PLO in 1969. In November 1974 he addressed the United Nations General Assembly and later that year Palestine was granted observer status in the UN. Following the Israeli invasion of Beirut in August 1982, PLO headquarters were moved to Tunis. On 15 November 1988, Arafat proclaimed the Independent State of Palestine on the West Bank and Gaza

Yasser Arafat, PLO chairman and President of the Palestinian Authority (1996–2004)

by the world's governments. Herzl was the leader of the Zionist movement until his death.

HAJJ AL-AMIN HUSSEINI, (1895–1974)

The leader of the Palestinians during the British mandate who led Palestinian violent activities against the Zionist movement. In 1920 he was nominated as the "Mufti" (Muslim religious position) of Jerusalem and later became the President of the Muslim Supreme Council. He incited the riots of 1920–1921 and was sentenced to ten years in prison but was pardoned by the British High Commissioner. He was among the perpetrators of the riots of 1929, and in 1936 led the Arab revolt against the British authorities. With the outbreak of World War II he left for Nazi Germany and supported the war effort

and propaganda of the fascist countries. After the war he escaped to Egypt, and from there, continued to work for the Palestinian cause. He presented an extreme and uncompromising position toward any idea of reconciliation with the Zionist movement. After the war of 1948 he was the major proponent of the right of return of the war's refugees.

El Husseini meets with Muslim S.S. soldiers

VLADIMIR ZE'EV JABOTINSKY (1880–1940)

A son of a wealthy family of merchants from Odessa (today Ukraine), Jabotinsky received both traditional and modern education. He studied law in Switzerland and Italy and published essays under the name "Altalena." He started his Zionist activities after the Kishinev pogroms (1903) and then advocated for the creation of an independent Jewish defense force. He initiated the formation of the Hebrew legions within the British forces during World War I. He founded the ZAHAR (the Revisionist Zionist Organization), representing the right wing of Zionism that did not envision any compromise with the Arab population.

THE LEAGUE OF NATIONS

An international association funded by the peace treaties that ended World

and was elected by due democratic process as president of Palestine on 2 April 1989. As PLO chairman, Arafat officially accepted the right of Israel to exist. This acceptance allowed the start of negotiations with Israel and eventually to the conclusion of the Oslo Accords in September 1993. In 1996, Arafat was elected by the first elected Palestinian Legislative Council as the president of the Palestinian National Authority. Arafat spent the last two years of his life in the Ramallah compound besieged by the Israeli army. After severe international pressure on Israel, Arafat was transferred to Paris in October 2004 after his health had worsened critically. He died a short time later.

ASHKENAZI JEWISH COMMUNITY (WESTERN JEWS)

A Jewish community from eastern and central Europe (Poland, Russia, and Germany), in addition to Jews who migrated to North America. They constitute about 90 percent of world Jewry.

BALFOUR, ARTHUR JAMES (1848–1939)

British prime minister (1902–1905) and leader of the Conservative Party for more than twenty years. He was secretary for foreign affairs in the war coalition government of Lloyd George (1916–1919). He issued the famous letter in 1917 which later became known as the Balfour Declaration.

BONAPARTE, NAPOLEON (1769–1821)

Born in the Island of Corsica. A great soldier and a shrewd politician who became emperor of France in 1804. He formed a great army, which seized neighboring countries. He prepared to invade Britain, but was defeated at Trafalgar in 1805. He invaded Russia and marched on to Moscow in 1812. However, the Russians burned Moscow before he entered it and was forced to leave Russia in the cold winter with only a small fraction of his army. After his ultimate defeat at the Battle of Waterloo in Belgium, Bonaparte was exiled to the island of Saint Helena, where he died in 1821.

BONE-BREAKING POLICY

The policy adopted by Yitzhak Rabin to crush the intifada which broke

War I. Its goals were to keep the peace, to mediate diplomatically in conflicts between states, and to help humankind address issues such as public health, welfare, cultural development, protection of minorities, and disarmament. Many problems impaired its activities, thus making the organization ineffective.

Lechi (The Fighters for the Freedom of Israel)

Yair Stern, the commander of the Lechi, next to the organization's anthem

An underground military organization that was founded by members who left the Etzel (Irgun) because it collaborated with Great Britain during World War II. The members of the Lechi (which amounted to a few dozen) focused their activities on personal attacks against British officials. They did not belong to any political wing of the *Yeshuv* and carried out their military operations separately and without the consent of, the *Yeshuv*'s political leaders.

Mandate

An authorization of legal authority. Historically it refers to the authorization that the League of Nations gave to certain countries, granting them the right to control a given geographical area in order to develop it and eventually to lead its people to complete independence (for example, the British Mandate in the Land of Israel).

Nationalism

A worldview that values a people's shared characteristics, such as ethnic origin, territorial contiguity, historical heritage, language, religion, and culture.

out in 1987 in protest of the Israeli occupation of the West Bank and Gaza. Israeli soldiers admitted the use of brutality against the Palestinians, including breaking the bones of protesters.

THE DISPLACED

Al-Naazihuun (in Arabic)—a term used to refer to those Palestinians who fled their homes in the West Bank or Gaza as a result of the 1967 Israeli aggression and who crossed the Jordan River and took shelter in Jordan.

HAMAS (ISLAMIC RESISTANCE MOVEMENT)

The military arm of the Muslim Brotherhood movement in Palestine. It became prominent in the Palestinian arena in the aftermath of the eruption of the 1987 intifada.

HUSSEIN, AL-SHARIF (1854–1931)

Al-Hussein Bin Ali Bin 'Awn Al-Qurayshi Al-Hashimi, the last sharif of Mecca, related by lineage to Al-Hussein Bin Ali, Prophet Mohammed's grandson. He is the father of King Abdullah of Jordan (King Hussein's grandfather), and the father of King Faisal I, king of Iraq after the end of World War I. He became famous for leading the Great Arab Rebellion against the Turks. He is also famous for the secret correspondence with Sir McMahon, in which the British promised to grant independence to the countries in the East in return for helping the Allies in World War I.

IMMIGRATION LAW

This law came into effect in 1920, permitting the Jewish Agency to bring 16,500 immigrants into Palestine each year, provided it was responsible for their keep for a year. But in May 1921, an order was published to stop immigration pending amendment of the nature of the application of the immigration conditions in the law. The Immigration Law was amended a number of times, and was finally replaced in 1928.

A nationalist movement aspires to political independence and sovereignty for such a people.

Palmach (Strike Forces)

The most professional military unit in the Haganah (the defense force of the *Yeshuv*). The unit was created during World War II, in 1942, in order to help the British forces defend the region against impending invasion by Nazi Germany and its allies. The first military operation of the Palmach was

in Lebanon. Later, the unit became the major combat force of the Haganah. During the War of Independence, the Palmach bore the lion's share of the fighting. In 1947–1948 the Palmach brigades numbered about six thousand fighters, out of which about one thousand were killed on the battlefield.

Palmach fighters

The United Nations

The United Nations (UN) was founded at the end of World War II. In the beginning it numbered fifty states, out of which five permanent members

of the Security Council had the right to veto any decision. Like its predecessor, the League of Nations, the UN aims to promote peace and security worldwide, as well as to resolve global economic, health, education, refugee, and human rights issues. UN membership today numbers more than 190 states.

The UN flag

The Western Wall

A supporting wall that King Herod built in order to enlarge the space of the Temple Mount. The Wall, known also as the Wailing Wall, is the only structural relic related to the Temple, though it is not a part of the Temple structure itself. The Jewish people view this wall as their most holy place, a remnant of their ancient sacred place of worship. Since the destruction of the Temple, Jews have prayed next to the Wall, waiting for the coming of

INTIFADA

A popular uprising or mass disobedience against the authority of the occupation or a Palestinian popular resistance movement which aims to liberate the Palestinian land from Israeli occupation. The most important intifadas are the first intifada (December 1987) and the second intifada (or Al-Aqsa Intifada) in September 2000.

JERUSALEM

A 5,000-year-old Arab city. Its oldest name is *Orshalim*, a Canaanite name that refers to the god Shal (god of peace). The Arab Jebusites called it *Yaboos*. It was occupied by the Israeli army in June 1967.

JEWISH AGENCY

The executive arm of the World Zionist Organization since 1922 in Palestine following the publication of the Balfour Declaration and the imposition of the British mandate over Palestine. Article 4 in the mandate document stipulated that "a Jewish agency shall be set up as a public body for the purpose of advising and cooperating with the Administration of Palestine in such economic, social, and other matters as may affect the establishment of the Jewish national home and the interests of the Jewish population in Palestine." The mandate document recognized the Jewish Agency as the Zionist organization whose central functions during the period of the mandate were to represent the Zionist movement and world Jewry before the mandatory authorities, the League of Nations, and the British government.

MANDATE

The appointment of powers granted to the Great Powers by the League of Nations to run the properties belonging to the countries defeated in World War I, especially the Ottoman Empire. In fact, it is the term which the colonial powers created to justify their colonialist plans. It was a compromise that excluded the character of occupation, though in the meantime didn't recognize the independence of the countries under a mandate because such a country is not prepared to rule over itself on its own and to stand on its own feet.

The Western Wall

the Messiah who will rebuild the Temple at the end of time. According to Muslim belief, Mohammed ascended to heaven from a rock that is situated at the summit of the Temple Mount and on which can be seen the footprint of his horse. Two mosques stand today on the Temple Mount: Al Aqsa (the Silver Tomb) and Omar (the Golden Tomb).

THE YESHUV

The Zionist Jewish community that immigrated to and settled in the Land of Israel. Following each wave of immigration this community increased its numbers. In addition, the *Yeshuv* progressed economically and militarily. In 1917 the *Yeshuv* numbered 55,000 people, which represented about 10 percent of the population. By 1947 the *Yeshuv* had grown to 650,000 inhabitants, about 33 percent of the population of the Land of Israel.

Marj Al-Zuhour Deportees

On 17 December 1992, the Israeli government decided to deport 418 Palestinians from Hamas and Islamic Jihad to Marj Al-Zuhour in south Lebanon in response to the kidnapping of Nissim Toledano, an Israeli soldier who was held hostage by a group of Palestinians. The soldier was later killed after Israel refused to release Palestinian prisoners in return for him. The deportees remained in Lebanon for one year, after which they were allowed to return to the occupied territories.

Nasser, Gamal Abdul (1918–1970)

Born in Alexandria on 15 January 1918. He joined military college in 1937 and fought with the Egyptian army in Palestine in 1948. He was the head of the Free Officers who led the Egyptian Revolution (1952) and became president of the Egyptian Republic (1956–1970). He nationalized the Suez Canal. He played an important role in the Arab independence movement and was a key figure in the nonaligned movement. He died in 1970.

Nationalism/Patriotism

Predicated on the basis of psychological bonds and other elements shared by a group of people such as language, culture, heritage, origin, history, land, goals, and destiny. Nationalism is the feeling of belonging to a group.

Refugees

The Palestinians who were forced to leave their homes and property in Palestine following the 1948 war. Today, there are four million refugees living in the West Bank, the Gaza Strip, Jordan, Syria, and Lebanon.

Right to Self-Determination

The legitimate right of all nations to determine their destiny and to shape their countries according to the will and freely expressed desires of their peoples. It is one of the most important principles advocated by American President Woodrow Wilson in the aftermath of World War I.

Sabra and Shatila Massacre (September 1982)

While the Israeli army was invading West Beirut in the aftermath of the assassination of Lebanese president Bashir Al-Jmayyil, the militia of the Lebanese Phalanges broke into the two Palestinian camps of Sabra and Shatila. During forty-eight hours, hundreds of unarmed Palestinians were massacred, including women, children, old men, and young men by machine guns, daggers, and axes. The world discovered the massacre on 18 September 1982.

Sadat, Anwar (1918–1981)

Born in 1918 to a simple, peasant family. He graduated as an officer from military school in 1938 and then was promoted to captain. He became a member of the Free Officers Organization in 1952 at the request of Jamal Abdul Nasser. He participated in the revolution that overthrew King Farouq of Egypt in

1954. President Nasser appointed him to the People's Court that prosecuted members of the underground Muslim Brotherhood who were accused of conspiring to assassinate President Nasser. Sadat became the president of Egypt following the death of Nasser in September 1970. He was the first Arab president to sign a peace treaty with Israel in 1978 as part of the Camp David treaty. On 26 March 1979, Sadat signed a treaty in which Egypt officially recognized Israel. On October 6, 1981, Sadat was assassinated by a member of a fundamentalist group during a military parade commemorating the October 1973 war.

Anwar Sadat (1918–1981), President of Eygpt

Sephardi Jewish Community

A community of Jews of nonwestern origins. They are also called "oriental" Jews. Some of them have Spanish, Portuguese, and African origins, and some come from Arab countries. The Sephardic community constitutes only 10 percent of world Jewry and speaks Spanish or Arabic.

STATUS QUO

A term meaning to leave everything as it was prior to 1917. This was a British policy which the mandatory government applied with respect to the holy places and aimed at the retention of the situation of these places as it was at the time of the Ottoman Empire.

SYKES AND PICOT

Sir Mark Sykes, a British diplomat, and George Picot, a French diplomat, met in London in November 1915 to negotiate a division of the Ottoman Empire in Asia. The Sykes-Picot agreement was named after them.

TRUMAN, HARRY S.

U.S. president (1945–1953) who played a major role in the establishment of the state of Israel in 1948.

UNIFIED COMMAND OF THE INTIFADA

Appeared on the Palestinian arena after the breakout of the 1987 intifada. It consisted of the representatives of the major Palestinian factions who were members of the Palestine Liberation Organization. It led the daily activities of the intifada through the communiqués it issued.

UNITED NATIONS RESOLUTION 194

Issued in December 1948 to resolve the problem of the refugees. Article 11 of the resolution stipulated that refugees wishing to return to their homes and live peacefully should be allowed to do so as soon as possible, and that compensation should be paid for the property of those who decide not to return; it also calls for compensation for missing people and for those who were injured. According to international law and justice, the responsible government and/or authorities must pay compensation for loss and damage.

UNITED NATIONS SECURITY COUNCIL

The fifteen-member executive body of the United Nations specializes in examining issues that threaten international peace. Its resolutions are considered binding to all member countries. It is made up of five permanent members and ten who are elected for two-year terms by the General Assembly.

U.N. SECURITY COUNCIL RESOLUTION 242

Issued after the June 1967 war. The resolution demanded Israeli withdrawal from the Arab territories (or territories) Israel occupied in the June 1967 war, putting an end to the state of enmity between Arab countries and Israel, and offering a fair solution to the problem of the refugees. It also called for the freedom of navigation in international waters. This resolution was considered the cornerstone of the concept of "land in exchange for peace."

WEIZMANN, CHAIM (1874–1952)

Born in Motol in Russia and studied in Germany and Switzerland. He taught chemistry at Manchester University from 1904 to 1914. In his studies, Weizmann discovered an advanced base of botulium acids and acetone for creation of cordite. The discovery made a contribution to the British war effort. He headed the Jewish negotiating team to the 1919 Paris Peace Conference where he worked to persuade the League of Nations to grant Britain a mandate for the administration of Palestine. He headed the World Jewish Organization from 1920 to 1931 and from 1935 to 1948. This is the organization that worked for establishment of a national home for the Jews in Palestine. He became the first president of the Israeli entity in 1949.

ZION

A mountain that overlooks the eastern part of Jerusalem. It was mentioned in the Old Testament in reference to a part of the city in which the Jebusite Arabs lived, who were the owners of the city of Jebus also mentioned in the Old Testament. When King David seized the city of Jebus from its inhabitants, he took hold of its fort, which was built on a mountain, and named it Zion.

ZIONISM

A colonialist political movement that bestowed a nationalistic characteristic over the Jews and a sense of ethnic unity. It called for a solution to what was termed the Jewish Problem in Europe. It opposed the assimilation of the Jews in their original homelands and convinced them to emigrate to Palestine, claiming that they had historical and religious rights in it. The interests of Zionism coincided with the aims of colonialism in establishing a Jewish state in Palestine.

REFERENCES

Abbas, Ihsan. *The Palestinian Encyclopedia*. Vol. 4.

Abd Al-Hadi, Mahdi. *The Palestinian Problem and Political Solutions 1934–1974*. Beirut: 1975.

Abd Al-Mun'im, Mohammad Faisal. *We and Israel in a Crucial Battle*. 1986.

Abdallah, Samir. *The Impact of the Occupation on the Productive Base of the Palestinian Economy*. Vol. 86. The Statistics Annual Book. Central Bureau for Statistics, 1986.

Abu E'leiwi, Hasan. *The Palestinian Encyclopedia*. Vol. 2.

Abu Hadba, Ahmed. *The Palestinian Economy and the Limits of Israeli Control*. Beirut: Economic Future, 1999.

Abu Zahra, Ibrahim. *The Zionist Movement and Colonization and Transfer of Palestinians*. Hebron, 1993.

Al-'Alami, Sa'd Al-Din. *Documents of the Supreme Islamic Council*. Jerusalem: Arab Press House, 1984.

Al-'Aqqad, Salah. *The Contemporary Arab East*. Anglo-Egyptian Library, 1983.

Al-Atrash, Azmi. *Palestinian Economy and Israeli Occupation*. Damascus: Dar Al-Wihda, 2003.

Al-Bitar, Firas. *The Political and Military Encyclopedia*. Amman: Dar Usama for Publishing and Distribution, 2003.

Al-Budairy, Musa, et al. *Palestinian Society on the West Bank and in the Gaza Strip*. Acre: Al-Aswar Publications, 1990.

Al-Deek, Mufeed. "Unpublished Pages from Moshe Sharett's Memoirs." American Universities Alumni Association.

Al-Duri, Abd Al-Aziz, ed. *The Palestinian Issue and the Arab Israeli Conflict*.

Al-Ghul, Omar Hilmi. *Palestinian Developments, 1967–1987*. 1st ed. Damascus: El-Wassim Printer and Publisher, 1992.

Al-Hout, Bayan Nuwayhed. *The Leadership and Political Institutions in Palestine, 1917–1948*. 3rd ed. Beirut: Institute for Palestine Studies, 1986.

———. *Palestine, the Cause, the People, the Culture*. Beirut, Lebanon: Dar Al-'Istiqlal.

Al-Husseini, Yousef Kamal Hassouna. *Palestine and Israeli Aggression on Islamic Holy Sites*. Hebron, 2000.

Al-Kayyali, Abd Al-Wahab. *Encyclopedia of Politics*. 2nd ed. Beirut: Arab Institute for Studies and Publishing, 1985.

———. *Modern History of Palestine*, 10th ed. Beirut, Lebanon: Arab Institute for Studies and Publishing, 1990.

Al-Khalidi, Walid. *Before Diaspora: A Pictorial History of the Palestinian People, 1876–1948*. Beirut: Institute for Palestinian Studies; West Bank: Bir Zeit University, 1988.

Al-Rajabi, Shahade Murshed. *The Jewish Community in Hebron*. Unpublished MA thesis, An-Najah National University, Nablus, 2000.

Al-Shar', Sadiq. *Our Wars with Israel, 1947–1973*. Amman: Al-Shuruuq Publication and Distribution, 1997.

Al-Sifri, 'Isa. *Arab Palestine Between the Mandate and Zionism (1917–1936)*. Jaffa, Palestine: New Library of Palestine, 1997.

Al-Tarazi, Nasri, and Hajjaj, Osama. *The Palestine Problem in Drawing and Words*. Amman, Jordan: The Association against Zionism and Racism, 1997.

Al-'Uwaisi, Abd Al-Fattah. *The Roots of the Palestinian Problem (1799–1922)*. Hebron: Al-Hussein Publications, 1992.

Aronson, Geoffery. *The Politicians of Fait Accompli in the West Bank and Gaza Strip*. Institute for Palestine Studies, 1999.

Ben-Gurion, David. *Diary of the War 1947–1948*. Ed. Gershon Devlin and

Walhrajan Oron. Trans. Samir Jabbour. Beirut: Institute for Palestine Studies, 1993.

Benvenisti, Meron. *The Economy of the Uprising.* Beirut: Institute for Palestine Studies, 1999.

Brief History of Palestine, the Nakba and the Determination. the Supreme Palestinian National Council for Remembrance of the Nakba.

The Campaign for Defending the Rights of Palestinian Refugees. *The Palestinian Refugees in Diaspora.* States Reports. Badeel.

Darwish, Marwan. *The Fourteenth Knesset Elections.* Nablus: Palestinian Studies and Research Center, 1996.

Declaration of the Independence of Palestine. 15 November 1988.

"Economy of the Private Sector in the West Bank & Gaza." Gaza: UN Coordinator's Office in the Occupied Territories, 1998.

Farsoun, Sameeh. *Palestine and the Palestinians.* Beirut: Research Center for Arab Unity, 2003.

Ghalyoun, Burhan. *Arabs and the Battle for Peace.* Beirut: Arab Culture Center, 1999.

Gujansky, Tamar. *The Development of Capitalism in Palestine.* 2nd ed. Culture Department, PLO, 1987.

Hadawi, Sami. *The Harsh Siege on Palestine, 1914–1979.* Amman: El-Tawfiq Press, 1982.

Hawatmeh, Nayef. *Oslo and the Other Balanced Peace.* Beirut: Bissan Institute, 1998.

Haydar, Aziz. *Palestinians in Israel Under the Oslo Agreement.* Beirut: Institute for Palestine Studies, 1997.

Hilal, Jamil. *Poverty in the West Bank and Gaza.* New York: United Nations, 1997.

Horovitz, Dan, and Lisak, Moshe. *Democracy and Security in an Endless Conflict.* Jerusalem: Institution of Israeli Arab Studies, 1995.

Hourani, Hani. *The Social and Economic Conditions in the West Bank After 1948.* Majalat Samed, 1988.

Hurst, David. *The Gun and the Olive Branch: The Roots of Violence in the Middle East,* London: Faber and Faber, 1977.

The Intifada and the Palestinian Nakba, 1948–2001. Jerusalem: Institute of Peace Roots, 2001.

Jbara, Taysir. *The History of Palestine.* Amman: Al-Shuruuq Publishing House, 1980.

———. *The 1936 Strike in Palestine.*

Kanafani, Ghassan. *Men in the Sun.* Salah Al-Din Publications, 1976.

Kattan, Henry. *The Palestinian Problem.* Trans. Rushdy A-Ashhab. Ministry of Culture Publications, PNA, 1999.

Khalaf, Salah. *A Palestinian Without an Identity.* Jerusalem: Palestinian Office for Journalistic Services.

Khalil, Sameeha Salameh. *From the Intifada to the State.* 1989.

Mir'i, Ibrahim. "The Village of Zir'in." In Shareef Kana'neh (ed.), *Destroyed Palestinian Villages*, Series no. 16. Bir Zeit University, Documents and Research Center, 1994.

Morris, Benny. *The Birth of the Palestinian Refugee Problem: 1946–1948.* Cambridge: Cambridge University Press, 1989.

The National Committee for Defending Arab Land in Palestine. "The Black Paper on Land Day (March 30, 1976)." Amman: Al Jalil Publishing House, 1985.

National Ministry of Defense, Lebanese Army. *The Palestinian Problem and the Danger of Zionism.* Beirut: Institute for Palestine Studies, 1983.

Oslo Peace Between Illusion and Reality. Damascus: Al Taqaddum al Arabi Institution, 1998.

Palestine: Its History and Its Question. Beirut, Lebanon: Institute for Palestine Studies, 1983. Cyprus: The Independent Company for Publishing Services, 1983.

The Palestinian Encyclopedia. Part 2: Special Studies. Vol. 3, Education in Palestine. Vol. 4, Civilization Studies. Vols. 6 and 7, Palestinian Issue Studies. Beirut: 1990.

The Palestinian Society in the West Bank and Gaza. Beirut. Institute for Palestine Studies. 1994

Sabra and Shatila in Memory. Tunis: South Publishing House, 1983.

Sayigh, Rosemary. *Palestinian Peasants from Uprooting to Revolution.* 2nd ed. Arab Research Institution, 1983. [In Uri Aveneri, *Israel Without Zionists*, New York, 1968.]

———, *Palestinians: From Peasants to Revolutionaries*, London, Zed Press, 1979.

Shabana, Luay, and Barghouti, Sufyan. "Unemployment in the Palestinian Territories." Jerusalem. Forum for Economic and Social Policy Research, 1999.

Shabit, Arieh, *Ha'aretz*, 21 July 2002.

———. *Ideology and Economy in Israel.* Jerusalem: Center for Alternative Information, 1998.

Shaker, Mahmoud. *Encyclopedia of Jewish History*. Amman: Dar Osama for Publication and Distribution, 2002.

Shaliv, Arieh. *The Intifada: Causes, Characteristics and Implications*. Translated by 'Ilayyan Al-Hindi, Arab Studies Society, Jerusalem, 1993.

Sharif, Hussein. *The Political Perception of Jews Through History from the Biblical Period to the Process of Negotiations, the Middle East from 1900 BC to 1995 AD*.

Shufani, Elias. *A Digest of Palestine's Political History: Since the Dawn of History until 1949*. Institute for Palestine Studies, 1996.

The Rough Road. Damascus: Al Taqadum al Arabi Institution, 1997.

Toma, Khalil. *Songs of the Last Nights*. Jerusalem: Salah Al-Din Publications, 1975.

Yassin, Salawati. *The Simplified and Extended Arab Encyclopedia*. Institute for Arab History, Beirut, 2001

Zeitawi, Nihad. "Deir Yassin." In Sharif Kana'neh (ed.), *Destroyed Palestinian Villages*. Series no. 4. Bir Zeit University, Documents and Research Center, 1987.

Zu'aiter, Akram. *The Palestinian Problem*, 3rd ed. Amman: Dar Al-Jalil Publishers for Palestinian Studies and Research, 1986.

TEACHERS' PERSONAL TRAJECTORIES

Twenty-four Palestinian and Israeli teachers participated in this project in order to learn and teach each other's historical narrative. Some teachers joined
the project at the beginning of the project; others joined after a while. They
all worked together effectively in uni-national and/or bi-national meetings
during the process of putting these narratives together. Afterward they undertook the task of teaching the new texts, which they themselves had authored,
to their own students. The experiences of the teachers participating in the
project varied according to their expectations. Below we present a summary
of what this project meant to the individual teachers in their own words.[1]

Abdulhakeem says: "This project is an effort to create a new atmosphere, or
relations between the two sides—Palestinian and Israeli—in an attempt to

---

1 The names of the Palestinian teachers who are quoted here: Abdulhakeem,
Maysoon, Amjad, Issa, Khalil, Sahar, Mohammad, Haleema, Rula, Ghadeer, and Eman.
The names of the Israeli teachers quoted here: Niv, Eyal, Sarah, Shai, Natalia, Eschel, Rachel,
Naomi.

convey the Palestinian history to Israeli students and to convey the Jewish or Israeli history to Palestinian students in the simplest way."

The project, with its innovative approach, was well received by both the Palestinian and Israeli teachers, and the opportunity for personal meetings with individuals from the other side was valued highly by most of them.

Maysoun: "This is the first time that I have met or talked to Israelis. I usually meet them at the military checkpoints while trying to move from one place to another inside my own country. Now I have to see them, talk to them, and listen to them so that we can work together toward our future on this land."

Niv: "Although I thought I knew the Palestinian narrative, it was only in my imagination. The meetings, sitting together, listening to the Palestinians, and reading their texts was the first time that I have actually read, or listened to, the Palestinian narrative, not imagined it. It was a very important experience for me personally."

Amjad expresses the impact of the meeting on his perception: "I discovered that the meetings were very fruitful. I never thought or experienced this way of exchange of views between sides with completely different viewpoints.

Palestinian and Israeli teachers discussing their narratives in Talitha Kumi school in Beit Jala

More horizons have opened in front of me and have created an interaction between my views and the views of others."

Several participants expressed their appreciation of the value of such a project to their students and to the students of the other side. At least three different aspects were listed by the participants as essential to the learning of two narratives.

For the Palestinians, the first aspect, as expressed by Issa, is the fact that it is very important for the Palestinians to learn their own narrative. "The Palestinians have to be aware that the Palestinian narrative, the narrative of the Palestinian student and the Palestinian people, is acceptable." As for the second aspect, adds Issa, "When we had the opportunity to know the Israeli narrative, we were able to understand certain issues and the historical developments of the other side."

Khalil also emphasizes the second aspect concerning the significance of learning about the other: "These encounters have provided us with a good chance to understand each other, particularly for me personally being a member of the Palestinian side, or the weaker side. Now I can understand the other side well and with an open mind. I also know how their kids think and what they learn and so I can understand the other side better."

Sarah: "It seems to me that such a project is extremely important in order for our kids to get used to 'seeing' the other side. I don't think that history is the only means through which we can deal with such a topic. Yet history is in fact an important and suitable tool since it allows us to offer other historical examples. Every part of the world has experienced some sort of conflict. Several countries have suffered a lot. However, these conflicts have been solved, and such countries now exist in peace. For example, the conflict between Germany and France, which went on for years, is non-existent now. This means that there is a future and hope that this might also happen here. It is important that we should provide our children with hope."

Eyal, on the other hand, points to the contribution of this project to the students' ability to learn about the other: "The Palestinian narrative offers a lot in comparison with what we and the Israeli students know today about the Palestinians. We are taking wide steps forward because if you were to go to any of our school libraries to learn something about the Palestinians, I don't believe you would find a lot of information."

Sahar and Mohammad point to the third aspect of the significance of learning the two narratives, which is when one side introduces their own narrative to the other side; or, as Sahar puts it: "To make your voice heard. There was an opportunity to discuss both our histories and to make our voice heard in regard to the issues we were discussing."

Mohammad: "I feel that history is a commitment that we have to convey far away; we also have to keep this commitment. It is good to take part in it and to contribute to the making of history and its facts so that we can convey these facts to the other side." Haleema stresses this aspect: "We can convey our viewpoint to the other side."

Teachers from both sides point to the difficulties of the implementation of the dual narrative approach in schools. For example, Rula and Sarah mention the objection of the education authorities.

Sarah: "I believe that someone should start such a project, though the time does not seem to be suitable since the [Israeli] Ministry of Education does not support these relations much."

Rula: "I wasn't allowed to teach the historical narrative at school because this topic is prohibited and because this idea is still not acceptable. I might be the only teacher who invited her students to her house. I explained the idea to my family and they had no objection. So I invited the students of Grades 9 and 10 and the room was crowded like a classroom."

Some of the other teachers were concerned about the difficulties facing the students.

Shai: "The beginning was pessimistic for me. I didn't think that something would come out of it. I thought that the situation was very tense and the students would not support this situation."

Natalia: "I recognize that it is not easy to teach both narratives, especially since I have had some experience with this type of informal education. I believe that the issue is more difficult at schools because students expect the topic to be far from politics or at least neutral. When you present the Palestinian narrative to them, they are most likely to tell you, 'Oh! You must be a leftist,' or something similar. I hope to be able to acquire a lot of tools here and to learn how I can do that correctly."

Ghadeer, on the other hand, describes the challenges of bringing the other's narrative to the students. "First, we should be honest in writing our own narrative. This requires us to be good researchers. And on top of that, we should be skillful communicators. This means that I should convey to my students truthfully everything that goes on during these workshops. Sometimes

Palestinian and Israeli teachers meeting in Braunschweig, Germany

a conflict arises about certain words or issues, so I have to be faithful with these things and be a good communicator."

Eschel: "I think that we are at an advanced stage where we can deal with how we can communicate these texts to the students themselves. We can see the difference between the teaching methods used by the Palestinians and those used by the Israelis."

Some teachers indicate that their teaching has undergone some kind of transformation after their experience with the project.

Shai: "I must say that a lot of my ideas have changed. First, as a teacher, this project has given me new ideas and different points of view. It has also affected my methods of teaching other subjects and not only the subject of conflict."

Rachel: "My teaching style has become interwoven with the Palestinian narrative even when I'm not using this booklet. I can't teach in a different way any longer. Also, I can't mention an incident in our shared history without some clarification, even a few words, about why the Palestinians behaved in a certain way and how they felt trying to explain their actions and decisions in a fair way, according to my understanding."

The teachers point out that despite a lot of challenges, their students were certainly affected by the project.

Iman: "What we had been used to until that time, students as well as teachers, was that students would read a single-sided narrative. But in this project, every student started to read the narrative not only from his side but also from the other side. And in this way, the individual student's vision and knowledge have become wider, and he/she has come to recognize through his own perspective matters that are important for him and for others as well."

Shai: "The feedback from the students gave me a lot of hope, because I recognized that students could see incidents in different ways and that it does not have a negative impact on them. I recognized that my students could understand why the Israeli leaders took this or that action. They also found in their hearts a place for the sufferings of the Palestinians. For me, this fact has its own significance and gives me hope to do more with my students in the future."

Like Shai, several teachers were very hopeful. Naomi, for instance, was looking forward to transferring the project to her own students and to extending the work she was doing together with the Palestinians inside Israel. "For several years, I had organized meetings in my school about the Palestinian-Arab cause, and definitely not from a purely Israeli point of view. Instead, we used to deal with this question as objectively as possible. And at the end of each meeting we used to go to Deir Hanna to meet the Palestinian youth there. At one time, we were able to bring the youth from Deir Hanna to visit us. In addition to the games, a lot of discussions were held. The meetings were really enjoyable. During the seven years that these meetings were held, we always parted with kisses. Afterward we were offered with the idea of getting in contact with the Palestinians there—I mean in the Palestinian territories."

Haleema: "We have the potential and we can make use of it. We hope to be able to teach these narratives at schools in the future, and that will lead to some sort of peace."

Natalia: "I'm happy to participate in this project because I believe that it is very important that we work for building peace. I hope, or believe, that teachers can bring more peace to the area through education."

Printed in the USA
CPSIA information can be obtained
at www.ICGtesting.com
JSHW020845071223
53406JS00003B/7